Hiding in Plain Sight

Pieter van Os writes for *NRC Handelsblad* and *De Groene Amsterdammer*. His published works include the books *The Netherlands in Focus*, and *We Understand Each Other Perfectly*, about his years as a parliamentary journalist. After having lived in Warsaw for four years, he now resides in Tirana, Albania. In 2020 he won the Libris History Prize and the Brusse Prize for best Dutch-language journalistic book of the year with *Hiding in Plain Sight*.

David Doherty studied English and literary linguistics in Glasgow before moving to Amsterdam, where he has been working as a translator for over twenty years. His literary work includes novels by award-winning authors Marente de Moor, Peter Terrin, and Alfred Birney. *Summer Brother*, his translation of Jaap Robben's *Zomervacht*, won the 2021 Vondel Translation Prize and was longlisted for the 2021 International Booker Prize.

Pieter van Os

Hiding in Plain Sight

*how a Jewish girl survived
Europe's heart of darkness*

Translated by David Doherty

SCRIBE
Melbourne • London

Scribe Publications
2 John St, Clerkenwell, London, WC1N 2ES, United Kingdom
18–20 Edward St, Brunswick, Victoria 3056, Australia
3754 Pleasant Ave, Suite 100, Minneapolis, Minnesota 55409, USA

First published in Dutch as *Liever dier dan mens* by Prometheus in 2020

Published by Scribe in 2022

Text copyright © Pieter van Os 2020
Translation copyright © David Doherty 2022

Typeset in 11.5/15 pt Dante by J&M Typesetting Services

Printed and bound in the UK by CPI Group (UK) Ltd, Croydon CR0 4YY

Scribe is committed to the sustainable use of natural resources and the use of paper
products made responsibly from those resources.

978 1 913348 89 2 (UK edition)
978 1 922585 03 5 (Australian edition)
978 1 957363 04 2 (US edition)
978 1 922586 68 1 (ebook)

Catalogue records for this book are available from the National Library of Australia
and the British Library.

This publication has been made possible with financial
support from the Dutch Foundation for Literature.

Nederlands
letterenfonds
dutch foundation
for literature

scribepublications.co.uk
scribepublications.com.au
scribepublications.com

To Henk and Heleen

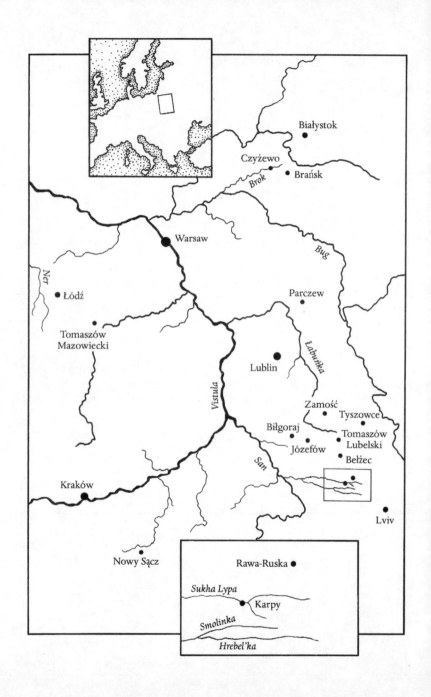

Family Tree

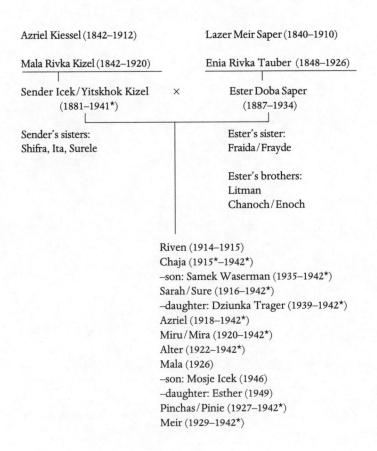

Azriel Kiessel (1842–1912)

Mala Rivka Kizel (1842–1920)

Sender Icek/Yitskhok Kizel
(1881–1941*)

Lazer Meir Saper (1840–1910)

Enia Rivka Tauber (1848–1926)

Ester Doba Saper
(1887–1934)

×

Sender's sisters:
Shifra, Ita, Surele

Ester's sister:
Fraida/Frayde

Ester's brothers:
Litman
Chanoch/Enoch

Riven (1914–1915)
Chaja (1915*–1942*)
–son: Samek Waserman (1935–1942*)
Sarah/Sure (1916–1942*)
–daughter: Dziunka Trager (1939–1942*)
Azriel (1918–1942*)
Miru/Mira (1920–1942*)
Alter (1922–1942*)
Mala (1926)
–son: Mosje Icek (1946)
–daughter: Esther (1949)
Pinchas/Pinie (1927–1942*)
Meir (1929–1942*)

* Approximation

Contents

PROLOGUE
The Bug

'Collect everything and sort it out after the war.'

–Emanuel Ringelblum, historian

When she went out to feed the pigs once a day, the farmer's wife tossed the family's leftovers beside the trough. Through a small opening in the floor, the food reached five hungry people hiding below.

Her husband had reckoned no one would go looking for Jews under a pigsty. He was right. Three of the five survived the war, though when liberation came they bore little resemblance to the people who had knocked on the farmer's door three years earlier.

A human being can barely exist on one meagre ration of leftovers a day. Crouching for days on end takes a dreadful toll on the body. The two who did not live to see liberation had briefly left their hiding place in the hamlet of Godlewo Wielkie to recover belongings they had hidden near their home. They probably hoped these goods would help them obtain more food from the farmer or offer greater protection from the rats, the frost, the rainwater, or the stink and the filth of the pigs. They did not survive their expedition.

The farmhouse is still standing, though today it serves as another farmer's shed, and decades of sun and rain have turned the wood a mousy grey. The new farmhouse is fifteen metres away, the plaster on its outer walls crumbling to expose the shoddy workmanship of large building blocks poorly laid.

The shed stands for a distant past, the farmhouse for a future that has already slipped away. Square and flat-roofed, the house looks like a miniature block of flats, with two floors and two identical balconies just big enough to hold a couple of bin bags. A satellite dish completes the picture. The Poles refer to these small farmhouses as *Kostka PRL-owskas* or 'little commie blocks': mini versions of the blocks of flats that sprang up in the big cities of the Polish People's Republic. Everyone calls them *bloki*.

For four years I lived in a city full of *bloki*: Warsaw, the capital of Poland. From there, I often travelled east, searching for people and places connected to a personal history that had captured my imagination. Most of these trips took me along the River Bug (pronounced 'boog' in Polish), and, as we drove, I would try to erase the square buildings from the landscape. One of the few certainties from the story I was chasing was its place in history: before 1946, a time when farmhouses did not resemble little blocks of flats.

And so, in a farmer's back garden some 100 kilometres from Warsaw, I concentrate on the wooden shed and picture it as it once was: a farmhouse at the time of the Second World War. With that image in mind, I go looking for the pigsty that must have stood beside or behind it.

The Jews dug the pit beneath the pigsty together with the farmer and his young son in the summer of 1941, soon after German forces seized control of this part of Poland. The Jews, the farmer, and his son dug to a depth of almost six feet. It took them two days.

I cannot find the place where the pigsty stood, and the *bloki*-farm's present owner is not inclined to help. To him, my story sounds odd at best and he drones on about never having met the owner from the 1940s. 'I'm new around here,' he says, which means he arrived in the fifties.

A Polish friend has come with me to interpret. As we drive back to Warsaw, she asks me what the Polish Jews hiding at the farm have to do with the book I'm writing. I come up with a halting answer or two. One is that they came from Czyżewo, four miles to the north. Now known as Czyżew-Osada, the town used to be a shtetl where my protagonist's mother and her parents once lived. Besides, I add, this is a story of Polish Jews who tried to survive the war in the Polish countryside, something my protagonist also tried to do for several months.

My Polish friend smiles. Go down that road, she says, and you can travel forever. She does the maths: in Czyżewo, 85 per cent of the population was Jewish, which adds up to a few thousand individuals. Are all their attempts to survive relevant to my book? Her calculations don't stop there. In 1939, Poland was home to approximately three-and-a-half million Jewish citizens, at least 250,000 of whom sought refuge in the countryside. 'Do you need to know all their stories, too, to gauge the value of your protagonist's story?'

The protagonist she is referring to is a woman who lives in the Dutch town of Amstelveen, effectively a suburb of Amsterdam. She grew up in an Orthodox Jewish family in a Warsaw neighbourhood that would go on to become the heart of the city's Jewish ghetto, in effect a public prison established by the German occupier. She was the only member of her family to survive the war—not by hiding under a pigsty, but by pretending to be somebody else, taking on different names and life stories at a time when your identity determined whether you lived or died.

My Polish friend and I drive on in silence, and I feign a sudden interest in the dozens, if not hundreds, of billboards we pass along the way. Often, they separate the road and a dry ditch from flat grassland with feeble rows of recently planted fir trees. There's a monotony to the world between Czyżewo and Warsaw. My friend ventures a question: 'Do we still need to go to Wrocław to interview Czesław Cholewicki?'

Cholewicki is the son of the farmer who hid the Jews under his pigsty in Godlewo Wielkie. After the war, as a boy of fifteen, he moved west to a place that had once been in Germany but became Polish when the borders between the two countries were redrawn.

Curiosity triumphs over common sense. Days later, we clock up a few more hours in the car and find ourselves side by side on a couch in the living room of a stone farmhouse near Wrocław. Cholewicki, a man of 88, tells us the tale as he remembers it. How he and his father dug a pit under the pigsty, covering it with two trees and a layer of mud and branches to make a new floor. How a kennel tacked onto the side provided a little fresh air, and how the Jews were allowed out for a short while at night to stretch their legs. His father had trained his dog not to react when it saw them, and luckily the farm was in a remote spot at the edge of the forest, so dogs on neighbouring farms didn't bark at every sound or move they made. Cholewicki's account of the Jews' fate is short and to the point. A few days after the two had gone in search of their belongings, his father found their bodies in the forest: murdered, and probably not by the Germans. At the time, Germans were thin on the ground in those parts. Besides, the Jews had not been shot. 'The Germans were known for gunning people down, not going at them with clubs or pitchforks.'

The three Jews who remained in hiding stayed put until two days after liberation, in the spring of 1944. Then they walked back to their looted homes in Czyżewo, which, unlike the larger houses on the main square, had not been occupied by Catholic Poles. News of their return spread like wildfire. A group of armed Poles paid them a visit, looking for money, gold, anything of value. 'People thought any Jew who had survived the whole ordeal must be very rich,' said Cholewicki. 'But those people had nothing.'

The armed Poles killed the father, mother, and daughter who had lived for three years in the pit beneath the pigs. Then they set out for the farm in Godlewo Wielkie. The Cholewickis' dog announced their arrival. Young Czesław ran out the back door and took cover in the bushes. From his hiding place, he heard the Poles screaming at his father.

'Where is the Jews' gold?!'

'Where have you hidden it?'

The men found nothing. 'They beat my father so badly, he could no longer stand.' Within days, he died of his injuries.

My Polish friend is right. This is a detour, one of many. Even so, I believe it to be worthwhile. Not only because its dispiriting brutality is typical of the detours anyone travelling back in time east of Berlin might make, but also because talking to Czesław Cholewicki made me realise for the first time that I had been chasing an illusion. I had spent too long trying to unsee all kinds of things: the *bloki* farmhouses, the billboards, the restaurants built to look like castles, the hundreds of roundabouts named after Pope John Paul II, the mint-green favoured by the residents of rural Poland when painting their plastered houses. By blotting them out, I had hoped to return to a time before 1946, to describe more vividly the world in which my protagonist lived. But after yet another tale of woe, I understood that I had been searching, obsessively perhaps, for a place that had probably never existed: a fairy-tale world of colourful settlements set among green hills and leafy landscapes, where birds sang, streams burbled, and wheat swayed in the fields. Where life was not only pure and simple, but alive with a rich sense of community.

Cholewicki's story was a final shove in the right direction. Despite the things I wanted to believe in, it had gradually begun to dawn on me that, even without the blocks, billboards, and rainswept roundabouts, my idealised world was not about to materialise. I understood that eighty years ago this place was every bit as flat, wet, grim, and cold. That its people, like people everywhere, were capable of terrifying ruthlessness, and that poverty was ugly and appalling. There was a good reason why, before the war, the little town of Czyżewo had been home to people smugglers: two men who, for a substantial sum, could arrange emigration to America, Canada, or Argentina, or at a pinch to Germany or Czechoslovakia.

Czyżewo's people smugglers lived alongside three egg sellers, an assortment of roofers, masons, peddlers, butchers, and bakers, a watchmaker, two carpenters, a hat maker, a blacksmith, and dozens of Luftmenschen (literally, air people, or what we would call dreamers), residents who had to rely on charity. A report from 1939 reveals that organised assistance was the only source of income for one in five Polish Jews.

* * *

Journalist Rafael F. Scharf survived the war. In 1939, he was living and working in London as a correspondent for a Polish newspaper. He devoted his later years almost entirely to spreading the word about the Jewish world in which he'd grown up. In countless lectures, he stressed the importance of steering 'a clear course between nostalgia and reality'. Yes, he wrote, over three million Jews had lived in pre-war Poland and had formed the 'the most vital, life-enhancing branch of Jewish life in the Diaspora'. They were 'a spring from which there flowed a contribution to the literary, musical, and scientific legacy of mankind, in disciplines as varied as Talmud studies and modern science'. Yet, at the same time, he argued, the crime committed by the Germans was so immense that it is impossible to increase the scale of its inhumanity by idealising the past. Idealisation can only stand in the way of the historical reality.

This insight informed my interviews with the protagonist of this book, Mala Rivka Kizel, whose survival story became my guide through the history of Central Europe in the twentieth century. Today she lives as Marilka Shlafer, just outside the Dutch capital. She was born in Warsaw, the sixth in a family of eight children, in February 1926.

In the pages that follow, she is Mala. To me, she is Mrs Shlafer. I visited her on several occasions at her charming yellow-brick home, tucked away in a small neighbourhood of terraced houses between the Bosbaan rowing lake and the River Amstel. In her light and airy living room with its round table, she welcomed me with coffee and biscuits. Her walls were hung with framed photographs — recent snapshots of her children and grandchildren, and of herself with friends from the local bridge club. One featured a bright-eyed Mrs Shlafer holding a silver trophy as beaming club members bunched in around her.

Mala is the daughter of Ester Doba Saper and Sender Yitskhok Kizel. The colours and brushstrokes in which she paints her childhood are a long way from Marc Chagall's dream-like visions of Jewish shtetl residents hovering above colourful wooden houses in the company of mythical, sometimes smiling creatures, the occasional fiddle tucked under one arm. Mala loved her parents. She grieved for them, and grieves to this day, almost eighty years after their lives were taken. Yet she has no qualms about telling me that, because she was a girl, her parents paid her little attention. 'You were better off as a boy,' she says. The children were never allowed too close to their mother, who suffered from an infectious illness, probably tuberculosis. And, health permitting, Mother was busy working in the toy shop she ran. 'I didn't see much of her,' Mala says. 'I only remember one kiss. On my leg, when she was tying my shoelace.'

Her father devoted his life to studying the Torah and teaching young Talmud scholars. Boys only, of course. 'My father believed you shouldn't so much as look at a girl, not even your sister. He impressed this on my brothers, who of course were expected to live by the tenets of their faith.' The birth of a boy was cause for elaborate celebration, complete with presents and sweets. Girls came into the world in silence. 'Father never showed me any real affection, not so much as a pat on the head.'

Mala is a short woman, neither slim nor plump. Perhaps robust is the best description. White waves of well-kept hair frame her sharp features and keen eyes. Recalling events that expose the deepest abysses of human nature, she speaks with remarkable lightness, a tone I have never really encountered in writings or discussions about the Holocaust. She smiles frequently, and rarely from a sense of awkwardness. Yet she trivialises nothing: her story traverses the abyss. Today's editorials on what we now call identity politics pale by comparison, or at least take on a different hue. Even so, the comparison is worth making. Mala's story is driven by humanity's obsession with nation, state, race, and identity.

Before I met Mala, I had already heard an abridged version of her story, told to me by her grandson, Amir Swaab—a friend I had lost touch with until the day I turned up at a venue in Warsaw to find him sitting at the piano. A pianist by profession, he was the accompanist to a one-woman show designed to delight Dutch expats with songs that poked fun at the bourgeoisie back home. Amir is a man with unruly curls and fine features regularly lit up by a roguish smile, suggesting a lightness of heart not easy to rhyme with his contemplative nature. After the show, he told me he had been to Warsaw before: his great grandmother lay buried in the Jewish cemetery, and he had once gone looking for her grave. We agreed to pay her a visit the next day.

Warsaw's vast Jewish cemetery is one of the few physical remnants of the city's Jewish community. We found the headstone we were looking for, and Amir, who had lived in Israel for a time, read the Hebrew inscription. His great grandmother had died in 1934 when her daughter, Amir's grandmother Mala, was just a girl. Sitting in the sunshine that day, Amir told me how that girl had survived the war. It is a story that has stayed with me ever since.

In the months and years that followed, I was seldom able to give a clear account of Mala's life. I would lose myself in the details that seemed to give so much value to a story as improbable as it is true. Those details show survival to be an intense version of growing up, one that draws on all the chameleon-like qualities that resilient teenagers develop along the way and that can become a matter of life or death when you are compelled to live outside your own group. Mala grew up in a world dominated by people who, however stark their differences, shared a belief in the evil of entire communities, in traits prescribed by ethnicity that could be ranked according to a hierarchy of origin, nationality, and race.

After my day with Amir in Warsaw, I visited Mala at home a number of times, and she told me her life story. By then, she had committed this story to paper, in a memoir entitled *How I Survived the War*. I transcribed our recorded conversations, and then—with the transcripts and her memoir to hand—I set out on a journey through time, tracking down the cities, towns, and villages, the people and the buildings that figure in her story, looking for documents, books, and eyewitness accounts to provide more context. This journey raised new questions at every turn, and I put these to Mala on subsequent visits. Email proved useful, too: Mala is a computer-savvy woman in her nineties who answers promptly. More often than not, her answers turned out to be repetitions, echoes of memories she had already shared.

Eventually, it dawned on me that her mind was not a reservoir of missing details I could simply tap into. In time, I learned not to bother her as much. I would have to make do with what she had already told me and written down, bolstered by what I could discover through archives, books, and conversations.

Poland had another lesson in store: people can simply vanish from the course of history. This happens elsewhere, too, but in Poland, Belarus, and Ukraine especially, entire families, villages, and communities have been carried off on the current of time. When writing his history of

Central and Eastern Europe around the time of the Second World War, historian Timothy Snyder chose to call it *Bloodlands*. A place where soldiers and civilians died in their millions, either murdered or wiped out by hunger, disease, and exhaustion. One-sixth of Polish citizens alive and well in 1939 did not survive the violence of the eight years that followed. As a percentage, it is the greatest loss of life in any country as a result of the Second World War. Hundreds of thousands, if not millions, more fled the country or were deported. Ethnic consolidation took place on a scale never before witnessed. The ruins and mass graves in the region between Berlin, Minsk, and Kiev formed a blank slate on which totalitarian leaders sought to construct a new, unsullied vision of the future. It was against this background that I set out to piece together a world that once was.

Mala's school is a case in point. 'The finest in Poland,' she called it. She even remembered the name of the street where it was located. A simple enough fact to check, you might think. Yet, even armed with this information, it took weeks and consultations with several experts to track it down. Or, more accurately, until I first laid eyes on proof that the school existed. Seventy-five years on, not a single stone remained of the building itself.

Another example: in an area that is now part of Ukraine but belonged to Poland until 1939, I went looking for a church where Mala had asked the parish priest for a baptismal certificate. 'You don't want to be baptised,' he told her. 'You want to stay alive,' and he gave Mala the certificate of a Polish country girl whose name she remembers to this day. This turned out to be no help. The region's church records had been destroyed in the ensuing violence and political upheaval. Letters to the Archdiocese of Lviv, a visit to an abbey near the church, an appointment with the ecclesiastical archives in Warsaw: nothing brought me closer to the priest who had helped Mala.

Chastened but not discouraged, I kept plugging away, probably spurred on by that old maxim from my training as a journalist: a single source is as good as none. I continued my travels, hungry for present-day confirmation of this story from a distant past.

Thankfully, there were other sources closer to home, not least the Jewish Historical Institute in Warsaw. Before long, this became the epicentre of my exploration of Mala's past. It is an institute with a remarkable history, founded on the discovery of two milk cans and a few tin boxes buried beneath the rubble of what had once been Warsaw's Jewish Ghetto. In the spring of 1943, historian Emanuel Ringelblum hid this unlikely archive under the cellars of several houses. At that point, Ringelblum knew the total destruction of the ghetto was imminent, having been told that its last surviving inhabitants planned to launch a desperate attack with whatever weapons they could lay their hands on: the Warsaw Ghetto Uprising.

The milk cans and boxes contained descriptions, documents, and statistics that Ringelblum and his staff had written, collected, and compiled since the earliest days of the ghetto. Their aim was to record as much information as possible about the last gasp of the Jewish community in Poland, and Warsaw in particular. Ringelblum's team consisted of between fifty and sixty historians, writers, journalists, and a handful of untrained volunteers. They collected German propaganda posters, children's drawings, ration coupons, writs, concert announcements, diary excerpts, and even sweet wrappers and tram tickets. They got medical professionals to draw up reports on the effects of hunger in the ghettos, they wrote their own accounts of the community's decline in all its facets, and they even managed to obtain information about the workings of the extermination camps in Treblinka and Chełmno; all so that future historians would not have to rely solely on the records of perpetrators, collaborators, and those who stood by and did nothing. This enormously labour-intensive undertaking and the diversity of the material was driven by Ringelblum's view of history. As a historian with a background in social work and journalism, he was keenly aware of how every chronicler colours and reshapes events by describing them. 'To ensure objectivity, to achieve as accurate and comprehensive a picture as possible of the War events in Jewish life,' he wrote, 'we tried to have the same incident described by as many people as possible. By comparing various accounts, the historian is able to arrive at the historical truth, the actual course of the event.'

Three of Ringelblum's team survived the war, one of whom helped search for the makeshift archive beneath the rubble of what had been the ghetto. The first milk cans were unearthed in September 1946,

followed a few years later by a second cache of boxes. A third milk
can remains lost to this day. Through the years, the institute — which
went on to bear Ringelblum's name — has added to the 35,000 pages
from the recovered cans and boxes, bringing together yet more pre-war
documents that survived the devastation: marriage certificates, birth
certificates, Yiddish newspapers, the paperwork of aid organisations.
The Ringelblum Institute also began to collect a growing number of
memoirs written by survivors, and established links with dozens of
databases digitised by organisations worldwide, granting access to
the spoken and written testimonies of thousands of survivors. The
institute helped me dig a little deeper when the questions I put to Mala
met with a candid 'I don't know' or 'I can't remember'. This was a
regular occurrence. As far as I could tell, Mala was seldom tempted to
interweave stories she had heard or read years later with what she knew
from her own experience. In fact, she only really did so when I kept on
at her, an approach that never gleaned worthwhile information. She
had already told me what she remembered. If I wanted more, I would
have to look for it myself. If I wanted to put her life in a historical
context, that was fine with her — 'Go right ahead' — but I wasn't to
keep badgering her. 'I've told you what I know.'

And so increasingly I began to make my own way through Mala's
world, in the company of people who had never known her or whose
paths never crossed hers. I immersed myself in the circumstances
that sent Mala on an odyssey that took her from Warsaw and western
Ukraine to the cities of Bremen and Magdeburg, on to Łódź and
Wałbrzych, and then to the Israeli city of Lod. Passing through these
places, I learned what life had been like when Mala was there and found
leads I was able to follow up at the Ringelblum Institute on returning
to Warsaw.

Driving along the River Brok towards the Bug, I find myself trying to
justify my detour to Godlewo Wielkie and my search for the vanished
pigsty in the farmer's garden. I present my Polish friend with fascinating
examples from other tributaries I have navigated on my expedition into
Mala's world, as if to convince her that the farm we have just left is
not so far removed from the great current of European history that

swept my protagonist along. I tell her the book I am writing not only contains Mala's own story of survival, but also observations from my own investigations, insights into my search for the fragments of Mala's story, and descriptions of the shores where I hope to find them.

Before it had dawned on me that turning up on Mala's doorstep with frequent progress reports wasn't such a good idea, I was surprised that she seemed to have no books—not even picture books—about pre-war Jewish life in Warsaw. She appeared to own no reminders of the time she grew up in, though her memories of that time were remarkably vivid. With this in mind, I decided to give her a present: a book of photos from the 1930s. Such picture books are incredibly popular in Warsaw; the bookshops are full of them.

The photos showed the district where Mala was born and raised: streets that, even before the war, were mostly home to Polish Jews. Bearded men in black overcoats peered out at us from under wide brims or fur hats. A closer look revealed their *payot* or sidelocks, curling down over their beards. Mala and I looked for photographs of Nowolipki Street, where her Aunt Surele lived and where, only two houses away, Ringelblum would later hide two milk cans crammed with archive material. We looked for pictures of Miła Street, where Mala herself had grown up. We looked for Dzika, the street where her father was born and where, as a girl during wartime, she found a gap that allowed her to sneak in and out of the ghetto.

It took me a while to notice that my own enthusiasm for the book far outshone hers. Searching for photos of a world that no longer exists is a task for historians or people of a nostalgic bent. None of this meant much to Mala, who was only playing along for my sake. She cherished none of the illusions about an idyllic world in a distant past that I had carried with me on my first forays into Eastern Europe.

Twice she looked me in the eye and asked, 'What are you hoping to find in that world that no longer exists?' What was I doing at that institute in Warsaw? What did it matter, if there was no way to find out exactly where and how her brothers and sisters had been murdered? In the end, that was all she really wanted to know. Facts that are nowhere to be found.

Staff at the institute tell me Mala is not alone in her desire to know the exact details. What happened to my family? What did they go through in their final minutes? Those are the questions survivors most often ask. 'It probably has to do with the precision and administrative zeal attributed to the Germans,' Noam Silberberg of the institute explains. 'Both are hopelessly overrated. The Nazis murdered most of their victims in Poland and further east without leaving a paper trail.' Fortunately, he shares my view that there are other reasons for trying to bring a lost world back to life with more than just memories. He works at the Ringelblum Institute, after all.

Yet the question remains: how? Let's start in Czyżewo. This shtetl on the banks of the River Brok was home to Mala's mother, Ester, when, at the beginning of the twentieth century, she was married off to Sender Yitskhok Kizel. This man Sender, or Sander, was an imposing figure with a big red beard, and his height earned him the nickname *Hoykher* (Tall) Sender. After living in Czyżewo for a while, the couple left for Warsaw. He and Ester may have travelled by donkey or perhaps by train; Czyżewo had joined the railway network a few decades before. One thing is certain: they did not travel by boat. Although the River Brok linked the shtetl with Warsaw and Gdańsk via the Bug and the Vistula, its waters were too treacherous to navigate, and remain so to this day.

Instead of footnotes

The words that introduce this prologue — 'Collect everything and sort it out after the war' — were spoken by Emanuel Ringelblum in 1941 and lived on in the memory of Hersh Wasser, one of only three members of Oneg Shabbat to survive the war. Oneg Shabbat means something like 'joy of Shabbat' a traditional reference to how devout Jews spend their holy day of rest. It was also the cryptic name given to the clandestine organisation led by Ringelblum. After burying the archive material that Oneg Shabbat had gathered, Ringelblum himself went into hiding with his wife and son, sharing the cellar of a greenhouse with a few other families in the garden of a Polish Catholic who lived near the Warsaw ghetto. This proved riskier than a pit beneath a pigsty. They were betrayed on 7 March 1944, probably by gardeners or a slighted ex-lover of the house's owner.

Ringelblum and his family were executed by the Germans, along with two non-Jewish Poles who had helped them go into hiding.

The quotes from Rafael F. Scharf date from long after the war, as does his statement, 'In mourning the past, it would be wrong to idealise it.' This comes from a lecture he gave in Kraków on 14 July 1991 as part of a summer programme called 'Tracing the Jewish Heritage in Poland', organised by Poland's Research Centre of Jewish History and Culture. It was later published as 'What Shall We Tell Miriam?' in the essay collection *Poland, What Have I to Do with Thee* (1996). Scharf's aim was to be as true to life as possible in bearing witness to the world of his youth. In this lecture, he drew upon what he called the 'only authentic descriptive record' of that world: the Yiddish and Hebrew literature of the 1930s. That literature, he said, was compassionate, but also 'mercilessly critical'. The authors 'portray the sordid conditions—the poverty, the powerlessness, the oppression, the obscurantism—and lash out against it.' Poverty was 'dire and widespread'.

Historian Bernard Wasserstein produced a study that echoes the anti-idealisation advocated by Scharf. The central theme of his impressive book *On the Eve: the Jews of Europe before the Second World War* (2012) is that the Jewish world before the Holocaust was in the throes of a major crisis. This, he argues, was not only due to external threats such as growing anti-Semitism and exclusive nationalism, but also to the internal pressures of secularisation, assimilation, demographic disaster, and growing poverty. *On the Eve* also includes a wonderful description of *Luftmenschen*, the destitute members of Poland's Jewish community.

Every word attributed to Mala in this prologue and the nineteen chapters that follow comes either from her memoirs or the conversations we had at her home in Amstelveen.

Work on this book began in 2015 and was completed in mid-2019. Mrs Marilka Shlafer died in late November 2020, at the age of ninety-four. As she lived to see the book's publication in the Netherlands, I have taken the liberty of rendering her words and recollections in the present tense.

1
The Brok

'A mouse being hunted by a cat doesn't pause to reflect upon
whether the cat is charcoal-colored or black.'

–Michał Głowiński, a writer who survived the Warsaw Ghetto

Although the River Brok was unnavigable, the people of Czyżewo found
a way to float tree trunks to the mills a few kilometres downstream,
where the wood was sawn into planks. Logging was the first economic
activity in Czyżewo that called for a degree of organisation. Later,
the production of *tsitses* began to take off, white garments worn by
Orthodox Jewish men under their black clothes, with dangling knotted
cords to remind the wearer of his religious duties. The name *tsitses*,
used by Orthodox Jews in Eastern Europe, refers to the dangling cords.

The production of these garments was the first real money-making
activity in Czyżewo. In demand throughout the Russian Empire, they
were later exported to America and Canada, too. Eventually, over a
quarter of the world's Orthodox Jews wore *tsitses* made in Czyżewo.

Around 1887, when Mala's mother, Ester Doba Saper, was born,
thirty families were able to earn a living from *tsitses*, which could only
be made by men. Until then, life in Czyżewo had been tough, even
compared to other shtetlekh in the region.

'The shtetl had no other distinction, except its poverty.' This quote
comes from Czyżewo's 'Yizkor book', a collection of commemorative

writing. Many vanished Jewish villages and towns that were once predominantly Jewish have one. The book of Czyżewo was published in Tel Aviv fifteen years after the Second World War, and is full of memories written by residents who survived the war. The poverty they describe is also reflected in the statistics from the early-twentieth century. The provincial archives, now housed in the city of Białystok, give the shtetl's population at the time as 1,495. 'Shtetl' is simply the Yiddish word for a settlement with a market, where many but not necessarily most of the population is Jewish. This was true of all but thirty-four of Czyżewo's residents.

For many years, Czyżewo's population did not expand, though families were large and children numerous. Its residents left for cities such as Łódź and Warsaw, also part of the Russian Empire at the time, or made their way to the port of Danzig and sailed for foreign shores. Infant mortality was high; the average age, low. Almost every severe infection was likely to end in death. The water from the village pump was so filthy that it only served to extinguish the countless fires that broke out in this town of wooden houses where, after dark, candles and oil lamps were the only source of light.

Czyżewo was an Orthodox shtetl. With only a few exceptions, everyone lived by the rules of the faith. However, this small community was also home to various schools of orthodoxy. At the end of the nineteenth century, a bitter feud broke out between the Hasidim and their opponents, the Misnagdim. The Hasidim came out on top, leaving the Misnagdim of Czyżewo no choice but to resentfully eat meat that they believed had not been slaughtered correctly.

Mala's family was Hasidic. Her grandfather inspected the religious schools in the district. A dispute also erupted within Czyżewo's Hasidic community between a group that followed the teachings of a spiritual leader from Ger (or Góra Kalwaria, as it is known in Polish) and a group that followed a rabbi from the Aleksander dynasty. The Ger camp were easy to recognise: they tucked their trouser legs into their socks. The clash led each group to establish its own separate place of worship.

Everyone spoke Yiddish to one another, and could get by in Polish when dealing with the police, postal workers, firemen, and other officials, and with the town's Catholic residents, whose number grew to around 200 in the 1930s. The Jews of Czyżewo also spoke Polish with the local farmers, who visited the town once a week to sell their produce on the main square.

Mala's parents married in 1905, first in Warsaw, then in Czyżewo. Mala believes her mother's marriage was arranged when she was thirteen, yet the official marriage certificate held by the government archives in Białystok gives the bride's age as eighteen, two years older than the legal age to be married. The bridegroom, Sender Yitskhok Kizel, was twenty-four. At the archive, I learn that separate agreements were sometimes made through a matchmaker, and in Ester's case this might have been when she turned thirteen.

Mala also tells me that her parents saw each other for the first time at their wedding—the kind of detail a marriage certificate can never reveal. An unlikely one, too, given that man and wife in a traditional Jewish match normally have the chance to meet in a chaperoned setting at least once. However, the certificate does state which family offered *kest*, the obligation to maintain the newlyweds for a period of time. It was usually the matchmaker who brokered such an agreement, along with arrangements as to who was to contribute what to the new household: Shabbat candle holders, menorahs, silver spoons, jewellery, and so on. In the case of Mala's parents, the *kest* lay with the family of the bride, which explains why the couple lived in Czyżewo for quite a while before leaving for Warsaw. They left shortly before the First World War. In the nick of time, you might say, as there was trouble ahead for the shtetl.

After the First World War, Czyżewo became part of Poland, a country resurrected on the drawing board at Versailles after 123 years of non-existence. The Russian armies set fire to countless homes as they retreated, and a soap factory and four windmills were among the other buildings torched along the way. Then came the forces led by Józef Haller, an anti-Semitic Polish nationalist. His 'Blue Army' of volunteers celebrated victory over the fledgling Soviet Union (1920–1921) by humiliating and even torturing the Jewish population, whom they saw as Bolshevik collaborators. They beat and kicked the men, shaved off their beards, and forced them to perform pointless tasks, such as leading cattle from one village to the next. Several residents of Czyżewo died at the hands of these 'Hallerists'. The same geopolitical shift led to the collapse of the local industry, robbing Czyżewo of access to the vast Russian hinterland that had been a crucial market for *tsitses*.

The shtetl's population did not return to pre-war level until the 1930s. Driven out by the increasing anti-Semitism in the surrounding villages, Jews came to Czyżewo. There they found safety in numbers, a sense of circling the wagons, to use the old American pioneering expression. And, sticking with the metaphor, it wasn't long before those keeping look-out saw trouble on the horizon. For the people of Czyżewo in 1939, this meant the advance of the Red Army.

In much of the world, this is a largely forgotten aspect of the Second World War. Not in Poland. The German Wehrmacht's offensive launched on 1 September 1939 was followed by a Soviet attack from the east sixteen days later, a coordinated strike by the two powers. In secret supplementary protocols to the non-aggression treaty that has gone down in history as the Molotov–Ribbentrop Pact, Stalin and Hitler had agreed to carve up Eastern Europe between them. One half of Poland, including Warsaw, was to become part of Germany. The eastern Polish lands, which at that time also comprised part of present-day Lithuania, Belarus, and Ukraine, would fall to the Soviet Union. Czyżewo lay in the Soviet section.

The Germans and the Soviets celebrated their victory in style with a joint military parade in Brest–Litovsk, on the newly drawn border between their two countries. In the months that followed, the Red Army rounded up over 300,000 inhabitants of the newly occupied region and deported them to places deep within the Soviet Union. Though they targeted intellectuals and landowners, the selection process could be fairly random. In some cities, towns, and villages, Soviet soldiers simply rounded up anyone who was wearing glasses, and branded them an intellectual. Another approach was to inspect people's hands. Those with soft skin and well-trimmed fingernails faced immediate deportation: they had clearly never done a hard day's manual labour in their lives.

The handful of communists in the region were tasked with helping

to decide who should stay and who should be deported. So, too, in
Czyżewo, where communists could be counted on the fingers of one
hand. Communists were atheists, after all, so why would they make
their home in a Jewish Orthodox settlement? One such man—big,
square-jawed, and sporting a crew cut—had been a teacher at the
shtetl's only public school. His name was Klar, and he was known as an
atheist rather than a communist, though his love for the dictatorship
of the proletariat was quick to surface in the first days of Soviet
occupation. He betrayed people he had treated as friends only a short
time before, people whose children he had taught. Years later, in
Czyżewo's book of remembrance, some survivors still felt the need to
vent their disgust in no uncertain terms. How could he have done such
a thing?

Almost two years after the Soviets arrived, the Germans came to
Czyżewo. Hitler had unleashed Operation Barbarossa in an effort to
bring the Soviet Union to its knees in a single summer. The Wehrmacht
stormed through the region, but not without receiving a warm
welcome from its Catholic Poles. They erected a makeshift triumphal
arch for the Germans on the western access road to Czyżewo. This
features in a report written by a Polish resistance fighter who travelled
through the area around Białystok at the time. He was an officer in
the Armia Krajowa or 'Home Army', Poland's largest resistance force.
It had a traditional command structure, and its leaders took orders
from the government-in-exile. Reporting to his superiors, the officer
confirmed what the government already feared: the region's Poles
saw the Germans as liberators. The officer, who had just come from
Lithuania, wrote that the situation further east was even worse.

The people of Czyżewo and environs were soon cured of any
initial enthusiasm. The Germans, like the Soviets, were aiming to wipe
the Polish nation from the face of the Earth. The locals were pressed
into the service of the German war machine, either by supplying
produce from their own land or by working in the industries of the
Third Reich further west. But in those early days, the departure of
the communists brought a sense of relief. Among the region's anti-
Semitic Poles, expectations also ran high as regards settling scores

with the Jews. Many saw Jews as collaborators, because in 1939 a small minority—men like Klar, the teacher—had welcomed the Red Army with open arms. During the late 1930s, the well-established myth that a Jew was a communist and vice versa had already been ramped up in the propaganda spread by Poland's National Democrats, 'Endeks' for short. The German occupation amplified this message. The resistance officer stated in his report that 'the enmity of Poles toward the Jews' had become so great that 'the local population does not imagine how normal relations could be re-established'.

In Czyżewo, the officer no longer encountered a single Jew. Some had fled with the Red Army. Others, he learned from the farmers in the region, had 'disappeared' between Zaręby and Czyżewo on a road that runs through a landscape of lakes and gorges. A reconstruction years later estimates that over 2,000 of Czyżewo's residents were killed there, not far from the village of Szulborze Wielkie, shortly after the arrival of German forces. A group of Poles had taken the presence of German soldiers as the start sign for a pogrom that, under German leadership, descended into a massacre.

Historians tell me that the exact details of the massacre are difficult to unpick. Reinhard Heydrich, head of the German Reich's Main Security Office, had decreed that same month that the aim was to provoke local pogroms without leaving traces. After the fact, local militias or farmers were not to be able to claim they had been following orders.

Two days after the Germans arrived, Cholewicki—the farmer from neighbouring Godlewo Wielkie, whose son I visited—walked past a place where he had heard hours of shooting. He saw the ground move, and put this down to the gasses released when bodies start to decompose. 'A hellish sight,' he would later tell his son. At least two members of Mala's family fell victim to this first wave of killings, including Fraida Saper, her mother's twin sister.

Has anything of pre-war Czyżewo survived to this day? Not really. The occasional wooden house with a pointed roof harks back to the old days, though most have been repainted in bright colours never seen before 1941. Some even have bright-blue roof tiles, which gives them a Lego-like appearance. Running water only reached the town in the

1950s, followed soon after by electricity. The contours of the small market square can still be traced, although nowadays traffic thunders across it, bound for Białystok to the east or Warsaw to the west. The church still stands. Its broad, creamy yellow façade seems somehow out of proportion, dwarfing the other buildings on the former square. It is also the only building not to feature advertising or a garish frontage. Pre-printed ad banners even veil the red brick of a synagogue that survived the war, one trumpeting the name of a major meat processing plant: 'Wipasz!'

The town also boasts a monument. I find it on a corner, opposite a blue-painted wooden house that serves as a post office. It consists of an upright chunk of granite with a copper-coloured plaque honouring the memory of 'the Poles who died winning back our country's independence'. This is a reference to the aforementioned war between the fledgling Polish republic and the equally young Soviet Union. The Poles who died in that conflict clearly did not come from the shtetl of Czyżewo. So how did this monument, erected in 1928, end up in an almost entirely Jewish town where restoring Polish independence was not exactly high on the agenda? A local historian tells me it's not unusual to find such monuments in the shtetlekh of the region. They should be seen as markers of electoral victories by the anti-Semitic Endeks, he explains. Standing by the ballot boxes, wielding clubs and other weapons, Endeks stopped Jews from voting, and once they were elected to the council that ran a Jewish town, they would thumb their noses at the Jewish residents by erecting a nationalist monument. 'This is Poland, and in Poland we celebrate all things Polish. That kind of thing.'

In 1940, the Soviets had the monument pulled down, and, balking at the idea of having to destroy something so massive, they buried it instead. The Poles unearthed it in 1981 and hoisted it upright once again.

* * *

Mala's father grew up on Dzika Street in Warsaw, just a few blocks south of the house in which Mala grew up. She believes her father's entire family came from the capital. This is probably because her

aunts — her father's three sisters — all lived nearby, in what was
Warsaw's most Jewish neighbourhood at the time. But the archives
tell a different story. Sender's mother hailed from Tyszowce, and his
father from Krasnobród. Both towns are not far from Zamość, which
lies around 200 kilometres east of Kraków, and for centuries fulfilled
a major role in the Jewish world in Eastern Europe. On 8 July 1864,
Mala's grandfather and grandmother married in Tyszowce. Both of
them were twenty-two, which in those days was relatively old for a
bride. Official figures show that over half the Jewish brides at the
time were under twenty-one. This altered rapidly in the decades that
followed, in just one illustration of an Orthodox Jewish world that may
have appeared static but, in reality, was seething with change.

Looking again at the marriage certificate from 1864, it's not so much
the age of Mala's grandparents that is striking, but their surnames.

Grandmother: Kizel.

Grandfather: Kiessel.

An archivist explains that this subtle difference in spelling was
probably the work of the registrar in attendance. In all likelihood, the
couple were directly related. This was not uncommon, nor was the
tendency of public officials to fudge the issue by altering the spelling.
The archivist sees his theory confirmed in the surnames of the children
born to the couple: in official documents they all bear the name Kizel.
The marriage certificate only gives this as their mother's surname, but
most likely it was their father's name, too.

'Unless the parents shared the same surname, you'd expect the
children to be called Kiessel.' It takes a moment for this to sink in.

What excites the archivist most of all is the language in which the
marriage certificate is written. 'This must be one of the last marriage
certificates in Polish.' Having crushed yet another armed uprising, the
Russian rulers banned the use of Polish in official documents, a ban
imposed in the year that Mala's grandparents were married. And, sure
enough, when the Kizels' son — Mala's father — gets married forty
years later, the registrar documents the event in Russian.

What else can this old certificate in Polish tell us? It tells us that
the father of Mala's grandfather was no longer alive. That his mother
earned a living from 'manual labour' on an estate belonging to one

of the Glogowskis, a family so wealthy that they owned the town of Tyszowce until 1944. Mother was the daughter of a grain merchant, the certificate states. Merchant may well be too grand a title: most likely, he bought grain from local farmers, had it ground at the nearest mill, and then sold the flour to other villagers from his home.

Lastly, the document tells us that no notary was present at the marriage ceremony, owing to 'a lack of property'.

Tyszowce was not a place of any great significance, but it certainly outshone Czyżewo. In addition to a Jewish past, it boasted a Polish history stretching back to the Middle Ages. Situated on a trade route, the town was enough of a prize to be repeatedly looted and destroyed: the Tartars laid waste to it in around 1500, the Swedes about a century later, and then came the Cossacks, not once but twice. Each time, Tyszowce was rebuilt. In the eighteenth century, the town became widely known for a special type of boot produced there. Known as *Tyszowiaki*, their major selling point was that the left and right boot were identical.

Jewish life in Tyszowce began to flourish when the town and the lands that surrounded it came under the ownership of a man called Jan Mier. In need of a middle class of merchants and people to collect taxes from local farmers, Meir encouraged Jews to settle in Tyszowce by offering them special privileges. Jews were far better suited to these roles than Polish serfs, because they could read (though not necessarily in the local language). Even in the darkest of times, Jewish parents invariably taught their children to read. The Jews were 'the people of the book', and anyone who could not read the sacred texts for themselves was ill equipped to take part in religious life. To be a practising Jew, you had to be literate.

In the Orthodox Jewish world, it was a vicious religious feud that put Tyszowce on the map. The trouble began in 1881, when Hasidic Jews accused the local rabbi of charging excessive prices for his kosher meat. The rabbi belonged to the opposing Misnagid movement, and the town's Misnagdim were incensed. Tensions steadily built, erupting into violence one year later. All the windows in the house of worship were smashed, and Russian soldiers had to be called in to restore order. The

Hasidim then reported the rabbi to the Russian authorities for helping draft dodgers escape across the border to the Habsburg Empire, only a few miles south. The Russians investigated but found no proof, leaving the Hasidim to resort to other means to rid themselves of the rabbi. By which means remains unclear, but disappear he did, and his position remained vacant for decades.

It was during those years that Tall Sender's parents, Mala's paternal grandparents, left Tyszowce for Warsaw, not a national capital at the time but a big city in the west of the Russian Empire.

Stroll through Tyszowce today, and you will mainly see cheap brickwork from the 1950s and the *bloki* farmhouses built from the 1960s onwards. Most have a white, rust-rimmed satellite dish clinging to a roof or balcony. The town had to be entirely rebuilt after the First World War and again after the Second, only this time without the Jewish population. None of Tyszowce's Jewish residents returned, not even the few who had survived the Holocaust deep in the Soviet Union. In September 1939, Red Army soldiers offered local Jews the chance to travel east with them, shortly after their annexation of the town and before they made way for the Wehrmacht under the terms agreed between Germany and the Soviet Union. About 1,300 Jews chose to stay. The Germans spared only those they considered strong enough to work in a camp on the banks of the Huczwa, a river that, like the Brok, flows into the Bug. Until October 1942, the camp's labourers were made to reinforce the banks to make the river navigable. Then they were loaded onto wooden carts and transported 18 miles south to the Bełżec extermination camp.

Today, Tyszowce is home to a mere 350 people, less than 5 per cent of the population in 1939. A small park now stands on what used to be the town square. The village elder, the *sołtys*, confirms that Tyszowce's main visitor attraction is its cemetery.

★ ★ ★

Mala grew up in a family of eight children. She was child number six, only ten months older than her younger brother. Another brother,

Meir, was born two years later. Their mother died at the age of forty-seven, not long after Mala's eighth birthday. She still remembers the bewilderment she felt. Where had her mother gone? After the funeral, she kept asking the mourners why Mother wasn't coming home with them. 'It moved everyone to tears, but no one thought to sit me down and explain what had happened.'

Mala's sisters and aunts filled the gap left by her mother. Compared to the dire poverty that was the norm in Warsaw's Jewish quarter, the Kizels were not badly off. They occupied a single floor of a building, the daughters sleeping in one room and the sons in another. There was no shower or hot water, even the toilet was outdoors, but their father was able to pay two housekeepers. 'A Polish woman came four days a week, and a Jewish woman, two days,' Mala recalls.

It's a distinction that gives pause for thought. It would be more accurate to distinguish between a Catholic Polish housekeeper and a Polish Jewish housekeeper, but in 1930s Poland everyone, like Mala, spoke of Jews and Poles. In modern-day Poland, little has changed. 'Here you are either a Pole or a Jew,' journalist Anna Bikont explains. It's a mindset she actively resists. She sees herself as both Jewish and Polish — a Polish Jew — and has done since discovering that her mother is Jewish, a discovery she did not make until she was in her thirties. Bikont's mother survived the war thanks to the false papers given to her by a non-Jewish Pole. The two fell in love, married, and decided to spare their children the ordeal of living as Jews in Poland. It's a decision Bikont does not accept, and now that she knows about her background, she wants to stand up and be counted as a Polish Jew. In a recent online survey, she discovered what an alien concept this is for the public records office. 'In order to tick a box to say I am Jewish, I first had to answer "no" to the question of whether I am Polish. I had to select Jewish from a list of options that included Ukrainian, German, Belarussian, and a few other nationalities. To this day in Poland, being Jewish is still considered a nationality.'

Returning to the Kizels, I will also refer to their Polish Jewish housekeeper and Polish non-Jewish housekeeper as Jewish and Polish respectively. Not only does it make for easier reading, but the notion of Jewishness as a nationality was also very fitting for the times. Mala explains that her father put more trust in the Polish housekeeper than the Jewish one, because she was better informed about the *kashres*, or Jewish dietary laws. She kept a close eye on the children, and made sure they did as they were told.

Father ran a school at the family home on Miła Street. From the front window, you could look across to no. 18, where the last doomed fighters of the Warsaw Ghetto Uprising fought to the bitter end in April 1943. The street had been pounded to rubble almost four years earlier in the 1939 aerial bombardment of Warsaw, a key element of Germany's blitzkrieg. At least 22,000 people died in the attack, over twenty times the death toll in Rotterdam — another European city razed by German bombers — and equalling the death toll of the notorious Allied bombardment of Dresden, six years later.

Before the bombs fell, Miła Street had been lined with tall houses, most with five floors and a large courtyard at the back where children played among the washing that was hung out to dry. At the end of the street lay Muranowski Square, with its market.

Tall Sender's religious school went by the name of *Grodzhisker kloyz*, after a rabbi who came from a Hasidic family with its origins in Grodzisk, a shtetl not far from the capital, and whose teachings Sender followed. *Kloyz* is a Yiddish word for a place of study. Among the host of Yiddish newspapers on the market in the 1920s and 1930s, I find two reports about the school. The first reveals that, four years after his wife's death, Tall Sender found himself in dire financial straits, facing eviction and the forced sale of his household goods. Mala has no recollection of this episode. The second item, from another newspaper and dated only days later, reports that Sender's financial problems have been solved, but gives no indication of what has brought about this change in fortune.

Mala does remember that the house was never quiet. Her father's pupils read aloud from dawn to dusk, interrupted only occasionally by a lesson from their teacher. Mala vaguely remembers the presence of supervisors, part of the regime in every traditional Jewish religious school. They made sure pupils did not shirk or smuggle in free-thinking literature such as novels or other light reading. News was also strictly forbidden. 'Newspapers were no good for us Orthodox folk,' Mala recalls. 'We had to pray and pray and pray. That's what I was taught.'

But there *were* books. Noam Silberberg of the Ringelblum Institute has found the name Sender Kizel printed in Hebrew books, theological studies published with his help. If enough people decided to club together to fund a publication, a subscription was opened. When there were enough subscribers, and therefore enough money, the book was published, and a list of donors was printed at the back: an early form of crowdfunding. Thinking back on the house she grew up in, Mala pictures entire walls crammed with books, from floor to ceiling. 'Father used a ladder to reach the books he needed.'

Unlike Orthodox parents in the shtetlekh, those in the capital were unable to build a wall between life as they believed it should be lived and the tumult of the ever-changing world beyond. They did try, however, and these attempts could ignite fierce intergenerational battles between fathers and sons. Meanwhile there were daughters who converted in order to run off with a dashing military officer, or who abandoned the God-fearing life to pursue a career as a singer, dancer, or actress in the city's burgeoning entertainment industry. Some parents responded by observing the official mourning ritual known as 'sitting shiva'. By making the huge sacrifice of pronouncing their wayward daughter dead, they hoped the shame would disappear and the natural order would resume. But anyone who lacked a talent for self-delusion could see how futile this was. Change was everywhere.

Paradoxically (or perhaps not) the rise of the nationalist Endeks and their violence against Jews went hand in hand with the flourishing of Jewish political parties, cultural clubs, and places of entertainment, to say nothing of a growing number of writers and poets who freely chose to work in one of the three languages available to them: Hebrew, Yiddish, or Polish. There was a particularly dramatic rise in the number of Yiddish publications, often expressing views on what today we would call issues of identity. Who are we? What is our role in society? How should we and others go about fulfilling this role?

Articles written during Mala's childhood reveal that Jews in Poland saw three options for themselves: leaving the country, assimilating into the majority Polish culture, or standing their ground while staying true to their Jewishness. Each option came in a variety of forms. Did assimilation mean abandoning your own faith and language, and even converting to Catholicism? As a self-respecting Jew, was it permissible to leave for America or Germany, or was the Holy Land the only decent option? And did standing your ground imply clinging to every last letter of the Jewish traditions and customs developed through the centuries on Polish soil?

For men like Mala's father, the answers to these questions were far from complex. The customs, traditions, and tenets of belief that his father before him had observed did more than shape his life — they were its very purpose. For Tall Sender, this was so self-evident that he failed to notice his children changing before his very eyes and their urge to live a life that was not dictated by tradition. Mala's older sister, Mira, is a perfect example. Her father would not let her go to high school. It was enough for a daughter to be able to write Yiddish. A woman's duty was to bear children and care for her husband. A good woman would also bring a measure of contentment and happiness to a marriage, but that was a bonus, not a requirement. Daughter Mira saw things differently. She wanted to attend university, and, without Tall Sender's knowledge, she put herself through a school that could give her that opportunity. She earned her tuition fees, often working deep into the night at a sewing machine, stitching embroidery on cushions and quilts.

Today, the practicalities of this are almost beyond our comprehension: how can you go to school without your father knowing? In Mira's case, her gender was a definite advantage: Tall Sender paid her less heed than he did his sons. As Scharf, our guide to this vanished world, puts it, 'The aspirations of the parents were focused on the male child.' Which made it even more of an achievement that Azriel, his eldest son, managed to do the same. Tall Sender hoped that all his sons would become rabbis: Talmud scholars who would one day reach a higher rung on the religious ladder than he had. These hopes were mainly pinned on his first-born, a clever but sickly boy. Tall Sender talked about how he and Ester had spent a small fortune taking Azriel to one doctor after another, even travelling as far as Vienna. They had also paid a hefty sum to keep him out of military service. But the apple of their eye did not have the calling, and secretly enrolled at a technical school.

It was not his father or mother, but Mala who found him out. At home, she discovered the parcel of clothes her brother took with him to change into before he entered the school. Mala was eleven years old at the time; Azriel, in his early twenties. She confronted her brother, and he admitted everything. It had all started with a part-time job in a factory, he explained, and made her promise not to tell their father.

It was a promise Mala was all too happy to keep. There were enough tensions in the family without Father hearing about this. Mala struggles to give examples of the strained atmosphere at home. That said, one fairly trivial incident has stayed with her: Azriel coming home one day with a chocolate cake in the shape of the Great Synagogue on Tłomackie Square. 'Azriel thought everyone would be delighted. Such a lovely cake, and delicious into the bargain. But my parents were furious with him. What were you thinking? How can we *eat* a synagogue?' The cake went untouched.

Later, Mala remembers another episode, one involving a red-haired teen from Czyżewo. The boy's parents had sent him from the shtetl into the care of Tall Sender. The idea was that he could continue his Talmud studies while doing something to improve his posture, which was in a very bad way. This was a common problem among young Hasidim and had to do with their schooling, which began at an early age. As soon as they could talk, they learned holy blessings from their mother. They soon went from Mother's care to Father's knee. And if Father was a scholar like Sender, he was usually at home poring over his books. Rocking back and forth with his father as he grappled with the meaning of the sacred texts, the little lad would pick up the sing-song melody of study. From the age of three, he would go to *cheder*, where little boys (not girls) learned the Hebrew alphabet and their first prayers, sitting in the same position as their fathers, hunched over the same texts. There was little opportunity to play outdoors and run around: the child was expected to devote around ten hours a day to *lernen* (studying). Scharf observes, 'That was how the young Jewish boy in the shtetl sat, from eight in the morning until six in the evening, five days a week and a half day on Friday, in a small often shabby and musty-smelling room in the home of the teacher, where fifteen or twenty children of different ages were crammed in together.'

'Lots of Hasidim were hunched from all the time they spent sitting and learning,' Mala remembers, 'but this boy was in worse shape than most: as a teenager he looked like a little old man.' The boy's parents in Czyżewo saw that something had to be done, so they dispatched the young yeshiva student to cousin Ester's family in the big city. Her husband, Tall Sender, had a sporting nephew who was a gym teacher. And as Sender was an exceptionally devout man, they had no concerns about entrusting their son to his keeping. In taking the boy on, Sender had his own agenda. He hoped that the deep-seated faith of a pious kid from Czyżewo might rub off on the not-so-pious sportsman.

Things took a different turn. The boy's faith in God Almighty proved to be no match for the gym teacher's conviction that He did not exist. And, unlike Tall Sender's sons, the red-haired boy made no attempt to disguise his inner turmoil. After every gym session, he confronted Sender with a series of unsettling questions, and things deteriorated to the point where Sender felt obliged to alert the family in Czyżewo. Mala doesn't know exactly what his telegram said, but she did witness the response from the shtetl. 'I can picture it to this day,' Mala says. 'Suddenly a big man with a long grey beard was standing in the doorway. He looked furious. The boy was sitting at the table. I was doing something else at the time, I can't remember what. The man marched up to his son, belted him one, hauled him to his feet, and dragged him out of the room. Not a word was spoken.' The boy's father took him straight back to Czyżewo: better to be a hunchback than godless. 'I never saw him again.'

The story brings back warm memories, Mala explains, because she liked her cousin, the gym teacher. David Rosenblatt was his name. She was especially fond of his mother, Aunt Surele. The affection was mutual. Surele called Mala 'Mamele', or 'little mother', because on her deathbed, Surele's mother—Mala's paternal grandmother—talked about the birth of 'a girl with my soul'. The next girl to be born was named after her: Mala Rywka (Rivka) Kizel.

Aunt Surele was a widow and lived at 51a Nowolipki Street, five blocks nearer the old city centre. Mala often dropped in to see her as a little girl, and Surele used to spoil her. 'She would wash my hair, something no one at home ever did.' Mala had to keep these visits to herself because her mother had no time for her sister-in-law. Surele was frowned upon for not raising her children devoutly enough, and, worse still, for not being honest about it. At Mother's instigation, a family boycott was imposed: the threat of secularisation was to be avoided at all costs.

One of Mala's elder sisters brought this threat even closer to home than Surele and her sporting son, confronting Mala's parents head-on with the ways of the new world. Sure—not to be confused with Surele—had a lot in common with her little sister. Like Mala, she was fair-haired and spoke Polish with virtually no accent, something she learned at a good Polish school she had attended without her parents' knowledge or in the shadow of their overwhelming indifference. She had found her own way in the world and ran her own kindergarten. Sure ended up falling in love with Henryk Trager, a man from an assimilated background who could not even understand Yiddish. Father intervened and locked Sure away for a month. The idea that his daughter would not marry a Hasid horrified him; a non-Orthodox man was bad enough, but an unbeliever without an ounce of respect for his own culture?

While Sure was under lock and key, her customers—mothers with young children—came knocking on Tall Sender's door. Where was their kindergarten teacher? Father did not answer.

Eighty years on, Mala finds it hard to judge whether her father really thought that denying Sure contact with her sweetheart for a month would solve matters, or whether it was a punishment born of panic and powerlessness. She remembers smuggling letters from Henryk to her sister. 'He paid me to take them to her,' Mala recalls. 'After four weeks, my father let Sure go and told her she could forget her dowry.' But there was no doubt who had lost. Sure's will was unbroken.

She was also in luck. A cousin of her mother's who had made his fortune as an industrialist in Berlin returned to Polish soil in the autumn of 1938, when the Nazis expelled all Jews with a Polish passport from the Third Reich, some 17,000 in total. Poland was reluctant to receive these deportees, and many found themselves in a camp set up by

Jewish organisations in Zbąszyń. Conditions there were rough, and the brush manufacturer from Berlin was wealthy enough to make his own arrangements. He moved into the Bristol, one of Warsaw's most exclusive hotels: a cream-coloured neoclassical building topped off by a domed pavilion and situated on the elegant Krakowskie Przedmieście, a sweeping avenue that ran from the monarch's seventeenth-century suburban palaces to the medieval city. As Mala tells it, Mother's affluent cousin always wore a white suit. He was very fond of Sure, and footed the bill for the wedding to her assimilated non-believer of a suitor. He also found them a home, not only advancing them a year or two's rent, but also fitting the place out 'right down to the toothbrushes'.

The cousin's contribution went further still. He even managed to convince Tall Sender to grudgingly accept the union between his daughter and Henryk. Sure's husband was also willing to make concessions. As an upstanding member of the religious community, the tall school director wanted his sons and sons-in-law at his side when he walked to the synagogue on Friday. Non-believer Henryk Trager was willing to indulge him. Sender supplied him with a prayer shawl to cover his head and shoulders. And Trager wore it.

In the end, Alter was the only son to live up to his father's ideal. He was only four years older than Mala, and became a rabbi at the age of nineteen, shortly before most of the ghetto's inhabitants were sent to Treblinka. Mala describes him as big, handsome, and blond. He was very strict in his ways. 'He would never hand me a bunch of keys. He always put them down on the table so he would not touch my hand. His little sister's hand!' Eighty years on, Mala still sounds incredulous.

To truly grasp the conflicts that rocked the Jewish world in the 1930s, it may be worth considering that, for Hasidim like Tall Sender and Alter, the world of marriage, boyfriends, schooling, and trips to the cinema was in no way separate from their own lives, dominated by the study of the Torah. This was not about book learning versus everyday life, although of course that is how it appeared, even to Mala. Matters relating to Halacha, that is to say all aspects of how to live one's life, are part of the Talmud, which incorporates the pronouncements of many sages from the early rabbinic period. There is a set procedure. After studying a matter from many different perspectives, scholars arrived at a definitive decision, not least on issues of fidelity and love. Halacha comes from the Hebrew for 'to go' or 'to walk'. This means that vast sections of Jewish religious texts are devoted to human relations, to the tensions that arise between spouses, to familial habits and matters of upbringing.

Tall Sender may have seemed unworldly in the eyes of a young urban generation, but that was certainly not how he viewed himself. He knew about human relations precisely because he spent all day, every day, poring over the sacred texts. At the same time, the definitive nature of the decisions taken by the scholars prevented him from adopting a certain freedom of spirit along the lines of 'new morals for a new age'. Another element at play is that the Torah is not structured chronologically. The answers to the questions addressed in the Scripture come from all ages, as do the comments on those answers. Present and past intermingle or, rather, they become one. Scharf describes how this worked in practice: 'The student in the yeshiva takes part in a debate between Hillel and Shammai, two great teachers from around the beginning of the Common Era; then he interrogates the viewpoint of a teacher from the seventeenth century to finally arrive at his own independent conclusion, which in turn is then ridiculed or greeted with approbation by his fellow students.'

When it came to Mala's schooling, the Talmud obliged Tall Sender to heed the law of the land. In Poland, the law stated that every child, including children from the Yiddish-speaking community, had to attend a government-approved school from the age of seven. But which school? Her sister Mira knew that 'a palace of a school' had opened its doors two years earlier, within walking distance of their home. It had been founded with money bequeathed by philanthropist Leopold Méyet, a lawyer and leading expert on Polish literature who died in 1912. In keeping with his principles, the school was an idealistic, multicultural project, intentionally located in one of the city's poorer neighbourhoods.

Méyet was a Polish Jew who wanted to bridge the wide gulf between the Yiddish and Polish cultures at a time when both were suffering under Russian repression. Though he did not advocate assimilation and had no desire to shrug off his Jewish background, he was very much a Polish nationalist. This combination was not unusual in the nineteenth century, when Polish nationalists were mainly focused on resisting foreign oppression, as opposed to targeting 'alien' elements among their own people. Nationalists could be anarchist, socialist, Jewish, Catholic, or any number of things. For Méyet, nationalism mainly meant elevating ordinary people — whether they were Catholic, Jewish, German, Lemko, Belarussian, or from any other minority — to become fully fledged citizens of a Polish republic that had yet to take shape. His writing reveals a preoccupation with raising the standard of living, combating illiteracy, and promoting Polish literature.

The tuition fees at Méyet's were affordable, and could be waived altogether for the poorest children. The school's directors also took care of clothing, and all pupils were given a free lunch. Mala remembers a theatre, a gym, and — the greatest luxury of all — showers with hot water. 'This meant I was the only one at home who was always clean.'

Multicultural idealism did not mean the school was what we would now call 'mixed'. While Jewish and Christian children were taught in the same building by teachers who shared more or less the same ideals, they did not share a classroom. There were Jewish and Catholic classes. In both, children were taught the national curriculum, and, in both, the emphasis was on language, literature, Polish history, and arithmetic. The Jewish children were also taught Hebrew and Jewish culture and history, while the Christians were taught catechism.

Mala was enrolled by her sister. But because her enrolment was late and the school was more popular with Jews than with Catholics, she found herself as one of the few Jewish pupils in a Catholic class. 'And the only one from an Orthodox family.'

It was a wonderful school, founded with the best of intentions, but as Mala soon discovered, the reality fell well short of Méyet's ideals. Catholic and Jewish children fought each other in the playground, and Jewish children like Mala who wound up in a Catholic class had it tougher than most. 'The other Jewish kids threw stones at us, and our Catholic classmates shoved us so we would slip and fall in the snow.' Mala had her classmates call her Marilka, in the hope of being bullied less. 'Not that it made much difference.'

One girl in particular made her life a misery. Jadwiga would sit behind Mala in class and tug on her braids. 'Non-stop. Once I got so angry, I slapped her full in the face. Just as well she was sitting down at the time, because she towered over me. The whole class went quiet, everyone was shocked. How could a Jewish girl like me dare to slap a non-Jewish girl? They began talking about what they were going to do to me. I was scared to death.'

The following lesson was catechism, which was taught by a priest. Usually, he dismissed the Jewish pupils, but, on this occasion, he told Marilka and Jadwiga to stay behind. 'I was terrified of the priest, because when Jews were beaten up it was often after church on a Sunday. I sat there shaking, and had no idea what I was in for. The priest beckoned me over and said, "My child, why did you hit her?" My child?! He was so kind, I could hardly believe it. I told him what had happened and how Jadwiga was always pestering me. Jadwiga admitted it. When the priest asked her why, she simply said, "Well, she's a Jew, isn't she?" At which, the priest said, "We are all children of God. We have to love one another." He asked us to kiss and make up, and we did. Jadwiga never tugged my braids again. For the first time, I discovered that priests weren't as terrifying as I thought.'

Mala fell in love with the school, and the school gave her a lot in return. 'I was a good pupil, though no one at home was the least bit interested in my report cards. Father least of all. He never so much as gave me a book or a notebook. Even at that age, I knew I'd have to take care of all that myself.'

Aged seven, Mala found herself a job packing chocolates. Other jobs followed. Later, she helped sort the produce at a fruit shop on Muranowski Square, at the end of the street. When she was ten, she tutored other children in arithmetic. School instilled in her a love of poetry and reading. 'Our house was full of books, but only religious works,' Mala says. 'Nothing that would interest a young girl. So I borrowed Polish books from the girls in my class. I was mad about those books. While my brothers were immersed in Jewish learning with my father, I was reading adventures about wicked stepmothers and forbidden love. I never went anywhere without a book. I loved stories, novels, and poems most of all. I learned dozens off by heart, and I could recite them, too.'

Her brothers looked down on so much secular or, even worse, Catholic pulp. Alter, in particular, made no bones about his disapproval. What was Mala doing at a Catholic school anyway? The very thought sickened him, and he regularly took his feelings out on Mala. 'One day when I was doing my homework, he knocked all my books off the table with a swipe of his arm. "*Avek mitn koshtshol!*" he shouted. Get rid of the church! I complained to Father, but that only made Alter angrier. "You'll see!" he fumed. "One day she'll turn Catholic."'

The sentiments expressed by Alter were not uncommon. Hershel Zimmermann survived the war, and later reflected on a childhood comparable to Alter's. On his deathbed in Miami, he told his wife how, as a high school student, he was disgusted by the Catholics he was forced to attend school with because the government didn't support any secondary schools for the Jewish community. Secretly, he relished the opportunity to leave the monotonous home schooling of the rabbi behind him and to learn about profane subjects such as Polish writing, science, geography, and music, but to the outside world he cursed the absence of a Jewish-run alternative high school. He kept insisting to the Catholic pupils that 'ours was the real God ... The gentile children called us names like "Christ-killers" and we often got into fights.' The ease with which the teachers separated the fighters was almost symbolic, Zimmermann mused, picking the Jewish boys out by their curly sidelocks, black kaftans, and round hats.

At the time, of course, Mala's brother Alter had no way of knowing that being assigned to a Catholic class would enable his little sister to survive the catastrophe ahead. The teachers at that palace of a school on Okopowa Street gave her a perfect command of Polish. She learned poems off by heart, verses she could recite in trying wartime situations to win the hearts of the illiterate daughters of Polish peasants. At school, she also picked up enough about the Catholic faith to reel off the prayers that every Catholic Polish girl was expected to know. The school had given her the confidence to enter a Catholic church with assurance. She knew how, where, and why to genuflect and make a sign of the cross.

Speaking Polish was not the norm in her family, much less speaking Polish without an accent. In fact, to the older generation, Polish was

entirely foreign. Their marriage certificate from 1905 describes both
Mala's parents as 'illiterate'. This was nonsense, of course, since Tall
Sender had his nose buried in the Torah on a daily basis, and his wife,
Ester, was also perfectly able to read. At the time, the word 'illiterate'
on a marriage certificate simply meant no knowledge of written Polish
or Russian, with its Cyrillic alphabet. In the eyes of Polish officialdom,
these were the only languages that counted.

All these decades later, Mala ponders the animosity between
Catholics and Jews in her youth and how her schooling changed
the course of her life. It was more than school, she says hesitantly,
that set her on a different path to her brother. 'I have an ear for
languages.' That much is undeniable. Her Dutch is excellent, though
she was in her thirties when she heard the language for the first time.
She has a good command of German, Hebrew, and English, and a
smattering of Russian. 'But I speak Polish best of all. I often catch
myself thinking in Polish. And I dream in Polish, too.' Remarkable,
considering that Mala has not been back to Poland since 1946, and
considering that Yiddish was not only her mother tongue, but the
language she spoke in her sleep when she was younger. In the story
of her survival, this seemingly unimportant detail would put her life
in the balance.

Instead of footnotes
The quote that opens this chapter comes from Głowiński's book *Czarne
sezony*, translated as *The Black Seasons* by Marci Shore.

Deportations from Poland to camps and prisons in the Soviet Union
between October 1939 and June 1941 were not researched extensively
until after the fall of the Berlin Wall. In the 1990s, Moscow's archives
were opened up to researchers for the first time, and since then the
consensus among them has grown: they now estimate that during
the Soviet occupation of Poland, between 309,000 and 327,000 people
were deported to the east. Of these, between 110,000 and 130,000 were
jailed. The rest were sent to labour camps.

The report by the Polish resistance fighter who travelled through
the area around Białystok in the summer of 1941 is referred to by

Polish–American historian Jan T. Gross in his book *Fear: anti-Semitism in Poland after Auschwitz: an essay in historical interpretation* (2006). Gross remarks that Poland's preferred version of its own national history dwells at some length on how the Red Army was welcomed by a section of the Jewish population in the towns and villages of eastern Poland, yet pays scant attention to the warm welcome the Germans received from a section of the Polish population in the same region less than two years later. Historians who point out the warmth of this reception can count on fierce criticism in Polish newspapers and magazines. Polish historians have informed me that even mentioning it in a footnote means I can wave goodbye to any prospect of receiving a subsidy for a Polish translation of this book. We shall see.

Not all of the Jews who remained in Czyżewo were killed in a joint massacre by Germans and Poles in the summer of 1941. Those who survived ended up in a labour camp in Zambrów. Eighteen months later, on 10 January 1943, they were sent to Auschwitz. On 20 March 1945, months after German troops had withdrawn from the region, ten Jews who returned to their homes in Czyżewo were killed by a group of armed Poles. They had escaped the Holocaust by travelling deep into the Soviet Union, only to die at the hands of their own neighbours. Other Jewish returnees got the message, and left the town for good. Most went to the United States or Israel. One or two journeyed back to Czyżewo years later, and described the thudding disappointment of their trip down memory lane. One such story is to be found in Czyżewo's Yizkor book, a complete copy of which can be found online.

An impressive number of these Yizkor or memorial books came to be made, and in many cases to be translated into English. The texts they contain constitute a monument to a particular town or village, often a place that only lives on in stories. These tend to be moving accounts, awkwardly written but with the aim of engendering a sense of fellowship among what journalist Anna Bikont calls 'decimated communities of former residents and their children scattered across the globe'. She, too, concedes that these books are not an especially valuable resource for capturing the history of a place: ultimately, their purpose is to sing the praises of life in the shtetl, not to reconstruct it.

Nevertheless, she rightly adds, they represent unparalleled material for cultural anthropologists by 'illustrating the process behind the myth of a happy little Jewish town'.

Rest assured, I made every effort to track down the larger-than-life character of Mala's mother's cousin, the benefactor in his impeccable white suit. Unfortunately, I did not succeed. The names and details supplied by Mala left me and every researcher I consulted drawing blanks. Even the Hotel Bristol's guest book contains nothing that resembles 'Josef Pogoda', the name that Mala remembers. The Bristol's management is still able to trace hotel guests from the 1930s, as it was one of the few buildings in Warsaw to survive the war: during the Warsaw Uprising in the summer of 1944, SS officers took up residence there. Other sensational family stories about our benefactor also led us nowhere, such as the tale that he was blinded by a spurned lover who threw sulphuric acid in his face after he refused to take her to Warsaw with him. He is also supposed to have squirreled away his fortune on a Swiss bank account, and to have arrived in Warsaw in an open-topped car driven by his personal chauffeur. By all accounts, the chauffeur was also installed at the Bristol, by no means a cheap place to stay.

After a lengthy search, Noam Silberberg of the Ringelblum Institute concluded, 'This is typical of the colourful family stories I often hear. Typical because the magical realism of stories like this gave Hasidic Jews and their secularising children an outlet for their astonishment at the tumultuous social changes of the day.' Be that as it may, Mala's recollections of the man are so clear and precise that it seems to me unlikely he did not exist at all.

The quotations from Rafael F. Scharf come from his article 'Kindheit en Jugend im jüdischen Schtetl', published in Werner Licharz, *Dialog mit Polen, Beiträge zur deutsch-polnischen Verständnigung*, no. 3, 1984, pp. 74–92. The English here is based on the Dutch translation by Rolf Deen and Philippe van Heusden.

Polish journalist Magdalena Kicińska found a number of articles about Mala's school. The most informative of these was published in the magazine *Kurier Wspomnień* on 13 December 2010.

Journalist Anna Bikont's battle to be included in the official records as both Jewish and Polish reveals an obstinate assumption held by

Polish public officials to this day: the notion that 'Jewish' is a nationality, even one that is inalienable. The case of Julia Brystiger, who has gone down in Polish history under her nickname *krwawa Luna* (Bloody Luna), provides another striking example. As a committed communist, Brystiger was rewarded with a senior position in post-war Poland's security services. In this capacity, she was occasionally expected to fill in her personal details on a form. Each time, she gave her nationality as 'Polish'. Today, these forms are held by the Institute of National Remembrance in Warsaw. On each one, the receiving official crossed out the word 'Polish' and wrote 'Jewish' beside it. By way of correction.

2

The Vistula

'The best political weapon is the weapon of terror. Cruelty
commands respect.Men may hate us. But we don't ask for their
love; only for their fear.'

–Heinrich Himmler, Reichsführer-SS

In the summer of 1939, the Polish government ordered thousands of gas masks to be distributed, and called on its citizens, out of love for the fatherland, to donate as much money as they could spare to help fund the army. Many wealthy individuals provided gifts in kind—sometimes a piece of artillery, sometimes a whole tank. Their efforts came to nothing: the sheer scale of the German offensive meant that Poland was crushed within weeks.

This was the first major test for the Wehrmacht, and its commanders intended to leave nothing to chance. On 1 September 1939, a staggering one-and-a-half million German troops invaded the country, from the west, the north (East Prussia), and the south, through Slovakia. They deployed 2,700 tanks and 1,900 fighter planes. Poland's 300 tanks and 392 aircraft didn't stand a chance. The Luftwaffe bombarded the Polish capital for 27 days. The bombs that reduced Mala's parents' home on Miła Street to a single floor fell on the feast of Yom Kippur, the Day of Atonement. Mala remembers how she, her father, brothers, and sisters walked through the streets hand in hand, so as not to lose one another in the chaos. The official surrender of the city followed three days later.

The Vistula—Wisła in Polish—became the Weichsel.

In Western Europe, the Germans hoped to occupy countries with a minimum of resources by maximising help from the indigenous population; the plan for Poland was far more hostile. The weekend before the invasion, Hitler told a number of his military commanders, 'The goal to be obtained in the war is not that of reaching certain lines but of physically demolishing the opponent.' He went on to urge, 'Be hard, be without mercy, act more quickly and brutally than the others.'

In their reports, high-ranking German officials wrote of the need for Poland to disappear as a cultural nation, to prevent uprisings like the ones that had taken place in the nineteenth century. The name Poland disappeared; the old borders disappeared. The west of the country was absorbed into the Reich, and the centre became a General Government to be exploited for profit, a kind of colony where the population was consigned to slavery. The east was left to Stalin.

The Germans set fire to archives, shipped art to the west, and commandeered countless churches and museums as barracks, stables, warehouses, and sports halls. Poles were only allowed to fulfil government posts at local level; all other positions were given to Germans or Poles of German descent. High schools, newspapers, and magazines were closed down. Heinrich Himmler, the head of the SS, wrote that four years of primary school was all the education the Poles would need. 'The objective of the *Volksschule* need only be: simple arithmetic involving numbers below 500, the writing of names, and to teach that it is God's commandment to obey Germans and to be honest, hard-working, and well-behaved. I consider it unnecessary to teach reading.' It would be better for the Third Reich if its slaves were illiterate. Himmler not only regarded the Poles as an inferior race; he intended to keep them that way.

Mala's school became a relief centre for those injured in the battle of Warsaw, and before long it housed around 2,400 people. Volunteers fed them with meat from the thousands of horses that had died in the bombing and lay scattered throughout the city. A bunker was built at the entrance to the school, where SS troops were billeted. In the schoolyard, SS soldiers burned books for days on end.

The writers of these books were targeted, too. The occupied territories had to be purged of all intellectuals. The *Generalplan Ost* insisted that the entire Polish elite had to perish. This masterplan for Central and Eastern Europe had been drawn up shortly before the invasion of Poland by the *Ostforschung*, a collaborative organisation involving researchers from German universities. The plan consisted of two phases: one for the short term, and one that spanned the next twenty to thirty years. The first phase set out the removal of the Polish elite, while the long-term aim was to create *Lebensraum*, or living space, for the superior German race. In other words, it envisaged the Germanisation of Eastern Europe. For this to happen, 45 million people had to disappear, through deportation to Siberia or other, more rigorous, means. Approximately 14 million inhabitants would be allowed to remain, pressed into service as unpaid workers for between eight and ten million German farmers, ethnic Germans (in which the Nazis included the Dutch), Danes, the German diaspora, and other people with the potential to undergo a process of *Umvolkung* that would allow them to be assimilated as inhabitants of Germany's eastern territories.

The short-term plan went into effect immediately, in the summer of 1939. It meant that any Polish citizen whose existence contradicted the German claim to superiority was in danger: doctors, artists, lawyers, researchers, and so on. Political affiliation was irrelevant. Even fascist, anti-Semitic intellectuals were not safe. Some offered their services to the Germans, but contrary to their later tactics in Western Europe, the occupiers rejected any such offers. In fact, the Gestapo went one step further and arrested these potential collaborators; anyone who aspired to a position of leadership was clearly a threat. In Hitler's words, 'Poles may have only one master—a German. Two masters cannot exist side by side, and this is why all members of the Polish intelligentsia must be killed. This sounds harsh, but such are the laws of life.' One-third of Poles with a university degree did not survive the occupation.

As early as June 1941, the Nazi top brass declared the implementation of the first phase of *Generalplan Ost* to have been completed.

Although the Germans regarded anti-Semitic Poles first and foremost as Poles, and therefore *Untermenschen*, they were nevertheless keen to fire up the anti-Semitic sentiment that already existed in Polish society. Assimilated Jews, as the memoirs of survivors attest, were shocked by the depth of hatred this unleashed. Before the German invasion, they were well aware that life as a Jew in Poland was no picnic, but few suspected how bad things could get when their compatriots were spurred on by their new rulers. Survivor Hershel Zimmermann, who had left his Orthodox youth in a shtetl behind for a new life in the capital, remembers how the people of Warsaw emerged from their air-raid shelters after four weeks of bombing. 'They looked and acted like wild animals, grabbing at any food they could get. The Germans set up bread lines, handing out a loaf of bread to each person in the line, but not to Jews. I was kicked out of bread lines several times when the Poles in line pointed me out to the Germans as a Jew.'

Throughout the war, Poles proved more adept than Germans at identifying Jews. After all, Jews and Poles had lived side by side for centuries. Besides, the desire for 'ethnic purity' was not exclusive to Germans. The Poles had their own version; in fact, the Germans themselves had been counted among Poland's undesirable minorities prior to September 1939: around 800,000 Germans lived in the Second Polish Republic, along with Belarussians, Ukrainians, Rusyns, and a few other minority groups, all of whom spoke their own language, while few were Roman Catholic. As Brian Porter's impressive study *When Nationalism Began to Hate* shows, from the end of the nineteenth century, hatred started to become a component of nationalism in Poland. In 1918, after the withdrawal of the imperial rulers, a new, independent Poland appeared on the map with signs that read 'Forbidden for dogs, Jews, and Germans'. When the Germans invaded, they were replaced by signs that read 'Access for Germans only'.

The Jews, of course, had it worse than anyone. Many authoritative accounts of the destruction wrought on Jewish life in Poland already exist, so I will only sketch the briefest of reminders here. First came the humiliations, as Orthodox Jews were mocked, and their beards shaved off or even pulled out. The bank accounts of all Polish Jews were blocked. Then came a ban on religious gatherings and ritual slaughter, and 'Aryan' directors were put in charge of all Jewish companies. In December 1939, it became mandatory for Jews in Warsaw to display a star of David in their shop windows. Every Jew over the age of twelve was obliged to wear a white band with a blue star of David on their right arm. Anyone who failed to do so risked summary execution at the hands of any German soldier, gendarme, or policeman who observed the offence—in other words, the man who checked their ID.

A small but aggressive section of the city's population then began to destroy Jewish shops and to assault Jews in the street. This gave the Germans a pretext to isolate the Jewish population even further. The propaganda of the day spoke of a Jewish threat to the Polish population caused by infectious diseases, and of threats to Jews by Poles with 'a score to settle'. Newspaper reports make it clear that the Germans sympathised with these Polish assailants while insisting that law and order had to be maintained. And so the occupier ordered the previously instituted Jewish Council to build a defensive wall around 'the area threatened by typhus'. The Jews had to pay for this wall themselves. Non-Jews in the neighbourhood, over 100,000 in all, had to move out, and an estimated 140,000 Jews from other parts of the city were relocated to take their place. Hand luggage and bedclothes were all they were allowed to bring with them.

This brief outline brings us to November 1940—Saturday the sixteenth, to be precise, the day the ghetto was closed to the outside world. The neighbourhood where Mala grew up had been transformed into a prison of less than four square kilometres. In March 1941, 450,000 people were living in this sealed-off section of city; no ghetto in occupied Europe housed as many inhabitants. They were packed in like sardines and systematically starved. The ration coupons they received were good for 500 calories, and that was only to start with. This was later reduced to 200 calories, though a human adult needs a daily intake of between 2,000 and 2,500 calories to stay healthy. (The average twenty-first-century European consumes around 3,500 calories a day. In the world's poorest countries, Congo or Malawi for example, much of the present-day population get by on around 1,600 calories a day.)

By the time the Germans came to deport the vast majority to the Treblinka extermination camp in the summer of 1942, around one in five of the ghetto's inhabitants had starved to death. Lifeless bodies lay on every street corner. They were collected at night and piled onto handcarts. In the dark days of December 1941, the crews collected 150 bodies a night. Food was always on everyone's mind, an obsession that fills the pages of the survivors' memoirs. Hunger and scarcity also ruled Mala's life, and she changed her name to obtain ration coupons. Ever since their street had been bombed, she had lived with the Wasermans: her sister Chaja, Chaja's husband, Majloch, and their little son, Samek. Mala could only obtain coupons by posing as Chaja's daughter, and so she came to be registered as Marilka Waserman.

Hunger can wreck the best of relationships. Mala's sister Mira fell out with a friend over a piece of bread. Mira had sent Mala over to the girl's house to fetch something, and Mala had to sit there while the girl munched on a baguette without offering her so much as a bite. When the girl wasn't looking, Mala broke off a chunk of bread and slipped it into her pocket. Later that day, the girl turned up at the Wasermans' door to complain. This sent Mira into a rage, and she lambasted her friend for not sharing in the first place. 'I'm only sorry my sister didn't run off with the whole loaf!'

Later, as the ghetto became even more overcrowded, hunger sparked a conflict between Mala and Różka, her best friend at the time. Różka lost her bread card, and because Mala had been to see her the day before, Różka's family were convinced she had stolen it and subjected her to an interrogation. Różka's father was the only one convinced of Mala's innocence: she came from a good family, after all, and was the daughter of a religious man. A brother-in-law dismissed his words, insisting everyone was willing to steal for bread. Mala was reduced to tears, at which the family locked her in a kind of storeroom filled with home-made soap and told her that's where she'd stay until she handed over the card—a card she didn't have. There was no bed, nothing to eat, and Mala can still remember the stink of the place. The next day, a man was caught trying use Różka's card at the baker's, and Mala was released.

Before long, Różka came to ask Mala's forgiveness; when Mala refused, Różka fell to her knees and begged. Friends who had arranged the meeting had to grab Mala to stop her storming off. In the end, Mala took pity on her friend. She understood that hunger can do strange things to people.

The starvation rations imposed on the ghetto meant that its inhabitants had to trade with people on the outside in order to survive. Hunger made smugglers of them. Adam Czerniaków, the head of the Jewish Council, estimated that forty times more food was smuggled in than entered through official channels. Getting provisions through and over the ghetto wall unseen called for agility, speed, a slight build, and a fearless disregard for death, which meant that the smugglers were mostly children. Mala was one of them. She remembers a loaf in the ghetto costing a small fortune: around 100 złoty, while the same loaf outside the ghetto sold for forty grosz (0.4 złoty). Her memory roughly corresponds with the price data collected by historian and sociologist Emanuel Ringelblum and his group, and later buried in milk cans and tin boxes.

'Outside the ghetto, we bought bread, butter, beans, buckwheat, and sometimes even fish,' Mala recalls. 'In the beginning, it wasn't dangerous: if we were caught by the Germans or the police, they just chased us back into the ghetto. Later, they confiscated our food and gave it to Polish children, who soon caught on and would stand around waiting. But after a while, smuggling meant risking your life.'

Mala had one distinct advantage: her appearance. *Dobry wygląd*, 'good looks', was the expression Poles used to describe Jews who did not look Semitic. Mala was fair-haired, and her eyes were blue with a hint of green. It also helped that she was a girl. Any boy with a suspect appearance or a Yiddish accent risked having his pants pulled down to see whether he had been circumcised. If a girl was stopped by the Polish police, they would make her recite a Polish prayer, something Mala could do without a trace of an accent.

Young smugglers told Ringelblum's frontline historians they were always on the look-out for a German nicknamed Frankenstein, who seemed to take particular pleasure in catching children. He would hunt them down for hours on end. A doctor by the name of Adina Szwajger recalled how he shot at children 'as if they were sparrows'. Two of Frankenstein's victims died the doctor's arms.

Mala's biggest fear was encountering someone she knew. Outside the ghetto one day, she bumped into Jadwiga, the braid–pulling classmate the priest had ordered her to kiss and make up with. Mala could tell instantly that Jadwiga was surprised to see her, a Jew outside the ghetto. Yet Mala even managed to convince a girl like Jadwiga that the situation was not as it seemed. She told her former classmate that her mother wasn't Jewish, and that she and her family lived outside the ghetto. 'Luckily, she believed me.'

Jadwiga's credulousness was definitely a stroke of luck. During the German occupation, many Polish children lost their capacity for empathy or compassion. Educational psychologist Irena Chmieleńska gave a startling account of this development in a Polish political-cultural weekly published in December 1945. Her article detailed the conclusions of a study she had carried out among non-Jewish children a few years earlier to discover how they had been affected by the war. Under the title 'Wartime Children', she explained how they steadily became more callous and self-centred, until taking advantage of every opportunity for material gain was what mattered most. The children Chmieleńska interviewed dismissed honesty, fairness, and consideration for the welfare of others as 'stupidity'. Qualities that were no good to anyone.

Boys between the ages of ten and thirteen 'spent entire nights watching by ghetto walls and blackmailing Jews who were climbing over.' Mala knew this. And it frightened her, too.

'I spoke with a ten-year-old boy from an upper-class intelligentsia family ... a so-called good family,' Chmieleńska noted. 'He said that the Germans were right to destroy the Jews because now, "We have more food; earlier Mommy and I were doing worse." Asked if he thought it would be just as fair to kill him and his mother so that some Jewish child and his mother had more to eat, he replied calmly, after giving the matter "serious consideration" that he would not consider this right "because, you see Miss, everybody is an egoist and has to think first about his own interest and it is better for me that way ..."'

In December 1945, Chmieleńska concluded, 'A German shot at "Jude," and a child shouted "Jude" whenever he met one ... That somebody else was beaten up or killed, not him, not his family, that he could watch this calmly with a feeling of personal safety, gave such a child a sense of pride—he felt better, untouchable vis-à-vis those who in his presence, and to his delight, were being humiliated.'

Chmieleńska believed that the Germans infected everyone with the concept of differentiating between human beings and people who were less than human. She cited a story that circulated in the underground press about a child turning to his mother after a shooting and asking, 'Mummy, was it a human being that was killed or a Jew?'

Danger was closing in on all sides. One early spring day in 1941, Mala had succeeded in returning to the ghetto with two loaves and some other provisions when she was stopped by a member of the Jewish ghetto police. He made her an offer: share your food with me and I'll let you go. Mala refused. 'What was he thinking? I was already in the ghetto!' The policeman threatened to hand her over to the Germans. Mala, who was fifteen at the time, could hardly believe her ears. 'The idea that a Jewish man would do something like that to a Jewish girl!' But that is exactly what happened. Mala recalls how the policeman grabbed her by the scruff of the neck and dragged her off. The first German soldier they met hit her full in the face with the butt of his rifle. 'I clasped my hand to my face and felt the warm blood running through my fingers.' She collapsed, and the next thing she remembers is waking up on a cellar floor. A group of onlookers had brought her to safety and were taking care of her.

Mala's brothers came to fetch her. They wanted to teach the Jewish policeman a lesson, but their father would not let them. Hitting someone was unconscionable; violence was out of the question. 'It was a while before I could get out of bed,' Mala says. 'My front teeth had been knocked out, and my whole face was swollen. But, worst of all, I had come home empty-handed.'

She went to see a dentist, who told her it would take bridgework to fix her teeth—an impossible expense for a girl like Mala. 'I told the dentist what had happened, and we both ended up in tears. She comforted me and promised she would fix my teeth for free. And she did.' Mala says the dentist restored her faith in humanity, which had been dealt a severe blow by the policeman's betrayal. 'Even so, it was difficult for me. I thought I was the only child in the world with false teeth.'

Dentures were the least of it. Mala had been hit in the face with a rifle butt at a time when many young smugglers were killed on the spot. Reports from the time reveal that the Germans were exasperated by Jewish policemen attempting to cut deals with the smugglers they caught, in the hope of sharing their spoils. At the start of 1942, they came up with a new system: every Jewish policeman in the ghetto was assigned a stretch of wall, between fifteen and twenty metres long. Any evidence of smuggling on a policeman's stretch, and he and his entire family would be executed.

Mala's elder sister, Mira, tried to stop her sneaking out of the ghetto in search of food, but to no avail. Especially after the daughter of a neighbouring family — another fair-haired girl from an Orthodox household — showed Mala a better route, but only once she had sworn not to reveal it to anyone. This took Mala to the northernmost point of the ghetto, not far from the railway platform where ghetto residents were put on the trains that transported them to the gas chambers of Treblinka. There, a section of the wall on Dzika Street consisted of several badly damaged houses where the neighbour girl had found an opening. It wasn't much of a gap, but just big enough for Mala to squeeze through.

With this new route came opportunities to trade, and Mala began to smuggle out clothes made by her sister Chaja at their home on Nalewki Street. Before the war, Chaja had worked as a seamstress for a prominent firm called Hopman. Her husband, Majloch, hailed from Tomaszów Lubelski, a town some thirty kilometres beyond the south-eastern city of Zamość. One of his hometown contacts bought the clothes from Mala and sold them on at a tidy profit. Demand was high: as the Jewish population in the south-east dwindled, so, too, did the supply of affordable textiles. Non-Jewish tailors were rare in that part of the country.

With the money she made from Majloch's Polish contact, Mala was able to feed the whole family. She was even able to put some money aside. While this struck me as bizarre in the context of the privations, the hunger, and the desperate circumstances in the ghetto, my initial surprise was tempered by studying Ringelblum's archive. One of his milk cans contained a study of smuggling. The daily income of a smuggler, no matter how young, was between thirty and 300 złoty.

Smuggling was so essential to the survival of the ghetto's inhabitants that it led to a redistribution of the few remaining assets in this condemned community. Mala says her smuggling activities made her 'rich', but rich is an overstatement.

Mala's new front teeth were a constant reminder of the risks she was running. And before long, the game was up. Outside the ghetto one day, her white armband with the star of David tucked in her pocket, she was warned that the Germans and the Polish police had encircled the area in a concerted effort to clamp down on the smugglers. The girl who had let Mala in on the secret route was also outside the ghetto at the time, and told her one boy had been shot dead.

Mala was too frightened to go back. Instead, she went looking for Majloch's contact. The man's name was Olszewski, and he was still in Warsaw. He offered to take her back to his hometown of Tomaszów Lubelski, where she could wait until the trouble had blown over and it was safe to return. And, sick with worry about how concerned her family would be, Mala desperately wanted to return.

The man and the girl travelled by train. It was April 1941, and Jews of any age faced execution if they were caught on a train. Mala was unaware of this, and could easily pass as Olszewski's daughter. No one asked them for their papers.

They arrived in Tomaszów Lubelski to a warm welcome from Olszewski's wife and two daughters, one of whom was almost the same age as Mala. She remembers the daughters as sweet and their mother as an exceptionally warm-hearted woman. When Olszewski explained why he had brought this Jewish girl home with him, his wife burst into tears. Mala had the impression that people in Tomaszów Lubelski knew nothing of the horrors taking place in the capital.

Mrs Olszewski told Mala that a Jewish family lived downstairs and that she could eat kosher with them. Mala took her up on the offer. The next day, she went to a baker's and bought fresh bread with the money she had earned. 'Bread rolls with onion, I remember to this day.

They were so tasty, I ate them all myself.' Then she bought buckwheat and beans, and sent them in a parcel addressed to the Wasermans in the ghetto. 'At the time, I just assumed it would be delivered.'

Instead of footnotes

The number of tanks and fighter planes attributed to the German and the Polish armed forces comes from *Poland: a history* (2009) by British-Polish historian Adam Zamoyski. The quote from Hitler and the figures for the Polish academics who were killed come from *Poland in the Modern World: beyond martyrdom* (2014) by Brian Porter-Szücs.

'War Children', the article written by developmental psychologist Irena Chmieleńska about the changes in the morality of Polish children, was published on 9 December 1945 in the weekly newspaper *Kuźnica*. Jan T. Gross cites her work in *Fear: anti-Semitism in Poland after Auschwitz: an essay in historical interpretation* (2006).

The estimate of goods smuggled into the ghetto was made by Adam Czerniaków, head of the Warsaw Ghetto Jewish Council, and appears in the diary he kept from September 1939 until 23 July 1942, when he committed suicide by taking a cyanide pill. It was the day after he had been told that the council would be expected to help arrange the deportation of many of the ghetto's residents to Treblinka and certain death. Szmul Zygielbojm, a leading Polish Jewish trade unionist and politician, took his own life ten months later. He was living in London as a member of the national council of Poland's government-in-exile, and killed himself on hearing the news that the Warsaw Ghetto Uprising had been crushed and the last inhabitants executed. In his suicide note, Zygielbojm wrote 'By my death, I wish to give expression to my most profound protest against the inaction in which the world watches and permits the destruction of the Jewish people.'

In his notes, Emanuel Ringelblum is full of admiration for the children who smuggled food into the ghetto. If a monument should be erected for anyone after the war, he wrote, let it be for them. That monument now stands at Warsaw's Okopowa Street Jewish cemetery, not far from where Mala's school once stood.

3

The Sukha Lypa

'What true Hasid isn't ready at a moment's notice to drink and
make merry?'

–Israel Joshua Singer, writer

After two weeks of staying with the Olszewskis and eating with the
Jewish family downstairs, Mala returned to her own family in the
ghetto. Enough time had passed for the most acute danger to have
blown over, or so she believed. It was her first train journey alone. If
someone had singled her out as a Jewish girl, she would not have lived
past the age of fifteen. On arriving in Warsaw, a new problem awaited
her. Too wary to take her secret route into the ghetto, how was she to
get back home? Though it was forbidden for Jews, she boarded a tram,
one that passed through the ghetto without stopping. A Polish police
officer stood guard, but Mala was in luck: she noticed a passenger
slipping the driver a small bottle of vodka, and, as the tram rounded
a bend, it seemed to slow more than was necessary. The passenger
jumped off. Mala followed.

The situation in the ghetto had become even more unbearable,
with an average of seven people crammed into a single room. When
she went to see Aunt Surele on Nowolipki Street, Mala learned that her
brothers Pinie and Azriel had fled the hunger and the hellish conditions.
Their plan had been to head east, across the River Bug to a region that
had been annexed by the Soviets. Surele's eldest son, the gym teacher,

had gone before them, and word of his safe arrival had already reached the ghetto.

Mala's sister Sure, the one who ran a kindergarten, had escaped the ghetto, too, and had gone into hiding with her husband, Henryk Trager, in the 'Aryan' section of Warsaw. Trager had served in the army and was well connected outside Jewish circles. Majloch, her sister Chaja's husband, was also convinced that his family, Mala and Mira included, had to get out of the ghetto and fast. 'This black pit will be the death of us all,' he said. He took the plunge, and asked his contact Olszewski to rent them a house in Tomaszów Lubelski, the town where he lived and where Majloch was born. He relied on Mala to deliver this request, in a letter that set the time and place for their rendezvous. Majloch's plan was to climb out of the sewer through a particular manhole outside the ghetto, and Olszewski was to be standing by.

Taking her usual route, Mala smuggled the letter out. The plan worked. A few days after Majloch got out, Chaja, and her young son, Samek, made their getaway, too. Mala was their guide, leading them through the narrow opening on Dzika Street. On her back, Chaja lugged the dead weight of her sewing machine, which was to be their main source of income.

They took a train to the town of Lublin, around 150 kilometres south-east of the capital, hoping no one would ask them for their papers. Mira followed a day later, and one of Majloch's cousins turned up in a truck to collect them all.

In Tomaszów, Chaja set about making thick, sleeveless waistcoats that could be worn as bodywarmers. Mala and Majloch sold them to farmers in the surrounding villages, while Mira took care of the housekeeping. Unfortunately, the weather soon turned milder, and the demand for bodywarmers dried up. Majloch advised Mira and Mala to find work on a farm; someone in his family knew of a likely farmer not far from Lublin.

At the time, many young Jewish Poles from the Lublin area were offering their services as farm labourers in exchange for board and lodging—a stay of execution. Many were on the run, not only from the Germans, but also from local Jewish councils ordered to supply the

Germans with a minimum number of labourers per day. In the spring of 1941, farmers were still happy to take these young Jews up on the offer.

Mira and Mala settled in at one of the larger farms, where they shared a room with another Jewish girl, Hanka, who was seventeen. Mira had already turned twenty. Mala describes Mira as bright and charming, but she had never been good with her hands, and had a knack of leaving most of the chores to her younger sister. On the farm, Mala says she wound up doing the work of two, afraid the farmer's family would send Mira packing if they had reason to complain. Yet, at the same time, Mala could see how the farmhands adored her sister. 'Everyone stopped by after work because Mira told such wonderful stories.' Dog-tired from the back-breaking work, Mala says she rarely stayed awake long enough to listen.

She no longer remembers exactly what her work duties were. Hershel Zimmermann, who dictated his own memoirs twenty-two years earlier than Mala, worked on a farm in the same region, and recalls his routine in more detail. 'The hardest and most backbreaking work was potato digging. This was normally considered women's work, but I was put to work doing that, too. One had to bend close to the ground to dig the potatoes and fill the baskets, which were later picked up by a wagon. The women were used to doing this type of work, as they did it all their lives ... At first, I could only do one row in the same time it took for them to do three, and by the end of that one row I thought that my back was broken. Eventually, I could work as well as they did. I did not want them to think a Jew could not work as hard as a Polish farmer. I did not want to reinforce commonly held misconceptions in Poland about Jews.'

Zimmermann led a horse and plough through the field, harvested with a hand scythe, dug onions, beets, and other vegetables from the garden, and, in the autumn, packed the farmhouse walls with dried leaves and branches to keep out the worst of the cold. He worked under the same conditions as Mala, her sister, and hundreds, perhaps even thousands, of other young, strong Polish Jews who worked in exchange for food and a place to sleep. Some nights, Zimmermann writes, he was too tired even to finish his food. During the day he wore clogs, like all the local farmers, and a straw hat. 'I looked so much like any other farm hand that you could not tell I was a city boy.'

There was one major difference between Zimmermann and the girls. He was the only labourer on the farm, and, as the winter of 1941 set in, there was enough work to allow him to stay on. For Mala, her sister, and Hanka, the work dried up when summer was over, and they had no choice but to leave. Another contributing factor may have been the decree issued on 15 October 1941 by Hans Frank, head of the General Government in Nazi-occupied Poland, that anyone who helped Jews would face the death penalty. The legal term for this offence was *Judenbegünstigung*. In light of the horrific loss of life inflicted by the Germans in the General Government, the number of Poles summarily executed on these grounds was surprisingly low: around 800. But as a deterrent, the measure proved extremely effective.

Then again, it is quite possible that the farmer Mala was working for knew nothing about the decree. Many people living on remote farms were cut off from the news. And in all her time at the farm near Lublin, Mala cannot remember seeing a single German. Following the invasion of the Soviet Union that same summer, very few Germans had remained in the area, and when they did appear, it was to make sure that the local farmers delivered their quotas. From July onwards, they sometimes returned to hunt down escaped Russian prisoners of war; the nearby forests were swarming with them.

Alongside the death penalty for helping Jews, Frank also imposed the death penalty on every Jew found outside a ghetto. Yet another year would pass before this decree began to be strictly enforced in the district of Lublin. There simply wasn't enough manpower, and the villages were too numerous and remote. The Germans did not return to the villages around Lublin and Tomaszów Lubelski in any great numbers until the spring and summer of 1942. But when they did, it was for what the soldiers and policemen themselves referred to as the *Judenjagd*: the hunt for the Jews.

By that time, Mala was working for a smallholder by the Sukha Lypa, a small river that runs through the remote, hilly landscape to the south of Tomaszów Lubelski. When Mala, Mira, and Hanka were forced to leave the farm, they headed south on foot. Hitching a ride on a horse-drawn cart, they travelled for an entire day, perhaps two, and wound up in the village of Karpy, around 135 kilometres south-east of Lublin. There, or, to be more exact, on a small farm just outside the village, Mala found a place with a family.

The cluster of farms and houses at the edge of the forest was known as Kolonie Karpy; it was common for small settlements in the area to bear the name of the adjacent village prefaced by the word *kolonie* or *kolonia*. Karpy itself was small enough, surrounded by wooded hills and only accessible by horse and cart over a rough track. It was home to 200 people at most, the majority of whom spoke a Polish dialect that overlapped with the Ukrainian spoken in the region. Mala moved in with the Gmitruks, a family of seven who lived in a house that consisted of a single room with a tiny extension by the door. The entire structure, even the roof, was made of wood. Only the chimney and the stove, which doubled as an oven, were made of stone. The family had five sons, three of whom were older than Mala. Their mother had died, and the woman of the household was the mother of the two younger boys—one aged seven, the other still a baby.

The family owned two cows, two pigs, chickens, and geese. They were grateful for Mala's arrival and the extra help she had to offer, not least because the man of the house was ill. As Mala remembers it, the three older boys fought almost daily over who was supposed to do what.

Mala has fond memories of her time with the Gmitruks, and still marvels at the primitive nature of the life they led—the life all of Karpy led, for that matter. The village had no running water and no electricity. 'Those people had nothing,' Mala recalls. 'They ate with wooden spoons they had made themselves. There were no chairs; everyone sat on a simple stool. The floor was trodden earth. Food was served without plates on a kind of large tray with raised edges.'

Even wood was a luxury. There were days in winter when the Gmitruks would not let their children get out of bed because it was too cold and they had no warm winter clothes. This was not unusual in small villages in the region. Hershel Zimmermann remembers a couple in the shtetl where he grew up waking after a particularly

cold night to find their babies frozen to death in their bed. Mala was
fortunate enough to sleep on top of the oven.

It was a life straight out of Van Gogh's *The Potato Eaters*. 'But,' Mala
says, 'the remarkable thing was that all the Gmitruks ate their fair share,
and no more. Isn't that something? And everyone was hungry, you
know. Hungry all the time.' Yet they took it in turns to eat a spoonful at
a time from that one big tray.

Mala was up at five every morning to milk the cows, feed the other
animals, and then help with the housework so that Mrs Gmitruk could
tend to her ailing husband. 'I did the washing, too. Without soap. There
was no soap in Kolonie Karpy. I soon got used to the way things were,
and the whole family treated me with respect. The Gmitruks were
illiterate, and so I would read to them, anything I could lay my hands
on. I read a passage from the Bible to Mrs Gmitruk every evening. I
spoke better Polish than anyone in Karpy, and I don't think anyone
there could read. On Sundays we went to church, which was about
three kilometres away. I walked barefoot. I only had one pair of shoes,
and I didn't want to wear them out.' People could tell she wasn't used
to walking barefoot. 'Most of them saw me as a city girl, not a Jewish
girl.'

For a time, the war seemed remote, though German forces had
stormed through the area not long before, bound for Moscow and
Stalingrad.

Mala's Jewish friend Hanka lived close by, and after a while her
sister Mira came to live locally, too. She found work with a doctor a few
kilometres away—a Jewish doctor, strangely enough. Because he was
the only person in the area with any medical knowledge, the Germans
had not yet sentenced him to hard labour or confined him to the ghetto
of Rawa-Ruska, some thirteen kilometres north-east of Karpy. The
doctor was widely respected in the community, so local farmers may
have hidden him whenever the Germans or other authorities came
to call. The doctor's wife had been taken away and either arrested or
murdered, which was why he was on the look-out for a young woman
like Mira—someone to take care of his three children and run the
household.

Mira was back in Tomaszów Lubelski when she heard about the

position with the doctor, and immediately set out on foot, a trek of about twenty-five kilometres. She was happy with the doctor and his young family. The feeling was mutual, and within a matter of months he wanted to marry her. Mala understands why. 'Mira was so pretty!' For her part, Mala made friends with a local girl called Amelka. They had met in one of the small fields outside the village, where the cows were put out to grass. The two girls were the same age, and before long they were confiding their hopes and fears to each other.

In this quiet place, the misery of the ghetto seemed far away, and for that very reason there was one thing Mala was determined to do: get her twelve-year-old brother, Meir, out of the ghetto, and bring him to the countryside.

Tall Sender had died early that summer, and young Meir Kizel was being looked after by Sender's widowed sister, Aunt Surele. Meir was in a bad way, and had somehow managed to get a letter to Chaja in Tomaszów. In it, he asked his sisters to help him.

Although her false teeth were a constant reminder of the blow from a German rifle, Mala remained undaunted. She resolved to make the trip to Warsaw: first on foot and then by train, a form of transport that, for Jews, was becoming more dangerous by the day. On the way, Mala bought a set of clothes for her little brother so that he might pass for a non-Jewish boy. She also took bread and buckwheat with her, a present for the dentist who had helped her free of charge.

Arriving at the ghetto, Mala overheard an animated discussion in Polish, a common discussion at the time, as the memoirs of non-Jewish Poles confirm. A Jewish boy had been shot dead after a Polish boy had turned him in or simply pointed at him, which amounted to the same thing. A German had shot and killed the young smuggler—that much was clear—but the bystanders were debating their own moral stance on what had just happened. Two years on, their everyday words would find an echo in Czesław Miłosz's poem about a fairground attraction that kept spinning next to the burning ghetto. People continued to make merry while the ghetto was destroyed. What should we make of this? What should we do?

In response to the boy's betrayal, Mala heard one man warn that

when the Germans were finished with the Jews, the Poles would be
next. She remembers a woman lamenting that the victim was only a
child after all. She can no longer recall the words of the bystanders who
justified or even welcomed the betrayal. But she clearly remembers
how their talk killed her sense of purpose stone-dead. 'I couldn't
summon the courage to go into the ghetto that day.'

Instead, she knocked on the door of a Polish couple she knew, and
asked if she could stay the night. Before the war, they had run a Jewish
ritual bath house not far from Mala's family home. When she was
younger, she and their children had played together. Now those same
children were being taunted at school because of the Yiddish accent
they had picked up from playing with Jewish kids. Mala realised how
unforgiving the times were becoming and how the Jews were being left
to their fate. Anti-Semitism had become the norm.

Miłosz called his carousel poem 'Campo dei Fiori', a reference to
the square where the heretic Giordano Bruno was burned to death on
the orders of the Inquisition:

At times wind from the burning
would drift dark kites along
and riders on the carousel
caught petals in midair.
That same hot wind
blew open the skirts of the girls
and the crowds were laughing
on that beautiful Warsaw Sunday.

Someone will read as moral
that the people of Rome or Warsaw
haggle, laugh, make love
as they pass by the martyrs' pyres.
Someone else will read
of the passing of things human,
of the oblivion
born before the flames have died.

* * *

That night, Mala was hit for the first time by the full reality of her father's death. He had left this life amid the hell of the ghetto, dead before the age of sixty. Not having lived with him since the bombardment of Warsaw, she does not have a clear sense of his final months.

Yet there are things we can say about Tall Sender's life in the ghetto, in the year he knew as 5701. We know that the son of the Rebbe of Grodzisk lived in Sender's neighbourhood and went about his work there. As one of three successors, he had been trained to lead his father's followers. He was eight years younger than Tall Sender, and, remarkably, the sermons he gave every Saturday survived the destruction of the ghetto. His name was Kalonymus Kalman Shapiro. He called himself the Rebbe of Piaseczno, which, like Grodzisk, is a small town very close to Warsaw, these days more of a suburb. Since the publication of a biography some twenty years ago, he is perhaps better known as 'the rabbi of the ghetto'.

Shapiro gave his sermons in Yiddish, not far from the bomb-damaged house where Tall Sender continued to live with his sons. He then transcribed them in Hebrew and put them in a tin that, in January 1943, he gave either to Ringelblum or to another member of his research team.

In 1956, a Polish-born resident of Israel went looking for Shapiro's teachings, and found them in the archives held by the Ringelblum Institute in Warsaw. No one had ever studied them. Five years later, they were published as a book in Hebrew, the language in which Shapiro had written them. The title was *Esh Kodesh*, which translates as *Sacred Fire* or *Holy Fire*.

Shapiro's congregation usually numbered about three hundred, until the summer of 1942, when between 80 and 90 per cent of the ghetto's inhabitants were sent to their deaths in Treblinka. Tall Sender was probably among those who came to listen to Shapiro. And even if that was not the case, Shapiro's teachings can tell us something about the faith, the mindset, and the life of a deeply religious Hasid such as Mala's father in those hellish final days.

To form an accurate picture of Tall Sender, it is important to appreciate that his faith was about more than a slavish obedience to the *mitzvot*, the commandments of the Torah—an impression I may have given when recounting his clashes with some of his children, especially his daughters. It is true that, in his obedience to the accepted interpretation of the precepts of his faith, Sender resembled members of what today we would call the ultra-Orthodox movement within Judaism, believers who are in some ways comparable to the orthodox Protestants of Northern Europe and North America. While such comparisons might be useful to the layperson, they fail to do justice to the religious experience of the Hasidim and the origins of this movement within Judaism—origins that lie in the rejection of an overly formalist and intellectual experience of the faith.

In the second half of the eighteenth century, Hasidism took root on Polish soil as a reaction against what its charismatic leader, the Baal Shem Tov, saw as an excessively dry approach that was laying waste to the Jewish faith. His appeal, and that of Hasidism, lay in the excitement that faith could bring, an ecstatic happiness that can occur when the faithful surrender themselves in rapturous devotion. While non-Hasidic Orthodox Jews regard the scriptures as the alpha and the omega of religious belief, the Hasidim cherish a more mystical orientation. Men such as Tall Sender and Shapiro were certainly strict adherents to the tenets of their faith, but at the same time they were in search of excitement and religious rapture, and that meant music, charismatic personalities (by no means necessarily scholars), and wine or something stronger, all with the aim of connecting with the divine through more than just the written word. Mala remembers how, every Saturday, her brothers and her father sang *zmires*, songs for the Shabbat table that had been handed down for generations. The words often dated all the way back to the Middle Ages and spoke of miraculous phenomena. Many charismatic figures from Hasidism had their own melodies. 'My brothers had wonderful singing voices,' Mala says. 'They could be heard all over the neighbourhood.' When they sang, home felt like a warmer, happier place.

The singing was accompanied by wine. For certain songs, rules had even been handed down as to the number of glasses to be consumed. Tall Sender made the wine himself in the cellar of his home. 'I remember farmers delivering cartloads of grapes,' Mala says. 'We always drank wine with our meals, even as children.' This wine was not to fuel drunken revelry, but to provide a good drink on set occasions. Nothing that would get in the way of Sander playing his violin. This, too, was among his talents, one he passed on to young Alter.

Alter was the son who fulfilled his father's aspirations and became a rabbi. Before that, as cantor, he would lead the synagogue in song. During the occupation, a marriage was arranged between him and the daughter of a respected member of the community. Mala could hardly believe it. 'My brother is going to marry? Impossible! He had never so much as looked at a woman!' But she was reassured when she talked to his bride-to-be, a lovely girl who told Mala that, when she and Alter met, it had been love at first sight.

In the 1930s, this more intense, more emotional approach to the faith was also Shapiro's response to the rise of secularisation. This emerges from the only book he published in his lifetime: *A Student's Obligation*. It took the form of a manual for the young people he had gathered around him, students he exhorted to carry out missionary work among their emotionally numbed contemporaries. In Shapiro's view, this numbness or lack of faith resulted from an excessive reining-in of the emotions. Such restraint could easily descend into matter-of-factness, feigned self-assurance, irony, and even cynicism, thereby jeopardising the social and religious continuity of the Jewish Orthodox world. Shapiro called on his students to arouse the power of the imagination among their numbed contemporaries, whose souls had to be pierced so that they could be inflamed. Emotional experience, he explained, was a divine substance, even though emotions can sometimes give rise to aversion or even disgust due to their physical manifestation. In his pre-war manual for students, Shapiro compares emotions to 'clear water in a filthy glass'.

Under the German occupation, the pressure on religious life intensified. Shapiro, who had lost a son in the bombardment of Warsaw, observed how the apocalyptic conditions affected different minds in different ways. When the streets are strewn with the bodies of the dead, taboos lose their hold over the living. Survivors' memoirs speak of brutalisation and faltering morals. Sex, violence, vengefulness, and suicidal despair gained the upper hand: a very different emotional release to the kind Shapiro had in mind. Koert Lindijer, a twenty-first-century Africa correspondent, gives a compelling account of what the unremitting presence of death can do to a person. In a refugee camp, he saw a row of bodies growing day by day, until there were hundreds. 'I wanted to shake off that leaden feeling of death. The remedy was to fight or to fuck. That surprised me at the time. And yes, perhaps I was ashamed. Because I still associated sex with intimacy and love. But death eroticises the senses and eats away at your values.'

Ringelblum, the ghetto historian, also recognised the pressures being brought to bear on religious life. There were poets who put God on trial, found Him guilty, and condemned Him to the gas chambers. (In Warsaw, no one had any illusions about Treblinka.) The poem 'An Account with God' by Władysław Szlengel, the ghetto's most popular poet, survived in one of Ringelblum's milk cans. It is a mocking accusation levelled at the Almighty. We obeyed your laws and what did it bring us? Starvation rations and Treblinka. It continues:

You told us not to eat pork,
we did not eat pork.
You told us to pray to You,
and we prayed to You.
And now, do You really expect
On the day after tomorrow, as in the Testament,
That I, on my way to the Prussian gas,
Will still say 'Amen' to You?

Yet Ringelblum also saw how hundreds of Hasidim appeared to withstand doubts that seemed inescapable in the face of so much hopelessness, amid so many atrocities committed against the weak, the ill, and the young. Walking through the ghetto, Ringelblum saw a sign that read 'Jews, Never Despair!' He went inside and saw Hasidim—like Tall Sender and Shapiro—dancing 'with the same religious fervour as they did before the war'. Ringelblum, a Zionist and socialist who lived a secular life and belonged to an influential Yiddish-supporting faction, was surprised but not indignant.

'After prayers one day,' he continued, 'a Jew danced there whose daughter had died the day before.' In their own way, the teachings of Shapiro, the rabbi of the ghetto, answer the question that Ringelblum appears to ask of posterity: how can a man dance so soon after his daughter's death?

To obtain that answer, you have to be able to read Shapiro's Shabbat sermons, and that is no easy task. Even in translation, his sentences appear to be written in another language or come from a distant past, a time when readers were not only familiar with Bible stories, but also knew their Talmudic and even Kabbalistic context. Shapiro's texts are seldom concrete. They never contain the words 'German', 'Nazi', 'SS', 'ghetto police', or 'Hitler'. Yet he does reflect on the concrete events of the day, as confirmed by a meticulous reconstruction of the history of the ghetto carried out by several historians. In other words, his community knew what he was talking about.

Shapiro's aim, the scholar Don Seeman argues, was to place the horrors he was living through in the narrative context of the Torah, a narrative that transcended time without being timeless. And, most importantly of all, he wanted to formulate thoughts that would enable him and his community to cope with the enormity of what was happening to them, thoughts that would give them the courage to go on living, to start a new week. In doing this, Shapiro did not shy away from the question so many were asking, especially at that time and in that place. Where is God in all this misery? How can these overwhelming atrocities be squared with the belief in an almighty God?

Shapiro's answer came in stages. In his earlier sermons, he presented relatively conventional answers for a deeply religious man. He saw the connection between crime and punishment. In the simplest of terms, a bad conscience could be cleansed through pain. Perhaps humanity, the Jews, had brought this upon themselves. But, gradually, this relationship between sin and retribution faded from Shapiro's sermons. The suffering was simply too great, the horrors no longer in proportion to any wrong the Jews could ever have done. The idea that the chosen people had to suffer until the coming of the Messiah was one thing, but why did the people of Israel have to endure so much, and so much more than anyone else?

If the answer was not to be found in atonement, perhaps it could be found in suffering itself. Could it be, Shapiro argued, that through this adversity, God was seeking to make Himself known to those with ears to hear Him? A few sermons later, Shapiro had become convinced of this. It is crucial to remember, he said, that however great one's suffering, God's own suffering is always greater, unfathomably greater. 'His pain from the affliction of Israel is boundless.' Human frailties prevent those who suffer and despair from seeing and experiencing the connection between God's untold pain and their own. God's suffering may be unfathomable, but perhaps the exceptional situation in which Shapiro and his followers found themselves would enable them to rise above such frailties. On a wing and a prayer.

In the Talmud, Shapiro found a story through which he could give shape to these thoughts about mass murder: the story of Rabbi Jose, who prayed among the ruins of a ravaged Jerusalem. As the rabbi prayed, he heard a voice 'cooing like a dove' that said, 'Woe is to me, that I have destroyed My house and exiled My children!' Later, the prophet Elijah appeared in a vision and revealed to the rabbi that the voice he had heard was the voice of God. And, more importantly, that this voice can be heard more clearly when Jews pray, as Rabbi Jose had done, among the ruins. There, and perhaps only there, can the house of prayer built by human hands open up to God. It is only among the ruins that the believer, himself a broken creature, can begin to grasp the immensity of God's sorrow at the destruction of His own people.

Such was Shapiro's argument, one that offers glimpses of the mystical orientation of Hasidism. Anyone who concentrates on the boundless suffering of God might find their own pain dissolving into it. And the overwhelming suffering visited upon the people of the ghetto might bring them closer to God.

It would be mistaken to view Shapiro as a joyous believer who saw a blessing in every form of adversity. He searched for meaning in the misery, but his own despair was none the less for it. This is revealed in the notes he scribbled in the margins of his work. Scholars who read the original handwritten manuscripts have tended to single out his final note, probably written in January 1943. All but illegible, the words were added to a sermon from December 1941. Shapiro continued to adapt and annotate his own sermons, even after he had delivered them. In this particular sermon, he had told his listeners that the catastrophe, however horrific, fitted a historical pattern of trials and tribulations for the Jewish people that stretched from their expulsions from Jerusalem and the destruction of that Holy City to all of the pogroms and persecutions that had taken place since. This is how ultra-Orthodox Jews view the Holocaust to this day. But not the rabbi of the Warsaw ghetto: revisiting his own sermon one year on, he scribbled a note in the margin that revealed a change of heart. By then, Shapiro was one of only around 55,000 people left alive in the Warsaw ghetto. He had lost both his children. And he wrote, 'However, as for the monstrous torments, the terrible and freakish deaths that the malevolent, monstrous murderers invented against us … from the end of 5702 and on—according to my knowledge of rabbinic literature and Jewish history in general, there has never been anything like them.'

Not long after he wrote this, the Germans transported the rabbi to a labour camp near Lublin. On 3 November 1943, under the bare branches in the woods that surround the village of Trawniki, he was killed during *Aktion Erntefest* (Operation Harvest Festival), a series of massacres ordered by Himmler on a vast scale to wipe out the last surviving Jews in the labour camps of the General Government. Members of the German Order Police and the SS, assisted by Ukrainians (mostly former prisoners of war), shot and killed 42,000 prisoners in the course of two days.

Instead of footnotes

The opening quote comes from the book *Fun a Velt vos iz Nishto Mer*, written in 1946 by Israel Joshua Singer, the brother of Isaac Bashevis Singer. An English translation by Joseph Singer, entitled *Of A World That is No More*, was published in 1970.

I write that the number of Poles summarily executed for helping Jews is around 800. It is important to emphasise that this figure does not include the hundreds, if not thousands, of Polish people who were sent to a concentration camp or labour camp for aiding Jews, and who were later killed there or died from exhaustion or torture. Members of Polish village-watch groups were also punished and, in some cases, shot. These groups kept guard at night to prevent Jews or resistance fighters sneaking into villages for food. If the Germans did catch Jews in the area, almost always as a result of a tip-off, they would kill them and exact punishment from the village watch.

Some Poles who sheltered Jews appeared before a *Sondergericht*, a court set up especially for this purpose, and were sentenced to death. In a few cases, the records of these improvised courts have been preserved. They show that the tracking down and killing of Jews, and the trial and execution of anyone who helped them, remained a priority for the Germans in Poland until the last day of the occupation.

Journalist Anna Bikont has written about the absence of German soldiers and policemen in this part of Poland after Germany invaded the Soviet Union. In the spring of 1941, there were swathes of territory where it was impossible to ensure that Jews could be 'dealt with', and reports complaining about the situation were sent back to Berlin. In some areas, police stations manned by five officers, at most, were expected to maintain order in over seventy villages, and to track down Jews, of course. The rapid German advance into the Soviet Union meant that the mobile killing units of *Einsatzgruppe B* found themselves operating further and further east before they had a chance to fulfil their task. This makes it easier to understand how Polish Jews such as Mala, who had fled the ghettos and were working as farm labourers, managed to lead relatively undisturbed lives in small villages such as Karpy until the hunt for the Jews began in earnest in the summer of 1942.

If someone did encounter German police officers and drew their attention to the presence of Jews in these rural areas, action was taken. The Jews would be tracked down and killed, or sent to the Lublin ghetto, which was sealed off from the outside world in March 1941 and entirely 'liquidated' in March and April 1942. A few months earlier, Joseph Goebbels, the Nazi Party's chief propagandist, had written a diary entry about the treatment of the Jews in the General Government, starting with Lublin: 'The procedure is a pretty barbaric one and not to be described here more definitely. Not much will remain of the Jews.' Of the 35,000 Jews who lived in Lublin before the war, only 230 survived the occupation.

The residents of Karpy called their river Sukha Lypa, a name it bears to this day. However, the pre-war Polish authorities referred to it as the Baszenka, and that is how it appears on their maps.

The lines of poetry by Czesław Miłosz quoted here, in a translation by David Brooks and Louis Iribarne, are taken from the collection *Czesław Miłosz: the collected poems 1931–1987* (1988). The lines from Władysław Szlengel's poem 'An Account with God' read as follows in the original Polish:

Tę blaszkę ... plac –
Te bony – czy Treblinki?
Czy jeszcze czekasz bym
Pojutrze jak testament
Pod pruski idąc gaz
Powiedział jeszcze 'Amen'?

The translation in this chapter is based on my own translation into Dutch, which in turn draws on Halina Birenbaum's translation into English and Hebrew.

On Shapiro, more widely known as the Rabbi of the Warsaw Ghetto since the rediscovery of his Shabbat sermons, US theologian Don Seeman of Emory University in Atlanta has written an in-depth analysis called 'Ritual Efficacy, Hasidic Mysticism and "Useless Suffering" in the Warsaw Ghetto', published by *Harvard Theological Review* in October 2008 (pp. 465–505). In 1994, Nehemia Polen, theologian and lecturer in Jewish Thought at Boston's Hebrew College, published a biography of Shapiro entitled *The Holy Fire: the teachings of Rabbi Kalonymus Kalman Shapira, the Rebbe of the Warsaw Ghetto*. It contains many excerpts from his sermons. The Professor of Jewish Studies at Canada's University of Waterloo, James A. Diamond, wrote an extensive article on Shapiro for online magazine *Mosaic*: 'The Buried, Raging Sermons of the Warsaw Ghetto Rabbi'.

4

The Smolinka

'Something like a glimmer of hope crossed my mind that the
gouged eyes could be put back where they belonged.'

–Jerzy Kosinski, writer

The next morning, Mala found the courage to go back to the ghetto.
She went to the north-eastern corner, and found that her secret route
was still there. To her surprise, she was able to enter unhindered. It
was 1942, and the situation inside the ghetto had changed dramatically.
Mala saw sights she would never forget: people who were nothing but
skin and bone, desperately ill, dying. 'I saw children drop dead in the
street. The first thing people did was remove the dead child's clothes,
in the hope that they could use them. The little body was covered with
newspaper and a stone placed on top.'

In the memoirs of ghetto survivors, paper is a recurring image. Not
so much newspaper as a kind of thin, pale cardboard. Remembering
his time as a child in the ghetto, Professor of Polish Literature Studies
Michał Głowiński describes how that paper somehow became bound
up with his experiences. It never failed to remind him of the hell he
had lived through as a little boy, a hell he struggled to find words for,
but could see in his mind's eye: '… that paper itself became for me one
of death's embodiments, one of its symbols.' That indefinable colour,
'neither white nor ash nor even gray—defines the colorscape of the
ghetto and imparts its tone'.

Arriving at Aunt Surele's house, Mala was confronted with two of Surele's children, twins roughly her own age. They begged Mala to take them with her. Mala had no idea how she was supposed to smuggle three children out of the ghetto. And assuming they could make it to Tomaszów, what then?

How could she explain that she was unable to help? In the end, she left without telling them. With Meir, of course, the reason for her journey in the first place. 'My little brother put on the clothes I had brought for him. Then I snipped the locks of hair by his ears.'

Mala and Meir made it to the station without a hitch. On the train, they were not so lucky. A woman pointed at the little boy and cawed, 'He's a Jew!'

'That's impossible,' Mala replied. 'He's my little brother!'

She claimed her brother was deaf and dumb, having drilled him before they left to keep his mouth shut, no matter what. His Polish was rudimentary at best, with a thick Yiddish accent.

Alarmed by the woman's public accusation, Mala and Meir got off at the next station. They had no idea where they were, other than somewhere between Warsaw and Tomaszów in the countryside of occupied Poland. It was Friday afternoon, and pouring with rain.

They knocked on the door of the first house they came to and asked if they could shelter from the downpour. The people who lived there—a couple with three children—turned out to be friendly. Meir continued to pretend he could not hear or speak.

'I told them we had to get off the train because my brother needed the toilet. The next train for Tomaszów wasn't due until the following morning. Glancing around the room, I noticed that the table had been laid with a white tablecloth. Under another cloth, I spotted a challah, the braided loaf eaten on Shabbat. I could hardly believe my eyes. I saw gefilte fish, too, the traditional Friday-evening meal. I plucked up the courage to ask if they were Jewish. You could have heard a pin drop. Then the son came up to me and said, "Yes, we are Jews."

'My brother was the first to start crying. Of course, then I told them all about the ghetto and our family in Tomaszów Lubelski. They turned out to be the only Jews in the village, and told us things were getting grimmer. They had been forced to close the shutters to stop local boys

throwing stones at the windows. Their house was our salvation. Meir
and I stayed until after Shabbat. There was plenty to eat. They even
gave us food for our journey.'

The family back in Tomaszów had given up hope of Mala returning
with Meir. They had been supposed to arrive on Thursday, so there was
huge relief when they finally turned up on Sunday. Mala was proud
that she had been able to rescue her little brother. Meir stayed with the
family, and she travelled the twenty-five kilometres back to Karpy. The
Gmitruks were glad to see her again, and so was her friend Amelka.

Amelka came from a troubled home, and so having Mala for
company in the village and down at the meadow with the cows meant
a lot to her. Her mother had died, and the new woman of the house
acted like the wicked stepmother from Cinderella. Amelka's brothers
had already left home, and she told Mala how her new stepsister had
lorded it over her from the moment she moved in, while Father turned
a blind eye. Amelka had made up her mind to run away, and she had a
plan. She was going to volunteer for work in Germany. And she wanted
Mala to come with her.

Though Karpy was largely cut off from news about the wider
world, Amelka knew this was possible because a handful of men
from the village had already left for Germany, the Gmitruks' eldest
son among them. Most of the Poles and Ukrainians who worked in
Germany had been pressganged at gunpoint. But others volunteered;
men from villages such as Karpy, who saw forced labour in Germany as
a way to escape the poverty at home.

Even by Polish standards, Mala recalls, the poverty in the region
was abject. Research confirms this, although only scant historical data
survives. Around 60 per cent of the population worked in agriculture,
even including cities such as Lviv and Kraków in the calculations.
Compare this to 11 per cent in present-day Poland or 2 per cent in
the Netherlands, one of the modern world's leading exporters of
agricultural produce. Serfdom had been officially abolished for almost
a century, but as Paul Robert Magosci writes in his monumental book *A
History of Ukraine*, 'Although the serfs were legally freed from bondage
in 1848, in a sense they remained economic serfs.' Serfs who had once

been the property of the landed gentry became tenant farmers who were obliged to pay their former owners, an obligation that left them worse off. The tiny plots of land they worked were too small for them to scrape a living from. In the 1930s, not long before Mala moved there, 45 per cent of the region's peasants had less than two hectares at their disposal, while a farmer needed at least five hectares to make sure his family did not go hungry. Another third of peasants had between two and five hectares. This left only a small percentage with enough land to make a decent living. The only solution open to peasant families was to sell their services to the local landowner for part of the year as a gardener, child minder, stable hand, lumberjack, or the like.

How had these plots of land become so small? The explanation is cultural. In many parts of Europe, it was the custom for the eldest son to inherit the farm, while younger sons looked elsewhere for a living. They joined the army or the clergy, went into government service, or tried their luck in far-flung territories, assuming their homeland offered such opportunities. In Poland and the former region of Galicia, a father divided his property and his land among all his sons, which often left no one with enough to make a living.

Mala experienced this first-hand. Not long after the head of the Gmitruk family had taken her in, his health took a turn for the worse. He eventually became bedridden. Mala was fond of him, and could tell that he was well-disposed towards her. He had stood up for her when she was picked on by their anti-Semitic neighbour, a man who claimed he had German roots. 'We had to clear snow, and the neighbour was in charge,' Mala recounts. 'After a while, he decided everyone could stop except me. Though he was far from well, Mr Gmitruk got out of bed and came to my rescue. I was frozen half to death.' The neighbour was told in no uncertain terms to lay off 'our Marilka'.

Mala had not seen Gmitruk's death coming. He passed away in early spring, 1942. She remembers crying and crying, kneeling at his bedside, praying with the others.

A day later, Gmitruk's second son arrived to divvy up the estate. He had brought along two men, a bottle of vodka, and his sister-in-law as a mediator. She was married to the eldest brother, one of the Gmitruks who had gone off to work in Germany. Mala suspected that she and the second son were having an affair. In any case, she knew that the late Mr Gmitruk had taken a strong dislike to this woman. Gmitruk's widow was taken unawares by the son's visit. 'She was still more or less in shock after her husband's death,' Mala says. 'It was all too much for her.' In the end, Gmitruk's property was split five ways, and the widow was left with only the house and the two cows. Before long, the second son had shacked up with his sister-in-law.

A small wooden house and two cows was nowhere near enough to live on. And Mrs Gmitruk still had a baby to feed. Perhaps some of her neighbours helped her out — Mala no longer remembers the details. From that time on, only the three of them lived in the house. 'She was keen for me to stay. After all, she would have been completely alone otherwise.' Mala read to Mrs Gmitruk, which made the long, cold evenings less monotonous for her.

Mala remembers her as a wise woman. 'She couldn't read or write, but she knew plenty.'

Mrs Gmitruk advised Mala to get baptised, an idea that Mala discussed with Amelka. Down at the meadow with the cows, she talked freely to her friend about her worries and her fears, about her life as a fugitive, about being Jewish in a country where that was punishable by death.

Amelka was always telling Mala she 'didn't look the least bit Jewish'. She, too, thought it was a good idea for her friend to see the parish priest and ask to be baptised as a Catholic. To Mala, this felt like a momentous step. In the eyes of the Germans, it made no difference: if a Pole had pointed Mala out as a Jew, it's unlikely that a baptismal certificate would have saved her. Things would also have looked very bleak for Mrs Gmitruk, regardless of whether the Jewish girl living under her roof had been baptised or not. At the start of 1942, mistrust was creeping into the villages of the General Government, and with good reason. One person pointing the finger could spell the end of everything.

I can state this with confidence, thanks to research carried out not only among witnesses and survivors, but also among perpetrators. A German who served in the region around Lublin as part of a Reserve Police battalion tasked with killing Jews told an interviewer in the

1960s that, from the winter of 1941, he and his fellow policemen shot Polish Catholics without any form of investigation if they had grounds for suspicion: 'denunciations or comments from envious neighbors sufficed for Poles to be shot along with their entire families on the mere suspicion of possessing weapons or hiding Jews or bandits'. He could not remember a single instance of his battalion providing information for an investigation that might have led to a trial, however improvised. That was considered a waste of time. Execution was the way to settle any doubts.

Mala knew nothing of this. The choice she faced was an existential one: to save her life or stay true to the faith in which she had been raised. She hesitated, remembering how her brother Alter had once furiously predicted that she — his own sister, the daughter of a respected Hasid — would one day betray her religion and bring shame on the family. Would she? Racked by doubt, Mala's nerve failed her, and she put off her decision again and again.

Meanwhile the relentless genocide of the Jews rumbled on. One day, a neighbour came charging into the house, tears streaming down her cheeks. Almost out of breath, she told them she had seen uniformed men shooting and killing Jews not far away, on the road from Rawa-Ruska to Karpy. It was April 1942. Those same men were approaching the village.

From eyewitness accounts, it is possible to give an impression of what had occurred: how German soldiers, shouting and firing their weapons, had torn through a section of the countryside in search of Jews. Some witnesses describe it as 'an orgy of killing'. One is the Polish doctor Zygmunt Kłukowski. He describes what he saw in Szczebrzeszyn, a village similar to Karpy, about twenty kilometres from Zamość: 'German and Polish police and members of the SS hunted down Jews for hours and hours. They dragged them from their various hiding places, broke down doors, smashed windows, and even threw hand grenades into cellars. The gendarmes from outside and the SS men left yesterday. Today "our" gendarmes and the Blue Police are at work; they have been ordered to kill every Jew they catch on the spot. They are executing this order with great zeal ... Throughout the day, Jews have been routed out from the most varied hide-outs. They have been shot on the spot or brought to the Jewish cemetery and killed ... there has been widespread looting. In general, the Polish population has not behaved correctly. Some have taken a very active part in the hunting of Jews. They pointed out where Jews were hiding, lads even chased small Jewish children, who the police killed in front of everyone.'

One Jewish woman, who survived the war by hiding beneath a pigsty, said that after two days of killing, the dogs no longer barked when shots were fired.

Before long, the neighbour's news reached Mira and Hanka, too, and they rushed over to see Mala. Realising the extent of the danger, Mira said they should escape into the forest, where they might find a group of armed partisans prepared to offer them protection.

Carrying little more than a loaf that Mrs Gmitruk had given them, they walked into what seemed like an endless forest. It was April. Their neighbour's breathless panic was in stark contrast to the quiet that closed in around them. 'All we could hear was the rustling of leaves.' Mira carved marks on the tree trunks in case they needed to find their way back to Karpy.

After walking for hours, they stopped to eat the loaf. At night, they huddled together and tried to sleep. It wasn't easy: the spring night was cold, their clothes too thin to keep them warm. 'It was almost dawn by the time we managed to nod off. We got up and continued walking. We were hungry. Then we came to the edge of the forest and saw a little house in the valley.'

The following account of Mala, Mira, and Hanka's escape through the forest around Karpy, Rawa-Ruska, and Radruz is more or less as Mala tells it in her own memoirs. I don't know what I could add without psychologising.

'I was wearing a small crucifix on a thin chain around my neck. I thought it would make me look more like a Catholic girl. I told the others that we could try to exchange it for bread. As we walked down into the valley, the smell of baking was coming from the house. We were already talking about how we would divide our loaf and keep some for later. I knocked on the door, and a young woman opened. I greeted her in Polish, and Mira asked her if we could exchange my crucifix and chain for some bread. The young woman took the chain and asked if it was real gold. Mira told her it was: 100 per cent gold. The woman called to her husband. He appeared with a pitchfork in his hand. As soon as he saw us, he yelled "Jews!" and jabbed the pitchfork at us. The woman held on to my crucifix and we ran.

'We scrambled out of the valley and managed to reach the forest. I lost a shoe. We kept on running through the forest, though it was all we could do to keep going. All three of us started to cry. We had no idea what to do next. There was blood on our clothes. The one thing we knew for sure was that we couldn't head back towards the house in the valley, so we set off in the opposite direction. After a while, we spotted another house, with nappies drying on a washing line. I suggested going down to the house alone and trying to steal a nappy from the line so that we could clean off the blood. Just as I was about to grab one, a dog attacked me. It gave me an awful bite. It wasn't a big dog, but it sank its teeth in. A man opened the door and told me to come inside. Not that I had any choice: the dog was still hanging onto my leg.'

Mala greeted him in Polish. They pulled up a chair for her, fed her bread and milk, and gave her a cloth to wipe away the blood. They didn't ask her anything. She remembers being so scared that she could hardly swallow. 'Even though I was incredibly hungry.'

When Mala tells me the story, she has to stop at this point. After composing herself, she continues, 'I had wanted a nappy to clean off the blood, but now there was even more blood. That dog had a hold of me and wouldn't let go. The farmer invited me in. He gave me bread and did not ask if I was Jewish. Those people existed, too, good Catholics, real Catholics who knew that if someone is hungry, you should give them food. If someone is homeless, give them shelter.'

Mala was in such a state that she had trouble talking as well as trouble eating.

'The man asked if there were more of us in the forest. I nodded. He told me to eat up and that he would give me bread for the others. His wife gave me a pair of shoes. They were too big, but at least it was something. I thanked them again and again. As I was leaving, the man said, "Listen, when it gets dark, you can come down and sleep in our loft. As long as you promise to leave early in the morning, so no one sees you."

'I returned to the others with bread and milk. We could hardly believe our luck. Mira and Hanka were afraid something had happened to me. When I told them we were allowed to sleep in the loft that night, we all jumped for joy—it was so cold in the forest. Once we were settled in the loft, we heard the man come up. We were frightened, of course, and had visions of betrayal and the Germans. But that good-hearted man brought us warm milk and something to eat. We were so emotional, we could hardly say a thing. Mira was the first to speak, and she thanked him so sweetly. She could always find the right words. We slept soundly that night, but we knew we had to be up at the crack of dawn. The last thing we wanted was for these kind people to get into trouble on our account.

'Back in the forest, we continued walking, and tried to figure out what to do. Later on, we ate some of the food we had been given, saving some for the next day. Night fell, and again we had no idea where to sleep. We kept walking just to try and stay warm. Suddenly, Hanka spotted a light in the woods, big and bright. Even though it was the middle of the night, we knocked on the door. Two girls lived there, kind girls. We told them we were lost, and asked if we could stay the night. They gave us the most delicious food. Mira overheard them say they should ask for our passports. Quick as a flash, she asked me what I had done with the bag with our documents, and I told her I must have left it behind. Our ruse worked, and after that the girls didn't bother about our papers.

'We were able to get ourselves cleaned up and have a good night's sleep, and in the morning they gave us the most wonderful breakfast. There was bread and butter, fried eggs, hot chocolate … all kinds of things you couldn't buy in the villages. We thanked them, and again it was Mira who said all the right things. Back in the forest, Mira told us the girls were probably prostitutes. I couldn't understand how prostitutes could be so kind, or why they would live in the middle of a forest.'

Thanks to the good night's sleep, the three of them felt a little fitter. Mira began looking for the marks she had carved into the tree trunks, and after a while she found them. They discussed what they should do. They agreed that many of the villagers were not anti-Semitic, perhaps even 90 per cent of them. But in every village there were one or two willing to help the Germans, and that could be enough to seal their fate. Mala had not forgotten about the Gmitruks' neighbour. What were they to do?

Following the tree markings, they found their way back to Karpy, to Mrs Gmitruk. She told them that all the Jews in the village had been killed or taken away. She also knew where they had been taken: a camp where people were burned. A place, so she had been told, where they had a big oven.

This was true. From March that year, a few weeks before the Germans came to the village, transports began arriving almost daily at the Bełżec extermination camp, named after the small town less than twenty-five kilometres from Karpy where it had been built. At Bełżec, the Germans would gas almost half a million Jews and 800 Roma, in addition to a number of Poles who had hidden Jews. Most of the victims were from the district of Lublin and western Ukraine, a region the Germans called 'Galizien'. Most were transported by train. Jews from Karpy and the surrounding countryside were taken to the camp in open wagons and later in army trucks.

Mrs Gmitruk once again raised the subject of baptism. Mala hated the idea, but hope won out over her better judgement. She remembers shaking like a leaf. 'As Orthodox Jews, we were brought up to believe that Catholics had no conscience. Of course, even before the war I had seen for myself that this wasn't the whole truth. At school, I had been in a class full of Catholics, and I learned the meaning of Christianity. It stood for a lot of things, but acting without a conscience wasn't one of them.'

Reflecting on the day she went to the church at Karpy, Mala brings up the priest at her school in Warsaw, the man who told her and her classmate Jadwiga that 'we are all God's children'. That must have given her some basis for trust, though she had just as much reason for mistrust: many a Catholic cleric was in no way inclined to save Jews.

Mala had to walk around three kilometres to the church, she remembers, which meant she probably went to one of two churches on the banks of the Smolinka, a narrow stream whose source is located a little further east. One church was Catholic at the time; the other served a Uniate or Greek Catholic congregation.

When Mala went inside, she found the priest reading. She told him she wanted to be baptised. The priest did not answer, but instead offered her a cup of tea. Later, he produced biscuits. 'Not that I could eat them. All I wanted from him was an answer.' He stood up and said, 'My child …' On hearing those words, Mala remembers, she felt a little better. The priest was very considerate and said he would help, but not by baptising her, as that was not why she had come. What he would do was help her survive.

'If you really want to be baptised,' he told her, 'come and see me again when the war is over.'

He handed Mala a document, a certificate of baptism. It was for another girl, but with the surname Gmitruk. And so Mala went from being Marilka Waserman to Janina Gmitruk.

She left the church and went straight to the meadow where Amelka was looking after the cows as they grazed. After the German raid, Amelka was amazed to see her Jewish friend alive. Mala showed her the baptismal certificate, and suggested they go ahead with Amelka's plan to leave. It was now or never. 'Everyone in the village knew I was Jewish. Staying was too big a risk.'

But first Mala took her Polish friend back to the church she had just come from. There she made Amelka from Karpy swear never to betray Mala from Warsaw. Amelka did just that. For her own part, Mala solemnly swore never to tell the truth about her own background to anyone. The next day, they left at dawn.

Saying goodbye to Mira was a wrench. The girls said nothing to Mrs Gmitruk. 'That was a hard thing to do. We were very fond of each other. But I thought it was for the best. If ever anyone asked her where I had gone, she wouldn't be able to tell them, even if she wanted to.'

Instead of footnotes

Mira, Mala, and Hanka hoped to find protection from armed resistance fighters in the forest. Such groups were certainly not far away in the spring of 1942, but the chances of running into them in such terrain were slim, and it is by no means certain that they would have greeted three young, unarmed Jewish women with much consideration. If Mira, Mala, and Hanka had really been in luck, they might have encountered the Jewish partisans who were active around Karpy. But this, too, was extremely unlikely. The region's forests were large, but not large enough in the end to offer sufficient protection. Armed Jewish resistance fighters only survived the war in a few very densely forested areas of Poland. Some of them will play a role later in this book.

The massacre in Szczebrzeszyn as described by the Polish doctor Zygmunt Klukowski comes from his *Diary from the Years of Occupation, 1939–44* (1993), translated into English by his son George and edited by his grandchildren. The doctor was a prominent member of the Polish resistance.

Mala remembers Mrs Gmitruk telling her that Jews from the local area were taken to Majdanek. In fact, it was Bełżec, but Mala's misremembering is understandable. For decades, the Bełżec camp was only known to a small group of experts, possibly a small number of SS and Wehrmacht veterans and, of course, those who lived nearby. The camp had been completely dismantled, and by the time the Red Army took control of the area, it was the site of a farm. In the months, years, and decades after the war, as Mala tried to grasp what had happened to her family, the name Majdanek probably found its way into her memory; a camp that gained notoriety immediately after liberation, and which stood in a suburb of Lublin. The haste of the German withdrawal meant that the liberators found the Majdanek camp still relatively intact. In the first weeks after liberation, the Red Army forced Lublin's residents to file past the mass graves and see with their own eyes the crimes that had been committed. Photographs of these viewings appeared in newspapers and endless government publications, cementing the camp's position in the public psyche.

Michał Głowiński, whose memories of the ghetto are bound up with the indefinable grey of the paper that was laid over corpses in the street, survived the war in a convent near Zamość. He wrote his memoirs in 1999. Six years later, they were published in English as *The Black Seasons*, in a translation by Marci Shore.

The opening quote about eyes gouged from their sockets is taken from *The Painted Bird*, written by Polish–Jewish writer Jerzy Kosinski (born Lewinkopf), who emigrated to the United States in 1957. The first version of the book, which is something between a novel and an autobiography, was published in 1965; a second was published in 1976. Kosinski describes how his first-person narrator, a young Jewish boy, survives in the countryside of occupied eastern Poland despite unremittingly brutish and excessive violence at the hands of peasants, villagers, and even Kalmyk soldiers of the Red Army. The world he claims to have been part of was further coloured by vivid descriptions of illiteracy, superstition, and swindlers. It is hard to imagine readers believing that Kosinski experienced all this first-hand, as he initially claimed, but it is certainly a beautifully written, fascinating, and disturbing work.

5
The Hrebel'ka

'What the nations can offer in good blood of our type, we will
take, if necessary, by kidnapping their children and raising them
with us.'

–Heinrich Himmler, Reichsführer-SS

I am going in search of the Gmitruks or their descendants. A man in his
thirties from the city of Zamość has come along to help me. He became
intrigued by Mala's story when he discovered that 'Kolonie Karpie', as
Mala remembers it, was absent from every map he consulted, either
Polish or Ukrainian. Even remarkably detailed local hiking maps had
nothing to offer. It was only on a military map used by the Germans
75 years ago that the words 'Kolonie Karpy' appeared, spelled a little
differently than Mala remembers. It is a small settlement just outside a
village that has been part of Ukraine since the Second World War, albeit
only a few kilometres east of the Polish–Ukrainian border. Satellite
images from Google Earth show why such a cluster of houses might be
called a *kolonia*, although they no longer bear that name. These days,
the 'colony' is lumped in with the equally insignificant village of Karpy.

My interest was also piqued by a village called Karp, about twenty-
five kilometres north-east of Tomaszów Lubelski and home to two
women born with the surname Gmitruk. However, Karp did not exist
in the 1940s. Nor does the bare, flat landscape that surrounds it match
Mala's description of the countryside she once lived in. The picture she

paints does evoke the leafy, hilly, and even scenic setting of Karpy.

The landscape between Karp and Karpy takes a picturesque turn near Tomaszów Lubelski, where the foothills of the Carpathian Mountains come into view and the pink and mint-green *bloki*-farms make way for the blacks, browns, and greys of their predecessors, wooden structures weathered by frost and sun. Beyond Tomaszów, the road to Karpy crosses the European Union border, and the contrast in wealth, infrastructure, and general well-being makes itself felt immediately, wreaking havoc with the car's suspension. The roads of south-east Poland are not exactly motorways, but they make for a smooth drive. As soon as we hit Ukraine, motoring is a matter of fits and starts. Juddering along, we swerve to avoid deep potholes in roads surfaced with cheap asphalt. Signs imposing a ninety-kilometres-per-hour speed limit bring a wry smile to the face of Daniel, my travelling companion: we're lucky to be doing ten. We seldom see another car, but get to admire the fluorescent tracksuits popular with locals out for a stroll along the ill-defined roadside.

Official figures confirm the sharp divide at the border between Poland and Ukraine. When communism collapsed, around 1990, both countries had roughly the same income per head of population. Economists at the time held out less hope for Poland than they did for Ukraine, with its natural resources, vast tracts of very fertile land, and an impressive industrial infrastructure. Yet today Poland's income per head of population is five times that of Ukraine. *Five* times: that's comparable to the gulf between Italy and Belarus, or between the Netherlands and Russia. And since Western Ukraine is considerably poorer than the east, the disparity is even starker along the border.

At diplomatic parties in Warsaw, there's an IMF representative who never tires of whipping out his smartphone to show satellite images of Poland and Ukraine taken at night. His point is clear: south-east Poland, like the rest of Europe, is a beacon of light. Immediately across the border, all is dark. Economic activity is minimal.

That said, this is a beautiful part of the world, with a landscape reminiscent of the Belgian Ardennes. Broad and free flowing, the River Hrebel'ka winds its way through the hills and the occasional forest of

mighty beech, chestnut, and even oak. It is a far cry from the copses
of feeble birch and stick-like fir that dominate the landscape around
Warsaw and Czyżewo.

While I daydream about the potential for tourism, my Polish
companion curses every time we pass a snow-white monument to
men such as Stepan Bandera and Roman Shukhevych. These statues,
numerous and modest in size, have been erected in the last five to
ten years to honour those who fought for Ukrainian independence in
the 1930s and 1940s—first against the Polish authorities, later against
Russian soldiers, and later still against German soldiers *and* Polish
citizens, most of them peasants. In 1943 and 1944, they killed around
70,000 people, mostly Polish-speaking peasants from Volhynia, an area
that now spans the north of Ukraine and west Belarus. One-third of
their victims came from further south, the area around Karpy. In the
same campaign, over 250,000 people fled the violence.

By no means an outspoken Polish nationalist, Daniel nevertheless
sees the glorification of these Ukrainian freedom fighters as a step too
far. 'Do they have no shame?'

This history of the slaughter of Polish peasants is one reason why
Daniel's hopes for our little expedition are anything but high. Mala says
the Gmitruks were Polish, which suggests three probable scenarios
after she and Amelka left in the spring of 1942: they were murdered,
they fled, or they were forced to move west. This last option was
because Stalin and Poland's new rulers saw these Volhynia massacres
as confirmation of the need for ethnic cleansing, both in the Soviet
Republic of Ukraine and the new Polish People's Republic. Or, more
accurately, the need for ethnic consolidation. A few kilometres west
of Karpy, a new border was drawn. The Ukrainians on the Polish side
were ordered to move to the Soviet Union, and the Poles on the Soviet
side to the Polish People's Republic. Locals who identified as neither
Polish nor Ukrainian, such as Lemkos and Boykos, were later removed
from their homes in a coordinated campaign called Operation Vistula,
and deported to places in the west of Poland.

Historian Timothy Snyder sums up this process as follows: 'Working
in parallel, and sometimes together, the Soviet and communist Polish
regimes achieved a curious feat between 1944 and 1947: they removed

the ethnic minorities, on both sides of the Soviet–Polish border, that had made the border regions mixed; and at the very same time, they removed the ethnic nationalists who had fought the hardest for precisely that kind of purity. Communists had taken up the program of their enemies. Soviet rule had become ethnic cleansing—cleansed of the ethnic cleansers.'

Then comes an astronomical figure, almost too unlikely to commit to paper, yet one that is well documented by both governments and reflects the current consensus among historians. In this post-war 'repatriation', 780,000 Poles from within the redrawn borders of the Soviet Republic of Ukraine were deported to the Polish People's Republic. A similar number came from Lithuania and Belarus to the new Polish nation further west. In other words, a total of 1,517,984 Poles left the Soviet Union in 1946. Conversely, the number of Ukrainians that the Polish army expelled from the Polish People's Republic to the Soviet Union was somewhere in excess of 483,000.

Daniel holds out the smallest glimmer of hope. The surname Gmitruk is more common in Ukraine than it is in Poland. He thinks Mala might have been mistaken, and that the Gmitruks were Ukrainian rather than Polish. 'Didn't she tell you she spoke better Polish than the villagers?' he reminds me. 'Well, the regional dialect, certainly back then, was something between Ukrainian and Polish, a Polonised version of Ukrainian. She might have interpreted that as poor Polish. What I'm trying to say is: they may not have been Poles. And if they were, and they survived everything that happened here, then it's a pity the border wasn't drawn five kilometres further east.'

Karpy can only be reached over a narrow, muddy path. Sunlight glints off the metal of corrugated roofing sheets and shimmers occasionally in the gilded onion dome of a Ukrainian-Orthodox church. Less conspicuous, though also domed, are the dark, almost black shapes of smaller wooden churches, many of them hemmed in by tall coniferous hedges. Until the war years, these belonged to the Greek Catholics, a denomination that combines Eastern Orthodox rites with obedience to the Pope in Rome. In Karpy, we find one such church, which now serves a Ukrainian-Orthodox congregation. Just beyond the handful of houses that make up the village, we come across another of those monuments that infuriate Daniel. Snow-white and recently planted on a low hill, it honours the men of the UPA, a Ukrainian nationalist paramilitary force. Sixteen of them were killed nearby, so the inscription says.

'By the Germans,' a farmer explains.

'By the Poles,' someone else tells us, later the same day.

'By the Red Army, who else?' sighs Karpy's oldest resident.

We are something of an attraction in the village. There is no need to ring anyone's doorbell; all the locals come out for a chat. Astounded that we have managed to find the place, they are keen to know how. On our phones? Through GPS? Our answer is cause for profound satisfaction. Karpy is not as obscure as they thought—it's on the digital map. 'A satellite has spotted us!' the cheeriest resident bellows to a bulky, bare-chested man leaning on his garden fence a few houses along. He pumps both fists.

It's easy to see how Mala would have believed she was safe here, if only for a while. The rest of the world feels far away. Walking in the shade of magnificent beeches on our way to talk to the village's second-oldest resident, the wind in the leaves is the only sound we hear.

Not a single Gmitruk lives in Karpy. No one can remember a Gmitruk ever having lived there, not even the oldest resident. She was already in her teens when she moved to the village, a time when all the houses were either abandoned or in ruins. A few people may have been living there already, she thinks, but they could just as easily have been newcomers like her who turned up a few weeks earlier. 'There used to be a lot of Germans,' a number of villagers tell us in Ukrainian, a language that, fortunately, Daniel speaks. 'Then all the Germans fled. And then we came.'

Ryszko is the most talkative of the villagers. His family came from the village of Horyniec-Zdrój, just across the border in Poland. 'We were Ukrainians, so we had to move here.' Had he ever gone back to see the place where his parents were born and raised, less than ten kilometres as the crow flies? 'I've only been to Poland twice in my life,' Ryszko tells us. 'And I'm 55 years old.'

An amateur historian in nearby Rawa-Ruska contests the view that Germans lived in or around Karpy. They were Poles, he says, and they had to leave 'because of the communists'. Then again, he adds, it's quite possible that they had already been killed or deported before the post-war campaign of ethnic consolidation began. This is not a reference to the Volynhia massacre, but to a fanatical racial segregation project launched by the SS, which took in the Polish city of Zamość and around 200 surrounding villages. *Aktion Zamość* was the first step towards implementing the long-term vision outlined in the Nazis' masterplan for Central and Eastern Europe. The operation was regarded as a trial run, and may well explain the Gmitruks' disappearance: deported or murdered, unless they had fled in advance.

Responsibility for implementing *Generalplan Ost* was in the hands of the Reich Security Main Office, founded in 1939 by Heinrich Himmler. The SS chief had several reasons for starting in the district of Lublin, one being that his loyal vassal Odilo Globocnik — nicknamed Globus — was the highest-ranking SS officer there. This fanatical Austrian had already proved his worth to Himmler in the death factories of Sobibór, Bełżec, and Treblinka, and he was more than eager for a new challenge. Governor General Hans Frank was less enthusiastic, believing that Germany should concentrate on winning the war before turning its attention to the ethnic cleansing of the Slavic population. In his words, 'You must not kill the cow you want to milk.'

Not that Frank was motivated by humanist tendencies. Still clinging to the hope of a final victory, he would later write, 'Once the war is won, then, for all I care, mincemeat can be made of the Poles and the Ukrainians and all the others who run around here; it doesn't matter what happens.' Yet even this goes against Himmler by insisting that such ruthlessness should be exhibited *after* the war. Victory first! Frank took the same view as the Wehrmacht commanders who thought it unwise to make thousands of enemies through forced migration: even 'inferior beings' were capable of putting up strong partisan resistance. Himmler and Globocnik pushed ahead regardless. They succeeded in persuading Frank — it is unclear how — and in November 1942 they launched *Aktion Zamość* with the aim of founding a purely Germanic colony in the east.

Why had this singular honour been bestowed on Zamość? Simply because Himmler had visited the city with a poet friend in the spring of 1940 and thought it too beautiful to be left to Jews, Poles, and other subhumans. The 1943 edition of the Baedeker travel guide to the General Government—yes, such a thing exists!—describes the city as 'a bastion of German culture'. The Germanic claim is historically baseless (Globocnik was supposed to have found the remnants of a German colony there), but the wartime Baedeker's praise for the architecture was certainly well founded. Worth a detour! The buildings were constructed 'from the same mould' by Italian architect Bernardo Morando, in keeping with sixteenth-century Renaissance ideals. Completed at the start of the seventeenth century, the project was financed by (and named after) nobleman and powerful politician Jan Zamoyski. UNESCO World Heritage status was conferred on the centre of Zamość in 1992.

The city's population has since dwindled, and today there is an air of dejection about the place. Everything you read about its dynamism so clearly belongs in the past. Almost eighty years have gone by since it was a melting pot of enterprising people with roots in Greece, Armenia, Italy, and even Scotland, including thousands of Jews from all walks of life, from dancing Hasidim to atheist revolutionaries. Zamość was the birthplace of communist activist Rosa Luxemburg and of Yitskhok Leybush Peretz, one of the most highly regarded Yiddish writers of all time.

In October 1942, all of the city's Jews—some 40 per cent of the pre-war population—were forced onto trucks and transported to Bełżec. One month later, the rest of the population had to disappear, along with the people of the surrounding villages. German statisticians record the eviction of approximately 116,000 people from 160 villages and settlements to make way for German-speaking colonists. Some 50,000 of those evicted ended up as forced labourers west of the Oder.

As for the children, 4,500 were also moved west. They were the 'chosen ones'. Following an inspection by race experts from the SS in Łódź, those with blond hair, blue eyes, and other Aryan traits ended up in Lebensborn homes, where they were brainwashed. Given a new name and primed with a sense of superiority about their Aryan roots, the children were adopted by SS families. Another 25,000 children from the Zamość region, assigned to a lower racial category by the same SS ideologues, were sent to concentration camps, in most cases Auschwitz or Majdanek. There they were given a lethal injection, or died of exhaustion and thirst.

Himmlerstadt. That was the new name sycophant Odilo Globocnik had come up with for a Germanised Zamość. But his boss was having none of it. No city or region had yet been named after Hitler, and Himmler was wary of stealing a march on the Führer. The wartime Baedeker therefore lists Zamość under P. For Pflugstadt.

Of the planned 60,000 German and ethnic German colonists, around 13,000 actually settled in the villages of the Zamojszczyzna, the area around Zamość. They didn't have it easy. The Wehrmacht commanders were proved right. Thousands of evicted Poles took to the vast forests of the region and formed armed resistance groups. They killed German colonists, ambushed German police units, and attacked military barracks and trucks loaded with supplies for frontline troops. The Zamość Uprising grew to become one of the biggest campaigns of armed resistance in all of Europe, with full-blown battles that are commemorated in Poland to this day. German reprisals were fierce: their troops flattened entire villages.

This was before the massacres carried out by Ukraine's independence fighters had even begun. These came later, starting in Volhynia and spreading to East Galicia from March 1943. That summer, the Ukrainian fighters stuck warnings to the trees in Polish villages and settlements: 'Leave within 48 hours for the far side of the Bug or the San. Otherwise: death!' In other words, the villagers were forced to flee westwards. For the people of Karpy, that meant crossing the River San. The Bug lay further north.

The word 'fighter' might suggest advanced weaponry: tanks, rifles, anti-aircraft guns. Nothing could have been further from the truth. In East Galicia, Ukrainian independence fighters set fire to Polish houses, and when the occupants tried to flee, they were forced back into their burning homes with scythes and pitchforks. Historian Timothy Snyder describes how these fighters sometimes displayed bodies that had been decapitated, crucified, torn apart, or chopped into pieces to

encourage the remaining Poles to leave. The power vacuum created by
the departure of the German army was filled with Ukrainian fighters.
They feared the Red Army more than the Germans they had initially
cooperated with and been trained by — not least in how to kill women,
children, and even babies. Besides, this was their chance. In February
1944, UPA leader Roman Shukhevych wrote in a command to his men,
'In view of the success of the Soviet forces it is necessary to speed
up the liquidation of the Poles, they must be totally wiped out, their
villages burned.' Two months later, a UPA commander wrote, 'Fight
them [the Poles] unmercifully. No one is to be spared, even in [the] case
of mixed marriages.'

The Gmitruk family lived in the twentieth century's own heart of
darkness, in Snyder's 'bloodlands': during the prolonged nightmare,
there was *Aktion Zamość*, the ethnic cleansing of Zamojszczyzna by
the Nazis between November 1942 and March 1943; the relentless
Nazi campaign to hunt down and murder every last Jew in the wider
region; the mass killing of Poles by murderous Ukrainian nationalists
in East Galicia; the massacres of Ukrainians by avenging Poles; and,
later, Operation Vistula, the forced resettlement in 1947 of Ukrainians,
Boykos, and Lemkos from the south-eastern provinces of post-war
Poland to the 'recovered territories' in the west of the country. Daniel
believes it is foolish of me to think we might find a Gmitruk in Karpy, or
to suppose that someone there would recall a girl called Amelka from
75 years ago. 'If the Gmitruks had been wealthy or owned property ...
Or if they had been able to write and send each other letters ...'

But we don't give up straight away. Instead, we draw a circle fifty
kilometres around Tomaszów Lubelski and visit every village where,
according to the public records, one or more Gmitruks live. As long
shots go, this one is manageable enough: our criteria limit the number
of villages to nine. We don't even need exact addresses. In a village,
anyone you meet will tell you which house or farm to head for — one
of the advantages of a community culture where reading, writing, and
screen-gazing are relatively unpopular pastimes.

When we ask them about Marilka and Amelka, the Gmitruks we
talk to dig deep into their memories. Can they recall a young Jewish

girl who came for a few months, tended the cows, shovelled snow, and then disappeared in the early spring of 1942? Their answer is no.

Fair enough; it is almost eighty years ago, after all. But perhaps they remember their parents mentioning a girl like that? A girl who read aloud from the Bible? One old woman, now in her eighties and the widow of a Gmitruk who died long ago, remembers her husband mentioning a Jewish girl in an anecdote he once told. 'An ethnic German wanted to betray her, but his father put a stop to it.' This might have been Mala. But that's all the woman can recall.

In the village of Wolica Śniatycka we also think we might be in luck. Two women, both born as Gmitruk, live next door to each other. They come from 'over the border', but unfortunately the name of their native village bears no resemblance to Karpy or anywhere close. The elder of the two's long-term memory functions perfectly well, but her short-term memory is so poor that she dishes up stories that have no connection to the questions we ask her. To discover whether she ever met a Marilka, we would have to spend days in her company hoping a Jewish girl might pop up spontaneously in a maelstrom of memories.

At which, Daniel pipes up, 'Yeah, but the name of the village isn't even a match.' We drive on.

People are only too happy to talk. Ask them about a girl in Karpy during the war, and they come out with a story of their own in which no Marilka appears. Most of these stories have to do with *Aktion Zamość*. People talk about buying back the freedom of captured children, about men jumping from trains, about older mothers who worked as housemaids in Bremen or Berlin and were abused by teenage boys in Hitler Youth uniforms. None of the Gmitruks is the least bit bothered about supplying evidence to support their stories. They are stories, after all; the Gmitruks are not in the witness box. Even the names of their protagonists are sometimes out of reach.

I ask about photos, and Daniel gives a pained smile. The photo albums that appear on the table are thin, and seldom go back beyond the 1970s. He is visibly embarrassed when I persist with my questions about the names of grandparents, and even great grandparents, in the hope of somehow getting closer to Amelka or the Gmitruks. Back on the road in his white Toyota, he points out the fault in my thinking: the blinkered notion that every farmer knows exactly who his forefathers are and where his roots lie. They can barely read and write, he says, so what are the chances that they have a detailed family tree all worked out in their head? 'It says more about you than it does about these people.' He's right. Hardly anyone we speak to knows their grandmother's maiden name, for instance. But they all have their stories. Some strike me as a way of processing past horrors; others, as a way of coming to terms with a guilty conscience, their own or that of a village community.

One Gmitruk tells the story of a butcher who did not have a butcher's shop. Instead, the locals would invite him to their small farms, where he would slaughter one of their pigs, and process the meat and fat into sausage, chops, ham, and lard. The butcher had two sons. One was killed in a road accident not long after the war; the other was felled by illness. The village of Zwierzyniec knew the reason for his misfortune. The butcher was cursed. During the war, he had murdered Jews with an axe. 'More than just a few.'

Another Gmitruk, this time in Koblo Kolonia, tells the story of a Jewish girl who survived the war and sailed for America. Years later, she came back to the village with her family to inquire after the people who had kept her alive during the war. They were mortified. 'If outsiders come looking for you, it usually spells trouble.' Much to their surprise, the Jewish girl's return proved to be a blessing. She helped the family who had saved her, gave them a tractor, and paid for their sons to come to America on holiday — an incredible luxury. Gmitruk makes a gesture that can only mean 'Wow!' He tells the whole story twice, and compares it to winning the lottery. We mumble something about courage and justice rather than luck. Gmitruk just laughs. It's hard to know why.

Two more Gmitruks offer us tea and cake. Sitting in the kitchen of their *bloki*-farm around ten kilometres from Zamość, we start to think we're on to something. This is family. In addition to sugar, Mrs Gmitruk produces a sachet from one of her wooden kitchen cupboards and stirs its sweet, powdery contents into our tea.

Her husband's face is etched with deep lines, his mouth set in a single crease. His ears stick out. He is a fine storyteller, serving up his tales with a certain cadence, as if he has rehearsed them.

Mrs Gmitruk is more careworn. She has sad eyes, and, like a litany repeated for the hundredth time, she reels off the reasons why her daughters have failed to get on in life. One is twenty-four and lives in England, as does her son. 'She calls and tells me, "This is no life. All I do is work and sleep."'

Her daughter would like to come back, Mrs Gmitruk sighs, but what future does she have in Poland? Her qualifications offer no prospect of higher education — 'Why did no one explain that to us?' — and at home they have no internet connection.

The hopelessness with which Mrs Gmitruk describes her children's plight imbues every story she tells, even her attempts to reconstruct the family history. Like her namesakes elsewhere, these attempts don't take her very far, but she does tell us her family comes from a border village that is now part of Ukraine. A village that sounds a lot like Karpy.

The Mrs Gmitruk who welcomed Mala into her home in the autumn of 1941 loved to listen as this Jewish girl from Warsaw read her Bible stories. The Mrs Gmitruk sitting opposite us listens to the radio. She tunes in to Radio Maryja, a popular station run by Father Tadeusz Rydzyk, a priest who is keen to point out that 'the word tolerance does not appear in the Gospels'. He rails against EU bureaucrats, multinationals, and feminists, and above all against the 'international movement of anti-Polonism' — an 'ism' that covers all things foreign.

The words 'Well, on Radio Maryja they said …' are never far from Mrs Gmitruk's lips. The station colours her thinking about history, delivering a wartime past in which Poles were either victim or hero, but never perpetrator. Mrs Gmitruk tells us about *Chapel of Remembrance*, a show that celebrates Poles who saved the lives of Jews. Incredibly courageous people, especially in the Poland of that time. Yad Vashem, Israel's state institution for preserving the memory of Holocaust victims, has recognised over 6,000 Poles as 'Righteous Among the Nations', an honour awarded to non-Jews who saved Jewish lives. *Chapel of Remembrance* glosses over what these righteous people had to endure in the months immediately after the war. Back then, Polish nationalists wanted nothing to do with them; now they are lauded as a source of national pride. The show on Radio Maryja has taught Mrs Gmitruk a thing or two. One: Jews were killed by Germans. Two: Poles tried to save them. 'And that's why it's so odd that the Jews are so ungrateful. Don't you agree?'

Mr Gmitruk informs us that you can call the radio station to suggest candidates for the show, which is why Mala's story has struck a chord with his wife. We hurriedly explain that Mala's time with the Gmitruks had been good and that they treated her well. But on no account did they save her. Mala left too early in the war for anyone to make that claim.

I had previously explained this situation at the archives in Warsaw, where I was hoping to trace the records of the churches around Karpy. 'That's a pity,' the archivist replied. 'If you'd been looking for someone who was righteous, I could get people on board. I might even be able to arrange a subsidy.'

These Gmitruks may have been related to their wartime namesakes from Karpy, but our conversation with them left us none the wiser. Oh well. On the way to the next Gmitruk on our list, Daniel says he was at least relieved that Mrs Gmitruk made no reference to Henryk Zieliński, a priest who makes regular appearances on Radio Maryja, 'spouting all kinds of typically anti-Semitic nonsense'. A few months later, Father Zieliński will go on to make statements on Polish public television that are picked up by Israeli media. Jews, the priest said, have 'a completely different set of values' and, more interesting still, 'a different concept of the truth'. According to Father Zieliński, 'For us, the truth corresponds to the facts. For the Jew, truth means something that conforms to his understanding of what's beneficial.'

For Mrs Gmitruk, the killing of the Jews is a subplot to the central narrative of the terror endured by her fellow Poles. What separates her from Zieliński is her complete lack of malice. She sincerely believes that the killing of the Jews pales in comparison to the horrors that the Polish people had to withstand. In this, she is not alone. A survey carried out in 2015 shows that only 33 per cent of Poles associate the word 'Auschwitz' with the killing of Jews. For 47 per cent, Auschwitz was 'primarily' a camp where Catholic Poles suffered. Among loyal listeners to Radio Maryja, that figure could well be twice as high. Around 75,000 Catholic Poles died in Auschwitz. Although it is difficult to give exact figures, the number of Jews who died there—Jews from all over Europe—was at least ten times that number.

As we drive back to Zamość, Daniel tells me what bothers him most about Mrs Gmitruk. It's not her ignorance of historical facts—'You can't really blame her for that'—but her lamentations about her daughter in England. 'Too many Poles think that way,' Daniel seethes. 'The whole world is to blame for their woes, no matter what. It's never their own fault... No *internet*?!' His laugh is a scornful bark. 'Every library, every public building has internet ... her daughter could have logged on anywhere.'

Perhaps this is a good time to say a few words about my travelling companion, Daniel Sabaciński. If only to show how every Pole has a turbulent family history, some more recent than others. His grandmother is descended from a prominent line of Polish nobility. She lived in a palace close to present-day Lviv, a city that is now in Ukraine, but that in her youth was under Habsburg rule and known as Lemberg. In 1918, the whole family abandoned their palace and headed west in a large covered wagon, on the run from the Bolsheviks. Their horses came to a halt 120 kilometres away in the Polish town of Biłgoraj, not far from Zamość.

Grandfather was there to meet them. He had fled Łódź, where the Russian authorities had sent him to work in the mines as punishment for his Polish nationalist activities. Grandfather had a degree in economics, and went on to become the mayor of Biłgoraj, an office he held for years until the Germans came. He and his wife survived the war, but, having been labelled class enemies, they had it tough in the Polish People's Republic.

Daniel came into the world while his father was in the United States. The authorities had given him permission to leave the country to undergo an eye operation, assuming that a father-to-be was bound to return. Not Daniel's father, who was a fervent anti-communist. In his younger years, Daniel's one dream was to follow his father, but when the Polish boy who loved all things American—'You should have seen my bedroom!' — finally got to spend a few months in Los Angeles, he came back disillusioned. Since then, Daniel has chosen to remain in Zamość, where he grew up as the only child of a single mother. He is the one student from his high school class not to have moved abroad or to a big city like Warsaw, Kraków, or Gdańsk. Daniel is what Poles call a 'local patriot', happy with his job in Zamość's fledgling tourist industry. 'We work hard to attract more visitors than just Israelis and American Jews who want to see the land of their forefathers.' He likes to tell foreigners about the resilience and the beauty of his region, which is why he has no patience with complainers like Mrs Gmitruk. They ruin his story.

Daniel imitates her weary tone: 'Why did no one tell us you can't go to university if you don't graduate from high school?' And then in his own voice: 'Don't make me laugh.' Neither of us does, probably because we suspect our laughter would ring with the condescension of two men with a university education. Perhaps that's why I am reminded of something Mala said about the Gmitruks she knew: 'They were too simple to be anti-Semitic.' A remark I immediately filed under 'amusing observations made by elderly ladies'. Surely, if anything gives you the wherewithal to overcome prejudice, it's education. But as Daniel and I speed along the canalised River Łabuńka, suddenly I'm not so sure.

This seed of doubt is fed by the memoirs and secondary sources I read at the Ringelblum Institute in Warsaw, many of which describe the mass killing of Jews in Poland. They reveal that nationalist students and their pre-war national democratic leaders regularly complained of the trouble they had convincing farmers to stop doing business with local Jews. Getting them on board was not so difficult, certainly not east of Warsaw in the area around Czyżewo, but to achieve a boycott of Jewish shops, the Endeks' main aim, it was going to take more than an abstract notion that Jews were vile creatures that should be driven out of Poland. Many farmers shared such views, according to the writer of one Endek article from 1936, yet they saw no reason to take action against Jewish neighbours with whom they had dealings. This incensed him.

At a Warsaw café, I meet historian Brian Porter-Szücs, who expands on this idea. 'Racial doctrine is also an ideology, a story that gives the world meaning. To open up to it, you have to be sensitive to ideological thinking. Many peasants had no such sensibility. They were unable to read, and they had a harvest to get in. Banging on about the excellence of the nation? That's idle city talk.'

One afternoon, I find myself at a small debating centre on the site of the former ghetto, where a radio presenter is talking about his experiences as a black man of Kenyan origin in the overwhelmingly white city of Warsaw. James Omolo talks about the surprise he often encounters in Poland. Complete strangers have walked up to him in the playground and asked whether his children's black skin will lighten now that they are growing up in Poland. As Omolo sees it, such questions have nothing to do with racism, only with ignorance. 'And racism doesn't come from ignorance,' he tells his audience that afternoon. 'On the contrary: racism requires knowledge. Little children see no difference between black and white. That comes later. Someone has to tell them about the hierarchy, that it's better to be white. That able-bodied is better than disabled, that straight is better than gay. Children have to take that in first, just as they take in that one and one are two.'

Maybe Omolo is right. Maybe the idea that ignorance leads to segregation and racism is not self-evident. And perhaps Daniel and I, through our love of history, have also absorbed prejudices that stand in our way rather than helping us. Our search for the Gmitruks is a good example. We are constantly wondering what they were: Polish or Ukrainian? Yet at that time, in the desperately poor area where they lived, this distinction was largely an academic construct. Olena Palko, a young Ukrainian researcher, explains, 'It was a successful construct, certainly, and when soldiers brought an obsession with race and nationality to the region, it became a matter of life and death. However, up to that point, it was anything but.'

Palko's research focuses on minorities in the Ukrainian interwar years. 'It's worth remembering,' she says, 'that the Gmitruks and their parents grew up as subjects of the Habsburg Empire. Karpy was in the province of Galicia. Did they think of themselves as Hapsburgers? No, of course they didn't. Did they call themselves Ukrainian? Possibly.'

A census from 1910 reveals that many of Karpy's residents did. In the wider municipality, there was more or less a fifty-fifty split between those who called themselves Ukrainian and those who called themselves Polish. In 1921 and 1931, by which time the region had been absorbed into Poland, the proportion of people who called themselves Ukrainian had increased slightly, but one finding among the figures from that time is even more telling: in 1931, no less than 707,000 residents referred to themselves as *tutejszy*, which, roughly translated, means 'from here'. The census officials were not happy about this categorisation, but it had proved impossible to slap a 'nationality' — Polish, Ukrainian, Russian, Jewish, or otherwise — on these people and make it stick.

Most of those who called themselves *tutejszy* lived north of Karpy, in what is now Belarus. Yet many others came from closer to the village. Unfortunately, the data from the 1931 census is not broken down according to village or rural municipality. Karpy does not merit a specific mention.

And what about the Gmitruks? What did they call themselves? My persistent questioning only serves to make Mala uncertain. There are a few things she knows for sure: they went to church and she was able to talk to them; the language they spoke was close enough to the Polish she had learned at school. 'My Polish was actually better than theirs.' Palko clarifies, 'In general you can say that townspeople from the area were often Polish. The same went for the large landowners, the few members of the intelligentsia, and the Catholic clergy. Farmers and other people who lived off the land were often Ukrainian, which is not to say that they necessarily referred to themselves as such.'

Palko argues that nowadays we are too inclined to theorise about nationalities that meant very little to the pre-war rural population. 'That's probably because later, during the war, those nationalities turned out to be crucial.' Soldiers from elsewhere brought an obsession with race and nationality to the region, she observes, one that turned out to be highly contagious. Yet for decades before the soldiers came, such notions had failed to catch on. The growing sense of nationhood in nineteenth-century Europe was 'first and foremost' a project of the lettered classes, and in and around places like Karpy the literate were few and far between. 'The main aim of nationalists was to counter the

idea that you came from here, from this village, from these estates,'
Palko explains. 'They wanted to do away with the idea that you were
one with that place and the local authority that governed it, that
you were a Zamoyski or a Lubomirski. Nationalists had to educate
people, to convince them they belonged to a nation. At that time, the
nationalist movement was about emancipation. There was no equating
stupidity with nationalism. If anything, it was the opposite.'

In other words, knowledge is not only a prerequisite for
discrimination, as Omolo argues, but also for a national consciousness.
And that kind of knowledge was something the Gmitruks probably
did not possess. They did not have patriotic singalongs, or declaim the
work of Ukrainian nationalist poets. There was no portrait of Piłsudski
on their wall. We will never even know exactly what language they
spoke, if for no other reason than they probably didn't really know
themselves.

A nationalist frame of reference makes it harder to understand the
region and its people, Palko says, and cites the example of the local
Greek Catholics. In the 1931 census, no fewer than 235,000 of them
said Polish was their mother tongue. 'Yet they were ethnic Ukrainian.
At least, that's how we academics refer to them. But ask a bunch
of academics what exactly they mean by the word 'ethnic', and the
answers you get will be pretty useless.'

Mala has no clear recollection of the church where she was given her
baptismal certificate. The Greek Catholic churches around Karpy
were built of wood so dark it was almost black, and often had domed
towers made of the same material. Roman Catholic churches had a
pointed steeple, and their walls were usually plastered creamy white.
As for Russian Orthodox churches, there were hardly any in the
neighbourhood.

During the war, Greek Catholic priests were more likely than
Roman Catholic priests to help a Jewish fugitive obtain false
documents. The senior cleric among the Greek Catholics, whose title
was 'Metropolitan', was appalled by the murderous violence he saw
around him. He hid Jews in Lviv, and sent a letter to Heinrich Himmler
objecting to the killing of Jews by the Ukrainian auxiliary police. If the

Germans were prepared to have these murders on their conscience, he wrote, they should do the killing themselves. In all Greek Catholic or Uniate churches, he instructed his priests to preach that murder is always a sin, whether or not your victim is a political enemy.

The Germans could have turned Ukraine into a collaborating satellite state without much trouble. The Ukrainians had endured extreme suffering under the terror inflicted by Stalin; millions had been starved in a famine engineered from Moscow. Yet, initially, the Nazis had no interest in establishing a satellite state in Ukraine. Hitler's plans cast the new *Reichskommissariat* in the role of colony, not of 'brotherly nation'. Its people were inferior beings to be got rid of or pressed into work as slaves. In November 1941, the new *Reichskommissar* of Ukraine, Erich Koch, banned all of the Ukrainian national and nationalist institutes whose leaders had looked to the arrival of the Nazis with such hope. Thousands were imprisoned or worse, and Koch went down in history as the man who said, 'If I meet a Ukrainian worthy of being seated at my table, I must have him shot.'

A Greek Catholic monk comes to greet us. A Friar Tuck belly helps lighten the sinister mood created by his black habit and the dark lines beneath his eyes. He lists countless reasons why it's impossible to discover whether a priest around 1942 issued a document to one Janina Gmitruk. Privacy is not among them. He talks about the fate of his church, the downward spiral that began after the war. It started with the death of the Metropolitan, upon which the Soviets intervened. They wanted nothing to do with religion, but turned a blind eye to Russian Orthodoxy while Greek Catholics and Roman Catholics were openly persecuted. Every last Uniate bishop was imprisoned. Churches were closed, burned to the ground, or converted into town halls, clubhouses, and gymnasiums. Many a priest ended up in a Siberian prison camp. Archives vanished. Good luck finding any baptismal certificates at all, never mind one issued under false pretences. The monk is living proof of the modest recovery made by the church since 1990.

In the weeks and months after Mala's departure, genocide found its way into every last corner of the General Government in Poland and the Reichskommissariat Ukraine. Looking back on this period decades later, Jewish–Polish historian Szymon Datner noted that, 'Practically every hamlet, village, town, and city in the General Government was witness to the murders of Jews who fled the ghettos, or escaped death trains.' Datner was the only member of his family to survive the ghetto of Białystok. After the war, he became the director of the Ringelblum Institute in Warsaw and the first leading Polish academic to study the cooperation between the German police and Polish peasants in the east of the country. At the time, he was hesitant to put numbers to his findings, a debate that historians have entered into only recently. The central question is how many Polish Jews survived the war in German-occupied territory that had been part of Poland before war broke out. The current consensus is as follows: approximately 250,000 Polish Jews attempted to hide in the forest, in self-made bunkers, or went into hiding with non-Jews. Around 200,000 of them were tracked down and murdered, which means that around 50,000 lived to see the end of the war.

In areas where there were neither forests nor partisans, almost no one survived. In the triangle between Białystok in the north-east, Lviv in the south-east, and Warsaw in the west, the chances of survival were slimmest. This was where the extermination camps of Bełżec, Treblinka, and Sobibór stood, the instruments of destruction at the heart of *Aktion Reinhard*, an operation named after Reinhard Heydrich. In the space of 100 days in the summer of 1942, 1.3 million people were murdered in these camps. In some districts within this triangle, less than 2 per cent of Jews survived, a terrifying figure for places that had been home to so many Jews. Entire villages had been Jewish, and Jews had made up half the population of towns such as Tomaszów Lubelski or Zamość.

The term *Judenjagd* or 'hunt for the Jews' was coined by the Germans themselves, by the Order Police and the gendarmes of the General Government. In the autumn of 1942 and the winter that followed, hunting down Jews became their main task, one they would continue to fulfil until the final days of the occupation. That is the picture to emerge from the accounts of German perpetrators, Jewish victims, Polish witnesses, and German police reports that record the number of 'bandits' arrested or turned in each day, often with details of the location and the locals who lent a hand. The impression is one of Germans ceaselessly on the hunt in the occupied Polish countryside, with local residents as the dogs who rounded up the quarry.

On the whole, that was how it worked. In every village, the Germans appointed a handful of locals who, in exchange for a small remuneration (often bottles of booze), were willing to be their eyes and ears. These helpful country folk, often referred to as 'citizens' militias', could turn the existing hierarchy in a village on its head. Fortunately for them, almost every farmer owned a dog, so a knock on the door in the middle of the night to ask for help seldom went unnoticed. Besides, the close-knit nature of village life in general made it especially difficult to keep a secret.

All of which means that, even if Mrs Gmitruk had been able to dig out a cellar or conceal Mala among her livestock, it would still have been nigh on impossible to disguise the fact that she was hiding someone. In one case, villagers tore an entire house apart in search of a Jew in hiding, simply because the man of the house had been acting strangely. They beat the children in the hope of forcing an admission from their parents, but found nothing. In the village of Bieniaszowice on the River Dunajec, local residents did discover one Pejka Kapelner. Their suspicions had been aroused when her protector had brought her a newspaper. In a village of illiterates such as Bieniaszowice, carrying a newspaper was the equivalent of shouting from the rooftops that you were hiding a Jew.

Jews who went into hiding usually paid their protectors. In many cases, the arrangement worked for a while, until the money ran out, or fear of the neighbours or the Germans became too much. In some cases, greed won out over compassion, and the farmer's family killed the hideaways for their possessions, though these seldom amounted to much. Władysław Nosek from the village of Janowice hid a woman of thirty in his barn until one day he decided to get rid of her. Why is not apparent from the testimony he gave after the war: perhaps he was afraid of being betrayed to the police; perhaps he had his eye on the two suitcases the woman had with her. Nosek confessed, 'I took a club ... and gave her a few hard blows to the head.' He buried her body in his field, and shared the contents of her suitcases among his family. They contained little more than clothes and bed linen.

Pitchforks appear regularly in memoirs and court reports from the time. Mala, Mira, and Hanka had to run for their lives from a pitchfork-wielding farmer. Another such story concerns Wojciech Pula, a farmer from the village of Dulcza who hid a Jewish tailor named Josek. His skills were much in demand, and the whole village reaped the rewards. For months, in exchange for his safety, Josek mended clothes for peasants and their families in the wider area. For Pula, this proved to be a nice little earner, but it also meant everyone knew he was hiding someone. Increasingly afraid his number might soon be up, he chose the least humane option. On the day the police arrived to order the villagers to hunt for Jews, he killed Josek with a pitchfork.

Fear often played a part in the murders of Jews committed by Poles. Researcher Tom Frydel studied many of the 30,000 court records from the post-war trials of collaborators and peasants who had committed offences, including crimes against Jews in hiding. Among peasants, in particular, Frydel discovered 'a communal fear bordering on mass hysteria'. Take the example of Podborze, a village comparable to Karpy. There, Polish policemen encountered peasants who begged them not to hand over any Jews they found to the Germans, but to shoot them on the spot. The peasants were afraid the Jews might identify them as their protectors. In the General Government, the dividing line between a selfless hero and a fearful killer could be remarkably thin.

Polish-Canadian historian Jan Grabowski writes that, during the war, the Poles 'had little to say in matters of life and death of the Jews. The only exception was the period of the *Judenjagd*, when the only way to salvation led through the hearts of the Poles. This was the only time, and the only situation, in which Poles (or, for that matter, Ukrainians, Belorussians, or Balts) decided which Jews would live or die.'

Did we know what was taking place? Could we have known? These are questions that have occupied many in Western Europe. Not in Poland. In Poland, everyone knew. The Poles asked other questions. How guilty are we? Do we tell our children? And if so, what words do we use? What stories do we tell? Or do we stay silent and act as if nothing happened?

An important voice in this discussion, even during the war, was Zofia Kossak-Szczucka. She was something of a celebrity in pre-war Poland, the author of popular books that were liberally sprinkled with anti-Semitism. Under the German occupation, however, Kossak decided to save Jews from the Warsaw ghetto through the Polish Council to Aid Jews, a secret organisation she co-founded under the codename Żegota. She was arrested and sent to Auschwitz, an ordeal she barely survived.

In 1942, she wrote an article or manifesto listing the crimes committed by the Nazis, followed by the statement, 'Anyone who remains silent in the face of murder is an accomplice to murder. Anyone who does not condemn approves.' Not a woman to change her mind, Kossak went on to insist in the very next paragraph that her 'feelings toward Jews' remained unaltered. She still saw them as 'political, economic and ideological enemies of Poland' who undermined the Polish nation and Christianity. Yet she denounced the way in which attitudes among Poles, especially Polish peasants, were changing. German barbarity, she wrote, had blunted their compassion and robbed them of their moral judgement. Why? 'Because lightning from the heavens does not strike the murderers of children, blood that was spilled is not avenged.' And so the peasantry had lost their fear of retribution, both earthly and divine, and had come to believe: 'Perhaps it is true that the Jew is a cursed creature, and can be killed with impunity. This explains why more and more peasants are taking an active part in the German action of extermination [of the Jews].'

Kossak wholeheartedly condemned such actions. The fifth commandment was as clear as day. Yad Vashem later recognised her as 'Righteous Among the Nations'.

Most Poles I meet are willing to talk about their country's turbulent history. Poland is also the only country — though Russia comes a close second — where over ten weekly publications entirely devoted to history can still turn a profit. But despite this love of national history, the hunt for the Jews remains a very sensitive issue. So sensitive, in fact, that many Poles, including those in positions of power, maintain that this period is not part of their history at all. After all, the country was occupied at the time.

Daniel, too, finds this an unsettling topic of conversation, though he does his best. 'We should be able to talk about everything.' He takes comfort in the fact that, in their memoirs, many survivors say the Ukrainians were even more anti-Semitic than the Poles, an observation he repeats several times. Whiling away the hours on our expeditions in his trusty Toyota, we wind up discussing whether his belief in a difference between Poles and Ukrainians stems from the same kind of ethnic group thinking that is at the root of anti-Semitism. Why is it so hard to think about the misery of the Second World War without falling into the same identity-based thinking that lies at the heart of all the misery?

Daniel ponders this for a while. 'Piss off with your politically correct bullshit' would be a valid-enough answer, but he takes the time to consider his reasons for rejecting my tentative accusation. After silently steering through a slalom of roadworks on the way to Zamość, he concludes that my anti-nationalism results in a soulless world where the only passion people have left is the latest iPhone.

'I see it in Warsaw among old classmates of mine from Zamość. They say they could never go back to the small-minded provinces. They say they pity me, but all they can find to talk about is which milk frother makes the best cappuccino.'

'Is that such a terrible conversation to have?' I venture. People who fret about froth are probably less likely to kill someone with a pitchfork. 'Besides,' I add, in an attempt to lighten the mood, 'who doesn't want their milk frothed to perfection?'

Daniel pulls a disapproving face. 'Soulless, that's what it is. And small-minded! The small-mindedness of the cosmopolitan tribe.'

Instead of footnotes

The quote that kicks off this chapter is from a speech Himmler gave in October 1943 to a gathering of senior SS officers in Poznań.

The murder of Poles in Volhynia and East Galicia in 1943–44 is a bone of fierce contention between Poles and Ukrainians. This also applies to Polish and Ukrainian historians, whose estimates of those killed differ dramatically. There are many websites devoted to the various calculations carried out by dozens of historians from as many countries. US historian Timothy Snyder, who both describes and provides figures for the atrocities committed in Eastern Europe, estimates that in East Galicia around 25,000 Poles were murdered by Ukrainian nationalists, and another 40,000 to 60,000 in the region of Volhynia to the north. Between 250,000 and 300,000 Polish-speaking inhabitants of those areas heeded the threats made by the Ukrainian nationalists and fled. In his book *Bloodlands: Europe between Hitler and Stalin* (2010), Snyder also provides a reasoned estimate of the total number of civilian fatalities on the territory that constitutes the present-day independent republic of Ukraine: approximately 3.5 million deaths, all between 1941 and 1945.

Radio presenter James Omolo's book *Strangers at the Gate: black Poland* was published in 2017, with financial backing from Kenya's Moyo International Investments Company.

The Jewish woman who noted that, after days of non-stop gunfire, the farmers' dogs no longer started barking, was Chaja Rosenblatt. She came from Radomyśl Wielki, a village near the city of Tarnów in southern Poland. Her observation comes from Jan Grabowski's book *Hunt for the Jews: betrayal and murder in German-occupied Poland* (Indiana University Press, 2013). Grabowski dug out anecdotes and personal accounts from police reports, memoirs, and witness statements that coalesce into a horrific picture of what befell the Jews in a single rural district just east of Kraków as they struggled to survive the occupation. Three examples are included in this chapter. In Poland, the figures Grabowski quotes are contested, not least his assertion that 200,000 Jews died as a direct or indirect result of actions taken by Poles. Grabowski himself regards this as a conservative estimate, as it excludes the victims of Poland's 'Blue Police'. A number of Polish historians argue that Grabowski's estimate is much too high. An exceptionally exhaustive Wikipedia page is devoted to this controversy: https://en.wikipedia.org/wiki/Hunt_for_the_Jews.

Catholic priest Tadeusz Rydzyk's assertion that the word 'tolerance' does not appear in the Gospels comes from Brian Porter-Szücs, who refers to it in his book *Poland in the Modern World: beyond martyrdom* (2014). Porter-Szücs also mentions another relevant survey about the self-image of Poles. In 2009, 81 per cent of Poles said they believed their forebears 'often' helped Jews survive the war, while only 11 per cent said their forebears 'often' handed Jews over to the occupying forces.

Polish Jewish historian Szymon Datner died in 1989. A few years before his death, he wrote about the attitude of the Poles during the occupation and the Holocaust that took place so close to home: 'Aside from passivity, which I regard as entirely justified in a situation in which every action was heroic, there also existed an indifference that I regard as negative ...'

In 2004, another scholar and Holocaust survivor from Poland, forensic psychiatrist Emanuel Tanay (born Tenenwurzel), wrote, 'The denunciations of the Jews who were hiding or were on false papers were not a sporadic activity, but an endemic problem. Virtually all Poles resisted, passively or actively, the German occupation. However, the majority of the Polish population assisted the Germans in their effort to annihilate the Jews.'

6

The Amstel

'It doesn't take much to change your memories. Talking about
them is often enough.'

–Douwe Draaisma, psychologist

On my travels between Tomaszów Lubelski, Karpy, and Lublin, it dawns
on me that all too often I am having to settle for shadows. It is proving
incredibly difficult to find written sources or living witnesses to flesh
out events from Mala's memory. She seldom remembers surnames,
and when she does, they have been transformed in the remembering.
She tells me her school was founded by a man called Majewski, but the
founder's name turns out to be Méyet. Mala's memory has probably
combined Méyet with Mościcki, the Polish president whose name was
associated with the Catholic section of the school. She cannot recall her
friend Amelka's surname. Though I should know better, I press her for
an answer, and in an effort to help me or to stop me asking questions,
she comes up with 'Passau'. But, as I soon discover, the surname Passau
doesn't occur once in all of Poland. I chalk it up as a lesson learned:
how likely is it that, 75 years on, this elderly woman will suddenly hit
upon a name just because I really want her to?

There is another process at work: when we put our memories into
words, we change the narrative in ways that are almost impossible to
reverse. Recounting a memory is not analogous to playing back a tape
of a pre-existing recording. Later events can colour or distort what we

think we remember. Dutch writer and comic-book creator Marten Toonder summed this up aptly when he said, 'Childhood events often turn out to be the consequence of an incident later in life.'

People don't just tell you what they remember. They incorporate aspects discovered after the fact, things that seem logical with the benefit of hindsight. The memoirs of Holocaust survivors regularly contain passages about the state of the nation; the tendency of Polish peasants to do this, that, or the other; or how partisans were likely to respond in a given situation. They frequently write about events they could never have experienced, not least because they only saw a sliver of the outside world from their hiding place. Perhaps that's why children's memoirs written directly after the war have the greatest impact. Children tend to stick to what they saw with their own eyes, and are seldom troubled by the urge to interpret. Without being tempted to theorise, they simply tell us what they went through.

In Mala's case, too, there are sometimes marked differences between the historical record and what she remembers, so marked as to try a researcher's patience. For example, after reading certain passages from Mala's memoirs, Ewa Koper of the Bełżec Memorial and Museum was no longer inclined to help me. Both charming and helpful, Koper knows all there is to know about how the Holocaust played out in Tomaszów Lubelski, the town where she grew up. In her thirties, she holds the office of Leader of Dialogue with the Forum for Dialogue, an organisation that works to facilitate communication between Catholics and Jews.

And that's not all. Working with survivors and their descendants, she set up a monument in memory of the town's murdered Jews. Obtaining extensive input from survivors in Israel and America, and liaising with a retired Israeli architect in Hod HaSharon, she facilitated a reconstruction of the pre-war town, which the architect then captured in a 3D computer animation. Anyone who wants to can now wander through Tomaszów Lubelski as it was in 1939, past each and every building, from the impressive seventeenth-century synagogue to the marketplace and the ritual bath house. The architect even managed to trace the names of the Jewish families who lived in the houses at that time. A native of Tomaszów Lubelski, his own name was among them.

All this is thanks to Ewa Koper, a researcher steeped in the history of Tomaszów. And then I turn up with the recollections of a woman from the Netherlands, not even a native of the town. A woman who claims that the Jews of Tomaszów Lubelski got on well with German soldiers and that anti-Semitism wasn't prevalent there at the time. One of Mala's abiding memories from her brief stay is the Olszewski family's incredulous response to her stories about the Warsaw ghetto. 'They thought I was lying.'

Ewa Koper finds another of Mala's statements striking, to say the least: 'In Tomaszów Lubelski, five of us lived in one room. We thought we had been saved, because the Jews there were very well treated.' Well treated? Ewa Koper, a lean young woman with a slender neck, strong jawline, and sad eyes, shows me photos from the time of the occupation: Germans carting off Jewish residents of Tomaszów Lubelski to a labour camp just south of the town. There they were given little to drink and forced to work in the burning sun. Anyone who fainted was buried alive.

Mala says Polish Jews in Tomaszów Lubelski did not have to wear an armband with a star of David. Ewa shows me photos that prove the opposite.

Ewa had no desire to help me, and so I went in search of another expert. Yet the seed of doubt had been planted. Had Mala really been in Tomaszów Lubelski? Perhaps, as Ewa suggested, she had stayed in Tomaszów *Mazowiecki*, a larger town closer to Warsaw?

On reading Mala's memoirs for the first time, I had assumed it would be relatively straightforward to find supporting evidence in Poland, to bring her story to life with characters, circumstances, events. Yet here I was, faltering at every step. Ewa's response stopped me dead in my tracks. It didn't help that Olszewski is the Polish equivalent of Smith or Jones, so tracking them down was never going to be easy. Mala had no idea whether these particular Olszewskis had lived close to a church, cemetery, hospital, school, or park, and now I had every reason to wonder whether they had lived in Tomaszów Lubelski at all.

In the hope of gaining a firmer foothold, I submitted a photo to a local newspaper in the other Tomaszów: Tomaszów Mazowiecki. It

was the only photo in Mala's possession dating from before or during
the war, given to her years later by a relative of her brother-in-law
Majloch Waserman. It pictures Majloch and his wife, Mala's sister
Chaja. Smiling for the camera, the couple are standing on a bridge, in
front of a distinctive stone statue of two giant putti intertwined.

I felt sure a reader would recognise the statue. By this time I had
taken a good look around Tomaszów Lubelski, and I knew it had no
bridges of note. A statue of two oversized cherubs would have stuck
out like a sore thumb among its modest streets, wooden houses, and
occasional barracks-like blocks of flats. It wasn't long before I had my
answer. Someone had recognised the statue and the bridge. Location:
Warsaw.

This was no help at all, but at least it made sense. Majloch had
moved to Warsaw, where he met and married Chaja, who was then
working as a seamstress for the textile firm Hopman. Out walking one
day, the young couple had posed together on a bridge.

It was months before I could say for certain that Mala had stayed
in the southern town of Tomaszów Lubelski, and not Tomaszów
Mazowiecki. Meanwhile, the Yad Vashem archives provided
confirmation that Majloch and his whole family had also been born
there. In the 1950s, one of his elder sisters added this information
to the official records in Jerusalem. She survived the war, having
left Tomaszów Lubelski with the Red Army when they withdrew
eastwards and left the town to the Germans. Her first stop had been
Rawa-Ruska, a few kilometres from Karpy. Later, she was put on a
transport to Siberia, where she first worked in east Uzbekistan and later
in the Kazakh city of Öskemen, then known as Ust-Kamenogorsk. At
Yad Vashem, she reported the death of her younger brother, Majloch
Waserman: born in Tomaszów Lubelski, moved to Warsaw, married to
Chaja Kizel.

Slowly but surely, more evidence of Mala's account began to
emerge. About Karpy, for starters. Mala remembers the village as being
twenty-five kilometres from Tomaszów Lubelski, a journey both she
and her sister had made on foot, Mira more than once. When you
set a compass to the scale on the map and draw a circle twenty-five
kilometres around Tomaszów Lubelski, the line passes through Karpy

in present-day Ukraine. And a few hundred metres from the village there is a small settlement, a few houses at most, which once bore the name Kolonie Karpy. The distance in Mala's memory is accurate. The other Tomaszów — Mazowiecki — lies almost 300 kilometres further west.

Following a long stream of emails and letters bearing the stamps of the Jewish Historical Institute, the Olszewskis finally surface in the archives of Tomaszów Lubelski: Jan Edward, the head of the household, and his wife, Julia. When war broke out, they were already in their forties. One year after peace was signed, they left the ruins of their hometown behind to start a new life in Breslau, moving into a house that the German occupants had been forced to vacate. Breslau, once a major city of the Third Reich, became the fourth-largest city in Poland when the borders were realigned. Its Polish name is Wrocław. The Olszewskis' migration was no exception. Shortly after the war, some four million Poles left their homes to start anew in the 'recovered territories'. About 1.5 million of them settled in the region around Wrocław.

But what about Mala's impressions? When she stayed in Tomaszów Lubelski, how had she arrived at the idea that the Jews there were on the best of terms with the occupying forces? That they were well treated? That they didn't have to wear an armband? That anti-Semitism was not a major concern?

Perhaps these are things she was told. To help support the family, Mala and Mira sold the clothes that Chaja made. The two younger sisters were able to pass as Polish Catholics, thanks to their perfect command of Polish and Mala's fair hair and blue-green eyes. And if they were recognised as Jews, they were not to worry. This wasn't Warsaw: anti-Semitism wasn't rife in Tomaszów; the Germans got along fine with the Jews. This untruth could be maintained because the townspeople did not know who Mala and Mira were. The fact that they were strangers allowed the arrangement to work for a time. And when the situation became more precarious, Majloch sent the girls to the countryside — first to the farmer near Lublin, after which Mala looked for other work and wound up as an unpaid housemaid and farmhand to the Gmitruk family, some twenty-five kilometres south of Tomaszów Lubelski.

Another question remains: why would the Olszewskis refuse to believe Mala's stories about the Warsaw ghetto? They may have been pretending. Mala had just turned fifteen at the time, and by all accounts she was a charming, clever teenager. Mala says Mrs Olszewski burst into tears when she spoke of the horrors of the ghetto, which suggests not only that her descriptions were vivid, but also that Mrs Olszewski was inclined to believe them. After a while, the Olszewskis may have sought to reassure Mala and calm their mother down. Reassurances along the lines of, 'Don't worry, that doesn't happen here.' Or even, 'The Jews here get on okay with the Germans.' In Mala's memory, such statements may have evolved over time and led her to conclude, 'They thought I was lying.'

This is all speculation, of course, but in the end we have little more to go on than the memory of a girl who was fifteen at the time, in combination with a handful of conflicting findings and other people's recollections. Even so, there are a few routes out of these contradictions. One is the issue of timing: Mala's arrival in Tomaszów Lubelski, in the spring of 1941, coincided with a lull in the atrocities. Before the war, the town had been home to a lively Jewish community. The same had been true of towns across the region, including Tyszowce and Krasnobród, where Mala's paternal grandfather and grandmother were born. Around half of Tomaszów's 13,000 residents were Jewish. There was a ritual slaughterhouse, a splendid bath house, and a huge brick synagogue dating from the first half of the seventeenth century. In September 1939, the Luftwaffe bombed the town mercilessly. Dozens of houses burned down, the synagogue lay in ruins, and around 200 people lost their lives. In the days that followed, Polish soldiers fought both German and Soviet troops in and around Tomaszów.

Having taken control of Tomaszów, the German soldiers spent seven days amusing themselves at the expense of its Jewish residents. They pulled out the beards of Jewish men, and made them dance, crawl, or run for hours. One survivor remembers how his father was forced to ride a horse round and round the marketplace. The man, who had never ridden a horse in his life, fell off, suffered several fractures, and died a few days later. A photo taken by a German soldier shows an Orthodox Jew with a swastika cut into his hair, surrounded by a group of laughing Germans.

At the end of those seven days, the Germans vacated the town and handed it over to the Red Army, in line with the pact sealed prior to the invasion. In another seven days the Germans were back, after the two totalitarian powers made a minor correction to their borders. The Red Army offered Tomaszów Lubelski's Jewish residents the chance to travel east with them. Some 4,500 Jews accepted this offer, including Majloch Waserman's sister; 1,500 stayed behind.

The German abuses then began in earnest. As early as December, they rounded up people with a physical or mental disability, locked them in a bunker, and filled it with water. Others were sent to the labour camp described by Ewa Koper. The town's remaining Jews were ordered to live in and around Piekarska Street, and were made to pave the street that led to the German gendarme station with stones from the wall of the Jewish cemetery. Gravestones were used to make steps in front of the house of the town's senior German commander, so he would not get his boots dirty.

Mala first arrived in Tomaszów months after all this had taken place. Beyond Piekarska Street, she would not have encountered any Jewish residents. Her brother-in-law told her she did not need to wear an armband.

I was eventually able to find the Olszewskis, but no trace of their downstairs neighbours: the large Jewish Orthodox family who allowed Mala to eat with them. Mala remembers the father's nickname: Awremele Królik, which translates as Abraham the Rabbit. Even the lively community of survivors from Tomaszów Lubelski who now reside in Israel, including one elderly lady with an exceptional memory, cannot remember anyone with that nickname. Which is not to say he did not exist.

Armed with printouts of the documents obtained from Yad Vashem, I return to put my hypotheses to Ewa Koper at the Bełżec museum. 'Could be,' she says. 'But hopefully you appreciate how hard it is for a researcher to acknowledge that people remember or experience one and the same reality in such completely different ways. To acknowledge that is to call into question the very worth of the testimony of all of those Holocaust survivors.'

We talk about the value of that testimony. Isn't it the case that researchers, writers, and even journalists primarily use it to illustrate the story they want to tell? In much the same way as TV shows that go searching for lost relatives only broadcast the searches which deliver the goods? Ewa finds her own hypothesis that Mala has never even been to Tomaszów Lubelski more 'appealing'.

Yet Mala *was* in Tomaszów Lubelski. Along with her sister Mira, her little brother Meir, her brother-in-law Majloch, and her sister Chaja.

Mala and her friend Amelka travelled from Kolonie Karpy to Lublin with the aim of finding work in Germany. To ascertain that she really was with the Gmitruks in Karpy, and not the Gmitruks in or around Karp, I ask Mala all manner of geographical questions. Were there hills around Karpy? Was there a railway line? What about a church with a domed tower, built of black, sun-baked wood? She seldom has an answer for me. But, blessed with an obliging nature and always willing to respond to a question, she often repeats the part of her story that fits the time frame of the question. Listening back to the tapes of our interviews, Mala's steadfast account and unwavering voice never fail to impress me. I hardly ever catch an inconsistency in her version of events.

I ask her how she and Amelka got from Karpy to a nearby railway station. Could it have been Rawa-Ruska? The station there had a direct line to Lublin at the time.

'We probably got a lift from a farmer,' she replies.

'In a car?'

'No, just on the back of his cart.'

'Pulled by a horse?'

'What else would it be pulled by? An ox?!'

'So a horse and cart took you and Amelka to the railway station?'

'I can't remember. I told you that already.'

Mala does remember leaving early in the morning. They were standing on the platform at 6.00 am. Mala had said goodbye to her sister Mira the night before. 'She cried and cried.'

In Lublin, the two teenage girls reported to the German office in charge of transporting workers to Germany. The gendarmes were surprised to see two girls volunteer for work; most of the workers they dealt with had been pressganged on the streets in raids that the Poles called *łapanki*, after a pre-war children's game. That said, Amelka and Mala's decision was not so out of the ordinary as to attract suspicion. Word had spread among hungry Polish journeymen that in Germany they could at least count on two square meals a day. For some, that was worth volunteering for.

Mala and Amelka had to wait three days before they could travel on to Germany. More workers had to be rounded up first. During the occupation of Poland, over 2.5 million people were shipped off to Germany to work. The girls killed time by wandering around the city in the company of Amelka's elder brother, the only person who was in on their plan. He had brought bread for them.

On the train, Mala was struck by how desperately sad her fellow passengers were to be leaving house and home. Almost everyone was in tears. Most hadn't even been able to say goodbye to their parents.

To get to know one another, the boys and girls in Mala's compartment each said a little something about themselves. They all came from Lublin or the surrounding countryside. Most were unable to read or write. 'Even a blind man could tell I wasn't a village girl. I spoke good Polish with no trace of an accent. So I had to come up with something.' She told the others she had been born in Kolonie Karpy, but that her family had moved to Warsaw, where she had attended a good Catholic school. They believed her. To lighten the mood, Mala began reciting poems she had learned by heart. 'Those verses were a great help to me during the war years. They cheered people up. I wanted to distract them, and it worked.'

Glancing down at my notes, I see questions like, 'How exactly did you spend those three days in Lublin?' and, 'Where did you sleep?' In the steadily dawning realisation that Mala volunteers all the information she remembers, I decide to skip them. I know she's not about to fill in the gaps just because I want her to. She has learned to live with the blanks in her memory.

Though I should know better, I can't help asking, 'Do you remember any of the verses you recited on the train?'

'Of course,' she replies, as if it's a question she's asked every day. Without a moment's hesitation, she launches into a long Polish poem, off the top of her head. Although she is in her nineties, her delivery is clear and lively. 'That'll do for now,' she says after a recital of almost ten minutes.

'That fairly rolled off the tongue,' I grin.

'I hope so,' she says. 'It must be sixty years since I spoke those lines.'

Back in Poland, I throw myself into a search for Mala's poem and find it in the pages of *Dzikie Życie* (*Wild Life*), a magazine for nature lovers. In 2002, a reader submitted it to the letters page. After all those years, Mala reproduced the hundred lines of the poem, word for word.

Tracking down the poet turns out to be trickier. The Polish experts I consult are stumped. All they can tell me is that it has never been included in a collection, though they happily point out a nod to Berthold Brecht in the second line: 'Mankind is kept alive by bestial acts.' It's easy to see how the poem cheered up Mala's fellow passengers; it was written to put a smile on your face. With this in mind, the literati steer me in the direction of a specialist in light verse.

Bożena Keff is a short woman with a roguish expression and stiff, black curls. She is 'almost 100 per cent convinced' that Mala's poem was penned by 'poet and raconteur' Ludwik Jerzy Kern. It's not just the style, metre, and wordplay that give the game away, but also Kern's love of animals. Keff backs up her theory with a wealth of historical publications on Kern, most dating from the post-war period when he garnered fame, mainly as a writer of children's books and nursery rhymes that were as popular with adults as they were with children; a figure akin to Annie M.G. Schmidt in Dutch or Roald Dahl in English. Keff, now in her seventies and a poet in her own right, reckons this must be one of Kern's early poems. It clearly dates from before the war but after 1928, the year Brecht wrote the line that Kern references.

The Polish title translates as 'Rather Animal than Human', although Mala remembers it as 'I Don't Want to Be Human', a phrase that recurs throughout the poem:

I don't want to be human
I'd be a horse, an ox, a dolphin
A kingfisher or a chimpanzee
One heck of a cow would be fine by me
There's just one thing I'd rather not be:
I don't want to be human.

This is followed by a list of torments that humans inflict on animals. A rider, for example, digging his heels into a horse's flanks without so much as a by-your-leave. 'Has anyone seen the opposite, though? / A horse sat on a human … I don't think so!'

Humans scoff eggs without appreciating the hens that laid them. Human mothers squeeze milk from a cow's teat for their children to drink. What if cows started milking human mothers to feed their little ones?

Kern concludes that all of these offences against the animal kingdom are beyond the pale, not least because animals are on a higher plane than us humans, not just ethically but aesthetically, too. After all, they achieve beauty without faking a smile, dyeing their hair, slapping on make-up, or dousing themselves in perfume.

It's a children's verse, of course, and a parable into the bargain. Yet it's both fascinating and poignant that Mala should recite it at a time when she and her family were threatened with murder. The differences between humans and animals find expression in different ways: self-consciousness, language, the use of tools and instruments, and certainly in the industrialised killing known since the Second World War as the Holocaust. Could animals capable of such a thing? The closing lines:

If I had to go back in time
Reclaim dozens of years from mortality,
If I came into the world once again
I'd not just be mad, I'd be fumin'
If I were born again as a human.

The past flows within us. Mala's voice has changed with the years, as has her pronunciation and her timbre, but she still knows the words.

They are there, suspended inside her, woven into the fabric of her brain, like the notes of a nineteenth-century symphony. Commit them to memory, and the score can be set aside. At her home in Amstelveen, Mrs Shlafer — a woman of 93 — recited a poem from her youth, effortlessly, word for word, with no need for improvisations. In doing so, she gave me the confidence to undertake the journeys to come, to travel to what is now Germany to find present-day traces of what she has told me about her past. I was going to need that confidence. Because there, in Germany, her story enters the realm of the improbable.

Instead of footnotes

The opening quote comes from Douwe Draaisma's 2016 book *Als mijn geheugen me niet bedriegt* (*If My Memory Serves Me Right*), which is also my source for the quote from writer and comic-book creator Marten Toonder.

Shalom Kelner is the Israeli architect who made a 3D animation of Tomaszów Lubelski as it existed on the eve of the Second World War. He was kind enough to give me a map of the town made by the Germans in 1941. The names of all the Jewish families are written next to the houses where they lived.

Charlotte Pothuizen, who translates from Polish to Dutch, helped me to translate the poem, most probably written by Ludwig Jerzy Kern and entitled 'Rather Animal than Human' or 'I Don't Want to Be Human'. Our Dutch translation forms the basis for the English lines included here.

7
The Weser

'So many of them are humorless and ready to accept somebody
else's word, devoid of that faculty to recognize bunk when they
see it. But it would be Nazism in reverse to say that only Germans
are capable of falling for that stuff.'

–Akiva Skidell, soldier

'As if everything was right with the world.' Through the window of the
train, Mala saw how daily life was going on in Germany, still untouched
by the war. It was the summer of 1942, and girls and boys her age were
sitting outside cafés enjoying the sunshine.

With Amelka and thousands of other Poles, she arrived in Bremen.
There, they were each allocated a bunk bed in a large dormitory.
Mala remembers Poles not being allowed to share a dormitory with
Czechs, who had arrived on an earlier transport and were given better
treatment.

Mala was put to work on a laundry production line. Her job was to
pull shirt sleeves over a mould for dry cleaning. She did her best to keep
up and satisfy her bosses, but her small frame put her at a disadvantage.
Ursula, her supervisor, saw Mala struggling and had her transferred to
another part of the same huge factory building to clean the offices of
the typing pool. The German typists were given lunch, while Polish
workers had to make do with a bread roll and a cup of coffee substitute
in the morning, and soup in the evening. Mala told this to the typists,

who complimented her on her German, even though it was sprinkled with Yiddish. Ukrainians and Poles were more attuned to Yiddish, but most Germans had never heard it spoken. Mala made up a story about her Polish father working in Germany and falling in love with a German woman. Back home in Poland, she said, her parents spoke German to each other and Polish to her.

'The German girls told me they knew right away that I wasn't really Polish. From then on, they always brought me a bread roll filled with sausage.' Mala used to save the sausage to give to Amelka. 'We would arrange to meet in one of the toilets.'

When the typists were on their break, Mala would sit herself down at one of the typewriters and try to teach herself to type, with some success. Her supervisor, Ursula, saw this, had no objections, and let Mala take over from one of the German typists when she went on maternity leave. The work was straightforward enough — mostly typing addresses on envelopes — and before long Mala's days as a cleaner were behind her. 'I was happy. My typing speed steadily increased, and it was clean work. I got on well with the other girls, and that was good for my German.' It also meant that Mala was paid in real currency instead of a handful of ration coupons. In the evenings, she would recite from her repertoire of Polish poems.

All the young people were given the weekends off. There were dances, and, for the first time in her life, Mala danced with a boy. Back in Warsaw, she had only been allowed to dance with other girls. One Czech boy asked her for dance after dance, and she learned the tango. 'I was glad to be dancing with a Czech boy rather than a Pole. It made him seem a little less non-Jewish.'

No one asked Amelka to dance. Mala thought this was because she didn't know how. Dancing wasn't the kind of thing you learned in Karpy. Besides, Amelka's stepmother had worked her like a cart horse, so dancing was out of the question.

* * *

In every Holocaust survivor's memoir, there comes a crucial moment when sheer luck takes over from intelligence, resourcefulness, and the will to live. Mala's moment of incredible luck came in the autumn of 1942. With the money she had earned, she bought sweaters, socks, and a shirt for her young nephew Samek, Chaja and Majloch's son back in Tomaszów Lubelski. She wrapped up the clothes, and addressed the parcel to the Olszewskis, who lived over 1,000 kilometres further east. Confirmation that the parcel had arrived came in a letter from Mr Olszewski telling her not to send anything else, as her family had been deported. 'Along with the other Jews in Tomaszów.'

The deportation had taken place in October 1942. The Jews were loaded onto trucks bound for Bełżec. Mala probably received Olszewski's letter in November or early December, according to the estimate of a historian with specialist knowledge of the postal service during the Second World War. Mala was distraught, so distraught that it only dawned on her gradually how lucky she had been: as a rule, all letters written to the laundry and office workers were screened by the same man. It was his job to censor them, or worse. Olszewski's letter left no doubt that Mala's family was Jewish. It would have exposed her in an instant and led to her immediate arrest and deportation to a camp. She knew this. The German typists had told her about a Jewish girl from Poland who had been betrayed by someone at work and put on the next train to Auschwitz. What they said led Mala to believe it was one of the typists who had reported her.

But, as Mala found out later, the man who screened the incoming mail had been absent the day Olszewski's letter arrived. This was the rarest of occurrences, an extreme coincidence.

At that moment, this was the last thing on Mala's mind. She ran to the toilet, locked herself in a cubicle, and cried. Ripping the letter to shreds, she flushed them away. She felt the urge to tell Amelka what had happened, but quickly decided against it. The less Amelka knew, the better it was for both of them. Mala had heard from the typists that the Jewish girl at work had been sent to Auschwitz along with a Polish friend who had kept her secret.

That night, Mala could not sleep. Should she have stayed with her family in Tomaszów? Where had the Germans taken them? Her memories of the ghetto made her fear the worst. Yet she also thought of a German woman she had met in Bremen, an encounter that stands out in Mala's accounts of her time in the city. During our conversations, it's a memory she often returns to. She first saw this kind woman, a total stranger, at a baker's shop within weeks of arriving in Bremen. In halting German, Mala ordered a loaf with the first of her wages. It was a Saturday, and of course Amelka was with her. As they left the shop, the woman approached the girls and invited them to her home for coffee. She treated them to homemade cake and, with tears in her eyes, she spoke of her two sons, both stationed in Poland. The woman said she hoped someone there would think to offer them coffee and cake.

In Mala's own words, 'She asked if we came from Poland and asked us to come her house for coffee. Isn't that amazing?! I mean, I thought all Germans were killers!' On another occasion, she reflects, 'It turned everything I thought I knew upside down. Unlike my brother Alter, I knew Catholics could have a conscience. But Germans, too? That had seemed impossible to me.'

The woman asked the two Polish girls if they would come back and visit her again.

Amelka was the only one who knew Mala's secret. She knew why her friend never ate the sausages she was given, a rare treat any of the other girls would have welcomed. This began to prey on Mala's mind, haunted as she was by the story of the Jewish girl who had been betrayed and deported. 'In those days, I had no way of knowing how bad Auschwitz was, but I knew it was bad.' It played on her nerves. If she saw Amelka talking to someone for any length of time, she couldn't rest until she knew exactly what had been said.

From the little money she earned, Mala was always buying things for Amelka. She remembers buying herself a hat, the kind worn by the German typists, and giving Amelka a sweater as a present. This may have been a straightforward token of affection, but at the same time she gave Amelka no reason to be displeased with her. Seventy-five years later, Mala finds it hard to unpick her motives, and would probably have struggled to do so even then. But she clearly remembers the day she had the chance to bid farewell to Amelka, the last person who could reveal what she was desperately trying to hide.

Mala was approached by Kaśka, one of the Polish friends who liked to listen to her poetry recitals. Kaśka would read out letters from her sister, who worked on a farm in Wolmirstedt, a picturesque little German town some 220 kilometres east. Kaśka missed her sister terribly, and thought working on a farm sounded far better than slaving away in the laundry. But, of course, she wasn't free to leave. Mala never refers to the work she did as forced labour, but that's what it was. Leaving meant escaping. Even so, Kaśka had her heart set on Wolmirstedt and was egged on by her friend Stefka, who'd had more than enough of the meagre rations at the laundry. The two Polish girls were hungry and determined, but, speaking no German, they asked Mala to help them buy train tickets. Kaśka and Stefka went to the station with Mala, and were amazed to hear her ask for three tickets instead of two. Delighted to have an interpreter along for the ride, they didn't mind a bit.

Unsupervised train travel was forbidden for foreign workers. Those from Poland were made to wear a diamond-shaped patch on their clothing, a purple 'P' on a yellow background. The girls had hidden their patches away and were careful not to say a word on the train, so no one would single them out as Polish.

It was spring 1943, and German citizens had become entirely accustomed to the phenomenon of foreign workers, or forced labourers. By the summer, a staggering 1.3 million people from the Polish General Government were working in Germany. That number eventually rose to 2.3 million, which meant there were more Poles in Germany than there were Germans in occupied Poland. In parallel with their plans to colonise far-off places, the Germans had brought about a colonisation of their own industry and agriculture. The factories and farms remained under German control, of course, yet throughout the countryside there was hardly a German male between the ages of 18 and 60 to be found. German men had to fight beyond the borders of the Reich.

As more territory was conquered, the number of workers from abroad rose, reaching 7.5 million in 1944: more than the population of the annexed German state of Austria, approximately double the population of Denmark, and considerably more than the population of

all three Baltic states combined. The aim of the war, the Germanisation
of Europe, also brought about the Europeanisation of Germany.

After a long day's train journey, the three girls knocked on the door
of the small farm where Kaśka's sister worked. The farmer's wife let
them in, and gave them something to drink. The sisters were thrilled to
see each other again, and Mala remembers the farmer and his wife
as 'nice, decent people'. Even so, Kaśka's sister had to eat separately,
though she was the only foreign worker on the farm. Racial mixing
was to be avoided wherever possible. That evening, the four girls ate in
the kitchen, while the farmer and his wife had dinner in the living room.

As the number of foreigners working in Germany rose, concerns
about 'racial pollution' grew deeper, especially among more
ideologically driven Nazis. Laws were passed to combat mixing and
intimacy. Even acts of kindness towards foreign workers — such
as giving them more food, drink, or tobacco than their official
ration — became punishable offences. The message was simple: avoid
these foreigners like the plague. The press hammered home the sin
of seeking contact with inferior beings such as Poles, Russians, and
Ukrainians, a crime characterised as 'contempt for our own blood'.
Sex, of course, was the greatest crime of all. Himmler decreed that
every act of 'illegal sexual intercourse' was punishable by death. Not
that this was followed to the letter; far from every instance of 'illegal
sexual intercourse' resulted in execution. On farms, especially, sexual
relations between German foremen and female workers from abroad
were commonplace. The decree was probably designed to have a
mitigating effect, and, as with many draconian Nazi measures, it was
a useful instrument in the hands of senior party officials who wanted
to intimidate someone of a lower rank. This happened frequently. In
the summer of 1942, a staggering 80 per cent of all Gestapo arrests in
Germany concerned people's dealings with foreigners.

The farmer allowed the three Polish girls to spend the night, on
the condition that they went to the police in the morning. He assured
them he meant well. Being caught by the police would only land them
in much deeper trouble.

The next day at the police station, the girls told the only officer on duty that they had come from Poland in the hope of finding work, and gave the same excuse Mala had used when travelling with her little brother, Meir: they had got off the train to go to the toilet and had returned to the platform to find that it had left without them.

Had a train from Poland actually passed this way? The lone policeman tried to verify their story, and went into the next room to make a phone call. After an anxious wait, Stefka decided to take matters into her own hands. 'She told us she was going next door to ask the policeman for a cigarette,' Mala says. 'But she was gone a long time. When they came back, both of them looked very pleased with themselves, and everything was settled!'

Looking back, Mala makes light of the incident, even insinuating that she knew at the time what Stefka had been up to with the policeman. But when I ask her directly, she denies this. 'What did I know of the world?!'

She recounts the story of Stefka and the policeman in her characteristic style: pithy sentences that call for an exclamation mark, with the occasional question mark thrown in for good measure. 'In those days, I thought kissing could make me pregnant?!' The Friday before she left for Wolmirstedt, she had refused to kiss the Czech boy who had taught her to tango. 'And believe you me, he tried!'

The three girls told the Wolmirstedt policeman that they had no ID; the last thing they wanted was to be sent back to Bremen. He gave them forms to fill in. For months, Mala had gone through life as Janina Gmitruk. So far, so good. But now she had to come up with a maiden name for her fictitious mother. In her panic, she recalled a shop sign in Bremen that bore the name 'Wassermann'. Things clicked into place. After all, she had passed herself off as Marilka Waserman when she lived with her sister and brother-in-law Majloch Waserman in the ghetto. Besides, the spelling on the shop sign — double S, double N — suggested the name was German, and she had already told the typists in Bremen that her mother was German. So, on paper, her mother became 'Maria Wassermann. Born and residing in Kolonie Karpy.'

There was no question of the girls being allowed to return to the farm where Kaśka's sister was staying; it was a small operation with

enough farmhands already. Instead, they were taken to a large estate
that employed over 100 labourers, all of them Polish. They called the
place *dwór*, Polish for a nobleman's country residence, and referred to
its owner, Friedrich Loss, as 'the baron'. In this new setting, Mala met
another friendly German in the shape of the foreman's wife. She was
an ethnic German, to be precise, from a Reich dependency in Silesia,
which had been part of Poland before the war. This meant she was
fluent in Polish. Mala soon felt at home, and took to reciting her Polish
verses during the lunch breaks. 'Everyone thought it was wonderful.'

Mala has fond memories of the weeks that followed. 'It was a happy
time.' But working the land was tough on her. Freeing herself of the
one person who might have given away her secret came at a price:
exchanging a pleasant, salaried job as a typist for hard labour. Mala
remembers plucking sugar beet as a particularly painful job: you had to
strip off the leaves in a single motion, without gloves. Before long, her
hands were swollen and bloody.

Her two Polish friends, Stefka and Kaśka, were delighted to have left
the laundry behind them. Farm work was something they had always
done, and in contrast to Bremen, they were given enough to eat. Both
girls soon found themselves a boyfriend, Polish lads from the baron's
sausage factory.

One day, the baron himself came riding out of the coach house on a
magnificent black horse with a glossy coat. To inspect his lands, and on
the look-out for a new housemaid. Out of the corner of her eye, Mala
saw him talking to the foreman at the edge of the field. The foreman
pointed in her direction, and the world stopped for a moment. 'My
heart was pounding in my chest. My first thought was that someone
had betrayed me.'

She was ordered to pack her things. Seeing she was anxious,
the baron reassured her that she was being given a position in his
household. Mala still remembers how charming and very well spoken
he was. 'He and the foreman's wife could see there was something
different about me. And there was. I was a city girl, while everyone
around me had been raised in the country.'

Friedrich Loss owned Wolmirstedt Castle, and lived in the adjacent
manor house, or *Junkerhof*. Mala had never seen such a beautiful

building, inside or out. For the first time in her life, she had her own
bedroom. The magnificent gardens were filled with flowering plants.
'Honestly, it was like a dream. I had never seen the like.'

In the Warsaw ghetto, not a tree remained standing.

* * *

I visit Elizabeth Ruddies, a niece of Friedrich Loss, in November 2016.
At her home in Wolmirstedt, she shows me pre-war photographs and
nineteenth-century watercolours. In contrast to the residents of Karpy,
Mrs Ruddies has thick albums with photographs that date back to the
earliest days of the camera. Every picture prompts a comment, often
in the form of an anecdote and always pinpointed on the family tree.
I couldn't have asked for a better guide to the manor house and its
garden during Mala's time there.

We take a tour of her uncle's house, still intact and recently sold
to a sculptor with vague plans to turn the place into a 'cultural and
therapeutic centre', assuming he can drum up the funds. Now in her
eighties, Mrs Ruddies often played there as a child. Her father was
Friedrich Loss's younger brother.

'Baron?' Elizabeth Ruddies chuckles. 'He'd have loved that!' Loss
was not a baron at all. He was only an aristocrat in the eyes of his
Polish labourers, who grew up in a world where large landowners were
almost always of noble birth.

Mrs Ruddies has fond memories of her uncle, a man with small,
round spectacles and the kind of haircut that was popular at the time:
shaved above the ears with a neat side parting in the thatch on top.
Though by no means an aristocrat, Friedrich did have the good fortune
to be born into a family of wealthy entrepreneurs. His grandfather
was a working-class boy made good who went on to found his own
company: Loss & Co. His son, Friedrich's father, oversaw a period of
enormous expansion, and died three years after Hitler came to power.
Friedrich himself was thirty-nine when he plucked Mala from the field.
In addition to the company farms, which raised sheep, horses, dairy
cows, and pigs for processed meat, Loss & Co.'s main earner since 1871
had been a large starch and sugar factory, which processed sugar beet

from miles around. The family even commissioned its own railway line to link its production facilities to the national network. Locals dubbed it 'the *Lossbahn*'.

I tell Elizabeth Ruddies that Mala remembers Uncle Friedrich with affection, but that she curses the memory of his wife. 'An absolute bitch,' Mala calls her, a woman who beat her staff and hurled abuse at Mala. 'You cursed Polish sow!' She remembers Madame Loss slapping her hard in the face for not plucking a game bird correctly. 'That woman was sick in the head! If I had stayed in Germany after the war, I would have gone to the police.'

Loss's niece nods sympathetically. 'I didn't like her either. Aunt Anni definitely had a screw loose. She did come from nobility, by the way.'

While Mrs Loss moved to West Germany in the 1950s, Elizabeth Ruddies stayed put and married a church minister in Wolmirstedt. While I listen to his wife's reminiscences, the reverend retreats to his study to dig out some old history assignments about the Loss family, the work of pupils from the local high school. He finds them. The splendour of the Loss family's life at the Junkerhof leaps off the pages. There was a botanical garden full of the exotic plants and trees that enchanted Mala. The milk produced by the cows was of such high quality, one pupil writes, that mothers unable to breastfeed their baby would travel miles to Wolmirstedt for milk from Loss's farms.

All this ended abruptly when the Soviets arrived. As early as 1945, everyone who owned over 100 hectares of land was evicted. For his assignment, one of the pupils managed to track down a document detailing the division of the Loss family's property. This included almost 1,000 hectares of land, a series of farms, a couple of factories, and another square kilometre of gardens. The land was divided among 143 previously landless Germans, including twenty-four settlers: refugees from the east. *Junkerland in Bauernhand* was the slogan of the day: 'noble land in peasant hands'. The factories came under public management as Saxony-Anhalt industrial plants.

Although Loss was not an aristocrat, strictly speaking, as a landowner and sugar magnate he was part of the 'Junkerdom', or landed gentry, that the Soviets were determined to weed out at the roots. This can be taken almost literally: even the trees were not spared.

Elizabeth Ruddies shows me photographs of the mighty beeches and oaks felled by the Soviets. There was something mean-spirited about the righteous division of property espoused by soldiers who had endured the toughest of conditions and been fed years of communist propaganda: equality wasn't so much about elevating the proletariat as it was about carting off the upper classes and either destroying their possessions or having them shipped deep into the Soviet Union. Making everyone poor and needy was one route to even-handedness.

The towering dovecote at Wolmirstedt Castle also perished. 'Far too beautiful for us Germans.' Elizabeth says it without bitterness, her tone so friendly and factual that she might have been discussing an item on the news.

Loss did not take all this lying down. His efforts to salvage his sugar factory gained the support of the newly appointed local government and the anti-fascist organisation *Antifa-Ausschüsse*. A letter signed by 130 employees and other residents of Wolmirstedt declared that Loss had never been a committed Nazi and that his social-minded approach through the decades had earned him the trust of the people. During the war, the letter continued, his generous treatment of workers from the east had led to clashes with Nazi officials. In other words, he fed his *Ostarbeiter* more than the prescribed rations. This policy was probably motivated by a combination of decency, habit, and self-interest, or at least his niece Elizabeth thinks so. Her uncle was accustomed to employing foreign workers. Even before the war, people came from afar to work on his land, and he was well aware that malnutrition, discontent, and exhaustion were bad for productivity. Besides, who were the Nazis to tell him how to run his company? His conflict with the officials became so heated that everyone in the area got to hear about it. Loss had also been reprimanded for allowing a union leader from the 1930s to work in his sugar factory. Nazis among his personnel wondered why the trade unionist hadn't been sent to a concentration camp. Loss found a way to smooth things over, and declared the man indispensable to the company.

After the war, it must have seemed logical to Loss that such incidents would work in his favour, but they ended up doing him no good. Until

1949, his part of the country was under Soviet military rule, and no matter how much confidence the new German local authorities had in Loss, the senior Soviet commander was in no mind to repeal the factory seizure. 'Of course, Uncle Friedrich was naïve to think it had anything to do with his political persuasions or his conduct,' Elizabeth says. 'The moneyed classes had to hand over their property and that was that. Their wartime conduct or their worldview were entirely beside the point.'

Loss did not flee to the west, nor was he among the wealthy landowners deported to the east. Instead, his expertise in the sugar industry earned him a position in the bureaucracy of the newly established province of Saxony-Anhalt, an office he held until his sudden death from illness a few years later. His family had been turfed out of their manor house five years earlier, and the building that had made such a deep impression on Mala was turned into a school. Loss's children went there, as did his niece Elizabeth. 'That was a strange experience. Only weeks before, I had been running around the place, playing with my cousins, and visiting my aunt and uncle. Suddenly, there I was, stuck behind a desk while the teachers played boss.'

Her reverend husband chips in a cheerful correction: 'They weren't playing boss, Elizabeth. They *were* the boss.'

Elizabeth Ruddies nods and smiles. 'True, true,' she murmurs, and goes on meticulously filing away the watercolours and photos she brought out to show me.

This class enemy lives modestly nowadays, in a terraced house emblematic of East German efforts to bring the communist promise of modernity to Wolmirstedt. Yet the Ruddies' two-up, two-down in a narrow street called Wiesengrund is alive with tangible expressions of the refinement, prosperity, and riches of a bygone age. The two Dutch landscape paintings on the wall date from the eighteenth and nineteenth centuries.

'The Russians took the best of it, you know,' Elizabeth says as she catches me sizing up the decor.

'Still, you've managed to hold onto some lovely pieces.'

'My family distributed their possessions for safe keeping. Friends, acquaintances, and employees hid them away, and gradually returned them to the family in the course of the 1950s. Well, what you see here, in any case.'

It is late in the evening before I pluck up the courage to ask Elizabeth about her left eye, which appears to have no movement. It turns out to be made of glass. The story emerges in shrugging asides, and when I ask for clarification she repeats, 'Oh, it wasn't that bad.' And once she adds, 'I was given chocolate when I was in hospital, by a couple of American soldiers who were still being treated there. An unbelievable luxury in those days.'

Elizabeth Ruddies lost her left eye when she was ten, six months after the official capitulation of Germany. In the stables that used to house Uncle Friedrich's horses, young Elizabeth and a few of her friends had gathered to watch as a couple of bored and boisterous Red Army soldiers used the rats for target practice. 'A piece of shrapnel flew into my eye. It was an accident. Collateral damage.'

* * *

Mala's stay at the Junkerhof in Wolmirstedt was the most luxurious time of her life. Even after the war, she never experienced anything like it again. She was one of three housemaids. 'Baron' Loss was civil and kind to his staff, and the setting was magnificent. But it was too good to last. Just when she had begun to feel relatively safe, things fell apart thanks to Iwan, a pock-marked young man from Ukraine. Iwan was of German descent, and so had risen to become a paid foreman at the sausage factory. While the labourers slept on bunkbeds in a barracks, he lived in a house in Wolmirstedt. Iwan made Mala's skin crawl, and she could not understand why her friend Zosia would want to kiss him. But Zosia did that and more, and when she found out she was expecting his baby, she moved in with him. This suggests there can't have been all that much to Iwan's German heritage—distant forebears, most likely—or such an arrangement would never have been tolerated. Poles were not allowed to openly enter into a relationship with Germans or ethnic Germans.

Despite her dislike of Iwan, Mala visited Zosia regularly. She lived close by, and they enjoyed chatting together in Polish. 'Speaking German all day could be a drain.'

Iwan and Zosia's baby was born, and the couple invited some friends from the farm to the baptism and then to their home for an improvised celebration. There was food and plenty of home-made vodka. The farm labourers were under curfew, and almost everyone had to be up at the crack of dawn in any case, so they all left relatively early. Mala — who lived nearer — stayed behind to clear up, and Zosia offered her a bed for the night.

As soon as she came down for breakfast the next morning, Mala could sense something was wrong. Out of nowhere, Iwan looked her in the eye and said, 'You're a Jew.' His tone was harsh, menacing. 'You spoke Yiddish in your sleep.'

Mala froze and said something like, 'Don't be daft. Of course I'm not Jewish.'

She knew there was no way she could bluff and claim he was mistaken. Iwan knew the difference between Yiddish and German. Mala can still picture the look on her friend Zosia's face as she sat there saying nothing at all.

Mala left Zosia's house feeling sick with panic. When the working day was over, she confided in a trusted friend, a man in his twenties or early thirties who had studied at a seminary back home in Poland. Everyone knew him as Janek Ksiądz, Polish for 'Janek the Priest'. Unlike her friends from Bremen, Mala had no desire to find a boyfriend at the farm, and felt safe with Janek, who had chosen a life of celibacy. Some of the farm girls warned Mala that Janek wanted to be more than friends, but she insists that at the time she simply couldn't believe it. With the benefit of hindsight, she admits, 'The girls were right, of course.'

Janek reassured Mala that Iwan probably wouldn't go to the police. And if he did, she was to say that Iwan had made advances towards her and that she had turned him down. That way, his accusation would look like the spiteful act of a thwarted lover. 'I think Janek even advised me to say that Iwan had tried to molest me the night I stayed over. And that, as a decent girl in the service of the Loss family, I had put him firmly in his place.'

Janek also tried to calm Mala by telling her that the area around Karpy was probably no longer in German hands, making any attempt to check her background extremely complex. Strangely enough, he did not ask Mala to confirm or deny Iwan's claim. 'He never asked me whether I was Jewish. He really was a special man.'

Mala's special man escorted her back to the Junkerhof, and once they arrived, he told her how difficult it was for him to leave her there all on her own. Mala made him a cup of coffee in the pantry. But then, she insisted, it was time for him to go.

Three days passed, and nothing happened. The other girls at the Junkerhof were as friendly as ever, though Mala was anything but her usual bright self. 'They assumed I was carrying a torch for some boy or other.' She bought a few more things for Amelka. After moving to the farm and then the Junkerhof, she had continued to give her friend gifts, sending parcels to Bremen without giving her own name and address. Mala remembers a nagging guilt about Amelka, knowing her friend had too little to eat and no one to slip her extra food. 'I wondered what she thought of me after I left. I sent her a parcel that day because I thought it might be my last opportunity. There was every chance I would be arrested.'

Sure enough, on the fourth day, an officer came to the door, and Mala had to accompany him. The police station he took her to looked for all the world like an ordinary house, but that was where prisoners were held in sleepy Wolmirstedt, more an overgrown village than a town. The guard who locked Mala up told her she didn't look Jewish. That was when she knew for certain that Iwan had reported her.

A day later, the guard opened the door to Mala's cell and took her upstairs, where he and his wife lived. They gave her something to eat. 'His wife was a kind-hearted woman. She was very good to me.' When Mala had finished her meal, the guard took her back to her cell. She had to spend the day there, because the guard was worried about inspectors, but after office hours it was a different matter, and Mala spent some pleasant evenings upstairs with her jailers. 'I get on well with people,' Mala reflects. 'I'm lucky that way. It's something you either have or you don't.'

After a week, the policeman who had arrested Mala at the Junkerhof came to collect her. The guard's wife was in tears, and gave her a small parcel of bread and cheese to take with her. The policeman was reluctant to handcuff his young charge, and instead made her promise not to run off. Mala assured him she wouldn't be any trouble. The policeman took her to the railway station, where he bought her an ice cream and joked that the people around them probably assumed they were father and daughter. They were off to the city of Magdeburg, less than ten kilometres away.

* * *

Mala was taken to the *Arbeitserziehungslager*, a 'labour education camp' for women, located on Schillstrasse. A pre-war factory building still stands on the site, and currently houses the Förster sack factory. Ignore the BMX racetrack, a bunch of East German allotments, and the looming viaduct of the Magdeburg ring road, and it's still easy enough to imagine the building as part of a prison camp. The wire fencing completes the picture. Schillstrasse has long since been swallowed by the ring road, but the narrow street that ran down the side of the hermetically sealed prison camp is still there: Slachthofstrasse, or 'Slaughterhouse Street'.

The former camp lies on the fringes of a rapidly shrinking city. In 1941, some 346,000 people lived in Magdeburg, not counting the foreign workers. Today, the population is 235,000. One in five of the city's houses stand empty. Since 1990, roughly half of the schools have closed; several have been turned into old folks' homes. The region that was once East Germany is now home to the world's oldest population, a place where the only excitement appears to be whipped up by politicians raging against immigration. They organise well-attended marches that do wonders for their chances of electoral success. Meanwhile, the region's governors are busy making deals with China to import nurses and carers.

Mala was told she would remain in the prison camp for as long as it took to investigate her background. This would turn out to be weeks, though it remains unclear how much effort the Germans put into verifying the accusations of the pock-marked Ukrainian of German descent and the accused girl's rebuttal that the man had assaulted her.

In the meantime, Mala was an inmate of the women's prison camp on Schillstrasse, where they made tarpaulins for military vehicles.

The archives reveal a number of things about the camp. In summary: a working day lasted twelve hours, the soup was watery, and the hygiene was poor. On the plus side, the guards were not especially cruel or sadistic. Mala's fellow inmates were mostly Russian and German. The Germans included criminals and other social undesirables, including a large number of *Mischlinge*, citizens who, according to the criteria laid down in the 1935 Nuremberg Laws, were half- or quarter-Jewish. In the language of the Nazis: a first-degree Mischling was someone with two Jewish grandparents out of four. A second-degree Mischling had one Jewish grandparent.

Mala remembers one other Polish woman in the camp. She worked in the kitchen, and sought out Mala's company. At night, she would climb into bed with Mala and bring her a potato. 'I was very happy with that potato, because we had so little to eat. You were always hungry. We would chat in Polish, and it cheered her up no end. She couldn't speak a word of German.'

The case of a young Russian woman at the camp was similar to Mala's, on paper at least. 'She was a natural beauty,' says Mala, who was not surprised to hear that the Russian had caught the eye of a German doctor at the hospital where she worked. When she did not give in to his advances, he reported her to the police. In the prison camp, she was refusing to eat. 'That Russian girl was convinced she was going to be executed. I told her life could take a different turn. In my broken Russian, I convinced her to eat something. And in the meantime, I fed her.' Mala does not know what happened to her.

Another memory from the camp was of a German prisoner who complained to the male governor that she had to shower with foreigners, while a German Mischling was permitted to shower with Germans. A half-Jew among full-blooded Germans! The director dismissed the complaint out of hand. In front of everyone, he reminded the woman that she was a criminal, while the Jewish woman had done no wrong. 'I was amazed to hear that from the mouth of a German,' Mala says. 'If you ask me, it was a dangerous statement to make in those days.'

This incident took place at morning roll call, where the women were assembled to hear the director's instructions for the day. Sometimes envelopes were handed to certain prisoners. A red envelope meant that the recipient was to be sent to a concentration camp, or even an extermination camp. A white envelope meant freedom.

When I ask Mala about her experience of the prison camp on Schillstrasse, she tells me about the bad food, the hungry nights, and the fear of being handed a red envelope. Yet she also recalls how appreciated she felt, memories that overshadow the deprivation. 'People were very fond of me, the director certainly. It was clear he thought that a young girl like me did not belong in prison.'

Mala's duties regularly included cleaning the director's office, and she could not resist the temptation to look for signs of progress in her case: in the worst instance, a red envelope with her name on it. She lived in fear that her luck had run out. 'After all, I knew I was guilty.' She found nothing. Then, one morning at roll call, she heard her name. 'I was so terrified, I couldn't stop shaking.' A Russian girl standing next to her whispered congratulations. She had seen that Mala's envelope was white. 'Knowing I was Jewish, I was convinced it must be some kind of mistake.'

Mala was allowed to wash and change into the clothes she had been wearing when she entered the prison camp. Then she was summoned to the director's office, where a stout man was sitting with the director at his desk. Impressed with Mala's command of the language, they asked if her mother was German. Wassermann, the maiden name Mala had filled in on her registration form, certainly sounded German. 'Yes,' Mala replied, without any hesitation. 'Exactly! I'm German.' The question dumbfounded her, but at the same time there was a logic behind it. Across Eastern Europe, the Nazis were actively seeking out *Volksdeutsche*, people of German descent who had migrated east decades or even centuries before and who were therefore seen as racially superior to the inferior races they lived among.

'They asked me if I was of German descent,' Mala tells me, seventy-five years on. 'Of course I said yes! If they'd asked me if I was Chinese, I'd have said yes. Anything to get out of that prison camp.'

The director—a man who apparently held the view that being a

Jew was not a crime — seems to have arrived at the conclusion that
Mala had not spoken Yiddish in her sleep, but an 'innocent' variety of
German. This is speculation. We have no idea what his reasoning was,
or if an investigation had even taken place. No paperwork survives.

However, we do know the identity of the stout man in the director's
office: Herman Holste, manager of the Magdeburger Bierhaus, a
hostelry in the city centre — no. 123 Breiter Weg, to be exact, within 150
metres of the cathedral. He and the director informed Mala that there
was no longer a place for her with the Loss family in Wolmirstedt. The
baron had already taken another girl into service. Nor could she return
to one of Loss's farms, where only foreign workers from the east were
allowed to work. If Mala was of German descent, something both men
appeared to believe, she would be better off working alongside both
German and Polish girls. The men had just the job in mind, serving
customers at Holste's establishment.

Mala left prison in Holste's company, and they took a tram to an
office in the city centre. After filling in a form or two, Mala was given
a document that granted her temporary status as a stateless person.
A racial assessment at a later date would determine whether she was
actually an ethnic German. An immediate consequence of her new
status was that she no longer had to wear a purple 'P'. Mala had gone
from Jewish to Polish to stateless.

Holste then took Mala to the Bierhaus on Breiter Weg. There, he
introduced her to the rest of his personnel: eight German and seven
Polish girls. Her job would be to help in the kitchen and prepare cold
snacks for the bar-restaurant, which was always busy. To her surprise,
she did not have to start straight away, but was shown to her new room
and given the day off.

What to do with her newfound freedom? She wrote a letter to Janek,
her trusted Polish friend on Loss's farm. Then she invited the Polish
girls to her room that evening. Not that she expected them to come.
Why should they want to associate with the new girl who didn't have
to wear 'P' on her clothes? But they did come, all seven of them. Mala
didn't tell them she had come straight from a prison camp, something
Holste must also have kept to himself — which came as a relief.
Instead, she rehearsed a new life story. She told her new colleagues she

came from a village in the east, but for as long as she could remember she had lived with her Polish father and German mother in Warsaw, which was why she could speak some German. And she had attended a Catholic school, which explained why she was fluent in Polish.

Each of the Polish girls then took it in turn to say something about herself. Mala can still remember their first names and even their ages, which ranged from fifteen to eighteen. They were all surprised by Mala's room, as six of the seven had to share a room that wasn't nearly as nice. Mala had no idea what she had done to deserve this privilege either. She suspected Holste might have wanted to atone for the wrongful imprisonment of a girl with a German mother, but she kept this theory to herself. Instead, she reprised her successful role as a performer of long and amusing Polish verses. 'I Don't Want to Be Human' went down a treat, Mala remembers.

Her memories of that first day and evening at the Magdeburger Bierhaus are vivid and plentiful. She remembers chatting deep into the night with the Polish girls, who went into great detail about the objectionable tendencies of the German girls. She remembers lying awake for hours, despite the comfy bed with clean sheets, a real pillow, and warm blankets.

'As I lay there, I could barely understand what had happened to me,' Mala recounts. 'I was so happy, not least because I had my own room, so no one would hear if I spoke Yiddish in my sleep.' Either it was something she hadn't done in prison, or no one had recognised her drowsy mumblings as Yiddish. Of course, she was terrified it would happen again. No matter how convincing her back story, what she said in her sleep was beyond her control.

Mala thought about Amelka again that night. Had she done the right thing in leaving her behind? Dwelling on her decision did not bring a change of heart. Though she suspected her friend from Karpy might be angry with her, Mala still believed a clean break had been for the best.

The first letter she received at the Bierhaus on Breiter Weg came from Janek the Priest: an urgent request to come to the farm near Wolmirstedt. Mala complied on her first day off, a Wednesday. Now that she no longer had to wear the 'P' for Pole, she was able to travel by train unaccompanied, and the trip was only a matter of minutes in any case. Janek was pleased to see her, and Mala once again found herself admiring this man, struck by his politeness and his calm demeanour.

Janek told Mala what had happened to her Ukrainian accuser, Iwan. Not long after her arrest, a group of Polish workers from the factory had ambushed him, throwing a blanket over his head before beating and kicking him half to death. They then shoved him down a flight of stairs and, caught up in the blanket, he had been unable to break his fall. Iwan fractured both his legs. The blanket meant he was unable to identify his attackers.

Janek was Iwan's only visitor in hospital. He was not yet a priest, perhaps he never would be, but he knew the mercy that came with his calling. Iwan told him about the note he had found in his pocket: if anything happens to Janina, it warned, your child will grow up an orphan. To prevent further trouble, Janek advised Iwan to go to the police and admit that he had falsely accused Mala. The length of time Mala spent in custody suggests Iwan did not take Janek's advice.

The second letter Mala received at the Bierhaus came from a man she had met one evening on the platform at Wolmirstedt station, a man with a feather on his little green hat. Mala had been visiting friends on the farm, Janek in particular, and the last train to Magdeburg was a long time coming. She remembers thanking her lucky stars that, as a stateless person, she was no longer under curfew. The letter writer, a German who worked for aircraft manufacturer Junkers, would soon steal a march on the Polish seminarian in Mala's affections.

As Mala recalls it, he introduced himself on the train as Erich Schulze. Mala told him her name was Anni, thinking it sounded more German than Janina, though she did tell him she was from Poland. Erich complimented her on her German, and in Magdeburg he walked her home to the Bierhaus. They talked and talked. When the time came to say goodbye, he took Mala's hand and held it for a long time. He insisted on seeing her again, and from that moment on he made the most of every opportunity to ask her out to restaurants, parks, cinemas.

In her written memoirs, Mala dwells at length on how Erich courted her in the weeks that followed. (She gives Erich's name its Dutch spelling: Erik.) Every detail made a lasting impression on a young woman — she was eighteen when they met — falling head over heels in love for the very first time.

In the beginning, Mala had no idea what to make of all this attention, and asked Ela, one of her Polish colleagues, for advice. From that very first evening at the Bierhaus, Mala had felt more of a bond with Ela than the other girls. She was clever, kind, an avid reader, and hailed from the city of Łódź. She was also anti-Semitic. 'Ela could be really nasty about Jews,' Mala remembers, but she thought that in time she could 'cure' her new friend of her prejudices. As soon as Ela heard about Erich, she was more than happy to step up to the mark as counsellor and cheerleader. She was fascinated by this German and his interest in Mala. She thought he was a splendid catch, and repeatedly told Mala how handsome and elegant all the Polish girls at the Bierhaus thought he was. Ela thought Mala was mad not to give in to his advances right away, and couldn't believe she had run away when he tried to kiss her late one evening, after another long day spent in each other's company.

As is so often the case with people who become lovers, Mala found Erich sympathetic at first, but little more than that. A nice man. She told him she thought she was too young to have a boyfriend. Erich was having none of it. There was a first time for everything, he said. 'We were in the middle of a war, and life went on,' Mala says. 'No one knew what tomorrow might bring. I'd have been hard pushed to contradict him.'

She agreed to the trips Erich proposed, as long as Ela could come along as her chaperone. Erich didn't seem to mind. The three of them would stroll through the parks of Magdeburg, have lunch, go to the pictures — it's unclear how they managed to smuggle Ela in with a 'P' pinned to her clothes — and go for picnics in the rolling hills around the city. Mala appreciates the irony of the company she was keeping: the unlikely trio of 'the German, the Jew, and the anti-Semite'.

Mala was bowled over by these outings. Erich took them out in a boat one day, and she remembers marvelling at the most beautiful landscape she had ever seen. It was August 1944; the weather was glorious. She was oblivious to the uprising in Warsaw that same month, in which the SS and the Wehrmacht would kill around 150,000 civilians by the start of October. When the killing was over, an SS unit roamed the streets with flamethrowers and dynamite, blowing up or burning down anything of value. Yet she was keenly aware that, a little more than a year before, she had been running through the forest in tattered clothes, escaping one farmer's pitchfork only to be bitten by another farmer's dog. Now she was eating sandwiches with home-made jam, potted and stored in the cellar of the summer house that belonged to Erich's parents. That evening, the three of them dined at a village restaurant. After another evening at the pictures, Erich kissed her hand.

Two days later, his letter arrived at Breiter Weg. 'A lovely letter,' Mala says.

Mala believes Erich was courting danger by pursuing her so openly. After all, Germans were strictly forbidden from associating with Polish girls, as laid down in the Polish decrees of 8 March 1940. But Erich was never at risk: Mala was no longer Polish, she was stateless. Her background was more of a problem for her than it was for him. She hesitated for a long time. 'I told Ela that if Erich had not been German, I would have wanted to marry him. She pointed out that my father had married a German and I spoke German, so what was the problem?'

Then came a day when two letters arrived, one from Erich and one from Janek the Priest. Between work and her outings with Erich, Mala had stopped visiting the farm, and Janek wrote that everybody missed her, himself most of all. But he was too late. Mala could hardly wait for Friday, for Erich to pick her up for another idyllic excursion. With Ela in tow, of course. 'Erich took my hand when we were at the pictures, and I felt warm all over.' That same evening, as she puts it, she let herself go. For Mala, not quite attuned to the present-day connotations, this means that she and Erich kissed passionately.

That night, she tossed and turned. She thought of her father, and knew beyond a shadow of a doubt that he would have seen her as a traitor to the Jewish people. To bring a Polish man home was shameful enough, but to come home with a German? It would have been the death of him. Yet she clung to a sliver of hope. Surely if her family could give Erich a chance and get to know him better, they would come to appreciate him for the wonderful, charming, decent man he was. He was the man she had fallen in love with, after all. Didn't that count for something?

It continued to eat away at her. A German! 'But I couldn't see Erich as German, not really. He was so very different to the Germans I had seen in Poland.'

Erich was not a committed Nazi. True, he wore the badge of Hitler's NSDAP on his lapel, a fact Mala had registered immediately during that first train journey from Wolmirstedt to Magdeburg. But he had taken her glance as a question, and explained that in order to work at Junkers he had to be a party member. He poked fun at the country's leaders, and cherished no illusions about the war. He knew that Germany was facing defeat within months, and dreaded to think what would follow. You couldn't believe the newspapers, he said. They only printed propaganda. He never spoke of the Jews, and never asked Mala to explain her background, though there was enough explaining to be done by a girl from Poland who did not wear a 'P' on her coat like Ela and the hundreds of Polish workers at the factory where he worked. Erich wasn't like the tens of thousands who had filled Magdeburg's Dom Square that summer in a mass show of loyalty to the Führer. Only days earlier, Hitler had survived an attempt on his life in the *Wolfsschanze* bunker complex in East Prussia, where he spent around two-thirds of his time since the invasion of the Soviet Union. The rally had been followed by a torchlit procession through the city. At improvised open-air services, clerics praised the Lord for saving their Führer.

Two days after the evening when she had let herself go, Mala received another heartfelt letter from Erich. In it, he wrote how thankful he was that they had met that night on the platform in Wolmirstedt. Another love letter arrived that same week. 'I was in seventh heaven. I decided that Erich and I belonged together. It was him or no one.'

Instead of footnotes

The quote that opens this chapter comes from a soldier in the US armed forces: Akiva Skidell grew up in a Jewish family in Poland, and while serving in Europe he wrote to his wife back in Brooklyn. This particular observation is taken from a letter dated February 1945, when he was stationed in Germany and saw action there.

It is impossible to find out what happened to a number of the main characters in this chapter. Mala does not know the surname of the young man everyone knew as Janek the Priest (Janek Ksiądz in Polish). Nor does she remember the name of the woman in Bremen who invited her and Amelka for coffee. She did provide me with the baron's surname, though Loos turned out to be Loss.

In his 1985 book, translated into English by William Templer as *Hitler's Foreign Workers: enforced foreign labor in Germany under the Third Reich* (1997), Ulrich Herbert provides a full record of the laws and decrees designed to prevent the mixing of races, along with issues, anecdotes, and fascinating facts relating to the millions of foreigners put to work in Nazi Germany. Herbert is my source for the high percentage of Gestapo arrests for inappropriate dealings with foreigners.

8

The Neisse

'The Ku Klux Klan, who saw Zelig as a Jew that could turn himself
into a Negro and an Indian, saw him as a triple threat.'

–The narrator of *Zelig*, a Woody Allen film

Mala's status as a stateless person meant she was awaiting an official
decision that might move her up a rung on the Third Reich's racial
ladder. The authorities at the women's prison camp on Schillstrasse in
Magdeburg believed that Mala had German blood, convinced by her
tall tale of a German mother whose maiden name was Wassermann.
The prison director had also been impressed by Mala's exceptional
command of German. Now her fate was in the hands of the men with
the power to confer the official stamp of *Volksdeutsche*.

Since the German invasion of Poland, millions had been given the
status of Volksdeutsche or ethnic German. An official memorandum
dating from 1938 described them as people whose 'language and
culture had German origins'. But for fanatical Nazis, the concept was
more than a dry definition. In their eyes, ethnic Germans were racially
pure foot soldiers in the Aryan race's battle for survival.

The Nazi leaders estimated that there were between 12 and 30
million ethnic Germans living in Eastern Europe, from the German
homeland to the Ural Mountains. German speakers in what had been
Polish Silesia and Polish Pommern (Pomerania) were made to sign a
document to distinguish them from the inferior Poles. Then came an

interview to confirm their privileged status and determine the category of German descent to which they belonged. Not every category qualified for official German status. It was, of course, accorded to Volksdeutsche who had actively supported the German cause before the war. But there were also those who had been completely absorbed into Polish culture and who had even expressed hostility towards the Germans. If a Pole of German descent refused to sign, they faced the threat of deportation to a labour camp, and in some cases even a death camp.

Threats aside, hundreds of thousands were only too happy to sign. The Nazis' planned Germanisation of what had until recently been western Poland turned these German-speaking Poles from an ethnic minority into part of a German majority. The plan called for the expulsion of most Poles to the Polish General Government, while those allowed to remain would be slave labourers housed in the barracks of a factory or farm, no different from the foreign workers that the Germans later drafted in from other countries. The long-term plan was for all Poles in the west to make way for ethnic Germans from the Baltic States and, following the invasion of the Soviet Union, from Ukraine, Belarus, and the lands around the River Volga.

The concept of Volksdeutsche or ethnic German was key to the racial ideology and policy of the Nazis. Not only was society to be cleansed of impure blood, but at the same time help was to be given to Aryans of all kinds, ethnic Germans first and foremost. The extermination of Jews and the advancement of ethnic Germans were two sides of the same coin. As historian Doris L. Bergen writes, 'In much the same way as Nazi authorities made laws, regulations and institutions to define and deal with Jews, they constructed a complex bureaucracy to handle ethnic Germans.' It was no accident that responsibility for the extermination of Jews and the advancement of ethnic Germans were entrusted to the same man: Heinrich Himmler. In addition to the logistics of extermination, it was his task to ensure that the homes and possessions of Jews and other unworthy people ended up in the hands of ethnic Germans. This represented a tangible fulfilment of the 'struggle for living space', a long-standing idea adopted by the Nazis that resonated broadly with the German population.

In letters sent home from Poland and the Soviet Union, SS officers and Wehrmacht soldiers often justified their own inhumane actions against 'inferior peoples' in terms of the benefits to ethnic Germans, members of their own superior race. Even *Einsatzgruppen*, the Nazi task forces that cut a murderous swathe through the Soviet Union in 1941, carried out a painstaking and well-administered redistribution of their spoils among the ethnic Germans they 'discovered' in the region. The loot included everything from children's prams and thermos flasks to harvesters, houses, and livestock — all duly noted.

A prime example of this link can be found in the person of Arthur Greiser, Reich governor of the Polish city of Łódź and founder of Chełmno, the first death camp. He took pride in the speed with which his SS men gassed vast numbers of Jews in trucks. In a letter to Himmler, he reports that his *Sonderkommando* (a special unit of 85 Jews who had to do the dirtiest work and whose death was imminent) had collected a sum of over 15,000 marks from the pockets of the gassed Jews. While they had probably done so on the orders of their SS guards, Greiser was keen to present this as a spontaneous act of generosity, and recommended that the money be donated to the orphaned children of ethnic Germans. In his reply, Himmler welcomed this initiative as an excellent idea.

An additional advantage of this redistribution of goods and financial resources was that it created a small group of loyal citizens on foreign soil. Beneficiaries of stolen goods are all too willing to support the argument that justifies the robbery; the firmest of convictions are born where self-interest and ideology coincide. It was robbery that made belief in racial distinctions so contagious — a belief that, especially in Eastern Europe, often persisted for years after the war had ended.

The concept of Volksdeutsche had also served the Nazis well in their earlier propaganda. It lay at the heart of a self-engineered problem that provided an excellent pretext for their ultimate goal: war. Ethnic Germans in other countries were being humiliated, Hitler insisted in speech after speech, a message Goebbels then relayed through films, newspapers, and books. And who were responsible for such humiliation? The inferior races of the east, subhumans. It was a narrative that allowed the Nazis to make a pledge to the people: the Wehrmacht and the SS would end this degradation, this disgrace. Germany would solve the problems of people whose existence, only a short time before, had been a matter of indifference to most Germans. Doris L. Bergen wryly observes, 'If the Volksdeutsche had not existed, the Nazis might have invented them.'

The SS played a greater role in identifying and 'saving' ethnic Germans than the Wehrmacht. Members of the SS staffed a new government department entirely devoted to this aim. Particularly following the invasion of the Soviet Union, this *Einwandererzentralstelle*, or Immigration Centre, processed several hundred thousand cases to establish whether or not someone merited German status. The centre came to be based in Łódź, a city the Germans had renamed Litzmannstadt. It subjected people who claimed German descent to rigorous testing, though only a minority of its staff had a medical or scientific background. They noted anthropometric data, such as hair colour, eye colour, and the shape of the nose. The set of the eyes and the distance from the forehead to the back of the skull were seen as particularly significant. They took an X-ray, and questioned the candidate about their childhood, education, and ancestry. On this basis, they arrived at a quotient for every potential German: the purity of their German blood expressed as a percentage.

The SS immigration officers took their work seriously. If in doubt, they made aspiring Germans come back again and again for further interrogation. Until the end of the war, they worked determinedly to maintain this quasi-scientific approach to determining the ethnic background of anyone claiming to be of German descent, despite an exponential increase in their workload as tens of thousands of people from the Soviet Union, Romania, and Hungary fled the Red Army's advance. Some of these refugees met the Immigration Centre's criteria for Germanness; many did not.

It was during these hectic days at the end of the war that Mala walked through the doors of the Immigration Centre. On 6 December 1944, to be precise. By this time, Germany's eastern front was unsettlingly close to Litzmannstadt, and, anticipating difficulties, the centre had split up into mobile units that could operate deeper inside the German Reich.

One such unit had relocated to Sudetenland, an area occupied by Germany since October 1938 in a move accepted by the West. The tens of thousands of Sudeten Germans in the region had been a key justification for German expansion. The racial assessors of the SS Immigration Centre had set themselves up in Reichenberg, now the Czech city of Liberec, thus sparing Mala a 600-kilometre journey east. Instead, she travelled 250 kilometres south-east, from the Elbe to the Neisse.

For her trip to Reichenberg, Mala's boss at the Magdeburger Bierhaus not only gave her four days' leave, but also ration coupons, a glowing letter of reference, and money for her train ticket, a sum well in excess of the actual price. Mala believes she owed this generosity, and her lovely room, to the publican's desire to make up for the time she had spent in prison. A foreman from Ukraine had falsely accused this sweet Polish girl, who had not only turned out to be innocent, but probably German into the bargain.

It was eleven below freezing when Mala stepped off the train. The streets of Reichenberg were thick with snow, and the narrow River Neisse had frozen over. Mala approached a woman to ask if there was a hotel nearby. The woman turned out to have a room to rent, and Mala accompanied her home, relieved she wouldn't have to spend her first-ever night at a hotel. Mala gave the woman her ration coupons, and asked her to cook a vegetarian meal. She was pleasantly surprised to find that the house had a shower. The woman offered her coffee and a slice of home-baked cake.

All was well—until she reported to the Immigration Centre the next day to find that her assessors planned to take a blood sample. This is it, Mala thought. My long journey ends here. My blood will give me away. One look, and they will know exactly what I am: Jewish. Rigid with fear, her only thought was, 'How do I get out of here?'

Seventy-five years on, Mala looks back and exclaims 'What did I know? I was a child!'

Did the assessors at the SS Immigration Centre really take blood samples? Unlike the Holocaust, not much has been written about the exact modus operandi for selecting ethnic Germans, except one weighty dissertation in German with an equally weighty title, which translates as *National Socialist Ethnic Politics and the Reorganisation of Europe: racial selection of the Central Immigration Office run by the head of the Security Police and the SD (1939–1945)*. Andreas Strippel, the man behind this study, calculates that from the start of the war until April 1945, the Immigration Centre registered approximately one million people as ethnic German. He frequently encountered fear of blood tests in the course of his research, even among German-speakers from the east who had nothing to hide. 'Some of them came from a premodern society deep in Russia or Ukraine. They had never had blood taken before. The whole setting in an institute like the Immigration Centre was a shock to their system.'

In reality, even the most fanatical and racially obsessed Nazi knew that blood offered no proof of whether or not someone was Aryan. The purpose of the samples, Strippel explains, was to detect any traces of the infectious diseases doing the rounds in Eastern Europe at the time.

Following her blood test, Mala was led into a room where eight SS officers were seated at a long table. The men looked into her blue-green eyes. They asked her about her cultural background, her education, her command of German. They asked if there were any Jews in her family. She gave them a potted history of her non-existent German mother's non-existent family. They had lived in Kolonie Karpy, she said, and had sent her to a German school. She told them she had volunteered to come and work in Germany.

Mala was a natural storyteller, and she knew it. But, shaken by the blood test, she no longer believed that this could end well. It was only a matter of time before she would be unmasked as a liar. Her own blood was about to expose her betrayal of her own flesh and blood.

How wrong she was. After another wait, she was summoned back in to face the council of eight. Their conclusion was clear: Everything is in order, you are a Volksdeutsche.

'I didn't know whether to laugh or cry,' Mala says. 'The place was full of people with no chance of ever being given their papers. And there was I, a Jewish girl who had not spoken a word of truth, approved as German. I was convinced that this was the hand of God.'

Mala may well have been mistaken about how many other candidates that day were to be denied German status. At that time, around two-thirds of those who appeared before the SS assessors received the papers they applied for. That said, it is not hard to understand Mala's thinking. At the end of the war, many applicants belonged to fatherless families, exhausted by their efforts to fend for themselves as they fled the Red Army. They must have made a wretched impression. To Mala, they did not seem especially German.

Strippel's research confirms the procedure Mala describes. The eight men she misled would probably have been delighted to see her: as a blonde, healthy, well-spoken girl, relatively fluent in German and with no resettlement issues to complicate matters, she was far from typical of the people who came before them. The assessors were often disillusioned by what they saw. The people they screened seldom lived up to the Nazi ideal of a superior German race. Theirs was an ideology of clear-cut categories, and many SS officers had expected to be able to pick out Germans with ease among the peoples of the east. Made in the image of their assessors, they would conduct themselves as true Germans: clean, thrifty, industrious, and dedicated to the Nazi ideals. 'Hard-working, punctual, neat, and tidy' was how the manager of the Bierhaus had described Mala in his glowing reference. But those who had left for the east decades or centuries before had adapted to their new surroundings as best they could, complete with mixed marriages and religious conversions, modifying their language, customs, and habits accordingly. In the eyes of many an SS officer, they were little more than boorish creatures babbling in odd dialects.

In short, the assessors found it hard to identify with these potential Germans. Since the fall of Stalingrad, military commanders had muddied the waters still further by calling on the Immigration Centre to relax their criteria so that tens of thousands more men could be conscripted into the armed forces. Even Himmler, who was ruthless in his adherence to racial doctrine and seldom turned a blind eye when it came to persecuting the Jews, called for a degree of leniency when it came to identifying ethnic Germans. He ordered the 'Germanisation' of 'racially valuable Poles', which amounted to granting ethnic-German status to collaborators who requested it.

Ideologically driven SS officers complained about this state of affairs. The authorities in Posen (Poznań in Polish) grumbled in one report about being forced to house ethnic Germans who lacked 'German family values'. The women, one officer reported, went to bed with Poles and Ukrainians whenever their husbands' backs were turned. And the men were no better, all too willing to sleep with Polish women and adopt Polish customs. The youth, meanwhile, were lazy and promiscuous. The one area in which these orphaned Germans did not disappoint was their anti-Semitism. But even SS officers found themselves wondering aloud whether this was a typically German trait: Jews were vile creatures, after all—you didn't have to be German to see that.

Another source of irritation was the way these aspiring Germans were forever using Christianity to justify their hatred of the Jews, presenting their Christian faith as ultimate proof that they were German. This cut no ice with the ideologically driven SS officers, for whom religious devotion was far from typical of the German race. If anything, they looked down on believers. Christianity created a slave morality, they said, echoing Nietzsche. Its values were incompatible with those of the *Herrenvolk*, a people born to rule, and propagated an ideal of equality that they despised. A true Nazi obeyed the laws of nature, and in nature the weak perish. To win the battle of the races, they thought, the Germans had to be as ruthless as the natural world. Churches and charitable organisations allow the weak to survive; true Germans throw them out of the nest.

Anyone with this mindset was bound to be exasperated by what they saw as the numerous blunders made by the German authorities when it came to the assessment of Eastern Europeans. There was righteous indignation at the number of 'racially inferior' foreigners being welcomed into the fold as Volksdeutsche. And so it came to pass that a young woman of eighteen found herself facing interviews, medical examinations, and blood tests before her Germanness could be determined by a panel of eight SS officers.

This was December 1944. Didn't SS officers have better things to do? I put this question to Andreas Strippel, the man behind the weighty dissertation. He takes my point, but explains that, 'in the final months of the war, the department worked harder than ever, a question of ideological zeal'. The men of the Immigration Centre were committed Nazis. They believed in the racial theory that formed the foundation of National Socialism, and genuinely thought that they were serving the highest possible ideal through their work. This sense of urgency was heightened in those final months, when they were working against the clock. 'We may lose the war,' one SS officer wrote in a letter to his parents, 'but we — and we alone — will keep German numbers at their proper level.'

'For them, this wasn't about saving lives, but about saving and even strengthening the race,' Strippel says. 'By bringing ethnic Germans into a German environment, they were preventing further racial dilution.' In other words, by uniting Germans, they were furthering the propagation of the 'pure-blooded' German, with or without new territories in which to prosper. In today's parlance, they were protecting the gene pool.

The racial assessors of the SS Immigration Centre continued to evaluate the Germanness of immigrants until February 1945. Remarkably, their work would continue to have an impact long after the war had ended: until 1990, the West German authorities continued to acknowledge the centre's findings when deciding whether someone had a right to settle in Germany. 'A very sensitive issue,' Strippel observes. 'It meant that people with a Jewish background who wanted to settle in Germany had far more trouble obtaining a residence permit than any number of Nazi collaborators from Eastern Europe who could hand over an official seal of approval from a bunch of SS officers.'

Mala was a young Jewish woman who could have handed over the same documents after the war, had she felt the need. She left Reichenberg as an incontrovertible Volksdeutsche, albeit under an identity she would no longer use when the war was over. Name: Anni Gmitruk. Mother's maiden name: Wassermann.

Stepping out onto the snow-filled streets, she was bewildered, but also delighted by what had just happened. What a pity Erich's not here, she thought. We would have had such a laugh about that pompous panel of SS officials.

Erich's response was a matter of conjecture, of course, given that Mala had yet to tell him she was Jewish. 'I took the train back to Magdeburg the next day. All I could think of was Erich. I was convinced that I had to tell him the truth, that I couldn't go on living a lie.'

Seventy-five years on, at home in Amstelveen, Mala says, 'I was planning to tell him. Honestly, I was!'

Her words are mainly for the benefit of her grandson Amir, who has joined us bearing coffee and biscuits. In a warm voice, tinged with scepticism, he asks his grandmother, 'Are you sure about that?'

'It would have made no difference to Erich,' she maintains. 'I'm sure of it. Just as it didn't matter to me that he was German.'

'That's not entirely true,' Amir replies. 'It did matter. You felt uneasy about it. And you must have realised that such a revelation wouldn't exactly have made his day?'

'I just *know*,' Mala insists. 'I remember telling him once: you know nothing about me, about my background, where I come from, who my parents are. And he said: You could be a gypsy, for all I care! It makes no difference to me.'

Amir and Mala's eyes meet, and they exchange a smile. Mala looks a little sheepish. Amir cocks an eyebrow.

'Okay,' Mala concedes, as if her grandson has put the question. 'A Jew would have been worse than a gypsy.'

Roma were persecuted, too, I pipe up. 'Twenty thousand Roma were killed in Auschwitz alone.'

Mala is not one for figures. 'When the occupation began, I remember hearing about someone who went into hiding among a band of gypsies not far from Warsaw. Probably not the wisest choice.'

Mala laughs; Amir and I smile. Suddenly, Mala returns to Erich and says, 'The main thing was that I didn't feel afraid when I was with him. He knew about the terrible things the Nazis were doing to Jews. And he thought it was awful.'

As for Erich's parents, Mala is not so sure. 'I never met them. We had a visit planned, but the bombardment put paid to that at the last minute. And when the bombs fell, I lost the letters with his address. What kind of welcome would I have got from them? From their neighbours? I mean, the Germans thought Jews were animals.'

* * *

Mala was not simply a Polish, Russian, Latvian, or Ukrainian girl who had slipped through the cracks in the race-assessment system. She was a Jew—not even a Jew from an assimilated family, but a girl who had grown up speaking Yiddish at the heart of an Orthodox community. Her mothers and aunts wore goat-hair wigs; her father and her brothers had sidelocks and beards, and wore fur hats. Her family consisted of people that most Germans only knew from propaganda films that depicted them as hunchbacks with deep-set eyes and sinister stares, a sly and unscrupulous nest of vipers that brought typhoid epidemics to Germany: the enemy within. Yet in Mala, one of their number had received the highest commendation from the sworn Nazis at the Immigration Centre: the status of an Aryan German.

Is Mala unique? In all his years of research into the SS Immigration Centre, Andreas Strippel knows of no other case like hers.

However, there is a story of a Jewish man who successfully passed himself off as an ethnic German. He, too, survived the war, and went on to write his memoirs. The son of a Polish immigrant who worked as a cobbler, Solomon 'Solly' Perel is ten months older than Mala and was born in the German town of Peine. Solomon's gender made his deception all the more remarkable: as a circumcised Jewish boy, he would never have made it through the SS selection system at the Immigration Centre. Yet circumstances somewhere between coincidental and astounding conspired to ensure that Perel never had to undergo a Nazi medical examination.

A Wehrmacht unit happened upon young Solomon Perel in the forest during the rapid German advance in the summer of 1941. He told the soldiers he was a *Volksdeutscher*; they took him at his word, and never thought to send him to the Immigration Centre.

How had Solomon ended up in the forest? In 1935, two years after the Nazis came to power, Solomon's parents had decided to leave Germany and move to Łódź in Poland, where a relative lived. The Nazis advanced on Łódź four years later, and the Perels ordered their three sons to travel east, although only two of them made the attempt. The brothers were separated in the chaos that broke out as they and thousands of others tried to cross the River Bug while thousands of Poles fleeing the advancing Red Army and the NKVD were trying to cross in the opposite direction. Solomon clambered into a small boat with dozens of others, but the boat was too frail to hold them and capsized. Solomon had left home wearing as many clothes as he could, and was struggling to stay afloat. A Russian soldier saw him going under and, without thinking twice, saved his life.

Solomon ended up at an orphanage in Grodno, a Polish city that had been occupied by the Soviets only days before. Today, it lies in Belarus. From the orphanage, he wrote letters to his God-fearing parents in which he extolled the blessings of socialism and atheism. He turned out to be exceptionally susceptible to both. Almost two years later, the Germans reached Grodno. As German fighter planes flew overhead and bombs exploded all around, the terrified children from the orphanage fled on foot. In the panic and chaos, Solomon lost touch with the group he was with, and before long German forces caught up with him and hundreds of other fugitives. Soldiers herded them into a forest clearing, and made them stand there for hours.

A German soldier went down the line. Solomon heard someone say that Jews and political commissars would be picked out and killed that same day. Salvos of machine-gun fire could be heard coming from the woods. He saw *politruks*, the Red Army's political commissars, tear the five-pointed red star from their sleeves. Solomon scraped a hole in the ground with the heel of his shoe, dropped his papers into it, and, keeping his hands in the air, stamped the soil back over them. He managed to do this unnoticed.

When the German soldier came and stood in front of him, Solomon said firmly and calmly in German, *Ich bin Volksdeutscher*. 'I am an ethnic German.'

'I hadn't thought of the consequences or how these fanatics for order and perfection would react when confronted by a boy without identity papers,' Solomon writes. 'But there was something like an intuitive faith, a spark of hope, and an inner voice whispering, "Everything's going to be all right, nothing will happen to you ..." A similar glint of hope probably flickers in the heart of anyone sentenced to death when the executioner opens his cell door and he must walk the last mile.'

The detail Solomon remembers most vividly from the moment that would determine the course of his life is the inscription on the belt buckle worn by the German soldier standing in front of him: *Gott mit uns.* God with us.

The soldier motioned to him to step to one side. Solomon did as he was told. As he stood there waiting, the soldier gave him an encouraging glance now and then, as if to let him know he hadn't been forgotten. Then the soldier went on barking orders at the people who were to be taken away.

Suddenly, a young Polish man pointed at Solomon and said, 'He … Jew!'

In that fraction of a second, all hope seemed to vanish. Then the soldier struck the Pole in the face and told him to shut up.

All the while, the sound of machine-gun fire was coming closer. A sergeant came running over. The soldier greeted him, then pointed at Solomon and said proudly, 'Sir, we found a young German among this human garbage.'

'Everything that happened after that was predestined,' Solomon Perel told a journalist fifty years later, following the première of the film adaptation of his life story. 'From that moment,' Perel said, 'I felt that I was playing the role of an extra in my own life.'

Slight of build with thick dark hair, Solomon Perel looked nothing like the ideal image of the German. But the soldiers on their murderous advance into the Soviet Union were more than willing to believe him. Discovering an ethnic German lent a noble sense of purpose to their campaign of destruction: they had rescued a sixteen-year-old boy from a life of misery among the Asian hordes. Not only that, but he came in handy as an interpreter when interrogating prisoners of war and the local population. On the very first day, the men of the 12th Panzer Division sat him on the hood of one of their half-track armoured vehicles. They christened him 'Jupp', and he became a kind of mascot for the division.

Everyone loved Jupp, Solomon recalls: 'One of the major goals of the Nazis was to bring all ethnic Germans back into the Reich. The soldiers around me were therefore filled with patriotic pride at the thought that they were participating, in a small way, in the realisation of such a great undertaking.'

On one occasion, his secret was almost discovered. The advancing division had commandeered a farmhouse and set up an improvised bath house in the kitchen. Thus far, Solomon had come up with all kinds of excuses to avoid being naked in the presence of the other soldiers. This time, too, he waited until the last man had left the kitchen. Then, carrying a towel and a piece of soap, he stepped into one of the tubs and began to wash in the warm water, singing along with the tune a soldier outside was playing on his harmonica. It was an aria from *I Pagliacci*, the opera about a group of travelling players dressed as clowns who cast doubt on what is real and what is pretence.

'Suddenly I recoiled. Someone nearby was whispering something. Before I knew what was happening, a pair of strong arms grabbed me from behind. I felt a naked body pressing against me. I froze. Thousands of bells went off in my head. As the man's erect penis tried to enter me, I jumped as though a snake had bitten me. It would have been smarter just to stand there, with my back to him, but I had instinctively freed myself from his embrace. Jumping out of the tub, I turned around.'

The inevitable happened. Heinz Kelzenberg, the brigade's medical officer, stared in bewilderment at Solomon's naked body and asked, 'Are you Jewish, Jupp?'

Solomon burst into tears, and begged the German to spare him 'Don't kill me! I'm still young, and I want to live!'

Fortunately for Solomon, Kelzenberg was neither a committed Nazi nor a sadistic anti-Semite. He walked over to him and said softly, 'Don't cry, Jupp, they mustn't hear you outside.' He promised Solomon that he would not betray his secret, and told him, 'You know, there *is* another Germany.'

Sixteen-year-old Solomon developed a special friendship with Heinz, who was thirty. He, too, had a secret to keep: his homosexuality. Weeks later, Solomon confided in him completely. Heinz was moved by his story, and stopped making sexual advances towards him. A few months later, Solomon, or Jupp, looked on helplessly as Heinz was hit by a grenade attack. Heinz's carotid artery was torn, and he bled to death in a matter of minutes. Solomon was shattered by this tragedy. He was alone with his secret once again.

Like Mala, Solomon Perel not only managed to slip through the tightening net, but at every turn encountered enemies who developed a fondness for him. Captain von Münchow, the unit's commander and a raging anti-Semite, was so fond of Jupp that he made plans to adopt him. He sent him to an elite school for the Hitler Youth in Braunschweig, so that in two years, when he had come of age, he could officially enrol in the army.

At Braunschweig, concealing that one undeniable piece of evidence of his Jewish background was no easy task. Solomon was always fiddling about with towels, and, without explaining why, wore underpants in the shower. His classmates thought this was odd—after the war, it emerged that they had even reported it as suspect behaviour to the teachers, but no action was taken. Solomon did not make it any easier on himself by falling in love with Leni Latsch, a member of the *Bund Deutscher Mädel*, the girls' wing of the Nazi Party's youth movement. As a devoted Nazi, Leni was anything but Christian or prudish. She believed it was her national duty to bear children, and the sooner the better.

Solomon was head over heels in love with Leni, but, afraid that his lack of foreskin would betray him, he avoided making love to her. In the end, it was Leni's mother who found out the truth about his background. The elaborate story Solomon had concocted about his German grandparents crumbled in the face of her persistent questioning. He broke down in tears and threw himself into the lap of Leni's mother. Fortunately, Leni was not present at the time, and her mother impressed upon Solomon that he was never to breathe a word to her about his background. Alarmed by her own daughter's fanatical Nazism, she felt sure Leni would not spare him.

Solomon Perel's memoirs are fascinating; the screen adaptation, less so. The film tends towards caricature, and contains a few instances of poetic licence that border on the ridiculous. Solomon himself begs to differ, and has praised the film in dozens of interviews around the world. You think the film is strange? 'The reality is even stranger,' he insists.

To illustrate his point, Solomon talks about a chance meeting, directly after the war, with the Race Studies teacher from the elite school he attended. This encounter is not in the film, though there is a scene in which the same teacher gives his class a lesson on racial characteristics. A Jew has a high forehead, the teacher says, and his excited pupils let out a low-pitched 'whoooo'. The Jew has a hooked nose — 'whoooo!' A flat back of the skull — 'whooo!' And he never looks you in the eye — an even louder 'whooo!' The teacher then imitates an ape-like walk, and warns that the Jew is intrinsically evil and can suddenly turn and seize you by the throat. He then summons Solomon to the front of the class and explains that, while his small stature and dark complexion indicate that his blood is not entirely pure, he is nevertheless a true Aryan of the East Baltic race. So much for the film.

'Imagine,' Perel said after the film's release. 'Out of everyone in the class, he picked me as his example for ethnology.' Perel also had to explain — and that is not in the film, either — why Jewish blood had to be wiped out. He knew these lessons inside out: the chapter of his textbook titled 'Characteristic and Distinguishing Features of Jews' told him all he needed to know. The Jew had the brains and the eyes of a human, but in terms of morality, he was lower than an animal. Unless he was eradicated, it would mean the decline of the West. Perel could reel all this off at the drop of a hat. He wanted to be the perfect pupil.

Solomon stood beside the teacher, in front of all his classmates. Larger-than-life photographs of Jewish faces looked down from the classroom wall, full-face and in profile. Beside them hung a before-and-after illustration of 'The Eternal Jew', the first showing a crooked little man with curly sidelocks in a threadbare black robe, leaning on a walking stick and with a bag of rags slung over his shoulder. Beneath the image, a caption read: 'This is how they came to Germany from the East.' The next picture showed a Jew with the same exaggerated features, but elegantly dressed, wearing gold and flaunting a diamond ring. He had a mighty paunch, a sly grin, and a cigar clamped between his lips. The caption read: '... and this is what they became in our midst.'

Standing there at the front of the class, Solomon was scared to death. What did this expert in ethnology have in store for the one boy in the class who looked nothing like the Aryan ideal? Then came the release, just like the film. 'Take a good look,' the teacher said. 'Here we have a typical descendant of the East Baltic race.' Later, real life did outdo the film. Two weeks after the German capitulation, Perel bumped into his old teacher at the railway station in Hanover. They recognised each other. Solomon came straight to the point, and told the teacher his mistake. 'Herr Borgdorf, I'd like to correct it now ... I'm of pure Jewish blood, from head to toe.'

And the teacher's response? Solomon Perel is not as consistent in his wording as Mala, and has told different versions of this meeting. But one constant is the teacher's unwavering self-assurance. If he hesitated at all, it was only for a moment before he said, 'I knew it all along, but I was trying to avoid hurting you.' Some adapted quickly to the new reality of post-war Germany.

Instead of footnotes

Andreas Strippel's dissertation was published in 2011 by the German publishing house Schöningh. Its original German title is *NS-Volkstumspolitik und die Neuordnung Europas. Rassenpolitische Selektion der Einwandererzentralstelle des Chefs der Sicherheitspolizei und des SD (1939–1945)*. For my understanding of the concept of *Volksdeutsche* (ethnic Germans), I owe a great deal to an article by Doris L. Bergen entitled 'The Nazi Concept of "Volksdeutsche" and the Exacerbation of Anti-Semitism in Eastern Europe, 1939–1945', published in the *Journal of Contemporary History*, vol. 29, no. 4 (October 1994), pp. 569–582. Two other valuable sources were Benjamin Goossen's article 'Measuring Mennonitism: racial categorization in Nazi Germany and beyond', published in the *Journal of Mennonite Studies*, vol. 34 (2016), and the book *Rasse, Siedlung, deutsches Blut* (*Race, Settlement, German Blood* (2003), by Isabel Heinemann.

As so often with moving and dramatic memoirs of Holocaust survivors, those of Solomon Perel have appeared in all kinds of editions. The first to be published commercially was in French. I read the German edition *Ich war Hitlerjunge Salomon*, published three years after the 1990 release of the film adaptation *Europa, Europa*, a French–German–Polish co-production, directed by Agnieszka Holland. The English quotations from the book are taken from Margot Bettauer Dembo's translation from the German, published in 1997 in association with the United States Holocaust Memorial Museum.

9

The Elbe

'April is the cruellest month, breeding / Lilacs out of the dead
land …'

–T. S. Eliot, *The Waste Land*

Mala had no choice but to wrap her arms around the waist of the
uniformed man. The stylised eagle on his red-and-black armband
clutched a swastika in its claws, and Mala was reminded of the SS
officers she had seen shouting insults and beating people in the Warsaw
ghetto. It sickened her to cling to such a man. But she understood that
this was the price she had to pay for her newfound status as an ethnic
German.

She had met the man at a gym hall in Zerbst, a walled town by the
Elbe, some forty kilometres south-east of Magdeburg. A picturesque
place, with houses that could have come straight out of *Hansel
and Gretel*. It was shortly before Christmas, and Mala had only just
returned from her trip to Reichenberg. That day, Allied bombs fell
on the Bierhaus, causing severe damage. Everyone ran for their lives.
Magdeburg was a prime target for the Allies, home to Polte, the largest
munitions factory in Germany. The chef at the Bierhaus forbade the
girls to go back inside the ravaged building. Instead, he told them to
stick together and follow him along the railway tracks, where they
would be safe from collapsing masonry. Homes were burning; the
air was black with smoke. Mala remembers total chaos in the streets,

everyone running like sheep in the same direction.

As they walked down the tracks, she recalled the bombs that had fallen on her parents' home, five years before. A brief surge of satisfaction soon gave way to pity for the wounded children and old people lying in the rubble by the roadside, abandoned. Some were crying out for help.

Germans further up the Nazi pecking order claimed the bombing was in fact a blessing. Goebbels expressed the view that there was no place in the modern age for a city like Magdeburg. Albert Speer, the architect who had been appointed minister of armaments and war production, and who had established a working staff for the reconstruction of bombed-out cities, presented the large-scale bombardments as a unique chance to rebuild Germany's cities along more efficient and aesthetically pleasing lines.

On the outskirts of the city, a line of vehicles was waiting for those who had fled. Mala climbed aboard a truck. When the bombs fell, she had run out into the street without the chance to grab Erich's letters. Not having committed his address to memory, she had no way to contact him. And he had no idea that she was on a truck bound for Zerbst.

At the large gym hall in Zerbst, Mala and the others were served sandwiches and drinks by youngsters from the Hitler Youth and the League of German Girls. Meanwhile, a committee was deliberating where these refugees were to be housed. The Polish girls from the Bierhaus were assigned to a labour camp at the edge of town. Mala wanted to go with them, but that was not an option. As a 'racially superior' Volksdeutsche, there was no question of her receiving the same treatment as a group of Poles.

A man from the committee came up to Mala and informed her that she would be going home with him. He had a motorcycle, and told Mala to climb on the back. 'Hold on tight,' he said.

An SS officer, Mala thought. This is what my lies have brought me. The man soon realised that she wasn't holding on tightly enough. He stopped his motorcycle and turned off the engine. Planting both feet on the ground, he reached back and pulled her arms tighter around his waist.

Otto Möller was not an SS officer, but a member of the *Volkssturm*, a militia that had been founded three months earlier. Membership was compulsory for practically all German men between the ages of sixteen and sixty who were not in the military, many of whom had been declared unfit for active service by the Wehrmacht. The men of the Volkssturm had very few resources at their disposal — no money, no uniforms, and hardly any weapons. However, they were supplied with armbands, and enthusiasts were permitted to kit themselves out with a uniform if they so wished. Möller was an enthusiast.

The primary duties of the Volkssturm militia consisted of digging anti-tank trenches, setting up roadblocks, and building barricades for the defence of German cities. Anyone who refused was sent to a labour camp. Some were even sentenced by 'flying court martial' and executed on the spot.

Refusal was the last thing on Möller's mind. He was a fervent national socialist. Mala also remembers him as well-to-do. She probably gleaned this impression from his uniform and his condescending yet friendly bearing. In fact, Möller was a fifty-six–year–old glassblower with a lower-than-average income by German standards, and little in the way of education. He was born in Geraberg, a town of glassblowers, and lived with his wife, Emma, and their married daughter at the small factory where he worked. The factory's owner–director, a man called Wilhelm Kramer, lived with his family at the same address. He was in the thermometer business.

By the time Mala entered their lives, the Möller family had already received word that their son-in-law had died in the Battle of Stalingrad. And from the younger of their two sons, the apple of his mother Emma's eye, they had heard nothing for quite some time. Immediately after passing his school exams, Emma's youngest had been called to arms and sent to the eastern front, aged sixteen. His parents told Mala how funny and talented he was; he had even been allowed to take his accordion with him to the front. Years after the war, his comrades would talk about the songs young Max Möller wrote and sang to keep them entertained.

It was not unusual for committed Nazis to take returnee and refugee children into their homes, often ethnic Germans or even children from the Lebensborn programme. Young Max's absence must surely have played a part in the Möllers' decision. Mala — Anni Gmitruk to the Möllers — was roughly the same age as the son they had waved off to war. They gave her his bedroom to sleep in.

On the very first evening, mother Emma Möller noticed the tears in Mala's eyes. She put her arm around the teenage Volksdeutsche and said, 'I will make sure we have a good life here together, despite the war.' Mala, whose revulsion had given way to sadness, felt a little better. Seven decades on, she says of Emma Möller, 'She really was a very warm, very kind-hearted woman.'

The next day, Emma Möller told Mala the family history, and read her a letter from her young son, the last they had heard from him. Emma thought, or rather hoped, that his lack of correspondence could be explained by disruptions to the postal service.

Emma took Mala everywhere with her. In an effort to stay kosher, Mala once again made the excuse that she was vegetarian. 'Mrs Möller cooked something specially for me every evening.'

Otto Möller turned out to be a calm and patient man. At the weekends, he taught Mala to ride a bicycle. When the weather turned nice, they spent time at the Möllers' small allotment just south of Zerbst, complete with a pair of lovely fruit trees. If Mala went to the pictures in the evening, Möller would fetch her so that she would not have to walk home alone after dark. This pleasant and sedate middle-class life was new to Mala. When her birthday rolled around in early February 1945, the party they threw for her came as a complete surprise. Mala had not grown up in a household where birthdays were celebrated. The Möllers invited friends over and showered Mala with gifts, including the bicycle that had belonged to their son Max.

On her birthday, Mala discovered that Emma had spent weeks knitting a sweater, a woolly hat, and matching socks for her, all gift-wrapped in brightly coloured paper. 'Never in my life had people been so nice to me,' Mala says. She was confused and overwhelmed by so much kindness. 'It was painful to discover that the Möllers were far kinder to me than my own parents had ever been. I had longed for love so much. My father only ever took my hand when we crossed the street. And my mother was always preoccupied with her sons, when she wasn't busy working to support the family. It was a genuine miracle to find so much love so far from home.'

This sense of gratitude left Mala wondering if she was being a traitor. Over half of the guests at her birthday party had sported an armband with a swastika, something that was by no means compulsory, as Mala well knew. Erich had never worn that kind of thing. The Möllers' friends actually wanted to wear the swastika, even to a girl's nineteenth-birthday party. 'Everyone toasted my good health,' Mala says. 'All I could think of was the home I grew up in, my own people. How could I be happy? I felt that I was betraying them by being there with those Germans.'

Mala's view of the world had been shaken by the first kind German she encountered: the lady in Bremen who hoped her sons would be treated with the same courtesy in Poland that she was extending to two Polish girls in Germany. Later, there was the policeman in Wolmirstedt who had let her out of her cell and into his own home to share meals with him and his good-hearted wife. And, of course, there was Erich, with his derogatory remarks about Hitler. To Mala, the Nazis were the SS officers and gendarmes in the ghetto, the guards in the women's prison camp, the soldiers who had marched into Warsaw: people from whom she expected nothing but calculating coldness and perhaps cruelty. They did not confuse her; the Möllers did.

She saw these nice people gather in awed silence around the radio to listen to Hitler's final speeches. On 30 January 1945, their Führer impressed upon his listeners that, in this 'fateful battle', there was only one command: 'He who fights honourably can … save his own life and the lives of his loved ones. But he who, because of cowardice or lack of character, turns his back on the nation shall inexorably die an ignominious death.' Hitler said he expected all Germans to make every sacrifice asked of them. 'I expect the sick and the weak or those otherwise unavailable for military duty to work with their last strength … I expect all women and girls to continue supporting this struggle with utmost fanaticism.'

Mala could reach only one conclusion: 'To the Möllers, Hitler was God.'

The Möllers also heard him warn of what the 'Asian hordes' would do to German women and girls if Germany lost the war. Among these prophecies of doom, their Führer also offered a degree of solace. For whatever might happen, at least one great victory had been achieved: 'The Jewish international enemy of the world … will not only fail in this attempt to destroy Europe and exterminate its nations, but will also end by annihilating itself.'

The Möller family felt a great and immediate fondness for the girl Otto Möller had plucked from the gym hall and brought to their home on a small industrial site just outside Zerbst. They had a sincere desire to help her, one of the beleaguered people in whose name Hitler had gone to war with Poland. The propaganda the family absorbed was full of tales of how the Wehrmacht was saving ethnic Germans from the clutches of cruel Poles and cunning Jews. One piece of propaganda, the popular 1941 film *Heimkehr (Homecoming)*, proved particularly effective at showing the urgency of liberating these downtrodden fellow Germans. The film was set in Lutsk, a city between the River Bug and the River Dnieper that lay in pre-war Poland. Its plot centres on the plight of 200 ethnic Germans facing execution at the hands of Poles until the Wehrmacht arrives just in time to save them. After their rescue, they travel to the new Germany, where heaven on earth awaits them.

The Möllers took their very own Volksdeutsche to one of the film's many screenings. It was preceded by the newsreel, *Die Deutsche Wochenschau*, a summary of the week's military triumphs. The voice-over insisted that morale at the front was riding high. German troops everywhere were fighting back bravely. This was January 1945, not long before Mala's birthday.

The main feature starred Paula Wessely, a big name at the time, and was shown until the very last days of the war. After that, it fell foul of an Allied ban, and remains banned to this day. Mala can still picture Wessely. She even recalls the opening lines of the patriotic song she sang in one of the film's most dramatic scenes: 'How I want to go back home / To my dear fatherland / Where they sing those happy songs / Where many a familiar word is spoken!'

Wessely's character, schoolteacher Maria Thomas, burst into song with her fellow Germans as they stood in a dark prison cell, up to their ankles in water. The day before, her fiancé had refused to join in when the Polish national anthem was played at the local cinema. A bunch of locals had beaten him up and left him for dead, and because he was German, the local hospital refused to treat him. To add to Maria's woes, a Polish man had shot and killed her father, a doctor. The 200 jailed Volksdeutsche could already see the barrels of the machine guns poking through the small windows of their cell. But they refused to give up. Because they were Germans. And because they had Maria, who lifted everyone's spirits, not only by singing, but also with a rousing speech. After the première, Goebbels praised the scene as 'the finest ever captured on film'.

In the build-up to this climax, Mala and the Möllers had already watched Poles smash up the classrooms of the German school where Maria taught. They had witnessed Poles murder a German innkeeper, and seen the innkeeper's wife assaulted by an unsightly man who ripped a necklace with a small swastika from around her neck. The unfortunate woman was then stoned by a crazed mob.

Mala looked over at Mrs Möller, and saw that her eyes were red from crying. 'Everyone was crying,' Mala says, throwing her hands in the air. 'They believed every last bit of it!'

The film, which had a budget of 3.5 million Reichsmark, is seen as classic Nazi propaganda. In the 'blood and soil' speech that teacher Maria gives in the prison cell, she sets out a glorious vision of the future. 'Just think, people, what it will be like, just think, when around us there will be lots of Germans—and when you come into a store, people won't talk Yiddish or Polish, but German. And not only the whole village will be German, but all around, everything surrounding us will be German.'

The joys of a homogenous society.

This must have made the Möllers feel good about themselves: they had saved a young German girl from these Polish horrors, a girl who deserved a close and loving family. They were acting in the name of a higher purpose, the well-being of the German race. As the film's protagonist says, 'And at night, in our beds, we'll awake, and the heart will suddenly know with a sweet shock that we're sleeping right in the middle of Germany, home and at home ... and all around, millions of German hearts will beat and quietly intone, you're home, home, home with your kin.'

On their way home, Otto Möller exclaimed, 'We cannot be rid of those cursed Jews soon enough.' Mala asked him if all Jews were like the ones in the film. 'My child,' Otto replied, 'you don't know the half of it.' In reality, they were far worse. They lied, robbed, stole, there was no end to their crimes. Mala asked him if he knew any Jews. 'No,' he replied, 'of course not.'

Mala sighs, 'I wondered how such a good-hearted and intelligent man could think and say such things.'

The whole experience had turned her stomach, a feeling that lasted well into the next day. At her birthday party, that sense of being a traitor became even more painful and more pointed, perhaps because the family's readiness to celebrate her special day instilled in her a mixture of gratitude and loathing. Mala tried in vain to ignore the question of whether the Möllers knew what their sons were doing in Poland or the Soviet Union.

No, she now concludes, they probably didn't. Such nice people would have been devastated to find out what was really happening in those places—that a son of theirs could shoot a Jewish man in the head simply for not raising his cap to him in the street. Mala believes they can't have been aware of such things.

But apart from what their parents did or did not know, the question remains: what did the Möller boys do in the east? How guilty were the Möllers and others like them for what was done to Mala's family and so many others? One widely held view is that they did very little out of the ordinary, that your average German was only following orders. They were cogs in the war machine of a Nazi regime that was bent on destruction. Another view, mainly popular in Eastern Europe, is that young men like the Möllers unleashed their murderous and sadistic urges on prisoners of war, Jews, and the local population.

It was American historian Christopher Browning who convinced me that both views are too simple. His book *Ordinary Men: 101 Reserve Police Battalion in Poland* is considered a classic among Holocaust researchers, and as essential reading for their first-year students. Familiar territory for many. Yet the story Browning uses to illustrate the insights he has gained into the Holocaust cannot be told often enough; it encapsulates the essence of Browning's position. It takes place on a summer's day in 1942, and rips up the view of the German mass murder I had formed through … what, exactly? How *do* people form their views on such matters? They pick them up from newspaper articles, books, their teachers, their parents, and, in my case, what passed for collective wisdom in the Netherlands of the 1980s and 1990s. A wisdom based on thinkers such as Hannah Arendt and Zygmunt Bauman. Browning had yet to feature.

To highlight the radical nature of Browning's contribution, it's important to say something about the others — Zygmunt Bauman, for example. A Polish-born sociologist, he survived the Holocaust, emigrated to Israel in the 1960s and later moved to the UK. There, he honed his ideas about the German mass murder, and produced an influential book entitled *Modernity and the Holocaust*. His analysis builds on the conclusions reached by Hannah Arendt in her role as a political philosopher who reported on the trial of leading Nazi Adolf Eichmann in Jerusalem. Her 1963 book on the subject bears the subtitle 'a report on the banality of evil'. She saw Eichmann as a banal, nondescript man who prided himself on having performed his duties efficiently. Not a monster, but a cog. The Nazis, Bauman and Arendt argue, could never have killed so many on the basis of monstrosity or sadism alone. It required a technocratic perspective, a focus on logical reasoning. They could not have attempted their project without a belief in social engineering, whetted on the ideas of the Enlightenment. While acknowledging that racial hatred can have roots that go back centuries, and understanding why the Holocaust is often seen as an extension of German Romanticism with its emphasis on a uniquely Germanic national character shaped by history, Bauman and Arendt maintain that the mass murder of the Jews was not a regression to medieval barbarity, but an expression of modern thinking. Where Romantics extolled the virtues of history and nature, Bauman argued, the radically modern man, with his indestructible faith in progress and social engineering, sought to put right what nature and history had spoiled. For the communists, this meant destroying the class enemy; for the Nazis, exterminating the Jews.

Bauman knew what he was talking about: as a Polish Jew, he had lost his family to the murderous ambition of the Nazis, and, as a communist working for the Polish security service shortly after the war, he had worked to destroy the class enemy. To exterminate his people, the Germans had rolled out a sophisticated, bureaucratic process founded on a division of labour, compliance with rules, and obedience to higher ranks. Science and technology were deployed in the service of murder.

Crucial to this was an element Bauman called 'moral blindness'. No one bore direct responsibility, except perhaps those at the pinnacle of authority. Eichmann, who came to symbolise the bureaucratic efficiency of the Holocaust, was assessed on the basis of figures: production targets drawn up by himself and his bosses. Bauman and Arendt follow Eichmann's own reasoning in this regard. Cogs do not work against the machine. As Bauman said in an interview with Dutch journalist Peter Giesen, 'If there is no room to choose, there is no room for morality.'

This notion spread far and wide as a defence of complicity, even among those who had pulled the trigger at the edge of a mass grave, those who had forced people onto trains that would take them to certain death, and those who built, guarded, and operated the gas chambers. 'What choice did I have?' they asked after the war. An order is an order. Their own moral responsibility was subordinate to hierarchical bonds of loyalty.

Browning has shown this to be untrue by shifting the focus from the memories of the survivors to the memories of the perpetrators.

Browning's story begins on 13 July 1942, in the General Government of Nazi-occupied Poland. German Reserve Police Battalion 101, a unit of just under 500 men, were billeted in Biłgoraj, the small town where Daniel's grandfather had been mayor. That summer's day, the battalion received its first major assignment.

In the 1960s, 125 members of the battalion were questioned extensively by German investigators, and these interrogations enabled Browning to reconstruct the events of that day in 1942. They also helped him gain a solid impression of the men themselves. They came from Hamburg. Some were middle class, but most were working class: builders, waiters, seamen, warehouse loaders, drivers. With an average age of thirty-nine, they were relatively long in the tooth, and this was partly why they had not been drafted into the army but were allowed to sign up for the reserve police. This made them 'Orpos' in German, short for *Ordnungspolizei* (Order Police). Relatively few were members of the Nazi party and, apart from a handful of First World War veterans, none of them had fired a gun at another human being until that day in July. In Browning's view, they were not exactly made of the right stuff to be remoulded into mass murderers.

At first light, the men climbed aboard military trucks that rattled their bones as they bounced along paths of sand and gravel, skirting the worst of the potholes. The men did not know where they were going or why. After almost two hours and thirty kilometres of slow progress, they arrived at their destination: the village of Józefów, less than twenty-five kilometres from Tomaszów Lubelski, where Majloch, Chaja, and Meir were living at the time. Around 2,200 people lived in the thatched, whitewashed houses of Józefów. Almost 1,800 of them were Jewish. The place was silent. The Orpos from Hamburg leapt from their trucks and formed a semi-circle around their commander.

Major Wilhelm Trapp was a fifty-three-year-old veteran of the First World War, decorated with the Iron Cross First Class. He had been a member of the NSDAP since 1932, one of the old guard, an *Alter Kämpfer*. Even so, there had been no place for him in the SS. Nor had he been given the equivalent of an SS rank, though this was common practice for valued members of the Wehrmacht, and in line with Himmler and Heydrich's policy of mixing the party and the state apparatus in the army and the police force. Trapp, Browning concludes, was evidently not regarded as SS material. Tellingly, the men of the 101 called him 'Papa Trapp'.

Twenty years on, the vast majority of those questioned commented on how pale and nervous Trapp seemed that morning. A few even said they saw tears in his eyes. The battalion, Trapp told his police reserves, had a fearsome and unpleasant duty to perform. He was not happy about it; in fact, he saw it as extremely regrettable, but the orders had come from the highest level. If it gave them any consolation as they carried out this duty, they should think of the bombs being dropped on their women and children in Germany as he spoke.

The battalion's task was to 'clear' the village of Jews.

Two decades later, a few of those under Trapp's command remembered him saying that the Jews were behind the international boycott of Germany. Two recalled Trapp telling them that Jews from the village had aided the resistance. Almost everyone remembered Trapp explaining that all Jewish men between the ages of fifteen and forty-five were to be separated from the rest, for transportation to a labour camp. The Orpos were then to execute the women, the children, and the elderly.

After giving these orders, Trapp made a noteworthy offer. He told the battalion that any man who did not feel up to the task should say so. Those who did would not have to take part. One man stepped forward. Another ten followed, perhaps eleven; the testimonies differ. These men then stood to one side to await further orders.

The shooting lasted all day. The killing of 1,500 people is a gruelling task, even for experienced gunmen. The army trucks that had brought the battalion to the village shuttled back and forth all day from the marketplace to the edge of the woods outside Józefów, fetching between thirty-five and forty women, children, and old people each time. The same number of Germans then took them into the woods, each policeman holding a victim by the arm. A captain led the columns through the trees and, like a parking attendant, directed them to a new place each time. On reaching the designated spot, the women, children, and old people were told to lie face down on the mossy ground. Every 'guide' then stood behind his victim, aimed the bayonet on his rifle at a spot between head and neck, and waited for the order to shoot. It was twilight, seventeen hours later, when the last bullets were fired into the heads of the unarmed victims. On the way home, it was quiet in the trucks. The men were exhausted and ill-tempered. This had been their first time. Bullets had regularly missed their target or only grazed the victim. Uniforms were drenched in blood, spattered with brain tissue and fragments of skull.

But not all the uniforms. As the day had worn on, more policemen had availed themselves of the opt-out that Trapp had given them. Some made themselves scarce. A small group spent hours hanging around the garden kept by Józefów's priest. Others pretended to have a job to do at the marketplace, where the waiting victims had been assembled. A number of the men carried out endless house searches, afraid they would be made to join the firing squad if they were found idling.

A thirty-seven-year-old tailor began the day as part of the firing squad, but after the first round of killing, it became too much for him. 'I was allotted a mother with daughter as victims for the next shooting. I began a conversation with them and learned that they were Germans from Kassel, and I took the decision not to participate further in the executions. The entire business was now so repugnant to me that I returned to my platoon leader and told him that I was sick.'

His platoon leader sent him back to the marketplace to help out.

Another man killed three people, only to be sickened by the fourth. He deliberately missed his target, ran off into the woods, threw up, and, as he remembers it, sat under a tree for two to three hours. Then he walked back to the edge of the woods, got behind the wheel of an empty truck, and drove back to the marketplace.

Two men made the mistake of asking a fanatical Nazi for permission to stop carrying out the executions. They had children of their own, they said, and could not go on. The Nazi, an SS *Hauptsturmführer*, answered with a simple 'No'. If they wanted to stop, he gestured, they could go and lie down beside the dead. Yet after the lunchbreak, another officer came and relieved the two men of their duties.

Reflecting on his study, Browning later wrote, 'the initial killing [was] quite traumatic and distressing to the men, but ... most quickly became brutalized, numbed, and accustomed to what they were doing. Moreover ... a significant minority became eager killers.'

Browning's book centres on the question of how, in a matter of weeks, ordinary citizens were transformed into perpetrators of mass murder. After studying the interrogations, he divided the men into three categories. The first consisted of the fanatical killers who, after

Józefów, often volunteered for such actions. The second consisted of men who did as they were told; nothing more, nothing less. The third group evaded the execution of unarmed civilians.

Did the evaders suffer as a result of their choice? Not really. The fanatical members of the battalion made it clear what they thought of them: weaklings, was their verdict; cowards perhaps. Their less fanatical comrades mainly saw them as freeloaders who were all too happy to leave the dirty work to others. More than other sections of society, the armed forces operate on the principle of 'one for all and all for one'. Yet none of those who refused were severely punished. Sometimes quite the opposite: one policeman, a timber merchant by trade, refused to kill 'defenseless women and children', and was later promoted. Trapp must have given him a positive reference. Another refuser even escaped disciplinary action after hitting a fellow policeman in the face for beating a Jewish woman with a club when the battalion was rounding up Jews in hiding. There was no official reprimand, though he was landed with Sunday morning cleaning duties, and ordered to stand watch at the most inconvenient times. That was all. Browning concludes that the men who refused at Józefów were never forced to take part in the killing until their time in the battalion was over.

After the war, lawyers defending German soldiers undertook a feverish search for documentary proof that soldiers who refused to kill unarmed civilians faced terrible consequences. No such document was ever found. German scholar Herbert Jäger later determined that there is not a single case of a soldier under the Nazi regime being officially punished for refusing to shoot an unarmed civilian. On 4 October 1943, Himmler gave a speech to SS officers in which he prized obedience as the essential virtue of every member of the SS. But in that same speech, he also cited one specific exception: someone whose nerves were shot, who was weak, might be told by a superior that he could retire from service.

When it became clear that ordinary soldiers could not base their defence on a document stating that they had been left with no choice but to murder unarmed civilians, lawyers in the 1960s resorted to the term 'putative duress'. In other words, their clients admitted that they committed murder, but only because they genuinely believed that they were under immense pressure to do so. The story of Battalion 101 demonstrates that this was not the case either. Day after day, the battalion's members saw fellow policemen being given other duties, never having to take that walk into the woods, and never volunteering to kill Jews. It was a group of 'willing executioners', usually around eight men, who set about killing all the Jews who had been dragged from their hiding places. By the end of the war, Battalion 101 had participated in the shooting deaths of over 38,000 unarmed Polish Jews and had deported another 45,000 to extermination camps. Browning's book does the maths for us: 'a total body count of 83,000 for a unit of less than 500 men'.

Daniel Goldhagen, another American scholar, examined the same interrogations as Browning and wrote a very different book. The two men then proceeded to clash in a series of public debates. Goldhagen's book, *Hitler's Willing Executioners*, put the emphasis on those who *did* want to take part in the killing, not on those who refused. In Goldhagen's view, the willing were driven by a deep-seated anti-Semitism that was typically German, centuries old, and shot through with genocidal longing. This longing was present in ordinary Germans, including the reserve policemen from Hamburg with children of their own. All their Nazi leaders had to do was unlock the cage of decency. It's an argument that could also be applied to the sons of the Möller family.

Browning and Goldhagen drew on the same sources to tell different stories, and the media have gone on to amplify these differences. And yet the similarities in their findings outweigh the differences. After studying the same interrogations, both men conclude that hierarchy was not the crucial factor. An order was not always an order. The defence that 'I was forced to take part in these massacres' simply doesn't hold up.

Browning points out that the men didn't have to take part. Goldhagen argues that they wanted to commit these atrocities, that there was no need for ruthless orders. Both men reject the analyses of Arendt and Bauman.

Arendt, they believe, allowed herself to be misled by Adolf Eichmann, who sought to conceal the full extent of his own responsibility for the massacre behind a smoke screen of apolitical professionalism: the expertise and banality of the bureaucrat whose only concern was carrying out his work correctly and hitting his targets.

Bauman and Arendt situate the problem within the system. Goldhagen blames German history, identity, and culture. Browning brings individual responsibility back into the discussion about war and mass murder. Everyone *can* become a mass murderer. But not everyone actually becomes one.

* * *

At the Möllers' home in Zerbst, the girl the family knew as Anni Gmitruk was also wrestling with the dilemma of individual responsibility. Mala was troubled by notions of collective guilt and whether behaviour is determined by nationality or even race. In the Warsaw ghetto, she had seen enough to know that the Germans were out to destroy her family. Yet here she was, surrounded by the kindness of the Möllers, who gave her more love than she had ever dreamt possible. Was she wrong to accept this love? This was the question that haunted her. Could the Möllers be exonerated by their ignorance? How ignorant were they? And that other question that would not go away: what were their sons doing on the eastern front?

Over seventy years after Mala's time at the thermometer factory, I travel to Zerbst in search of the Möllers, in the hope that they can answer that question. The first stop on my search is the municipal archives. Unlike my experiences in Wolmirstedt, Magdeburg, Lublin, and Tomaszów Lubelski, here I am assisted by an exceptionally helpful and inventive young woman. With calm and friendly German precision, she finds permissible ways to circumvent the privacy laws that make historical research into life stories so complicated. It's a promising start.

Zerbst, she explains, used to have no fewer than five thermometer factories, all relatively small-scale operations. In fact, the town was once Germany's centre of production for clinical thermometers. In the 1930s, some 90 per cent of their glass-blown products were shipped abroad. Because the Möllers lived on the premises, we hunt for Möllers at the factory addresses. (Mala remembers the Möllers as Millers, but there are no Millers living in Zerbst.) We hit upon a Möller whose address corresponds with that of thermometer manufacturer Wilhelm Kramer: Altbuchsland 14, 39261 Zerbst/Anhalt. Surely this is our man? Mala has mentioned the Kramers, too.

Past meets present, and the address leads to a small industrial site. Ringed by state-of-the-art fencing, I find an assortment of landscaping companies, plumbers, and manufacturers of front doors — 'Your Home's Very Own Calling Card', as one firm's slogan would have it — all housed in what looks like a pre-war building, albeit obscured by stacked wooden pallets, a fork-lift truck, and a pile of soil bags several metres high. I spot a date, writ large on the brick façade: 1909. The building houses industrial units, but also residential properties, complete with residents. The name Möller doesn't ring any bells with them. This is not a huge disappointment: having consulted the1982 *Zerbster Heimatkalender* — an annual brochure for local businesses — I already knew that Kramer's factory closed down in the 1960s. The brochure's heavy-duty prose also revealed that in 1982 the town's annual output was 1.1 million thermometers produced by a mere 25 people, none of them called Möller.

I discover that Otto Möller died in 1958, at the age of seventy. His wife, Emma, passed away nine years later. Mala remembers that their daughter had a son who was seven when the war ended. That would put him in his eighties.

The friendly young archivist finds out that the Möllers' daughter married a man named Kurt Spahr shortly before war broke out. A soldier who died in the Battle of Stalingrad, exactly as Mala was told by Emma Möller.

According to the telephone directory, someone with the surname Spahr lives in one of the apartment blocks fifty metres from Kramer's former factory. In 1944, the street was called Friedrichsholz, renamed Waldfrieden under East Germany's communist regime. Could this Spahr be the son of the Möllers' daughter?

The five-floor apartment blocks have never had a lick of paint, and the plasterwork consists of a thin layer of cement applied to a polystyrene panel with wire mesh, the cheapest of the bargain-basement construction methods widely employed in the German Democratic Republic. The result is the dullest of greys.

An elderly man opens the door. Spahr, he explains, moved a few years ago, and now lives a long way off. He points us in the direction of a neighbour who knew Spahr well.

'A long way off' turns out to be a ninety-minute drive away. And yes, Wilfried Spahr *is* the grandson of the Möllers from Altbuchsland, Mala's surrogate parents. The grandson is in his seventies, and has lived almost his entire life within a few hundred metres of the thermometer factory where his grandfather worked.

I give him a call. Spahr remembers the Volksdeutsche Anni well, he says: the girl his grandparents took in. 'The interpreter', he calls her. He agrees to meet me in Bestensee, where he and his wife have moved to be closer to his son. Plus he needed a flat with wheelchair access. Wilfried Spahr has Parkinson's disease.

Before I head for Bestensee, I take a stroll through Zerbst. Tourist leaflets cling to the memory of a picturesque medieval town. 'Welcome to beautiful Zerbst/Anhalt, over 1,050 years old.' But seventy years after the war, little of that beauty remains. Only the city walls are still intact, with a Cistercian monastery and a single gatehouse attached. The moat beyond is filled with water from the River Nuthe and surrounded by sturdy chestnut trees and expansive oaks. Inside the walls, medieval times have been banished, and the trees are scrawny and newly planted. Featureless four-storey apartment blocks in pastel shades stand like barracks amid unkempt stretches of grass, an incongruous setting for the ruins of what used to be the Church of St Nicholas. One of the first stone churches to be built east of the Elbe, it was once a vast edifice. Now grass grows between its high walls. A flower bed has taken the place of the altar, beautifully tended, as if to celebrate the radical nature of transience.

The fact that Zerbst's city walls now surround streets full of prefab concrete buildings is a legacy of the conflict in which Otto Möller was caught up in the first months of 1945: a clash between those willing to surrender and the fanatics determined to fight on to the bitter end.

The mayor wanted to capitulate, in the hope that his town would be spared, but Zerbst's senior Nazi politician dismissed any such notion, even though all was lost. The architecture of the town today tells you how this conflict ended. Zerbst is a monument to the ruthless Allied bombing of Germany's heartland and to the pig-headedness with which fanatical Nazis fought on.

After the war, the Soviets would not hear of reconstruction. 'They wanted us to be a model communist town,' the young archivist tells me. Others insist that Zerbst was punished. Among them is the baker, a small woman with short red hair and plenty of zip. 'For people like you, the Second World War exists in films or in books. Here in Zerbst, we live every day with what happened on that one day of destruction. Everything was wiped out.'

The local bookshop bears witness to the power of nostalgia. The handful of books and DVDs about the town are filled with before-and-after photographs. Some present the images side-by-side to invite comparison. A Facebook group devoted to 'views of Zerbst, old and new' has several regular contributors. Three years as a follower leaves me wondering what stuff you have to be made of to devote your leisure time to posting photographs of Zerbst before and after Allied bombs laid it to waste. A more dispiriting pastime is hard to imagine.

Schicksalstunde, they call it. The fateful hour. In fact, the destruction of Zerbst took more than a single hour. On the morning of 16 April 1945, an operation codenamed 'Young Girl' dispatched four waves of planes. Two were enough to consign the medieval town to history forever.

Some of America's conquering heroes were troubled by the town's fate. Tony Vaccaro, soldier and photographer, had travelled east from Normandy with the 83rd Infantry Division. When the rest of his unit departed, he stayed behind in Germany as a correspondent for US Army newspaper *The Stars and Stripes*, and spent months capturing images of the conflict's immediate aftermath. His photographs grace the covers of many a book about the Second World War. In a documentary filmed in 2001, Vaccaro is interviewed on Zerbst's main square, an empty expanse of cobbles surrounded by post-war buildings. In his broad Italian-American accent, he says he is amazed anyone at all survived the Allied bombardment. 'It was the most bombed little town I have ever seen in my life.' He was proud of winning the war, but could not be proud of what he witnessed in Zerbst. Vaccaro was no stranger to wartime devastation, but for him this was the saddest case of all. 'It's difficult to digest.'

A dentist and teacher from Zerbst decided to collect eyewitness accounts of people who had lived through the bombardment. German suffering at the hands of the Allies was not a welcome topic in communist East Germany, even though the bombs had been dropped by the capitalist, imperialist enemy. The testimonies he collected could only be published after the death of Stalin and, even then, they had to be preceded by an introduction stating in no uncertain terms that the people of Zerbst only had themselves to blame for failing to rise up against their leaders. Instead of declaring every town, village, and home to be a fortress, true German patriots should have called for an end to Hitler's war: '*Schluss mit dem Hitlerkrieg!*' If they had tuned in to Radio Moscow five days before the bombardment, the writer says, the people would have heard Walter Ulbricht tell his future East German citizens, 'What your lives will look like depends on what you do to prevent the destruction of your town. Liberate your hometown from the rule of the Nazi bosses and you will be saved!'

The people of Zerbst had not tuned in to Ulbricht. But common sense had led some to conclude that nothing good could come of continuing the fight. A group of women sawed through the thick tree trunks that the men of the Volkssturm — men like Otto Möller — had used to block the access roads. A soldier ordered them to stop. The women only obeyed when he drew his pistol.

Meanwhile, the mayor was engaged in frantic efforts to convince the Americans not to destroy his town. Fair enough, the Americans said, as long as you surrender unconditionally. In other words, the capitulation of the mayor and the civil authorities was not enough; the military forces stationed in the town had to lay down their arms, too.

By this time, the town's senior Nazi official had abandoned his post, and Major von Busse of the SS had come to Zerbst, heading a unit of around 100 soldiers who had fought in the east. Von Busse said his orders were to turn Zerbst into a fortress. Despite the mayor's best efforts, von Busse dismissed the idea of surrender outright. The logbook of the US regiment records one last-ditch attempt by the mayor to avert disaster. Then came the bombs and the devastation. The Americans entered the ruined town to find that von Busse had arrested the mayor shortly before the bombardment and had planned to sentence him to death for communicating with US forces without military clearance. Confirmation of this verdict never came, and, in the meantime, von Busse himself had fled.

The Nazi's second-in-command was still in Zerbst. American GIs found him in a hospital bed, hoping to avoid imprisonment by posing as a patient.

Days later, the Americans handed the town over to Soviet forces. The border of the Soviet zone of occupation ran along the River Elbe, a little to the west. Before long, the river would mark the border between East and West Germany.

The ruthless nature of America's campaign of shelling and bombing is perhaps best explained by a mixture of cynicism and exhaustion. The men of the 83rd had landed at Omaha Beach at the start of June 1944, and went on to fight in Normandy, Brittany, Luxembourg, the Battle of Hürtgen Forest, the Battle of the Bulge, and even along the Elbe, where the regiment encountered yet more pockets of unexpectedly fierce resistance, some of it led by boys of fifteen and sixteen, cadets at a military academy not far from Zerbst. In addition to the fighting, they made gruesome discoveries. Coming across a number of smaller labour camps, they saw conditions that brought home the cold-blooded nature of the National Socialist dictatorship—evidence of reports that, until then, many had dismissed as propaganda invented by their own army's news service. On 11 April, in Langenstein, they liberated a satellite camp of Buchenwald. The prisoners they found were more dead than alive. Many more perished after their liberators arrived.

Lieutenant Frank Towers and a number of men under his command freed prisoners from an abandoned freight train on its way from Bergen-Belsen to Theresienstadt. It stood not far from the estate of Friedrich Loss, where Mala had worked alongside other

Polish labourers. The wagons were unguarded, SS officers having fled the scene minutes earlier. Only the driver remained, awaiting orders. Unable to feed the malnourished prisoners on the train—well over 2,000 of them—Towers and his men sought help in nearby Farsleben, a small town three kilometres from Wolmirstedt. There, he demanded that they take in the Jewish prisoners, wash them, and feed them. Hunger had not yet reached this part of Germany, and Towers' demands were no great hardship. Yet, decades later, he recalls that the German townspeople only complied after an American commander put a pistol to the mayor's head. Even then, they went about their task grudgingly.

For the rest of his life, Towers would wonder why so many Germans—soldiers and civilians—remained so cruel until the very end of the war, why they held to the course that had been set. This may have something to do with the 'breathtakingly rapid brutalization' observed by Browning, a process that these Germans were apparently unable to reverse themselves. To do so, they needed the intervention of Towers and his men.

There was a terrifying irrationality about the energy that German prison guards, SS officers above all, invested in driving together prisoners and shooting them in the final hours—in some cases, even minutes—before the Allies arrived. Why take yet more lives? One theory is that they wanted to deny the victors living evidence of their crimes. Another is because they actually believed the world would be a better place without these 'racial dregs'. Or, as some scholars have suggested, had they become addicted to the power they wielded?

Decades after Lieutenant Frank Towers came upon a train full of half-starved Jewish prisoners near Farsleben, he became friends with a man whose life he saved when soldiers under his command stormed the Polte munitions factory in Magdeburg. As a young man, Ernest Kahn must have looked fit and strong; at every selection, SS officers picked him out from the rows of Jews being sent to their death. The strong could work first and die later. At the age of nineteen, Kahn ended up in the Kaiserwald concentration camp near Riga before being shipped to Stutthof near Danzig in 1944. During the last months of the war, he was transferred to a subcamp of Buchenwald and put to work at Polte. Every day, the prisoners were marched from the camp to the factory, which lay around fifteen kilometres to the south.

Following the air raids on 16 April 1945, the day Zerbst went up in flames, the Germans evacuated the camp. As there were no more horses, the guards loaded their luggage and personal belongings onto a large wagon that the prisoners were made to pull and shove. As the column trudged past the Polte factory, Ernest and three other prisoners made a run for it and slipped inside the gate of the vast factory site. The factory had been disabled by the air raid. There was no water or electricity, but the men found some German overalls, which enabled them to ditch their prison uniforms. Not that this was much of a disguise: with their shaved heads and starved bodies, they barely looked human. They spent one night in the attic of an office, but woke up to find four SS officers staring down at them, guns drawn. 'Out, you swines! Hands up!' the Germans shouted, and marched them down to the factory yard where around 100 prisoners were already lined up with their hands in the air. Every five to eight minutes, ten of the prisoners were driven off in a small truck.

'I was standing with my hands up and I said to the guy to my left, "This is it, we made it up until now" — and lo and behold, an air raid started! The US Air Force, low-flying bombers came. You could see the pilot's eyes — that's how low they dropped the bomb load. The guards chased us into the adjacent air raid shelter ... they posted a guard in front of that door and as we passed he said, "I'm innocent, I never did you any harm." He was an old, old man, older than me today. So when I heard that, it was music to my ears. I had never heard something like that from any guard.'

The guards left the shelter and locked it from the outside. The prisoners could hear the bombs falling and see smoke seeping in under the door, but in their hearts, they were singing and praying for a direct hit to put them out of their misery. Ernest Kahn leaned against the door and, to his amazement, it opened. He never found out whether the air pressure of falling bombs had blown the heavy lock off, or whether it had been opened for them. Decades later, he said he would still like to know, as if longing for a sign of humanity from at least one of the guards.

The prisoners scattered in all directions. Ernest took cover in a lift shaft along with three other prisoners, and waited there until the bombing was over and a deathly quiet settled in. They sent one of the prisoners to see what was happening, and thirty minutes later he returned with a big pan of soup and the news, 'Boys, we are free. The Americans are here!'

* * *

In his apartment in Bodensee, Wilfried Spahr is wearing black sweatpants that have long since lost their shape. They bear the words 'American Sport' in creased white letters. He repeats the confirmation he gave on the phone: he is the youngest grandson of Emma and Otto Möller, the National Socialists who took Mala into their home so lovingly.

Spahr turns out to be a friendly man who can talk at great length about his aches and ailments. Two artificial hips and an artificial knee have compounded the problems of Parkinson's disease, which may explain the smile that seems to have died on his lips. His features are handsome enough. He has a low forehead, and wears his thinning grey hair in a neat side-parting. He grew up without his father, who died in action before Mala came to stay with the Möllers. In the early 1950s, the government let the family know where his father was buried, but, as Spahr explains, there was never enough money to make the long journey from Zerbst to Volgograd, formerly Stalingrad. The grave remains unvisited.

Of the Möllers' sons, only the elder returned from the war. Released from a Russian prisoner-of-war camp in 1947, he came back to Zerbst, where he became a baker. The younger brother, Max, who played the accordion, served on the front somewhere near Minsk. He went to fetch water with one of his mates, and the two of them were never seen again. On one occasion, someone who worked for the Red Cross told Emma that Max had been seen alive in a prison camp after the war. But she was told not to share this information with anyone, and so didn't know what to make of it.

Emma's daughter, Wilfried Spahr's mother, remarried two years after the war. The new husband left her not long afterwards to start a new life in West Germany with another family. Mother went into service as a housemaid and nanny for a Russian air force officer; the military airfield at Zerbst remained in use after the war. 'She was always well treated,' son Wilfried recalls. When the officer moved away, she found work at a soap factory that no longer exists.

As a little boy, Wilfried joined the Free German Youth, the official youth organisation in communist East Germany. He learned to dance, and played in the brass band, complete with uniform. 'Every first of May, I did my bit.' Little Wilfried grew up to be a metalworker rather than a glassblower, and when his failing joints put an end to his active working life, he was still able to train apprentices until early retirement beckoned.

We look through photographs from years gone by. The house at the thermometer factory seems barely to have changed. The photos confirm something else Mala said: Otto Möller looks considerably younger than his wife, though in fact she was two years his junior. Emma's hair is grey, and the deep lines under her eyes give her a mournful expression.

We search until we find some photos that must have been taken in 1943 or 1944. But none include Mala. Spahr looks frantically, convinced there must be at least one picture of the person he calls 'the interpreter' or 'the girl'. Spahr remembers his grandmother Emma being especially fond of her. Both his grandparents and his mother thought it odd that they never heard from Anni again after she left. 'My grandparents helped her. They were always willing to help people, and I have raised my own children to do the same.'

He illustrates this point with stories about himself and his grandparents in the years directly after the war. He tells me about the Russian soldiers who, for days on end, were posted right around the corner. They were there to direct the tanks, and on no account were they to abandon their post. A driver was dispatched to pick the soldiers up in the evening, but sometimes they were forgotten and had to spend the night by the roadside. His grandmother felt sorry for them, and would always make sure they got something to eat. Spahr also talks about the deserters he helped, or tried to help. 'But they were always caught in the end,' he sighs with a dismissive gesture. 'A nasty business.' He leaves it at that.

And what about Grand-dad Möller? Did he ever talk about Germany before the war, about his faith in Hitler and the National Socialist cause, about the war in which he lost his youngest son? No, Spahr says, he didn't. At least, not that he remembers.

The word 'simple' keeps cropping up. Wilfried Spahr often refers to himself as a 'simple man' and the Möllers as 'simple folk'. He likes to think his own children are cut from the same cloth. When I tell him that Anni Gmitruk was born Mala Rivka Kizel, and that she was not a Volksdeutsche but a Jewish refugee from Warsaw, there is a short silence followed by a halting sentence that contains the words 'our simple ways'. Then, more clearly, he says, 'We are simple people.' Another silence, and then: 'If Gran and Grand-dad had known about that girl, they wouldn't have said a word, not to anyone.' He says it so quietly that even my German friends need to replay the recording a few times to be sure of his words.

Spahr regains his composure by launching into another lengthy anecdote about how his mother helped Russian soldiers shortly after the war. He does not steer the conversation back to Mala. When I do, he reverts to short answers, and the word 'simple' reappears. For Spahr, the word appears to stand for honesty and integrity, to leave no room for doubt. Or is it more to do with culpability? Not shrewd enough to act immorally? Not savvy enough to fathom the evil of Nazism? Incapable of understanding, never mind influencing, grand political movements?

Listening to the tape of the interview, my German friend Thomas swears loudly at this display of 'simplicity as a virtue'. He is thirty-one, just old enough to have been born in East Germany. Disgusted by what he has heard, he calls Spahr 'a typical representative of German post-Biedermeier culture'.

Of *what*?

'It's a culture in which everyone is always banging on about their own simplicity and domesticity. An antiheroic, bourgeois culture,' Thomas explains. 'But, if you ask me, that simplicity is mainly an excuse to dodge questions about your own responsibility, or that of

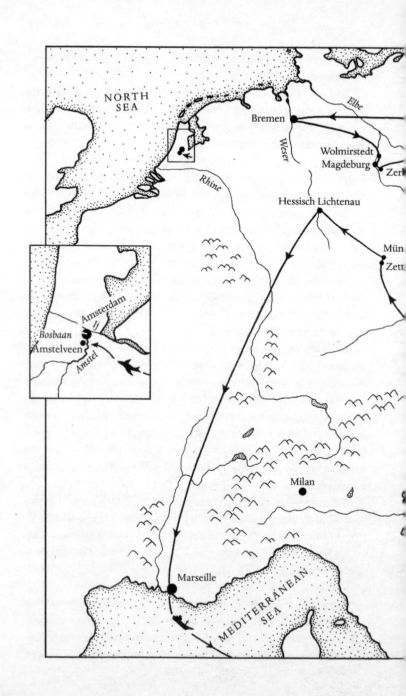

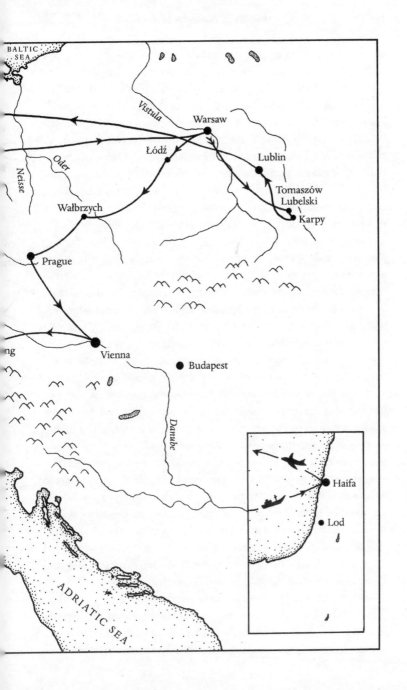

your parents and grandparents. Spahr's Nazi grandfather was just a simple man … of course he was. It lets everyone off the hook.'

Thomas tells me about his own grandparents, who hail from Görlitz. They, too, like to sing the praises of the simple life, and they, too, were committed Nazis. 'Of course, my grandfather was as innocent as could be. He was a train driver during the Second World War … yes, *those* trains included. He can wax lyrical about how quickly they could repair bombed or sabotaged tracks. But try to talk politics with him, and you hit a wall of simplicity. Once or twice I got him to let his guard down and speak his mind. And then he was perfectly clear: the country has never been better off than under Adolf Hitler's leadership.'

The stories that Wilfried Spahr and his wife tell about their time under Soviet military rule bear little resemblance to the dark tales of the Ruddies back in Wolmirstedt. Unlike the descendants of 'Baron' Loss, Spahr and the Möllers were not class enemies. They were glassblowers who made thermometers. Yet even the working-class Möller family did not escape the widespread suffering as a result of hunger, looting, and even rape. Had his mother been a victim? It's not something he wants to talk about. A nod of confirmation is as far as he will go.

Zerbst is mentioned in the books written about the sexual abuse of German women on a massive scale by soldiers of the Red Army. The town's newly installed mayor, a communist since 1926, could hardly wait until the Americans left to make way for the Soviets. He dismissed the rumours of rape in the east as typical Nazi propaganda. But not long after the Soviets arrived, the first victims of sexual assault reported to his office. Within minutes, the mayor and the women were yelling at one another. Initially, the mayor simply could not or would not believe their accusations. But the reality was undeniable. 'Rapes, assaults, murders, one after the other. Over a hundred raped women were cared for just in the local school. These women had been manhandled by the Russians in the most horrible, animal-like manner.'

The hatred felt by Soviet soldiers ran deep, born of the loss of friends and family, and fed by the continuous stream of propaganda to which they were exposed. This helped dehumanise the Germans. Where German propaganda declared the Russians to be less than human, Russian propaganda succeeded in reducing all Germans to savage beasts. One telling remark comes from a report by a Russian general. Advancing on Berlin, he passed through a devastated town in East Prussia, and saw German children desperately searching for their parents. 'What was surprising,' the general wrote, 'was that they were crying in exactly the same way as our children cry.'

Spahr would rather talk about Zerbst Castle, once home to the ruling house of Anhalt, including a teenage Catherine the Great. After the American bombardment, one wing remained intact, only to be blown up by the soldiers of the Red Army. But, more relevant to Mala's past, Spahr knows what happened to the motorcycle that had once been Otto Möller's pride and joy. Directly after the Americans arrived, he hid it not far from his home, in a pit where they dumped the ash from coal-fired stoves. A few months later, a neighbour gave the game away. Russian soldiers found the motorbike and, of course, confiscated it.

'It had seemed like such a good hiding place,' Spahr sighs.

We both agree that nothing can outwit betrayal.

After a moment's thought, Spahr amends this conclusion. 'Maybe not nothing,' he says. 'But certainly not much.'

Instead of footnotes

On her trip to the pictures with the Möllers, Mala remembers seeing a Jewish butcher serving ground rat to a German mother instead of the minced beef she wanted to feed her sick children—another scene that moved Mrs Möller to tears. Though the title escapes her, Mala thinks it was from *Heimkehr*, the film in which Paula Wessely stars as a tormented, downtrodden, yet undaunted young Volksdeutsche who finds liberation in her German homeland.

But Mala is mistaken. There is no such scene in the surviving copies of *Heimkehr*. In fact, only one Jewish character appears in the entire film, a merchant by the name of Salomonsohn. Experts on Nazi propaganda films, such as Isa van Eeghen (the author of a dissertation on the Nazification of the German film industry) and Susan Tegel (author of *Nazis and the Cinema*), do not rule out the possibility that the scene may appear in another version of the film, or that it comes from a short film screened before the main feature. The anti-Semitism in such films was often laid on more crudely and thickly than in major productions. *Der ewige Jude* (1940) infamously features footage of scurrying rats as a metaphor for the Jews who are said to be overrunning Europe. It may be that Mala saw this film, which was presented to audiences as a documentary, and conflated the rat scene with a long and graphic depiction of the kosher slaughter of a cow. During the slaughter scene, the voice-over says that the Führer has prohibited these cruel practices. 'And as with slaughter, Nazi Germany has done away with all Jewry.'

Heimkehr was a huge hit. The Polish actors who played the cruel Poles in the film were jailed after the war. Their defence — 'I spoke no German, so I didn't understand the plot' — cut no ice with Poland's war tribunals. The only exception was big-name actor Bogusław Samborski, who played the film's leading villain, the mayor of Lutsk. He escaped punishment by fleeing to Argentina. The Germans and Austrians who worked on the film got off lightly or even scot-free. Paula Wessely's stage comeback in Vienna ruffled some feathers among the Soviet occupiers and a handful of Americans, who lodged an objection with the Austrian authorities. After all, Wessely had been one of the 'faces' of Nazi propaganda, and had earned the astronomical fee of 150,000 Reichsmark for her role in *Heimkehr*. But the Austrians did not budge an inch. Gustav Ucicky, the director, also went on to make countless films. The English translation of the lines from *Heimkehr* comes from Johannes von Moltke's 2005 book *No Place Like Home: locations of Heimat in German cinema*.

Christopher Browning's book *Ordinary Men: Reserve Police Battalion 101 and the Final Solution in Poland* was published in 1992. Fortunately, these free-form footnotes give me the opportunity to relate what happened to Wilhelm Trapp, the First World War veteran who gave his men the option of stepping back from the killing of women and children before his battalion's first murderous operation in Józefów and who, some said, was seen sobbing as he took refuge in the village school. Shortly after the war, a member of the battalion reported by his ex-wife gave Trapp's name while being questioned during a war crimes investigation. The interrogation concerned a reprisal in the town of

Talcyn, where Battalion 101 took part in the execution of 78 Poles. The man not only mentioned Trapp as the battalion's commander, but also his first sergeant and the timber merchant who had refused to take any part in what he called 'the killing of defenseless women and children', whether or not they were Jewish. In other words, the man reported by his ex-wife only named battalion members who had shown some signs of conscientious objection. The occupying forces in Germany extradited the three to Poland in October 1947 for a trial that focused solely on Talcyn. In consultation with the town's Polish mayor, Trapp had selected the Poles who were killed. He was sentenced to death, and was executed in December 1948. The sergeant was sentenced to three years behind bars; the timber merchant, to eight years. The severity of the sentences went according to the military chain of command, not the individual conduct or personal views of those convicted.

Daniel Goldhagen's book *Hitler's Willing Executioners. ordinary Germans and the Holocaust* was published in 1996, four years after Browning's book.

The book *Zerbst im April 1945. Eine Chronik, nach Berichten von Augenzeugen* (*Zerbst in April 1945: a chronicle based on eyewitness reports*) dates from 1955. It was reissued in 2008, with additions by Claus Blumstengel. Fear of punishment, Blumstengel confirms, may have played a role in the fanaticism of the German soldiers in the final days and hours of the war. It was unclear to many of them whether surrender amounted to high treason. Just twenty days before the Allied bombardment of Zerbst, German *Werwölf* fighters assassinated Franz Oppenhoff, the mayor of Aachen, on the orders of Heinrich Himmler. The Allies had appointed Oppenhoff to the office after their victory in the Battle of Aachen. Nazi Party newspaper the *Völkische Beobachter* reported his killing as a 'just deed'.

This was late March 1945, one month before Hitler's suicide, and desertion was still punishable by death. During the war, the Germans executed around 20,000 of their own men for desertion. Tens of thousands more ended up in penal battalions, few of whom came out alive. If a German deserter did escape punishment, the authorities were quick to track down his family. These figures come from Niall Ferguson's 2006 book *The War of the World: history's age of hatred*.

The DVDs about Zerbst, for sale in the local bookshop, are called *Zerbst zur Schmalfilmzeit: Vor der Zerstörung* (*Zerbst in the Film Era: before the destruction*), 2009 and *Zerbst zur Schmalfilmzeit* (*Zerbst in the Film Era*), 2008.

The stories of Lieutenant Frank Towers and Ernest Kahn appear on the website teachinghistorymatters.com run by writer, historian, and teacher Matthew Rozell.

I have based my account of the disillusioned communist mayor of Zerbst on Norman Naimark's book *The Russians in Germany: a history of the Soviet zone of occupation 1945–1949* (1995/2001). Russian general Maslow and his surprised observation that German children were human, too, comes from Antony Beevor's *Berlin: the downfall, 1945* (2002).

I could not have written this chapter without the help of David Cohen. He travelled with me to Zerbst and to Bestensee to visit Wilfried Spahr, the Möllers' grandson.

10

The East River

'In human beings, differences are not like the physical barriers of
mountains, fixed forever—they are fluid with life's flow'

–Rabindranath Tagore, writer

Emma Möller would always remember the day she had to flee her
home. Zerbst was burning. Her husband was somewhere among the
sea of flames defending the town. Her daughter had taken cover in
an air-raid shelter with her seven-year-old grandson, Wilfried. Emma
herself was lying face down on the sodden brown earth, twenty or
thirty metres from her home at the small thermometer factory on
Altbuchsland, surrounded by the saplings of a newly planted wood.
Her neighbours lay beside her; among them were the factory's director,
Wilhelm Kramer, his wife, one of his daughters, and his three young
grandchildren. Mala was there, too, of course: known as Anni to Emma
Möller, and as Janina to her Polish colleagues from Magdeburg who
had been put to work at the munitions factory in Zerbst.

Whenever the Allied bombers flew over, the Möllers and the
Kramers would always shelter in the wood and then return to the
factory. But that day, the trees no longer provided enough cover: the
onslaught was too severe. Emma Möller could see flashes of gunfire
coming from the aircraft as they buzzed low. It was only a matter of
time, she thought, before they would be shot, too. She decided to take
Anni and make a run for it. Her plan was to reach the tiny village of

Bias, two to three kilometres further south, and shelter at the farm where her sister lived with her husband and two teenage daughters. It was a short walk away, but not when bombs were falling all around, when the air was black with smoke, and thick with the moans and screams of the wounded. People were lying everywhere, on the road, on the verges, in the fields.

After thirty minutes, Mrs Möller said she wasn't going to make it, and ordered Anni to go on without her. 'You are still young,' she said. But Anni would not hear of it, and stayed with her. Seconds later, Emma Möller stumbled and fell flat into a hole in the road. A searing pain shot through her right leg, and she pleaded with Anni to leave her behind. 'Go! Run!' At that, Anni said something Emma Möller had often asked her to say, a word she had been longing to hear: 'Mutti'. For the first time, Mala called Mrs Möller 'Mum'.

Mala took her mutti by the hand, and they reached the farm together. The tiny village had been spared.

The farm was home to the Königs family. Mala liked them. The father was not a member of the Volkssturm, and the two daughters were her own age. Unlike the Möllers, they had no illusions about how the war would end.

Mala remembers a heated exchange. Knowing the Americans would be among them soon, the two daughters quarrelled about how to behave towards them. One said it would be best to look sad to arouse their pity. The other insisted they should stand proud: chin up, head held high.

But for the moment the only soldiers who called at the farmhouse in Bias were German. They had no desire to talk about the war. 'Enjoy every day while you still can,' one of them said. The Königs daughters, Mala, and the soldiers listened to music, while Mr and Mrs Königs sat in the cellar with Mrs Möller. The soldiers promised to return the next day with wine and real coffee, an untold luxury in those days. They also promised to bring someone else along, an officer, on condition that 'the blonde' would be there, too. 'Then we can dance.'

The blonde was Mala. She told the Königs girls that she didn't want to dance with the men, that she already had a boyfriend, Erich. She insisted she was taken, though she had no idea how she was supposed to find the man she was in love with.

In preparation for the soldiers' return, the two daughters set about tidying up the house and baked a cake. They asked Mala to help, but she chose to stay downstairs with her mutti. Mala was determined to take good care of her: 'I had never had a mutti!'

All at once, they heard gunshots close by. Mala came up from the cellar to see what was going on. Through the window, the girls saw three German soldiers — *their* soldiers! — being led away by a group of men in lighter-green uniforms. They had to be Americans. 'We saw the Germans look in our direction.' The Königs girls forgot any notion they had of how to act in front of Americans, and dived into the cellar as quickly as they could.

For Mala, sheltering from the bombs by the factory on Altbuchsland was also the last time she saw the Kramers: the factory director and his family. Mala had regularly looked after Kramer's three granddaughters, the youngest of whom was still a baby. She also used to take the eldest daughter, who was five, on little outings into town. Air raids terrified the little girl and, if they had to shelter, Mala would shield her with her body and calm her by whispering comforting words in her ear, so the blasts would make less impact on her eardrums. 'She was very fond of me.'

During one of the last bombardments, shielded by Mala, the little girl resigned herself to death. 'Dear Fräulein Anni,' she told Mala, 'I want to go and meet the Good Lord now.' Mala recalls being moved to tears, but at the same time she couldn't help wondering what the little girl's father was doing in Poland. 'He was an officer in the German army.'

Wilfried Spahr, the elderly grandson of Emma and Otto Möller, says Anni's name was mentioned in the Möller household long after she left. At birthday parties, for example, when Wilfried went to visit his grandparents. There, he often heard the same story. How, after the war had ended, Russian soldiers had come looking for Mala. 'They kicked down the door and yelled at them to fetch the Polish girl.'

As Spahr tells it, in the local dialect, Mala had hidden under a loose plank in the floor. But it was no use. A soldier drew his gun and threatened to shoot someone unless she appeared. 'As soon as she heard that, she came out.'

In Mala's story, the soldiers who came looking for her at the farm in Bias were American. This suggests that Spahr's memories of the tales told at birthday parties have become mixed with other memories. Or, more likely, mixed with other stories he heard as a boy in the months after May 1945, when the Americans withdrew and handed military command over to the Red Army, the men who looted and raped. Little Wilfried was not at the farm in Bias. As the bombs fell that April, he was sheltering with his mother at the hospital in Zerbst.

It is not hard to understand why Wilfried thought the soldiers had come looking for Mala in order to abuse her. Mala never told the Möllers why American soldiers had suddenly come looking for her, and why they threatened the family unless she came out of hiding immediately. The Germans were always left guessing about the hours Mala spent with the Americans upstairs in their living quarters. The fact that Mala refused to say anything about it told them all they needed to know. Or so they thought.

The truth was very different. A few hours after the German soldiers had been led off without so much as seeing the cake the girls had baked for them, Emma and Mala heard voices and climbed the cellar stairs to see who was there. It turned out to be five American soldiers, who said they were going to spend the night in the house. 'They were trying to speak German,' Mala recalls, 'but it sounded more like Yiddish. I could hardly believe my ears, but it was true. I couldn't understand or speak a word of English, so it couldn't have been that.'

A few hours later, Mala and her mutti went up to the kitchen to make themselves and the Königs something to eat. One of the Americans asked her for a drink of water. 'He was bare-chested and, as I was fetching it for him, I noticed he was wearing a silver chain with a mezuzah on it.' In Poland, nearly every Jewish home had a mezuzah, a long, narrow case attached to the doorpost containing a small parchment scroll with a prayer from the Torah that begins 'Hear,

O Israel the Lord our God, the Lord is One'. The miniature silver-coloured or gold-coloured versions that some American soldiers wore on a chain around their neck were often a gift from family members to offer protection, and did not always contain a scroll.

Mala could hardly believe her eyes. 'I couldn't stop myself trembling.' Downstairs in the cellar, she started crying, tears she could not explain to anyone. 'How could I tell them I was Jewish? I wouldn't have known where to start!'

The next time she and Emma went up to the kitchen, she continued cleaning and washing up, even after her mutti had returned to the cellar. The soldiers were outside on the front porch, cleaning their weapons and singing a song in Yiddish. Mala sang along, softly. She was alone with the soldiers at this point.

'Suddenly one of the soldiers came up behind me and asked sternly, "Who are you?" He could tell something wasn't right: I called Mrs Möller "Mutti", yet here I was singing along with them in Yiddish. Not only that, but I was wearing the Polish sign.'

Mala had always kept the yellow patch with the purple 'P' on it, and as soon as the Americans arrived, she had pinned it to her clothes again. Mutti did not comment on this, and seemed to understand that, under the circumstances, Mala thought it was better to be seen as Polish than German. Now Mala wanted to let the soldiers know she was Jewish, too, but without revealing her secret to the others.

'Of course, I sang along with them in the hope that they would understand that I was Jewish. But the soldier was so gruff that I started to cry again. It was such a crazy situation. For years I had been terrified of being unmasked, afraid people would discover that I was Jewish. And now here I was in the same house as Jewish soldiers, but on the side of the enemy. Not really, of course, but still ... it was so confusing. I ran back down into the cellar.'

While Mala was struggling desperately with her existential plight, Otto Möller had also arrived at the farmhouse, having ditched his Volkssturm armband. His efforts to defend Zerbst had come to nothing, but at least he had survived the blaze unscathed. In the cellar, he told everyone they should thank their lucky stars that the Americans had reached them before the Russians. He saw Mala in tears and went back upstairs to assess the situation, but returned almost immediately, looking shocked. He told Mala the soldiers were looking for her and that she should hide immediately. Everyone tried to help. At first, Mala went along with this plan and tried one hiding place after another, but suddenly she stopped, told the others not to worry, and climbed the stairs alone, closing the cellar door behind her.

Mala had decided to convince the soldiers that she was Jewish, though after years spent concealing her background, she had no idea how.

'Upstairs, I told them I only wanted to talk to the Jews. Three of the soldiers were Jewish, two weren't. The non-Jewish soldiers put an arm around the shoulder of their Jewish comrades. "We are one," a soldier said in Yiddish. "It's safe for you to talk." I had to tell my story to all five of them. Yiddish and German are similar, and after speaking nothing but German for months, my Yiddish was peppered with German words, and they didn't believe me right away.'

However, they were intrigued. They asked Mala which Jewish festival they had just celebrated. Having lost all track of the Jewish calendar, she didn't know. The soldiers thought this was suspect. Pesach or Passover had just come and gone; in 1945 it fell in the period from 28 March to 5 April. When Mala couldn't answer, one of the soldiers asked her how she had celebrated Pesach in the past. Mala told them about the *seder*, about reading from the *Haggadah*, drinking four cups of wine, about bitter herbs and unleavened bread. Then one of the soldiers fetched a book of Hebrew prayer, a *siddur*. Mala read from it without any difficulty.

The soldiers were wide-eyed with wonder. That, at least, is how Mala remembers it. 'As I read, I could see out of the corner of my eye that all five of them were moved to tears.' To her astonishment, the non-Jewish soldiers seemed to be even more emotional than the Jews.

She told them her story: about the ghetto, how she had rescued her little brother, Meir, how an SS officer had beaten her, how her sister lived in the home of a Jewish doctor in Karpy. 'I also told them how the Germans had driven Jews from the villages and forced all Jews into ghettos. They told me what they had heard about Warsaw. That the ghetto there had been razed, that everyone had been sent to the gas chambers. I couldn't believe them. It was all too terrible. Besides, I knew Germans. They just weren't like that. I knew they had done terrible things in Poland, but nothing that horrific.

'They wanted to know how pro-Nazi this German family were. Because the Möllers had only ever shown me kindness, I lied. They had been like parents to me, they really had. Besides, I just couldn't believe that they were a military threat. They worshipped Hitler, of course, they were absolutely mad about him, but why should I tell the Americans that?

'The soldiers advised me not to go back to Poland, and offered me their help to get to America. They wrote me a letter to give to a senior US officer. He was Jewish, too, they said, and they told me where to find him. They assured me I would be able to travel with a transport of wounded soldiers.'

The soldiers showered Mala with presents, and even gave her a diamond bracelet. She knew most of these things must have been confiscated from Germans, and she was reluctant to accept them — 'in my eyes, it was all worth so much' — but they insisted, and in the end she did. 'At the time, you never knew what tomorrow might bring.' She also took the letter they had written for her. 'But I didn't go looking for the officer they mentioned. I couldn't believe that my whole family was dead, so I didn't want to go to America. Besides, I wanted to find Erich.'

The soldiers sat Mala on a tank in front of the farmhouse and took a photograph of her. She then rejoined the family in the cellar and, switching back to German, told them the Americans were impressed that they, the Möllers, had been so kind as to give a Polish girl a place in their family. She said nothing else about what had happened upstairs, and her silence may have fed the stories young Wilfried Spahr heard in the years that followed, about soldiers from the Red Army who had come looking for her. It was true that soldiers had been looking for Mala and that the Möllers had tried to hide her, but the family would always wonder what had happened to her when she went upstairs to see the soldiers of her own free will. She never told the Möllers she was Jewish, and they never heard her speak Yiddish with the Americans.

What were the chances of the American soldiers at the farmhouse in Bias being Jewish? Not as slim as I initially thought. During the Second World War, some 550,000 Jewish Americans served in the US armed forces. In other words, over half a million American soldiers had an 'H' for 'Hebrew' on the metal dog tag around their necks. A staggering statistic: it means that about 11 per cent of the Jewish community in the United States heeded the call to arms at some point.

This data is to be found in *GI Jews*, a book by Deborah Dash Moore. The author helped me search for the three Jewish soldiers who encountered Mala at the Bias farmhouse in April 1945. It soon became clear that the men belonged to the 329th Infantry Regiment, part of the 83rd 'Thunderbolt' Division of the US Army that, following the Battle of the Bulge, advanced swiftly to Berlin and then on as far as Zerbst.

Dash Moore remembers a soldier from the 329th telling her about a meeting very like the one with Mala, though he probably was not there in person. 'Yes, I doubt that would have been the case,' the soldier's son, a historian, confirms. 'Otherwise he would have told me about it. I mean, it's quite a spectacular story.'

The soldier in question, Harold Freeman, was born and raised on the East River, the stretch of water that divides Brooklyn from Manhattan. He worked for the Army Signal Corps, the section of the army that takes care of communication links. In this capacity, he was not obliged to fight overseas, and to begin with that was fine with him. But in 1943 he felt compelled to put words into action. As a committed socialist, he had been warning his friends about Hitler for years. In his view, America couldn't declare war on Nazi Germany quickly enough. Nazism, he said, was a more demonic force than capitalism. In addition, the Soviet Union had become an ally of the US, and since 1942, Freeman had been wise to information that confirmed his worst fear: the mass murder of the Jews.

The realisation hit that the world his parents had come from was being wiped out. 'In a romantic vein,' he wrote to his wife Bea, 'I likened my voyage to Europe to a crusade to combat the very forces of evil that some 40 years ago had plagued my parents.' Around the turn of the twentieth century, his parents had left Piotrków Trybunalski, a

Polish town where Jews once accounted for up to 30 per cent of the population.

Freeman, who saw months of frontline combat, told Dash Moore that in Germany a group of men from his platoon, battalion, division, or regiment had met a girl who was 'pretty and half-Jewish'. They found her, Freeman told her, in a house with two women, one of whom had a son who had been killed on the eastern front. The identity of the soldiers in Freeman's account can no longer be ascertained. At the time of writing, Freeman is 101 years old, and his son explains that he is no longer able to talk about his memories.

My first reaction was that this couldn't have been Mala. After all, she was not half-Jewish. But two years of research, scores of contradictions, and countless memoirs have expanded my view of what is possible. Not only could this conclusion be explained by the turbulent passage of time and the vagaries of memory, but also by the confusion that Mala herself may have caused. The soldiers heard her call one of the German women in the house 'Mutti'. And when asked why a German family would take her in as their own daughter, she told them: because they think I'm a Volksdeutsche from Poland.

This assertion prompted more questions: how had she become a Volksdeutsche? It was a status given to her by the Nazi Immigration Centre. Would they really have given that label to a girl who was 100 per cent Jewish? That must have seemed unlikely.

Another thing about Mala that didn't quite add up was that, although she spoke Yiddish and knew her prayers, she defended the German family. That was something the Americans were not used to. In France and Belgium, they had liberated Jews who had survived the war by going into hiding with French and Belgian citizens. Every last one of them cursed the Germans. Later, they had encountered the Jewish survivors of concentration camps such as Ohrdruf, people who looked nothing like Mala, and not just because of her blue-green eyes and fair hair. Barely clinging to life after everything they had endured, those survivors were in themselves a living indictment of the Germans, an indictment beyond words. They had no trouble believing that the Jewish community in Warsaw had been wiped out and that almost everyone was dead. Yet, when the Americans told this to Mala, she refused to believe them. Of course the Germans had done terrible things, she had seen them with her own eyes, but she did not think them capable of murder on such a scale. And she said this to the American soldiers.

In light of all this, Freeman's conclusion that the girl was half-Jewish is not hard to understand.

Unfortunately, no descendants of the veterans of the 329th were able to provide me with confirmation of Mala's story, much less trace the photograph of Mala on a tank. Harold Freeman's son confirms that his father spoke Yiddish, but also says he could not be the soldier with the mezuzah around his neck. He was 'entirely secular' and had no qualms about 'eating ham for Uncle Sam', to quote a basketball cheer of the time. The trail of Mala and the Jewish GIs ends here.

* * *

Mala knew that being Jewish carried the death penalty. She was also aware that in America things were different, and that non-Jews were capable of love and kindness. What she was not aware of, and had never experienced, was an ordinary, pleasurable, or even loving interaction between Jews and non-Jews. The friendliness shown to her by Poles and Germans stemmed from the fact that she lied about who she was. Amid the friendliness, she heard those same Poles and Germans — not least, Ela and the Möllers — say the most terrible things about Jews. For Mala, mutual aversion had been the norm. In her own family, too, hardly anyone had felt the need to associate with non-Jews. 'For my father, even having dealings with a non-Orthodox Jew was a problem.' Apart from brother-in-law Henryk Trager and her mother's mysterious white-suited cousin, assimilated or assimilating Jews barely featured in Mala's life. 'We are one.' That statement made by the non-Jewish soldiers and their Jewish brothers-in-arms at the farmhouse in Bias knocked her sideways and was something she would never forget. They put their arms around each other's shoulders to show her that they belonged together.

Of course, this was far from proof that America was free of anti-Semitism. In the 1930s, many members of Congress were openly anti-Semitic. Universities worked with quotas to restrict the number of Jews among the student population, newspapers were full of job vacancies to which 'only Christians' needed apply, and not all property or land could be sold to Jews. Father Charles Coughlin, a Roman Catholic priest with a popular radio show, railed against American Jews on a weekly basis, tarring them with the same brush as communists, supporters of Roosevelt's New Deal, and other traitors. In September 1941, aviator Charles Lindbergh, an enormously popular public figure and an admirer of Nazi Germany, gave a speech in Des Moines, Iowa, in which he entreated the American people not to let themselves be dragged into a world war, a speech in which he portrayed the Jews as a danger to the country, thanks to 'their large ownership and influence in our motion pictures, our press, our radio, and our government'.

But as awareness of Germany's crimes grew among American citizens, so too did the unease that they and their authorities felt about their own anti-Semitism. On top of this, half a million Jews in the US Army did a great deal to diminish anti-Semitism in American society. In *GI Jews*, Dash Moore makes the point that the concept of a 'Judeo-Christian tradition', often taken as a given today, was partly a product of military expediency. The US armed forces introduced the term in its newspapers during the Second World War, and it was soon adopted by the mainstream press.

Through the twin concepts of 'Judeo-Christian tradition' and 'Judeo-Christian civilisation', the heads of the American armed forces sought to boost motivation among their troops. This need was something they had identified during the First World War, when a great many fighting men found themselves asking fundamental questions about why they were risking their lives. The rank and file began to wonder whether they had more in common with the men they were shooting than with the officer classes who sent them over the top and into the line of fire. To avoid similar tensions this time round, the Second World War had to be seen to serve an inspiring and ideologically sound purpose. The emphasis in articles written for the fighting men therefore came to rest on the struggle to defeat dictatorship and barbarism, and to uphold democracy, 'Judeo-Christian civilisation', and the 'Judeo-Christian tradition'.

Of course, the unthinkable atrocities committed by the Germans did much to further this cause: there was no need to exaggerate the crimes of the enemy. But a concerted effort was needed to give substance to the Judeo-Christian tradition. For most Catholics, Protestants, and Jews, the only traditions they had shared for centuries had been mutual distrust, exclusion, and worse. The US Army's drive to turn this around as a motivational tool for its forces was so successful that, as Dash Moore wrote in 2004, what 'was largely a creation of the American military in World War II' is nowadays assumed by 'educated Americans' to be 'a real tradition, that has existed for centuries.'

While it is important to acknowledge that brotherhood for all was first and foremost an ideal and not a reality, countless stories from that time show American soldiers doing their best to put that ideal into practice. Ideas have consequences. Take the actions of Master Sergeant Roddie Edmonds, who does not appear in the book *GI Jews*, but is featured in a 2017 documentary of the same name. Edmonds wound up in a German prisoner-of-war camp. Ahead of a roll call, the camp commandant ordered that only the Jewish prisoners were to assemble. Edmonds refused, and instead ordered all the American camp inmates to line up. In answer to the furious response of the Nazi commandant, he said, 'We are all Jews here.' The commandant drew his pistol. What happened next may seem too much like a Hollywood movie to be true, but many eye-witness accounts confirm it. 'Major, you can shoot me,' Edmonds said, with the barrel of the gun pointing at his head, 'but you will have to kill all of us … and you will be tried for war crimes when we win this war.' The German camp commandant muttered something under his breath, turned, and stormed off.

Mala was shocked that the soldiers to whom she revealed her secret did not immediately believe that she was Jewish. What she didn't know was that they had been drilled in distrust. In France, they had been allowed to celebrate with the liberated civilians, but as they pushed forward into Germany, they were under strict orders not to display the same behaviour. The German people had brought Hitler to power, and so suspicion was the only appropriate response. Anti-fraternisation measures were in place: Germany was no place for brotherly understanding. In the spring of 1945, all American soldiers were shown a thirteen-minute instruction film, *Your Job in Germany*. Over a soundtrack of Beethoven, a sombre male voice intones: 'Keep your wits about you. Don't relax that caution now ... The German lust for conquest is not dead.' The film shows magnificent landscapes and well-dressed people with fair skin and fair hair. The voice-over continues, 'Somewhere in this Germany there are two million ex-Nazi officials.' Out of uniform, 'you won't know them, but they'll know you.' As the camera shows scenes of children playing, the sombre voice says, 'These are the most dangerous: German youth. Children, when the Nazi party came into power. They know no other system but the one that poisoned their minds. They're soaked in it.' Do not argue with them or try to change their point of view, the voice warns, and more importantly 'you will not be friendly. You will be aloof, watchful and suspicious ... Fraternization means making friends. The German people are not our friends. You will not associate yourself with German men, women, or children ... Trust none of them.'

GIs were not allowed to clasp the hand of the Germans in friendship, to play sports with them, or receive gifts from them. Nor were they to accompany them in the street or kick a ball around with them.

Among Jewish soldiers there was broad support for these anti-fraternisation measures. For Akiva Skidell, who like Freeman wrote to his wife in Brooklyn, complying with them was no hardship. He was repelled by the Germans. He even loathed the children, 'tho [sic] I know well enough that they are not to blame.' Germans were at their worst when they whined and proclaimed their innocence, Skidell wrote. He called them 'expert t.l.ers', which stood for *tukhes-lekers*. First-class arse-lickers, in other words.

Imagine Skidell in that German house in Bias, confronted with a blonde, well-dressed, well-fed teenager who claimed to be Jewish yet called a German woman 'Mutti' ...

The concentration camps made a deep impression on every American soldier, high-ranking or low-ranking, Jewish, Christian or unbeliever. Nothing could have prepared them; everyone was sickened by what they saw. While inspecting Ohrdruf, a satellite camp of Buchenwald liberated at the start of April by the regiment to which the soldiers in Zerbst belonged, General George Patton was physically sick, and a witness said of General Dwight Eisenhower that 'he was green, actually green'. Eisenhower later wrote to a fellow general, 'the things I saw beggar description.' The writer J.D. Salinger, of Lithuanian Jewish descent, served with the 12th infantry regiment when it liberated Kaufering IV, a subcamp of Dachau. Decades later, he told his daughter, 'You can never really get the smell of burning flesh out of your nose entirely, no matter how long you live.' US Army reporter and later TV executive Sergeant Fred W. Friendly wrote in a letter home that he would never forget the strange sound of men clapping who had no flesh on their hands. And Henry (real name Heinz) Kissinger, who fled the Nazis with his Jewish parents and who returned as a soldier to the German Fürth of his youth, decided then and for all time to assume the worst in human beings, a promise the staunch realpolitiker and winner of the Nobel Peace Prize always kept.

The time spent among those who had barely survived the horrors inflicted by the SS, the Nazi regime, and Germany was very important for the camaraderie between Jewish and non-Jewish soldiers. The man who had shown Eisenhower around Ohrdruf, Sergeant David Cohen, later wrote 'I felt good as a Jew to see these officers and men had the same feeling I did.'

The horrors of the camps stoked American distrust of the German people. All this suffering was their fault: they had made it possible, turned a blind eye. For all the GIs knew, the Germans whose house they were commandeering had been party to these crimes against humanity. In any case, their sense of revulsion was enough to make them wary if a girl in a German family claimed to be Jewish. At the same time, the solidarity kindled by their own army's propaganda and consolidated by horrors they witnessed was strong enough that, when Mala asked to speak only to Jews, a group of Jewish and Christian soldiers responded by throwing their arms round each other's shoulders and insisting, 'We are one.'

Instead of footnotes

Almost all of the Americans who captured Zerbst have since died. Neither those who survive, nor the descendants of the deceased GIs I contacted, had any recollection of a photograph of a young Jewish girl on a tank. The National Museum of American Jewish Military History in Washington DC has no record of such a photo. One of the three Yiddish-speaking soldiers at the farmhouse in Bias was probably Sidney Fink, a soldier in the 3rd battalion of the 329th infantry regiment. Sidney was not much of a letter writer, and said little about his wartime experiences later in life. His descendants know nothing about the meeting with Mala in Bias. He passed away in his hometown of Scranton, Pennsylvania, in 2002.

The senior officer to whom Mala was supposed to give the letter written on her behalf by the GIs must have been Samuel Magill, a lieutenant colonel with the 329th who took care of Jewish survivors. Magill died in 2013, in Munich. While he helped thousands of Jews leave Europe, this Jewish American eventually decided after living in several different places to make his home in Germany.

The US armed forces' anti-fraternisation campaign ended up being a partial failure. In the autumn of 1945, a US Army survey revealed that over a quarter of its soldiers had engaged in sexual intercourse with a German woman. In April and May, sex mainly meant rape, around 500 cases a week, according to the army's own estimates, but by July and August most of the sex was consensual. Akiva Skidell, the soldier in this chapter who was repelled by all things German, was exasperated by his fellow GIs' reluctance to stay away from the local women. In a letter to his wife, Ettie, he wrote that he could think of only one mitigating circumstance: some of the men 'say [sex] isn't fraternization anyway—as long as you don't talk. And talking isn't essential.'

Deborah Dash Moore, whose book *GI Jews* is a key source for this chapter, helped me in my search for the American soldiers who spoke to Mala in Bias, as did Rachel Weinstein, Avinoam Patt, and Joshua Freeman, the son of Harold Freeman. Unfortunately, our efforts were in vain.

11

The Volga

'The death of one man: that is a catastrophe. A hundred thousand deaths: that is a statistic!'

–French diplomat in 'Französischer Witz',
an essay by Kurt Tucholsky

To examine the shifting front lines in Europe towards the end of the Second World War is to see the incredible speed at which the Third Reich imploded from December 1944. Before Christmas, the Red Army was east of the Vistula, and the armies under the command of the Americans and the British were still locked in battle in the Belgian Ardennes. But less than four months later, the advancing Soviet and American forces met in the German heartland. The meeting took place only a few kilometres from Zerbst and just across the River Elbe, some 120 kilometres from Berlin. On 30 April 1945, Hitler took his own life.

Few in Germany had expected things to move so fast. Mala certainly hadn't. In the autumn of 1944, she was still enjoying romantic excursions with Erich around Magdeburg, chaperoned by her anti-Semitic Polish friend Ela. The war felt distant, and those days among the placid beauty of nature seemed endless. Erich, the aviation engineer, had been looking forward to Christmas, when he would take his beautiful German-speaking Polish sweetheart to meet his parents. At least, that was the plan.

The bombs that rained down on Magdeburg put paid to everything. That fateful day came shortly after Mala's return from Reichenberg, the trip that had given her the official status of a Volksdeutsche. She fled the bombs and the chaos, and was taken in by the Möllers in Zerbst. And that same evening, folding her clothes in the bedroom of the Möllers' missing son, she realised that she had left Erich's letters behind.

The shock of this realisation was like a knife to the heart: without those letters she had no address. 'It was a crushing blow,' Mala remembers. 'At that time, Erich was the most important thing in my life.'

The last time she had spoken to him was on 13 December, before her trip to Reichenberg. She had gone to see him in Halle, travelling by train and turning up unannounced. By that time, she couldn't bear to be without him. 'It was driving me mad.' In a letter, Erich had explained that the division of Junkers where he worked had gone underground in the city, and gave her the address of his lodgings. An older woman opened the door to her and recognised Mala immediately as the girl in the photograph on Erich's bedside table. The woman let her in, and they drank coffee together.

Erich hadn't been lodging with her long, the woman said, but he had already told her all about Mala. Why didn't she call him? The landlady had Erich's work number, and there was a phone at the post office. They went there together.

'When I heard Erich's voice, I couldn't say a word,' Mala remembers. And so it was Erich who spoke. He tried to calm her. He told her to go back to Magdeburg, and promised he would write again soon. Then Erich's landlady took Mala to the station. Mala was bitterly upset. She couldn't stop the tears.

Back at the Bierhaus, Ela immediately saw the state her friend was in. She did her best to lift Mala's spirits, but it was no use. In the end, Ela suggested they go to the pictures. And that's what they did. 'I couldn't sit there crying all day, now could I?'

Erich's promised letter arrived a few days later. He said he was very sorry, but he was unable to come and see her. There was nothing to be done; the country was at war, after all. He hoped that they would still be able to spend Christmas together at his parents' home.

Mala and Erich never saw or spoke to each other again.

* * *

I travel to Magdeburg, not only to see the prison and the Bierhaus, but also to discover what happened to Erich after the war. The chance that he is still alive is slim. Mala, in her nineties, thinks Erich must have been at least ten years older than she was. And working at a German aviation plant, there is every chance he did not survive the Allied bombardments in the final weeks of the war.

When she hears his name, the archivist in Magdeburg can't help but smile: Erich Schulze is the German equivalent of John Smith in English. But, buoyed by my success, I gamely plough my way through the addresses I find in the wartime telephone directories. Unfortunately, Erich turns out to be more elusive than the Möllers, not least because Mala has given me far less to go on. I return to my notes again and again, and the same scant details stare back at me: engineer ... worked at Junkers ... stationed in Halle at the end of the war ... a critical NSDAP member involved in the manufacture of fighter planes ... wore a green hat with a feather in it.

For a long time, I dismissed this last detail as evidence of an outmoded dress sense, but the German historians I speak to immediately associate Erich's headgear with a love of hunting. Alas, the federal hunting association tell me they no longer have records from the Second World War, so even this unexpected lead runs cold. I seize on another snippet of information: Erich once told Mala that his parents ran a furniture store. I consult the 1943 telephone directory, which is practically identical to the 1938 directory, except for a sharp rise in the number of widows. German telephone directories from back in the day reveal more about a business owner than just their name and address. These bonus details also enable me to pick out engineers called Erich Schulze from all the other Erich Schulzes.

Having scanned for furniture stores and skimmed through the ads, I head for Cecilienstrasse 39, only to find that it must have been destroyed by the bombs in 1945. The building that has taken its place is boarded up. And so I move on to Grusonstrasse 7b, still home to someone by the name of Schulze. No relation, it turns out. One particularly promising lead takes me to Hospitalstrasse and what was the home in 1940 of retired furniture-maker Walter Schulze. He lived there with his wife and their son, Erich. This, too, turns out to be a dead end: different Schulzes.

My next line of inquiry is Junkers Flugzeug- und Motorenwerke, the aircraft and motor works founded by pacifist Hugo Junkers. In 1936, one year after his death, the Nazis nationalised the company, which employed 40,000 people at the time. One of the best-known Junkers aircraft is the trimotor Ju–52, nicknamed 'Auntie Ju' and known for its distinctive corrugated body. A transport plane, it was used to drop parachutists during German air offensives. At the Halle plant, Erich worked on new models of another well-known Junkers aircraft, the Ju–87, also known as the Stuka dive bomber. One of its distinguishing features was a piercing siren, which increased in volume as it dived. This was by no means a design flaw: the aim was to trigger a stampede of panicked civilians and add to the chaos on the ground.

American aviator Charles Lindbergh was impressed by Junkers. He visited the company's factories shortly before war broke out and, brimming with admiration, told his British friends that Germany was well on its way to becoming the world leader in aviation, if it wasn't already. In the summer of 1945, he paid the company another visit, this time under the protection of US troops. He left the equipment, but took all of the company's paperwork, everything from blueprints to the payroll administration—which must have included Erich's details. Frustratingly, the documents Lindbergh took back with him to the United States have disappeared without trace. Even after the fall of the Berlin Wall, German aviation experts and historians were unable to track down the archive material. 'Top secret' is the official line taken by the US authorities. But the current consensus among those in the know is that 'secret' could well be a euphemism for 'lost or destroyed'.

Two years and countless emails later, I pick up Erich's trail after all, thanks to a German journalist in Berlin—the same chap who saw the Möller's grandson Wilfried as the embodiment of post-war Biedermeier culture. He finds a reference to Erich in a CIA information report, based on an interview with a Russian defector in 1950. The report was released in 2001, long after the end of the Cold War, and can be accessed online. We stare at the screen in disbelief, then read and re-read what we have found. A rapid-fire exchange of ideas leads us to the same conclusion: it's him!

CIA involvement makes it sound like the stuff of thrillers, but this particular report is short on high-octane espionage. The agency had someone draw up a thirty-nine-page account of aircraft production in the small Russian town of Podberezye: how it was organised, who reported to whom, and the make-up of the various teams. The aircraft development facility in Podberezye (spelled 'Podberesje' in the report) was largely staffed by German specialists who had been brought to the Soviet Union in October 1946. Among the list of employees, the name 'Erich Schulz' appears, a German working in a machine workshop with about twenty of his fellow countrymen and some 250 Soviet citizens. He is listed as a 'layout man', which means he transferred the engineers' designs to the production material, which was then cut and welded. More to the point, in 1946 Erich Schulz had been working at the Junkers factory in Halle.

He may be an 'e' short of the surname supplied by Mala, but Erich Schulz is our man. He was whisked off to Podberezye as part of Operation Osoaviakhim, a paramilitary operation led by the Soviet NKVD, a predecessor of the KGB. In the course of a single night and a single day, 2,000 scientists, engineers, and highly skilled workers were taken from their homes. They were told they were going to serve the advancement of communism, and were permitted to bring their families and even some of their household goods. This was not a punitive exercise: members of the Communist Party were also required to cooperate.

In addition to key people and the expertise they brought with them, the Soviets seized everything they thought might serve the further development of the nation: machines, sketches, laboratories, aircraft, and even tools. Much of it ended up beyond the Urals in Kuybyshev, present-day Samara, the centre of the Russian aerospace industry at the time. Even four complete wind tunnels were dismantled and loaded onto trains. The Soviets saw the operation as part and parcel of the reparations the Allies had imposed on Germany at their joint conferences. The amount Germany owed had yet to be fixed, and not long after the capitulation it became clear that agreement on this issue would not be forthcoming any time soon, if at all. Stalin decided not to wait. While Western Europe — including the French, British, and American occupation zones in Germany — was gearing up to receive Marshall aid, German infrastructure was being dismantled on an epic scale in the Soviet occupation zone.

The Russians had over 4,000 of the 17,000 major companies and factories in the Soviet zone shipped east by rail as Ikea-style self-assembly kits. As for underground factories like the one in Halle, the Soviets often blew up the entrances, to hammer home the message that the rise of communism in their own Soviet federation also meant the demolition of Germany. Their approach was a mix of reparation, looting, punitive measures, and communist propaganda. A popular ditty in the Soviet occupation zone at the time sums things up: 'You liberate us from everything, from cars and machines / Watches, rings, and other things. / We cry for joy.'

The Germans spirited off to Russia were there to ensure the expansion and modernisation of the Soviet Union's air force. These engineers, former employees of Heinkel, Siebel, and Junkers, were paid a salary and were not treated as prisoners. In Podberezye, they even earned more than their Soviet colleagues. Since they had signed a contract, often on the train heading east, this could hardly be called 'forced labour', yet most of them had been seized in the dead of night or at the crack of dawn, and refusal had not been a genuine option. Spouses who did not want to accompany their partners were allowed to remain in Germany, and some of them did.

The US intelligence services report the case of one Dr Ludwig, which illustrates the terms and conditions offered. Ludwig worked at an AGFA nylon factory in Wolfen, between Zerbst and Halle. Nylon was considered important for the textile industry in the Soviet Union. One week after Erich's deportation to the Soviet Union, Ludwig was approached on the street by a Russian in civilian clothes and presented with two contracts. The first read, 'The undersigned obligates himself to assist in the reconstruction of the Soviet Union by going to Russia and working for two years in building up the Nylon Works. In return, the undersigned will receive the double allowance of 1,500 rubles or 3,000 marks per month.' That was a huge sum in those days. 'Families do not have to go. Quarters with hard and soft furniture will be available.' The second contract simply read, 'The undersigned herewith declares his unwillingness to assist in the reconstruction of the Soviet Union.' The Russian told Ludwig he was free to choose, but Ludwig knew all too well how 'free' this choice was. He left for Russia.

During Operation Osoaviakhim, the city of Halle — where Erich worked — was the only place where the Soviets had to resort to force. There, NKVD units had to actively pursue factory employees who tried to escape deportation. Some even had to be clubbed into submission before they abandoned their attempts to resist.

News of those beatings did not reach the Western press, but the operation itself did. German newspapers in the British and American zones of Berlin alleged kidnapping on a large scale. Reports like these angered the Soviets, who vented their frustrations in the Berlin consultations between the Allied occupying forces: why was press criticism reserved only for Russia's recruitment drive, when other countries were doing the same? In Operation Paperclip, hadn't the Americans laid claim to leading German engineers, not least rocket scientist and SS man Wernher von Braun? (Braun went on to become the driving force behind the US space programme that put the first man on the moon in 1969.) We kept a lid on things during the American operation, the Soviets said. Why couldn't the Americans keep their own press under control?

Podberezye means 'under the birches'. Russia is full of birch trees, and it's a name shared by dozens of towns and villages across the country. These particular birches stand on a peninsula between the Volga and the Ivankovo Reservoir. Podberezye's houses now form a suburb of Dubna, a city that lies on the Moscow Canal, dug by Gulag prisoners in the 1930s. When the German engineers lived there, giant statues of Soviet heroes stood by the canal and were lit up at night. Where the Volga flows into the canal, a fifteen-metre statue of Lenin was erected. It survives to this day, and is now the largest Lenin in all

that the engineers were mainly waiting for their return to Germany, something the Soviets had repeatedly assured them would happen, although no one knew when. When that day could come tomorrow, why make the effort to adapt or build a life for yourself? This state of suspended animation dampened motivation and morale. At the end of 1949, various Russian observers reported that the German engineers saw their work at the plant as temporary and a matter of coercion. As a result, the mood within the collective was dominated by the desire to return home, and, with the exception of a small group, their work was slow, sloppy, and demonstrated little in the way of initiative.

None of the memoirists write about Erich Schulz, so I track them down and call them up. Although no one has personal impressions to share, they confirm his presence in Podberezye. His name also appears in a Russian document that one of the Podberezye deportees obtained at a reunion in Russia. While the Junkers documents confiscated by Lindbergh seem to have disappeared into thin air, Soviet records listing the engineers brought to Russia have been preserved. Among the names listed is 'Erich Schulte'. The spelling is different, but the biographical details contained in the document all point to our man, Erich Schulz.

Erich was born in 1909 in Dessau, a town halfway between Magdeburg and Halle. He was unmarried when he was enlisted by the Soviets, which made him an exception within the group of German engineers. In Podberezye he lived at 39 Lenin Street, where he shared a house with two families, the Nebels and the Heinzes.

> Education: Mechanical engineering school
> Marital status: Single
> Place of work: Experimental Design Bureau no. 1 (OKB–1)
> Role: Group leader

The most striking detail is Erich's year of birth. This makes him thirty-five when he tipped his green hat with the feather on it to an eighteen-year-old girl on the platform at Wolmirstedt railway station and struck up a conversation. According to Mala, he still lived with his parents.

These new details make my search easier, not only in the municipal archives in Dessau, but also in Halle and Magdeburg. Yet I find nothing, not even when I enlist some serious help. The trail left by Erich Schulz appears to run cold in Russia. Somewhere in that vast country, he disappears. Perhaps, unlike the overwhelming majority of the German engineers who lived under the birch trees, he assimilated or at least integrated into the local population. Perhaps he struck up a conversation with another girl on another railway platform; Mala insists that he was by no means racist.

The only possible lead I find, in a place not far from Dubna, is a public house with the German name 'Bierhof'. According to the local records office, it is registered in the name of 'Henrich Schulz'. A couple of phone calls to the pub are enough to dampen my enthusiasm. 'Oh, it's just a name,' the barmaid says. As the owner explains to me later, it's a name with an air of dependability about it. 'There's no German grand-dad around here.'

Instead of footnotes

The chapter's opening quote—'The death of one man: that is a catastrophe. A hundred thousand deaths: that is a statistic!'—is often attributed to Stalin. This first occurred in a 1947 column in *The Washington Post* and has since been repeated thousands of times in various forms. However, there is no credible evidence from Stalin's inner circle to suggest that he ever spoke these words. The Tucholsky essay in which this line is attributed to a French diplomat dates from 1925.

Much of the information on the Soviet occupation zone in Germany in this chapter comes from the book by Norman Naimark mentioned in the notes to Chapter 9.

The memoirs of the children of Podberezye are Klaus H.A. Jacob's self-published book *Bevorich's vergessen könnte: Ein Bericht aus meiner Zeit* (*Before I Could Forget: a report from my time*), 2016; Heinrich Sparrer's *Chronik des Deutschen Schachclubs Podberesje 1946–1950* (*Chronicle of the German Chess Club in Podberezye 1946–1950*), 1981; Dieter Scheller's *Abenteuer Podberesje* (*Podberezye Adventure*), 2016; Helmut Belitz's account on the website of the Haida family (s.a.); Renate Clausnitzer's *Reiseziel unbekannt. Zeitzeugenbericht über das Leben deutscher Flugzeugbauer, die nach dem Zweiten Weltkrieg in die Sowjetunion deportiert wurden* (Destination Unknown: contemporary witness report on the life of German aircraft manufacturers deported to the Soviet Union after the Second World War), 2017.

Another important source was Christoph Mick's book, *Forschen für Stalin: Deutsche Fachleute in der sowjetischen Rüstungsindustrie, 1945–1958* (Research for Stalin: German experts in the Soviet armaments industry 1945–1958), 2000.

I received help from Konrad Eulitz, the son of one of the Germans brought to Podberezye, who has become an expert on all of the German aviation personnel who were shipped to Russia. His lecture 'Deutsche Luftfahrtspezialisten in der UdSSR 1946–1956. Entführung oder Deportation' ('German Aviation Specialists in the USSR 1946–1956: abduction or deportation'), which he mainly gives to Rotary Clubs across Europe, proved to be very helpful.

The CIA report that includes the name 'Erich Schluz' can be found at https://archive.org/stream/CIA-RDP81-01028R000100100011-7/CIA-RDP81-01028R000100100011-7_djvu.txt.

Klaus Jacob supplied me with the photograph of the Russian document that contains the name and details of Erich Schulz. I must also thank Hubert Smeets, who speaks Russian and made the telephone calls that aided my search for possible descendants of Erich around Dubna and Tver, by the Moscow Canal.

12
Return to the Vistula

'It seemed to me that I was walking on corpses, that at any
moment I would step into a pool of blood.'

–Janina Godycka-Ćwirko, writer

Mala had gone back to wearing a 'P' for Pole on her coat. Her status
as an ethnic German had been short lived, and it is worth asking
what good it did her. True, she had been more comfortably off and
better fed than her Polish friends from the Magdeburg Bierhaus who
had been put to work at the munitions factory in Zerbst. And, with
hindsight, she had been safer. Paradoxically, the closer you were to
the centre of power, the smaller your risk of being unmasked. This
was just as well, because Mala had been heard speaking Yiddish in her
sleep again. When the air-raid alarm sounded one night, the Möllers
had dashed into Mala's room and heard their Volksdeutsche speaking
a foreign language—not German, but not Polish either. In the
morning, they asked her, 'Did you know you speak an odd language
in your sleep?'

Most Polish and Ukrainian workers would have recognised Yiddish
in an instant. The Möllers, however, had probably never even met a Jew,
and their view of all things Jewish had been formed by propaganda, not
least the posters on display throughout the country depicting Jews as
hunched little men with sinister smiles and huge noses. In the entire

twentieth century, Jews had never accounted for more than 1 per cent of Germany's population.

What about Zerbst, where the Möllers lived? In 1933, the town was home to sixty Jews, all of whom spoke German. By 1939, that number had fallen to less than half: from the moment Hitler came to power, the number of Jews in Germany plummeted. Of the twenty-nine who stayed on in Zerbst, only one woman survived the Holocaust. She returned from a women's internment camp in May 1945, unable to relay any information about the fate of the town's other Jews. She had lost her mind.

Mala was relieved that the Möllers had not recognised her sleep-talking as Yiddish, but was terrified she might give herself away again. From then on, she put a chair behind the bedroom door. This habit stuck with her even after the Americans arrived and she had no real reason to fear discovery. She knew the tables had turned.

This became abundantly clear after she and the Möllers said goodbye to the family in Bias and returned home to Zerbst. That same night, Mala got up to go to the toilet. Crossing the hallway, she saw Otto, Emma, and their grown-up daughter in the living room. They were burning documents in the open hearth, and were clearly startled to see her. Mala reassured them immediately. There was no need to worry, she said. She had told the Americans that they were not Nazis.

In the days that followed, Mala only saw the Möllers in the evening. Her days were spent out and about with her Polish friends, especially her anti-Semitic friend Ela. Mala felt no urge to Ela what she had been keeping to herself all this time. She did want to tell the Möllers, who were pleased that Mala came back each night to sleep under their roof. Spooked by tales of foreign workers robbing local houses, they felt safer with Mala around, hoping she would be able to reason with any intruders. She had already sent a couple of Yugoslavians packing when they tried to loot the Kramers' house, telling them to do their stealing somewhere else instead of picking on 'good Germans'.

'Deep down, I wanted to tell the Möllers that a German in the ghetto had beaten me half to death,' Mala says. 'I wanted to ask them what they knew. I wanted to know if they were aware that German soldiers had killed little children.' Uncertainty held her back. 'I didn't know what tomorrow would bring. Or even if there were any Jews left. It occurred to me that I might have to spend the rest of my life with the Möllers. I already had German identity papers.'

And there was Erich, of course. Mala was determined to search for him. 'I was still hopelessly in love.' She fretted about him constantly. 'The Russians were terribly heartless to the Germans. They raped the women and killed the men. Night after night, I dreamt they were about to shoot him and that I threw myself in front of him, screaming "Don't shoot! Don't shoot! He's a good German."'

Mala's Polish friends had moved into the homes of Germans who were now being made to sleep in the barracks and the warehouses that had housed their foreign workers. Her friends were busy making plans to leave for Poland, but Mala was hesitant. 'I still had Erich to find.' She was sure he was looking for her, too. 'Through newspapers or aid organisations. Of course, he was looking for a Polish girl in Magdeburg. How was he to know I was with the Möllers in Zerbst?'

If Erich had gone in search of her before being transported to Russia in the autumn of 1946, he would doubtless have gone to the Bierhaus in Magdeburg. And at the address on Breiter Weg, he would have found only the shell of a bombed-out building.

Things haven't changed much. When I went looking for what was the most popular bar-restaurant in Magdeburg in the first half of the twentieth century, all I found was a gaping hole in the heart of town: a pit about thirty metres long, eight to ten metres wide, and four to five metres deep in the middle.

What options did Erich have? The population was frantically trying to keep the Russians at bay, with varying degrees of success. As a German man looking for a foreign girl, a worker from Poland, his chances of finding her were slim.

Meanwhile, Mala's friends were out on the town most days. Suddenly everyone had money to burn, she remembers. Only her friend Ela had reservations about joining in. Her anti-Semitism was accompanied by a strong sense of decency.

The area between Magdeburg and Zerbst and on to Halle saw some of the worst looting in post-war Germany. Gangs of Poles, Ukrainians,

Balts, and Russians stripped entire villages bare. These liberated labourers took horses, livestock, clocks, pianos, furniture, and even household implements—everything, in fact, that they could load onto the carts and vehicles they commandeered. According to one official estimate, by the autumn of 1945, the number of cattle in the Soviet occupation zone had sunk below 50 per cent of pre-war levels. Another report mentions areas in Saxony 'where villages have no cattle and around 100 villages ... where there is not a chicken left either'. This was a serious problem for German farmers under orders to feed the Red Army.

After the war, around 700,000 Poles found themselves in the Soviet occupation zone, an area that stretched from the Elbe to the new Oder–Neisse line in the east. Around half returned to Poland in those first few months, and Mala was among them. She travelled by horse-drawn cart, in a column that consisted of twelve carts and many more horses.

'Remember I told you what the Americans had said to me about Warsaw?' she says. 'Well, I still couldn't believe it. So I went to Warsaw, to find my family.'

Of course, that meant leaving the Möllers behind. It was hard for Mala to say goodbye. Mrs Möller cried. 'I couldn't see her as an enemy of the Jews,' Mala says. 'All I could see was a remarkable woman who had taken me in as a daughter.' With tears in her eyes, Mala rode off on the bicycle the Möllers had given her for her birthday, the bicycle that had belonged to their youngest son, still missing in action on the eastern front.

Mala travelled homeward with a group of people her own age. Nearly everyone was between fifteen and twenty-five years old. Many of them were couples. Mala stayed close to Ela throughout the journey. The group spent the night in villages that had been abandoned as the Red Army advanced. If they ran into soldiers along the way, they were forced to hand over belongings. The wristwatches were first to go, Mala remembers. Not that her travelling companions felt any great sense of loss, she says. Those same watches had been on German wrists not long before.

The Soviet soldiers were not unfriendly, Mala remembers. They simply explained that they had a right to the watches in exchange for giving the Poles their freedom. They also made one young lad who had raided a shoe shop hand over his spoils — not to them, but to the rest of the group: an ad-hoc lesson in communism. The soldiers looked on approvingly as the young Poles sat around trying on the shoes to find a pair that fitted.

Although she did not feel threatened by the Soviets, Mala understood what was expected of her when one soldier took a dress from her case and held it up to the light, perhaps with a leery twinkle in his eye. The dress had been a present from the Möllers. Mala gave it to him and also accepted the proposition made by another soldier: his horse in exchange for her bicycle. 'It wasn't as if I had a choice.'

She had never sat on a horse before, never mind ridden one. But she was in luck: the animal was docile and obliging enough to go easy on her. 'I rode into Poland on horseback.'

At the border by the Oder, Mala handed her papers to a couple of Soviet soldiers. These were the papers she had been issued by the local policeman in Wolmirstedt, the officer who had been softened up by Stefka, one of the Polish girls from the laundry in Bremen. They stated that Mala was Polish. By this time, she had disposed of the German documents conferred on her by the SS Immigration Centre. On hearing that the trains were still running in Poland, she gave her horse to one of the border guards. 'What was I going to do with a horse?!' Her friend Ela was bound for Łódź, while Mala's next stop was Warsaw. They parted. Ela couldn't stop crying.

On the train, all Mala could think about was Erich. 'He really was the love of my life,' she says. She dozed off and dreamt that Erich was at her side. In her dream, they arrived in Warsaw together and made their way to the home she grew up in, the house at 21 Miła Street. 'Everyone was gathered at the table, and he had a long, wonderful discussion with my father about faith and religion. I dreamt that Erich had sprouted *payot*, you know, curls in front of his ears. Little blond ringlets.' She can't help but laugh. 'Once they get to know Erich, they will all fall in love with him. That's what I thought, or rather what I hoped. Laughable, of course: my father wouldn't even have stood for his daughter coming home with a non-Orthodox Jew. As for Erich, my

big problem was not knowing where to look. I didn't know his parents'
address, and I would never have been able to find that house in Halle
again. At the time, it felt like losing those letters was the worst thing
that had happened to me in the war. That was before I found out that
my whole family had been murdered.'

* * *

On seeing Warsaw again, Mala was overwhelmed by the scale of the
devastation. The city barely existed; everything was in ruins. In the
final summer of the occupation, over a year after the ghetto uprising,
the people of the city had risen up against the Germans under the
leadership of the Armia Krajowa or Home Army, the main Polish
resistance force, which took its orders from the government in exile
in London. The Red Army was only some fifteen kilometres from the
city, but its advance had stalled. The reason for this remains a subject of
heated debate among dozens of historians, who bombard one another
with theories, eyewitness accounts, and official records. One theory
is that Stalin deliberately reined in his forces to allow the Germans
to bring in enough reinforcements to finish off the Polish rebels, the
vast majority of whom were anti-communist and likely to be equally
resistant to Stalin's plans to turn Poland into a Soviet satellite state.
Besides, a fierce battle with the Polish resistance could only deplete the
German forces still further.

Stalin would later tell Churchill that the advancing Soviet troops
had been halted by unexpectedly stiff German resistance near the
Vistula. While neither Stalin nor Churchill count as particularly reliable
sources, an increasing number of historians are nonetheless willing
to consider the truth of this version of events. Whatever the reasons,
without Soviet support, the uprising brought disaster on the city and
the Poles. Over a million people lived in Warsaw at the start of 1944,
but when the Red Army finally crossed the Vistula in January 1945,
it encountered an urban wasteland that was home mainly to rats and
a handful of unbelievably resilient stowaways who emerged from the
ruins. Among them was Władysław Szpilman, a musician who came
to international fame posthumously as the protagonist of *The Pianist*,

Roman Polanski's film of his life. German soldiers had carried out mass executions with estimated death tolls well in excess of 100,000. An SS brigade made up of convicted criminals under the command of Oskar Dirlewanger shot about 40,000 civilians in just two days. The rest of the city's residents were transported out, some 60,000 of them to concentration camps such as Ravensbrück, Mauthausen, and Auschwitz.

The uprising and the mass slaughter have not been forgotten. The reconstructed Warsaw is a city of memorials. Among the younger generation, a cult of commemoration is on the rise, as evidenced by all kinds of T-shirts and graffiti. At one home match, supporters of the football club Legia Warsaw unfurled a giant banner covering an entire stand, which read in English: 'Warsaw, the city that survived its own death.'

The ghetto was even flatter than the rest of the city. When they quashed the ghetto uprising in 1943, the Germans torched the buildings one by one, and later had them demolished. Only the prison remained standing. Later, a concentration camp appeared among the rubble, with the full Nazi complement of watchtowers, barbed wire, barracks, and crematoria. Several thousand Jewish prisoners from Auschwitz, many of them from Western Europe, were put at the disposal of the camp commanders for the purpose of clearing rubble and dragging off any corpses they found for incineration. Every last physical memory of the ghetto had to be wiped out. During the Warsaw uprising, one year later, a Polish resistance unit freed a few hundred of these inmates, the only ones left alive.

During her time in the ghetto, Mala had seen SS officers shoot people in the streets. In the hills around Karpy, she had run for her life from a pitchfork-wielding farmer. On the train to Germany, she had absorbed the anti-Semitism of her Polish peers. In Bremen, she had received a letter from Poland with the news that her sister and her little brother had been deported. In a cinema in Zerbst, she came to understand that kind and even loving Germans fervently hoped that Jews would be wiped off the face of the Earth. Yet she had always kept some hope. She had never taken her darkest thoughts to their ultimate conclusion.

The distance between her and her family had allowed her to keep hope alive, until she came to the ruins of Warsaw. Now, for the first time, it occurred to Mala that everyone might be dead; for a moment, she lost all hope.

Mala sat down on a stone amid the expanse of rubble, and saw the ghost world shown on the cover of this book. The photograph was taken in April 1946. The girl pictured is younger than Mala; the shoes she is wearing are much too big for her. She looks out across the devastated ghetto, the section where Mala's family home once stood. Remarkably, the contours of the old streets were still visible among the rubble. The prisoners of the Warsaw concentration camp had dragged carts along them, bearing corpses and belongings from the ruins.

One such street was called Zamenhofa (a name that has since been restored), after L.L. Zamenhof, an ophthalmologist from Białystok, who created an entirely new language: Esperanto. He even came up with a new religion or philosophy: Homaranismo. The aim of both the language and the belief system was to defuse the tensions that existed between the many communities in the city of his youth and, ultimately, between the peoples of the world. Zamenhof died in 1917, and so did not live to see those tensions spiral into mass murder and the destruction of the world in which he lived. The multicultural society he had wanted to save no longer existed. Poland became monocultural.

To experience how different life in Poland once was, look no further than the Jewish community of Mala's parents and forefathers. In the mid-eighteenth century, around two-thirds of the world's Jews lived in the Kingdom of Poland. Their migration had begun at the end of the eleventh centry, sparked by massacres and expulsions associated with the First Crusade that began in 1096, especially in the region that is now Germany. In places such as Spain, Bohemia, and Moravia, they led to the deportation of long-established Jewish communities. The Kingdom of Poland offered Jews a relatively safe haven. In sources from the late Middle Ages, the term *paradisus iudaeorum* appears in connection with Poland: the Jewish paradise.

Many Polish nobles encouraged this immigration by giving tax benefits and privileges undreamt of by Jews living in Western Europe.

Polish landowners hoped, especially after the murderous campaigns of the Mongols, that immigrants could bring more villages and even towns to their sparsely populated lands. The Jews were thought to be particularly well suited to this purpose, as their own traditions were not rooted in agriculture, and relied on skills and services the nobles could not expect from their own serfs, a mostly illiterate peasant class who struggled to scrape a living for themselves. What Poland needed in order to thrive was a population of millers, innkeepers, brewers, cobblers, tailors, and the like.

No one who was anyone in Poland at the time thought that the Jews were depriving others of these jobs. It is also important to realise that the worldview of the nobility in the Middle Ages was more aristocratic than it was Christian, a view steeped in the ethics of honour propagated by classical thinkers such as Cicero and Tacitus, for whom work, production, and trade only went so far in terms of furnishing human life with a degree of dignity. For the nobleman, an honourable life centred on virtues that could be demonstrated on the battlefield, during a hunt or a tournament, and possibly at court. A good-enough reason to leave work, production, and trade to others. And it mattered little if these others were also completely 'other', as the Jews were perceived to be.

Having settled in Poland, Jews would for centuries bridge the gulf between nobility and peasants. They functioned as a kind of middle class in this feudal society. The Catholic church resisted their presence, but the nobility went ahead with its plans. As time passed in this 'paradise', Jewish culture and religion developed distinctively Polish characteristics, to which Hasidism — which was founded and first became a mass movement in the Polish lands — made a prominent contribution.

At the end of the eighteenth century, the Kingdom of Poland was wiped from the map, and three ambitious empires shared the spoils: Russia, Prussia, and the Habsburg Empire. A series of Polish armed uprisings were all to no avail. Every quashed uprising triggered a wave of more ruthless repression, especially by the Russians. In the meantime, Polish nationalism thrived, and when at the end of the First World War the country was reinstated on the drawing board, and then achieved international recognition at Versailles, a large proportion of its Catholic Polish-speaking citizens believed that the republic was exclusively theirs.

Some twenty years later, life had become increasingly tough for Poland's Jews, who represented around 10 per cent of the population. The death in 1935 of Józef Piłsudski, the undisputed leader of the republic, was a particularly significant blow. Piłsudski had been the standard-bearer for a multicultural Poland, a popular statesman who explicitly rejected anti-Semitism. Not so the colonels and generals who succeeded him. They introduced laws excluding Jews from all manner of government positions, made Saturday a mandatory day of work, and nationalised Jewish-dominated areas of commerce, such as tobacco and alcohol production.

The country's leaders turned a blind eye to the boycott of Jewish shops imposed by the nationalist Endeks and supported by a large section of the Catholic clergy. A true Pole, the Endeks insisted, did not buy from a Jew. The government bolstered the nationalists' campaign by obliging every business to display the name of its owner—in nice big letters, if you please. This made it easier for Endeks to post young people outside Jewish-owned shops to harass non-Jewish customers and take their picture for publication in their pamphlets, a regular occurrence. The people of Poland, the Endeks maintained, had a right to know about the 'national betrayal' being committed by their fellow citizens.

Meanwhile, universities introduced what were known as 'ghetto benches', the only seats in lecture theatres where Jews were allowed to sit. Politicians were fanning the flames of hostility. Nationalists spoke of 'the foreign element', and came out with slogans such as 'Polish land for the Poles!'

By 1935, this kind of language had become the norm. Three years later, national radical activist Kazimierz Halaburda went further still when he declared, 'The Turkish way is the best!' This was a clear reference to the genocide of the Armenians committed in the Ottoman Empire decades before. In Warsaw, Mala remembers, there were posters everywhere with the text, 'Jews, go home to Palestine'.

By the late 1930s, many Polish Jews wanted to do exactly that. But it was easier said than done. Palestine was a mandated territory under British control, and the British were only allowing a few thousand European Jews into Palestine each year for fear that a greater influx would upset an already precarious balance of power. The immigration permits issued by the British were in such high demand that they fetched astronomical sums on the black market, putting them well out of reach of the vast majority of Polish Jews. In response to the economic crisis, Canada had all but closed its borders, too, while more anti-Semitic motives had led the United States to restrict Jewish immigration from Europe since the early 1920s. Other Western countries—the Netherlands and France among them—had no desire to welcome what they saw as the 'lumpenproletariat' of Eastern European Jews. The Dutch government even borrowed the Nazi term *Ostjuden* to distinguish 'Eastern Jews' from the 'more civilised' German Jews that the Netherlands was prepared to admit in small numbers. Meanwhile, the Polish government was actively exploring the possibility of a more distant destination for the Jews: Madagascar, off the east coast of Africa. Poland even sent a delegation to the French-controlled island territory, but plans to settle 50,000 Jewish colonists in the short term met with local opposition and were shelved.

By the late 1930s, Poland's Jews were caught between a rock and a hard place. Their main hope of safe passage to another country was through the clandestine smuggling operations that occasionally managed to get people out.

The term lumpenproletariat as applied to Jews from Eastern Europe did not come out of nowhere. In the industrial city of Łódź, 70 per cent of Jewish families in the 1930s were living in a single room. A quarter of Warsaw's Jewish population of 350,000 people were suffering from the effects of malnutrition, even before the German invasion. Writer Sholem Asch was in his thirties when he emigrated to the United States in 1914 and went on to write bestsellers about the Polish Jewish community in which he grew up. Returning in the 1930s to revisit the world he had left behind, he was shocked by what he saw. In a letter home, he wrote of Warsaw's Jewish quarter, where Mala was living at the time: 'every second person was undernourished, skeletons of skin and bones, crippled, candidates for the grave'. After visiting the same district around the same period, British Jewish leader Neville Laski observed, 'I have never seen such poverty, squalor, and filth. It made me despair of civilisation.'

In the shtetlekh, the situation must have been even worse. In Czyżewo, where an aunt and uncle of Mala's still lived in the 1930s, hardly anyone emigrated, due to the Orthodox Jewish belief that departure to the Holy Land would only be possible after the coming of the Messiah, an event for which they were still waiting. In the summer of 1922, the Brukarz and Rubinowicz families broke with this tradition and left anyway. Thirteen years later, they returned briefly to visit friends and family. It was a huge shock. Dov Brukarz writes, 'We had lived in Eretz Yisrael for 13 years and had not stopped longing for the simple, primitive shtetl ... until we made the excursion.'

* * *

Sitting on a stone in what had once been the ghetto, Mala realised there was nothing left of this world, and that she, too, had nothing. No photographs of her parents, her brothers, or sisters, not even a simple keepsake. Nothing.

A memory came to her, an image of her father. After the bombing in the first days of the war, there had been no water in the house. Mala's sister Sure was pregnant at the time, and kept fainting from dehydration. Mala found a bucket and headed for the broad, flowing waters of the Vistula. She walked to the end of Konwiktorska Street, ran down the steep slope to the beach along the river, then struggled back up the incline and set out on the two-kilometre walk back home, her bucket brim-full of water. When she arrived, her father looked at her in wonder and said, 'My child, you will survive this war.'

There, on the stone, she recalled something else her father had told her. That the Germans would never be able to do what, in the end, they had done: to annihilate the Jews or 'clear up the Jewish question', as Hitler had proclaimed in his speeches. 'They will never succeed,' her father had said. 'There are far too many Jews here.'

Mala looked down at her wrist, at the diamond bracelet the American soldiers had given her at the farmhouse in Bias. She also had a stash of thermometers from Otto Möller, something to barter with in uncertain times when goods were worth more than money. At that moment, these things meant nothing. All thought of survival left her. 'I could feel that none of my family were alive. Life lost all meaning. How was I supposed to go on without a family?' Looking back on that moment, Mala repeatedly exclaims: 'I didn't want to go on living!' And 'How could I live in this world alone?!'

She no longer knows how long she sat in despair among the ruins. But after a while, she recalls, a man came up and asked her if there were any Jews left in Warsaw. She had seen him wandering among the rubble, searching for a past beneath the stones. He told her that Jewish survivors were being looked after in Łódź, where some of the buildings were still standing, many of them empty. He gave Mala an address: 15 Franciszkańska Street.

That same evening, after travelling over 100 kilometres south-west, Mala arrived at the geographical centre of the new Poland and knocked on the front door.

* * *

But what of Warsaw? The ghetto? What can be seen today of the neighbourhood where Mala was born and raised? There is a stark contrast between the tasteful publications about Jewish life in pre-war Warsaw and the indifference of the architectural mess that has risen on the ruins of the ghetto. From the eerie chill of the mirrored office blocks to the crumbling flats from the 1950s, not a trace of Isaac Bashevis Singer's colourful tales of the neighbourhood remains. The weather seldom lends a hand: Warsaw has more than its fair share of grey and misty days. Having lived there for four years, the image that sticks with me is a haze of broad, mint-green apartment blocks against a white sky.

Undeterred by the absence of landmarks from the past, thousands of Jewish visitors, mostly Americans, visit the neighbourhood each year for a guided tour of 'the Warsaw ghetto'. What seems like a strong concept on paper turns out to be a challenge in visualisation. I have taken the tour myself. Per square metre, considerably less remains of the ghetto than of Rome's ancient Forum Romanum. And in the

Eternal City you are at least spared the indignity of seeking out a vanished world amid the urban detritus that has taken hold among Warsaw's eroding concrete since the 1990s: the billboards, kebab shops, and stores flogging sex toys and second-hand phones.

At the turn of the century, in an effort to offer visitors something tangible, the city authorities marked out where the ghetto wall once stood. The only remaining section of the original wall was once part of the 'small ghetto', an area to the south that formed part of the main ghetto until July 1941. To reach it, you have to cross the courtyard of a pre-war apartment complex that has remained intact all these years. In the 1990s, the property was returned to the descendants of the original Jewish owner, some of whom even turned out to be living in Poland, though the youngest had no notion that he was of Jewish descent. 'My mother thought it best not to tell me.'

This same man, Krzysztof Gutkowski, now manages the complex. We meet over coffee at a major international chain, and he talks about the lengths to which his mother and grandmother went to keep his Jewish roots from him. Later, he takes me to the last remaining section of the ghetto wall, around twenty metres long. Visitors from abroad have written on it. A tenant who lives next door has stuck a photograph of Pope John Paul II in his window, facing outwards to greet the ghetto's visitors. 'We've had a word with him about it,' the young manager says, 'but it's his window. He felt like the Israeli and American tourists were taking over his courtyard.' He laughs. 'You could see the pope as a kind of ineffectual scarecrow.'

Gutkowski understands. 'Hordes of tourists yakking away at the top of their voices right outside your window. Some guides even have megaphones. And it's always the same tale of woe.' His tenant's silent protest doesn't bother him personally, he says, because John Paul II was the first major Polish religious figure to consistently speak out against anti-Semitism. 'The way I see it, the pope in the window is a symbol of reconciliation.'

Instead of footnotes

Mala lived her post-war life in the belief that her entire family had been murdered. But Noam Silberberg, an Israeli genealogist at the Ringelblum Institute in Warsaw, discovered that a maternal cousin and his family did survive the war. Morris Saper from Białystok was the son of Litman Saper, the brother of Ester Doba Saper, Mala's mother. Morris died in 1946, but his widow, Bertha Tauber-Saper, and their son, Louis Max, later emigrated to the United States. There, they established the spelling of the family name definitively as Saper. (Up to that point, it had been spelled a number of ways, including Sapir and even Safer, depending on the person writing it down and their mother tongue.) Louis Max went on to have a family of his own. His son, Mark Aaron Saper, is still alive, has children, and has even posted his family tree on a private website for those interested in genealogy.

Pauline Broekema and Helma Coolman's 2013 book *In het puin van het getto* (*In the Rubble of the Ghetto*) is a study of the concentration camp in Warsaw where the prisoners were forced to clear rubble and burn the bodies of the dead. The claim that the SS brigade led by Oskar Dirlewanger executed 40,000 civilians in two days (in addition to raping thousands of women) comes from Timothy Snyder's *Bloodlands* (2010).

The quote from the national democrat activist Halaburda comes from *The Populist Radical Right in Poland: the patriots* (2010) by Rafał Pankowski.

Details of the living conditions in Łódź, and Warsaw as seen through the eyes of visitors Sholem Asch and Neville Laski, come from Norman Goda's 2012 book *The Holocaust: Europe, the world, and the Jews, 1918–1945*. Dov Brukarz's account of his family's journey to Poland forms part of Czyżewo's Yizkor book.

The quote at the start of the chapter comes from an autobiographical story by the Polish writer Janina Godycka-Ćwirko, describing her return to Warsaw in 1945. The English translation comes from Anne Applebaum's book *Iron Curtain: the crushing of Eastern Europe, 1944–1956* (1990).

13

The Ner

'For the first truckload my hand trembled slightly when shooting,
but one gets used to it. By the time the tenth truck arrived I was
already aiming steadily and fired surely at the many women,
children and infants.'

–Walter Mattner, soldier

Before the war, Łódź was Poland's second city and home to the country's
second-largest Jewish community. As in Warsaw, that community was
condemned to live in a ghetto established in a neighbourhood already
considered poor before the German occupation. Its residents lived
packed together behind the almost featureless façades of blocks built
around central courtyards. In Łódź, unlike Warsaw, many of these
blocks are still standing eighty years later, including the building known
as the Bursa where Mala sought refuge in the summer of 1945.

A school until the ghetto was sealed off, the Bursa went on to house
Jews from Prague. Along with many Jews who had been trapped in
the Łódź ghetto before it was liquidated, they were murdered at
Kulmhof on the River Ner, a place called Chełmno nad Nerem in
Polish, and better known to the world as the Chełmno extermination
camp. Among the victims were two of Franz Kafka's sisters, Valerie
and Gabriele. The former school then became a warehouse for the
underwear that the ghetto's inhabitants produced for the Wehrmacht.
When Poland was liberated, the Central Committee for Jews in Poland

took over the building to house survivors of the camps and Jewish repatriates from the Soviet Union. Exhaust fumes have turned its plasterwork charcoal-grey.

Still reeling from her experience in Warsaw, Mala went there directly from the station. She arrived in the evening. A doorman asked her, 'What do you have to do with Jews?'

Just down the street, at number 29, was a light-blue church belonging to the Mariavites, a group of believers who seceded from the Roman Catholic Church in the late-nineteenth century under the leadership of a nun. Miraculously, the statue of Our Lady outside the church survived the occupation, thanks to a protective wooden frame, someone explains to me. One door down, at number 27, was where the ghetto police had its headquarters, and number 18, some fifty metres from Mala's new place of residence, had been home to the Perels, the family of young Solomon, the Jewish boy who fled the city and survived the war in the guise of a Volksdeutscher under the unwitting protection a German panzer division. Internationally, Łódź is primarily known for its film academy, which has turned out renowned directors such as Krzysztof Kieślowski and Roman Polanski. Polanski himself is a child Holocaust survivor: his father helped him to escape the Kraków ghetto on the day that thousands of its inhabitants were herded onto trains heading for the camps.

Twenty years after the war, Łódź was still home to a Jewish community with its own Yiddish-speaking culture, complete with a theatre and even a newspaper or two. Then it all came to an end. A telling illustration of the Jewish absence in the city today is the little plastic figure that mock-Jewish restaurant Anatewka gives to its customers along with the bill: a cartoonish caricature of an Orthodox Jew — complete with black coat, long beard, and *payot* — clutching a 1 grosz coin, the equivalent of a penny. The restaurant's walls are filled with gilt-framed oil paintings of bearded Orthodox Jews counting coins and poring over cash books. Many Poles are completely oblivious to the stereotyping that underlies these plastic figures and popular genre paintings. The restaurant is a proud exponent of Yiddish cuisine, so how can it be accused of anti-Semitism?

Again in contrast to Warsaw, few of Łódź's 200,000 Jewish residents actually resembled the Jews in these paintings. A minority of the city's Jews were Orthodox. Many were labourers; some had their own business. They had settled in the city from the mid-nineteenth century onwards, attracted by the wealth of jobs in the booming textile industry. Situated on the fringes of the tsarist Russian Empire, Łódź produced clothing for millions of Russians, and earned itself the nickname 'the Manchester of the East'. In some respects, it even outdid its British counterparts. While the cities of northern England's industrial heartland doubled in population between 1850 and 1900, the population of Łódź shot up from 16,000 to 321,000. By the time the First World War broke out, fourteen years later, it had doubled once again.

The population was mixed. In the 1931 census, around half of the city's residents identified as Polish and some 10 per cent as German, while around 30 per cent referred to themselves as Jewish. These groups lived side by side without any major friction. In Łódź, tensions tended to run along a different axis: a socioeconomic faultline with tens of thousands of socialist workers on one side and the factory owners, employers, and their foremen on the other. German historian Karl Schlögel argues that the city gave rise to 'homo Lodziensis', a being whose connection to the city instilled a distinctive mindset that took precedence over tribal or religious loyalties. Everyone in Łódź was an immigrant, Schlögel maintains, and so their identity was not defined by where they came from, but by their future prospects, prosperity, and the pursuit of success. As a result, the rest of the country viewed Łódź as a den of iniquity where godless socialists and capitalists held centuries-old Polish traditions in contempt.

The Nazis had big plans for Łódź and its German minority. It was to become Litzmannstadt, an eastern outpost named after Karl Litzmann, the moustachioed general who had led the offensive on the city during the First World War. Under Nazi occupation, it soon became the site of a ghetto, but the Jews confined there met a different fate to those in the dozens of other ghettos across Poland. The city's status as an industrial powerhouse enabled the autocratically inclined chairman of its Jewish Council, Chaim Mordechai Rumkowski, to put a viable proposition to

the Germans: this district fenced off with barbed wire could be turned
into a low-cost production hub contributing to the German war effort
on an industrial scale. And so it came to pass. The Łódź ghetto was
sealed off from the outside world more rigorously than other ghettos
(smuggling and escape were simply impossible), and was transformed
into one big labour camp. In countless craft workshops and factories,
the inhabitants produced everything from ammunition to underwear,
keeping the German forces in uniforms, caps, and boots. For their
work, they were paid in *rumki*, the unofficial name for the currency
printed specifically for use in the ghetto, and prominently bearing
Rumkowski's title and signature. By the standards of German-occupied
Poland, 'King Chaim'—as he became known—was granted unheard-
of privileges. In his speeches, compiled by a Statistics Department set
up for the Łódź ghetto, he repeatedly emphasised the link between
work and survival 'Experience has made it clear that, in our times, the
basic law is that work protects us from annihilation.'

This servile adaptability gave the two biggest ghettos in occupied
Poland a very different character. While the Warsaw ghetto was built
for starvation, the Łódź ghetto was geared towards production and
exploitation. In Warsaw, the occupying forces faced an armed ghetto
uprising in the spring of 1943, and responded by torching every building
that remained standing. In Łódź, it was a long time before Himmler
and the most race-obsessed Nazis were given free rein: the ghetto was
not liquidated until August 1944, when the last 74,000 inhabitants were
transported to Auschwitz to be murdered. For this reason, Łódź is
often referred to as 'the last ghetto', a phrase used in the title of several
books on its history.

At the Bursa, Mala was shown to a large dormitory, where she lay
down on a straw mattress and sobbed quietly to herself for a long time.
They were tears of joy, she says, looking back. She was overwhelmed
by feelings she finds hard to describe. 'In that place, I could see that
Jews were still alive … It had to do with that. I was no longer the only
one in the world.'

It was no accident that Łódź was designated a place of refuge
by the recently established Central Committee for Polish Jews, with

backing from the country's caretaker government. The Germans had not only wiped out the city's large Jewish community, but they had also expelled much of the Polish population to make room for tens of thousands of ethnic Germans, most of them from Bessarabia, Galicia, and Bukovina. As the Third Reich crumbled, these new residents then fled west to escape the advancing Red Army. Due to its relatively intact infrastructure and the large number of vacant houses, the authorities even considered making Łódź the new capital of Poland.

The city's archives contain a card proving that Mala was a resident of the city. Address: 15 Franciszkańska Street. Name: Mala Rywka Kizel. For the first time since war had broken out, she was registered under the name she was given at birth.

Mala has vivid memories of her first evening in Łódź and of waking up the next morning. She opened her eyes to find a group of girls gathered by her bed, staring down at her. 'They looked like dead people, terribly thin and bald. I was dumbstruck.'

The Yiddish newspaper of the day, *Dos Naye Lebn* (*New Life*), gives an impression of life at the Bursa, which operated something like a student halls of residence. In 1945, it housed 150 people aged between eighteen and twenty-eight, most of whom had survived the camps. Later, they were joined by repatriates from the Soviet Union and a handful of Polish Jews who had survived the war as partisans. Most wanted nothing more than to finally complete the schooling that had been interrupted by war, and to go on to university. The building was full of future engineers, physicists, and even one or two Holocaust researchers. 'We started to live a new life in that house at Franciszkańska 15,' resident Rachelka Kaufman remembers. 'Living with that group of people who had survived the horrors of war, and a feeling of togetherness, strengthened us.' Another resident, Adam Broner, speaks of 'a new home and family'. He was one year older than Mala, and had returned to the city of his youth as a soldier in the Red Army. 'It was there that we started a new life and formed long-time friendships.'

Mala became friends with a young woman called Różka. She was one of the 74,000 people who had been allowed to continue working in the Łódź ghetto until August 1944, along with her parents, brothers, and sisters. In Auschwitz, she was the only member of her family not to be sent straight to the gas chambers. When SS guards fled the camp five months later, on the run from the Red Army, they left her behind with the sick and the dying. By the time the Soviet soldiers arrived, Różka was too weak to walk. One of them carried her to a nearby house and ordered the occupants to take good care of her, warning that he would be back to check on her progress. Time passed, and she grew strong enough to return to Łódź.

When they first met, Różka was still very thin and practically bald, but Mala watched her recover day by day. A young man called Sewek came to visit Różka: he was in his twenties, and looked healthy and strong. In August 1944, he had been one of several hundred inhabitants of the ghetto who were spared transportation. He was assigned to a group of men made to stay behind and 'clean up' the ghetto. It was filthy work. Their duties were to drag the remaining corpses from the houses, and unblock, clean, and dismantle toilets and latrines. Worst of all were the swarms of rats and flies that had taken over the houses. To add to the ordeal, the weather was unseasonably warm in Łódź that September, and the bodies were soon crawling with maggots and ants. Yet these men were the lucky ones. In the houses they were forced to empty, they found food enough to keep them alive.

Sewek wanted to know if Różka had any news of his wife. The two women were close friends, and had been transported to Auschwitz at the same time. Różka was able to share all kinds of memories with Sewek, but she could not tell him what had happened to her. Sewek's wife, her close friend, never returned, but Różka and Sewek continued to see one another. They married a few months later.

At the former school on Franciszkańska Street, a man with only stumps for legs introduced Mala to another Auschwitz survivor. She shook him by the hand, and he took a long time to let go. 'I had been trying my hardest to forget Erich, but the warmth of that hand in mine made me think of him.'

The Auschwitz survivor was called Nathan Shlafer. A few years older than Mala, he was a skilled technician. During the war, he had done all kinds of odd jobs in the Łódź ghetto, eventually earning himself a position with the city's electric company. His work was restricted to the ghetto, of course.

To keep the production lines running, he would rush from one workshop to the next patching up the power supply. He had a special annotation on his ID card, and an armband that permitted him to be on the streets at all times, even after curfew. He knew the layout of the ghetto like the back of his hand, and when the Germans began rounding everyone up for transport in August 1944, he escaped across the rooftops. On the other side of the wall, he ran into a couple of people he knew—friends or perhaps acquaintances—and thought he had been saved, but they handed him over to the Germans.

This was not the most shocking thing that Nathan experienced during the occupation. Almost two years previously, on a sunny day in September 1942, he had been walking through the ghetto on his way to a job when three military trucks turned the corner. They pulled up outside a hospital, and the soldiers went inside. From passers-by, he understood that the soldiers had come to drag the sick from their beds to take them to the camp on the River Ner. It wasn't long before a crowd of people from the ghetto descended on the hospital, probably in an attempt to save their friends or relatives from transportation. The Jewish ghetto police held them back. As fighting broke out, Nathan looked up to see infants being thrown from a third-floor window.

Mala could not or did not want to believe this story. Germans would never do such a thing. She knew that; she had lived with a German family. It took her years to accept that this had really happened, after hearing the accounts of others and seeing them printed in black and white. Several survivors of the Łódź ghetto have spoken about this atrocity. The babies thrown from the window were not the figment of someone's traumatised imagination. 'Stories like that made me doubt my faith in God,' Mala says.

Before the Red Army reached Auschwitz in January 1945, the SS forced some 56,000 prisoners to leave the camp and march westward through the snow in temperatures that were well below freezing. With the benefit of hindsight, we can conclude that Nathan managed to keep going just long enough. When the death march began, the Germans shot any prisoners who fell by the wayside. By the time Nathan collapsed, they left them to die. Why waste a bullet on someone who was too weak to stand and was sure to freeze to death? This reasoning was Nathan's good fortune. He did not freeze. When the desperate procession was out of sight, he was able to drag himself by the elbows to an empty house. German soldiers had abandoned the place in haste. He found some milk, and was able to drink a little. Luckily, he had learned enough about hunger to know that too much food could kill a starved body.

Nathan slept for days, in a bed with a feather quilt. When he finally woke, he ate from a clean plate. Each time when he had eaten his fill, he threw the plate out of the window: a harmless enough way to vent the rage he felt inside.

He found a chicken, which he slaughtered, plucked, and cooked. Every day, he ate a little more. He discovered pots of jam, but would not touch them. Once, in Auschwitz, he had found an empty barrel that contained jam. He had climbed inside and licked what was left from the wood. Soon after, he fell ill with bellyache and diarrhoea. There was no toilet paper, so he tore tiny strips from his clothing to wipe himself. If anyone had discovered he was ill, it would have been the end of him: the sick bay was a portal to death. He stank, of course, and his fellow inmates gave him a hard time in the barracks, but no one betrayed him. He never ate jam again.

When all the plates had been smashed, Nathan was strong enough to move on. He took two smart suits with him, a pair of shoes, and the feather quilt, and set off for his hometown of Łódź, in the hope of finding friends, acquaintances, and of course his mother and sister. He knew that, like him, they had escaped the first selection for the gas chambers on arriving in Auschwitz. But there was no one left alive.

Speaking at his graveside decades later, Nathan's grandson recalled that, even as an old man, he could recite the addresses and phone numbers of the friends and family he had lost.

* * *

Nathan told Mala about Julian Weinberg, another survivor of the Łódź ghetto. Weinberg had studied mathematics in France and, returning to Poland years before the outbreak of war, was put in charge of the city's electricity supply. Nathan sang Weinberg's praises to Mala. It was said that he had memorised every last cable in the city's network, knowledge that made him indispensable to the German occupier, both inside and outside the ghetto. And so, unlike his employee Nathan, he was not deported to Auschwitz in August 1944, but remained behind with the clean-up crew.

To save his wife and children from deportation, Weinberg hid them in an electrical substation, assuming that neither soldiers nor police would think to conduct a thorough search there. He was right. The Weinberg family were among the 600 survivors able to conceal themselves in the ostensibly empty ghetto until the arrival of the Red Army in January 1945.

From Julian Weinberg, it is only a small step to another remarkable figure: David P. Boder. The two men met in Paris in the summer of 1946. Boder was an American psychologist who worked for the Illinois Institute of Technology. Born Aron Mendel Michelson into a large Jewish family in tsarist-ruled Latvia, he later converted to Christianity with the aim of smoothing his path to academic success—a move that prompted his wife to leave him. In 1919, after the Bolsheviks came to power, he and his second wife fled to Mexico, where he changed his name to David Pablo Boder. Six years later, he moved to the United States, and during the 1930s he gained a measure of celebrity as a psychologist, with media-friendly research on children's letters to Santa Claus, and one study that involved attaching sensors to young people's heads to gauge their responses to horror films. His work even merited a mention in *Time Magazine*.

The war changed everything, even for him. The large family he had left behind in Latvia were murdered, including his ex-wife, who was also the mother of his daughter. Following Germany's capitulation, he felt compelled to return to Europe at the first opportunity to interview survivors, perhaps in an attempt to gain some kind of personal understanding. On his grant applications, he wrote that his aim was to study the influence of extreme suffering on the personality—applications that were rejected for months on end. Even a visa to travel to a liberated and reconquered Europe proved elusive until the spring of 1946. Having made it at last, he went on to carry out the most important work of his career. In a single summer, he interviewed over 100 survivors in sixteen different locations and in at least seven languages; his command of each was sufficient to conduct a serious interview.

The survivor memories that Boder recorded stand out among the thousands of other such recordings because they are so fresh. The people he interviewed were not in a position to see the bigger picture and to situate their personal stories within a broader narrative. They spoke of the atrocities they had endured and witnessed at a time when a general vocabulary of wartime experience, a shared language that became the mainstay of later memoirs, had yet to develop. Boder's interviews took place ten years before the word 'Holocaust' came into circulation. One interviewee who survived a death march told Boder his story without ever referring to it as such: the term had yet to enter the lexicon. Boder, too, was operating without a context. He can be heard asking people how to spell place names such as Auschwitz. In his transcripts, he writes 'Mingel' when someone tells him about a doctor by the name of Mengele.

On his return to the United States, Boder set about analysing, transcribing, and processing the eyewitness accounts he had recorded. Until his death, it was practically all he would do. In the meantime, his public profile dwindled. Sixteen years after the war, he would die in anonymity as an unpaid research associate. *I Did Not Interview the Dead*, his 1949 book based on the interviews, found only a small and select readership. It was not until forty years after his death that his former employer, the Illinois Institute of Technology, digitised the recordings and published them online under the title 'Voices of the Holocaust'. This time, the response was huge. People were finally ready to hear them.

The encounter between the psychologist Boder and the mathematician Weinberg took place at The Grand Hotel in Paris. By this time, Weinberg had returned to the Electric Works in Łódź as the managing director. He had stipulated in advance that the interview should not exceed thirty minutes. This was a departure from Boder's usual method, and it made him audibly nervous. The two men spoke

German, with Weinberg throwing in an occasional word of Yiddish and French. His background was typical of the more affluent section of the Jewish community in Łódź: he came from an assimilated Jewish family, and Polish was his first language. While Boder's interest in what Weinberg has to say is evident from the recording, he can't help coming across as a schoolmaster from a bygone age.

Weinberg tells Boder about his first real experience of sadism. It was during the first year of the war. He had just buried his mother, and was walking back home. Out of nowhere, a young man grabbed him by his coat and dragged him through a gate and into a yard to join a group of about fifteen other Jews. Weinberg took the man to be an ethnic German, about twenty-one years of age, and he was brandishing a whip that he clearly enjoyed using. He and a group of fellow Nazis ordered Weinberg and the others to unload sacks of coal from a cart and carry them to a cellar. On discovering that Weinberg was an engineer—an intellectual—they made him stay behind for hours to lug the coal from one cellar to another, and then back to the first. 'Pure chicanery,' Weinberg and Boder conclude: a pointless task designed solely to humiliate.

Perhaps because they only had half an hour, or because Boder was still too inexperienced to ask Weinberg the questions he hoped to be asked, the interviewee appears to take control of the conversation. He tells Boder about the elimination of the last 74,000 inhabitants of the ghetto, announced in the first days of August 1944. 'A commission of generals decided that Łódź was near the front ... and it was not right to keep so many Jews near the front.'

That commission included a German ghetto commandant who had once given a speech that began 'My Jews!' In light of the catastrophe approaching from the east, the commandant said, Germany had radically altered its policy. The hard-working Jews standing before him would be saved, every last one of them, to carry out the essential work that needed to be done in the bombed-out German cities further west.

Those hard-working Jews were all too willing to believe him, Weinberg says, and the Łódź ghetto had been so rigorously isolated that the truth about the massacres only began to filter through late in the war, very late indeed. The workers reported to the railway platform willingly, and, as an added incentive, the Germans made it their only food distribution point, so hunger drove people to their deaths. In the meantime, Weinberg said, the ghetto police and the German police, assisted by the Polish fire brigade, combed the entire ghetto. 'All the Jews were evacuated, but not to the bombed-out cities,' Weinberg concludes. 'Everything [sic] went through Auschwitz, through the famous extermination camp.'

Rumkowski of the Jewish Council was also sent to Auschwitz, on the last train to leave the ghetto. There is a photograph of the Jewish elder on the platform: white-haired, suited, a yellow star pinned to his coat. The German ghetto commandant is escorting him, as cordially as can be. It's one of almost 500 colour slides that turned up in 1987 at an antique shop in Salzburg. They were taken for propaganda purposes by the ghetto's Austrian accountant, a Nazi, and were intended to show how the parasitical Jew could be put to work in an orderly and profitable slave camp. This was grist to the mill for German officials, who took a highly practical view of the ghettos. Heinrich Himmler, keen to avoid any hitches in his campaign of mass murder, actively combatted such pragmatism. One photograph, in particular, highlights the cruel irony of Rumkowski's situation: it shows him surrounded by laughing German soldiers as he welcomes Himmler himself with full honours. The Reichsführer-SS remains seated in his car: a green, open-topped BMW with the number plate 'SS–1'.

Weinberg can also be seen in one of the Austrian bookkeeper's photographs. As a prominent member of the ghetto operation, he is pictured at Rumkowski's side. During his thirty minutes with Boder at The Grand Hotel in the summer of 1946, Weinberg distances himself from the autocrat on a German leash. Weinberg insists that he took little part in 'community affairs' because the Łódź ghetto was run by a Jewish elder, Rumkowski, who was eager to handle things alone. As Weinberg puts it, 'He got his orders directly from the ghetto management, and he carried them out to the best of his ability. I did not want to participate in these things directly … I was opposed to the entire policy, so I had to keep away from that whole business.'

Weinberg, who remained in communist Poland all his life, seems to be pre-empting a later debate between historians, one that centres on a question asked at the time by survivors of the Łódź ghetto: how was Chaim Rumkowski to be judged? Was he a heartless collaborator interested solely in his own glory and fame, a man who thought he was God, as Emanuel Ringelblum had heard in Warsaw? Or was he a man who, in brutally unequal negotiations with the Germans, tried to do the best he could for the Jewish community?

A 'what if' often arises during this debate: what if the Red Army had not halted its advance on the eastern banks of the Vistula in the summer of 1944? What if the Soviet forces had forged ahead at the murderous pace they had maintained earlier that year? Then Rumkowski might have gone down in history as the man who, as sole chairman of a Jewish Council, had saved tens of thousands of Jews. But the Soviet advance did halt, and Rumkowski is portrayed as an obedient instrument of the Nazi executioners; an unpleasant, pompous, and dictatorial instrument at that. An autocrat who made sure that his political opponents were top of the deportation lists.

Many analysts look at Rumkowski and see proof that Adam Czerniaków, his counterpart in Warsaw, took the right decision. On receiving the order to hand over tens of thousands of ghetto inhabitants to the Germans for transport to Treblinka, the head of Warsaw's Jewish Council took a cyanide pill. Rumkowski took orders, not pills, and continued to do so even when the Germans ordered him to hand over all children and non-productive old people. Which begs another question: even if the Red Army had arrived earlier, and Rumkowski had saved thousands of lives, hadn't the sacrifices already made been too inhumane? The order to hand over the ghetto's children is the most agonising example. On 4 September 1942, Rumkowski gave a speech in which he told the people of the ghetto not to hide their children. His first words to the huge crowd gathered before him were, 'A grievous blow has struck the ghetto. They are asking us to give up the best we possess—the children and the elderly.' He explained that there was no choice, that limbs had to be cut off in order to save the body. If they did not obey, Rumkowski said, the Germans would come to claim the 20,000 lives they demanded and more, a terrifying prospect.

It's a familiar argument: 'If we don't do it ourselves …'

Of course, Rumkowski said in his speech that he had tried everything to have the order reversed. Whatever the truth of that statement, he did not succeed. Where he did succeed, he claimed, was in reducing the number of children to be taken and making up the shortfall with the sick, regardless of age. Common sense dictated, Rumkowski insisted, that salvation had to be reserved for those who had a chance of living long enough to see it. And because the healthy shared their meagre rations with the sick, they ran a greater risk of becoming ill themselves: this was a noble sacrifice, but one made for those 'who haven't the slightest chance of recovery.'

He concluded, 'A broken Jew stands before you. This is the most difficult of all orders I have ever had to carry out at any time. I reach out to you with my broken, trembling hands and beg: give into my hands the victims. So that we can avoid having further victims, and a population of 100,000 Jews can be preserved.'

Less than two weeks later, over 15,000 inhabitants of the ghetto — children, the sick, and the elderly — were deported. One further detail: to make sure the Jewish police cooperated in full, the officers were promised that their own children and direct family would be spared deportation. It wasn't long before the Germans broke this promise, too.

When even Rumkowski had been deported to Auschwitz, the last of the ghetto's inhabitants listened in secret to a radio they had found in one of the abandoned houses. Learning that Russian forces had advanced to within a few kilometres of Łódź, they understood that the endgame had begun, and that the Germans would come and finish them off. With nothing left to lose, these last survivors hid themselves away in the empty houses. The recording shows the precision of Weinberg's thinking. In his interview, he recalls how the Germans captured twenty-three survivors on the first day, about seventy on the second, and a few more the day after that. Though a grave had already been dug, they were locked up rather than shot. For once, delay brought consolation. It soon became clear that the Germans had fled, leaving Weinberg and the rest to free the captives.

* * *

In Łódź, Mala could once again be Jewish. But one secret had made way for another: her love for Erich, a German aviation engineer. It was clear Nathan wanted nothing more than to be with her, and she fretted constantly about her reasons for pushing him away.

'What was I supposed to tell him?' Mala exclaims. 'That I was in love with a German?! It would have been a huge shock. And what would the others have thought, after everything they had been through in the camps? A German!'

And so she kept her secret. In time, Nathan would be the first person to hear the story of Mala's love for Erich. But first they had another city to reach, and two more rivers to cross.

Instead of footnotes

The growing popularity in Poland of little wooden and plastic figures of Orthodox Jews with money in their hands ('a Jew with a cent', as the Poles call them) is the subject of an academic study by Erica Lehrer and Joanna Tokarska-Bakir. Both researchers believe that anti-Semitism is not the only explanation for their popularity, arguing that the rather crude iconography belies a nostalgic longing for Jewish Poland, comparable to the nostalgia behind the popularity of wooden statues of native Americans ('cigar store Indians') in the United States.

Karl Schlögel writes about Łódź in his 1996 essay in 'Lodz – Suche nach dem Gelobten Land' ('Łódź – Search for the Promised Land'), originally published in *Die Zeit*. Gordon J. Horwitz gives an authoritative account of the city's wartime history in *Ghettostadt: Łódź and the making of a Nazi city* (2008).

David Pablo Boder, the psychologist from Latvia who wound up in America and returned to Europe after the war to interview survivors, is the subject of 'Before It Had A Name', an episode of the podcast *This American Life*, no. 197, October 2001. The transcription of Boder's interview with Julian Weinberg can be found at https://voices.library. iit.edu/interview/weinbergJ.

Several survivors of the Łódź ghetto have given accounts of German soldiers throwing babies out of the hospital windows, including Dr Donat Szmulewicz-Stanisz, in Jerzy Lewiński's *Proces Hansa Biebowa*

(*The Trial of Hans Biebow*), published in 1999. A translation of Bronka Szyldwach's account is included in *Preserved Evidence: Ghetto Lodz*, edited by Anna Eilenberg-Eibeshitz (1998). Julian Weinberg also appears to refer to this same incident in his Paris interview with Boder, when he talks about seeing children being taken from the hospital and thrown directly onto the waiting vehicles.

My description of the building, known as the Bursa, where Mala stayed after the war, is drawn from *Life in Transit: Jews in postwar Lodz 1945–1950* (2010) by Shimon Redlich. The quote from Adam Broner, one of the Bursa's residents, comes from his memoirs, translated into English as *My War Against the Nazis. a Jewish soldier with the Red Army* (2007). The Holocaust expert who lived among the engineers and other scientists at the Bursa was Lucjan Dobroszycki. His own account, *The Chronicle of the Lodz Ghetto* (1987), contains Rumkowski's notorious 'Give me your children' speech.

The Austrian head of bookkeeping in the ghetto who took the photographs of the deportation is called Walter Genewein. The Movex 12 camera he used had previously belonged to a Jewish resident of Łódź. The Jüdisches Museum in Frankfurt purchased the photographs, exhibited them, and published them on its website. The photograph of Himmler in the green open-topped car is catalogued as Lodz-A024.jpg.

The quotation that starts this chapter comes from a letter dated 5 October 1941, sent by Austrian Wehrmacht soldier Walter Mattner to his pregnant wife in Vienna. He served in the area around Minsk where, by his own account, he shot and killed hundreds, if not thousands, of Jews.

14

The Sołokija

'A man alone was nothing—a Jew alone was even less than that—but with a partisan group, a man had half a chance. Or a quarter of a chance.'

–Kalmen Wewryk, escaped Sobibór prisoner

In the days after the American forces rolled into Zerbst, Mala saw a small group of GIs gathered around a campfire in the street. She couldn't quite believe her eyes. Moving closer, she saw it was true: they were burning money, cases full of German Reichsmarks. Banknotes that bore the swastika were being taken out of circulation. Mala asked if she could have some. Sure, help yourself, came the reply. She took as many notes as could fit in her bag. You never knew ...

A few weeks later, at the station in Łódź, she discovered that Reichsmarks were still welcome in Poland, swastikas or not. Unlike the złoty, the national currency, the value of the German banknotes was stable. For a fraction of the money in her bag, Mala was able to buy herself a ticket from Łódź to Tomaszów Lubelski. Still clinging to the last of her hope, she was going in search of her sisters, Chaja and Mira, her brother-in-law, Majloch, her little brother, Meir, and her nephew Samek. The train took her through Warsaw and Lublin.

Even after the devastating realisation that hit her among the ruins of Warsaw, Mala's openness to others remained intact: on the train she got talking to two sisters, both in uniform—complete with holster and pistol. They told Mala that they had been confined to a ghetto in Parczew, a small town not far from Lublin, but had escaped into the forest shortly before the ghetto was liquidated. One of them told Mala they were going to find her daughter, who had been left in the care of a trusted farmer and his family.

After escaping the ghetto, the sisters had stumbled upon a band of Jewish fugitives in the forest who employed a very different strategy from the vast majority of Polish Jews trying to survive in the countryside. Instead of paying farmers for protection, they used the last of their money to arm themselves and stayed hidden in the woods. They dug themselves dens in the sandy earth, covering the walls with straw, and making a roof out of twigs and branches.

Obtaining weapons was crucial, but far from simple. It could take weeks for a group of around fifty men—women were very much in the minority—to get hold of a single pistol or rifle. Once they did, life became a little easier: with a weapon you could not only fend off attacks by farmers and force them to hand over food, but you could also ambush a Polish policeman or a German gendarme, and build your armoury.

The partisans the sisters from Parczew met in the forest had escaped from Lipowa 7, a concentration camp in the middle of Lublin where many of the inmates were Jews who had served in the Polish army. In other words, they were trained soldiers who had seen combat. From their base in the forest, they battled to survive, to avenge their families, or, if nothing else, to go down fighting. After braving a harsh winter, the Lipowa 7 group was able to join forces with a Jewish partisan unit under the leadership of Yechiel ('Chil') Grynszpan, the son of a horse trader from Sosnowica, a village south-west of Parczew. Chil was what you might call a born leader: an engaging, decisive, and charismatic figure. He knew his way around the difficult local terrain, with its marshes and barely passable trails. His father's trade with Polish farmers meant he also had a fair idea who could be trusted.

That day on the train, Mala did not hear the full story of Chil and his fighters. That would come later, much later. Yet the encounter with the Jewish sisters made a deep impression on her. The mere fact that they existed, that they had survived, and the knowledge that other

Jews had fought their way through the war rekindled the hope that she might still find at least some of her family. The hope that not everyone had been killed.

Listening to their story, Mala had no way of knowing how miraculous it was that the sisters were alive at all. The chances of survival in the Polish countryside were minimal for Jews, even those who were armed and living deep in the forest. The climate was unforgiving. Temperatures could drop below minus ten Celsius for days on end. The environment was hostile: there was a price on their heads, and any sympathy that did exist among the local population crumbled in the face of the unrelenting terror instilled by the occupier. So how had the sisters cheated death? From the testimonies given by Chil's fighters immediately after the war and the memoirs they wrote years and sometimes decades later, an answer is forthcoming.

One man in particular, Hershel Zimmermann, attempted to reconstruct his life as a partisan as faithfully as possible. Like the sisters, he found himself in Chil's unit. He appears in this book's early chapters as a young man who, like Mala, came from an Orthodox family and fled the Warsaw ghetto to work as an unpaid labourer on a farm near Lublin in exchange for board and lodging. Like Mala, he stayed with the farmer and his family until the spring of 1942, by which time the Germans had wiped out all the ghettos in the region and were enlisting the help of the local population to track down every last Jew. Zimmermann took refuge in the surrounding forest, where he endured months of extreme hardship before managing to obtain a shotgun from the farmer he had worked for.

To survive, Zimmermann said, you had to threaten and steal from the local farmers. Even more importantly: if you wanted to make it, you had to act on those threats.

Chil's fighters liked to steal their livestock whole. Pigs were their preferred prize because the meat could be kept underground for quite some time, unlike beef, which soon began to rot. 'Under the circumstances,' Zimmermann noted decades later, 'there was no question of trying to keep kosher.' The farmers soon cottoned on to the partisans' preference for pork, and started hiding their pigs in barns and cellars, even digging pits to keep them out of sight. But the partisans had their methods when it came to searching out hidden animals. One comical turn proved especially effective: roaming around the farmyard making pig noises until they got a reply. 'Once we found a pig, we would kill it on the farm, quarter it, and transport it to the base by wagon.'

The desire for vengeance, Zimmermann knew, had the power to keep some fighters going in the brutal conditions in the Polish forest. Most of the partisans came from villages in the area. They knew who had hunted down Jews, and sometimes they knew who had relished the killing and who had been a passive participant. He tells the story of Fajga, a young woman who had roamed the forest around Parczew with Zimmerman long before they met up with Chil's group. She came from Zamołodycze, a small village on the fringes of the forest. One day, almost every man in the village went hunting for Jews. There were at least seventy of them, armed with clubs, sticks, and pitchforks, led by a policeman from the only town in the area. They found twenty people hiding in a forest dugout, among them Fajga and Zimmermann.

At the time, Zimmermann did not have a shotgun. His only weapon was a sharp knife. The villagers dragged the Jews out of hiding and walked them back to the village, under guard. On the way, Zimmermann noticed that only one of the men had a proper rifle, and decided to take a risk. In a commanding voice, he suddenly shouted 'Everybody scatter, full speed!' They ran in all directions, with the villagers in pursuit. One came after Zimmermann, who took the knife from his pocket as he ran. His pursuer grabbed him by his coat, at which Zimmermann turned in his tracks and drove his blade into the man's flesh as hard as he could. The villager fell to the ground with barely a whimper.

Fajga, too, had managed to get herself to safety. Twelve of the group were not so lucky. The villagers managed to recapture them, and took them to the house of Zelik, Fajga's father. There, they kept watch on their human spoils while one of them alerted the nearest German army post, around five kilometres away.

The Germans came riding into the village on horseback and had the Jews brought out of the house one by one. The residents of Zamołodycze gathered outside the house and watched as one Jew after another was gunned down by a German. 'These people had grown up together,' Zimmermann recalls. 'They had done business with one another. Zelik was the village shoemaker.'

One of his sons, a brother of Fajga's, managed to jump from an attic window and make a run for it. A group of villagers chased after him, caught him, and dragged him back to the house. That day, Fajga would lose her mother, father, brothers, and sisters.

A year later, Zimmermann, Fajga, and two fellow partisans returned to the village to exact revenge. By this time, they had been able to obtain firearms, including the rifle that had once belonged to the farmer Zimmermann had worked for.

It was a Sunday evening, and as they approached the village, they heard music. It was coming from what had been Zelik's house, the home Fajga had grown up in. As the only unarmed member of the group, she had grabbed an axe from a barn along the way. The closer they got to the house, the more incensed Fajga became. She stormed in, and the music stopped dead. Fajga saw that one of the men was wearing her father's boots. The partisans shot him and took the boots. The other villagers begged for mercy. Zimmermann recalls, 'Fajga was enraged, like a wild animal. She knew each of the partygoers by their first names. She ran around her house, breaking everything with her axe and calling out their names as she did so. We were planning to burn down the house, but the people who ran out sounded an alarm and soon we heard the bells of the church ringing.'

A crowd of villagers was coming towards them, and they heard the sound of rifle shots. Zimmermann and his comrades returned fire. One of them was armed with a flare gun, which he had only ever used to threaten local farmers because it looked like a shotgun. He had never fired it—why would a group of Jewish fugitives hiding the forest want to light up the dark?—but this was as good a time as any. The partisans' first flare lit up the sky above the village for a moment or two, just long enough to strike fear into the villagers and stop their advance. Zimmermann, Fajga, and the others ran full pelt into the forest, spurred on by the adrenaline rush of that fleeting taste of power: the knowledge that the villagers had seen armed Jews who had come to take revenge.

Not long after this act of vengeance, Zimmermann and his small band of poorly armed fugitives were able to throw in their lot with Chil Grynszpan's larger and better-armed partisan unit. Together they carried out daring raids on German police posts to obtain uniforms. A year later, they even managed to seize a few machine guns. By the autumn of 1943, around 400 fighters were permanently defending and supplying over 1,000 people—many of them sick, elderly, or children—hidden away on a few islands in a marshy area deep in the vast forest. There they cooked, made their own clothes, repaired their own shoes, and preserved and buried provisions in the summer that they could dig up to see them through the winter.

The group also picked up a few survivors of the Sobibór uprising, prisoners who had fled the death camp and had been able to reach the forest. Towards the end of the occupation, Chil's unit began collaborating with the Armia Ludowa, a Soviet-backed armed resistance force made up of Polish communists. Using guerrilla tactics, they blew up bridges, and attacked a number of town halls, a police station, and several farms that were supplying the Germans with food. They cut telephone lines, and lured truckloads of German gendarmes into ambushes. When liberation came, many of Chil's fighters were absorbed into the new Polish army formed in the Soviet Union. Others joined Poland's newly installed police force.

The two sisters Mala met in the train had been part of this world and had survived. Little wonder that they were uniformed, and that each carried a pistol in a holster.

* * *

The welcome Mala received from the Olszewskis in Tomaszów Lubelski was anything but warm. 'They were shocked to see me,' Mala remembers. 'They hadn't thought I would still be alive.' Mala was shocked, too. These people who had once been so kind and generous to her were suddenly distant and cold. She thinks the Olszewskis were afraid that she had come to reclaim her sister Chaja's belongings, things they had probably claimed as their own. But Mala did not ask after her sister's belongings. She asked if Chaja was still alive. And she asked about her brother-in-law, her little brother, Meir, and her sister Mira.

The Olszewskis repeated what they had told Mala in the letter they had sent to Bremen: Mala's family had been deported. Only Majloch had managed to avoid deportation at first, they said. But he, too, was captured in the end. About Mira, the Olszewskis knew nothing.

Mala's impression that the Olszewskis felt they had somehow been caught out was not unusual. In their memoirs, various survivors describe returning home after everything they had endured only to hear the people who had moved into their house complain, 'Of all the Jews who were carted off, why did *mine* have to come back?' Possessions were seldom returned to their former owners, so that could not be the reason for this self-pity. The return of 'their Jew' was unsettling, because it led them to an undeniable conclusion: I am a profiteer. The return made it harder to reason away any lingering guilt.

The Olszewskis felt caught out. At another moment, Mala says they had become 'nasty … just like the other Poles'. This could well have been the case; Mala was there, I wasn't. Yet it's worth considering that the family's position may have been more ambivalent, and that fear may have had a role to play: fear of the neighbours, of the community they lived in. This was a time when people who had helped Jews were shunned or even denounced outright. These 'Jewish uncles' had gone against a new set of norms—Jews were to be reported, not protected—and anyone who violates the norms of a close-knit community can expect repercussions.

Chaja's belongings may have been a concern, not because the Olszewskis feared Mala's wrath, but the wrath of the town. The vast redistribution of wealth across Poland in those days was bound up with violence and the fear of violence. Three million Polish Jews had disappeared, an entire social class, in fact: a middle class of traders and craftsmen. Many in rural Poland believed that much of the Jews' wealth had found its way into the pockets of the few who had protected them, or at least tried to protect them. After all, they had been paid by the Jews they had hidden. This made them profiteers in the eyes of the community, people who had taken advantage of the situation. Enough Polish peasants felt there was a score to be settled.

A study of the fate of Jews in a rural district of southern Poland led Polish-Canadian researcher Jan Grabowski to conclude that after the massacre of the Jews, their wealth came to be widely regarded as common property, 'and individual attempts at hiding Jews were considered egoistic assaults against the community'. Grabowski regularly encountered the notion, or the conviction, that those who had betrayed, hunted, or killed Jews had more right to the victims' possessions than others. He cites a case in the village of Brnik. In a large-scale manhunt, the local population tracked down dozens of Jews and handed them over to the Germans, a few villages away. After the Jews had been killed, two Germans and a couple of Polish policemen brought bags filled with the victims' clothes and possessions back to the village — thanks for a job well done. Quarrels broke out over who was entitled to these belongings; some of the villagers came to blows, and the Polish police had to intervene. The officers decided that only those who had participated in the manhunt had a right to the loot. Anyone who had not taken an active part did not deserve to gain.

Far from everyone is convinced that the shift in the balance of wealth accounts for the violence against Jews who returned and those who had helped them. Journalist Anna Bikont adds a third reason: the simple fear of being prosecuted for crimes committed during the hunt for the Jews. The perpetrators of such crimes were afraid they would be reported to the new authorities by Jews and people who had attempted to help Jews. While the years immediately after the German withdrawal were chaotic, they were not entirely lawless. The new regime wanted to bring order and peace, and this involved punitive measures, including the punishment of crimes committed against Jewish citizens. And so, Bikont concludes, the guilty saw a reason to get rid of witnesses, whether or not they were Jewish.

Mala says the Olszewskis tried to discourage her from searching for Mira. As she remembers it, they told her, 'The people who have stolen from the Jews are now killing Jews as well.'

There is another possibility, put forward by historian and sociologist Jan T. Gross: an attempt by the perpetrators to drive out their demons by demonic means. Or, as Metallica once put it, to fight fire with fire. The return of Jewish survivors was hard to stomach for those who had been involved in crimes against Jews. People whose lives had been worth less than nothing were now returning from the camps, emerging from the pigsties, or finding their way back from far-flung places in Russia, and were threatening to become a permanent reminder of their misdeeds. Gross quotes leading Polish intellectual Stanisław Ossowski. In 1947, when the violence in rural Poland was far from over, he wrote, 'those whom fate has destined for annihilation can easily appear disgusting to others and removed beyond the pale of human relations'. It's true: pity is not the only conceivable response to the fate of the downtrodden or the persecuted. As Tacitus wrote 2,000 years earlier 'It is human nature to hate the man whom you have injured.' Thousands of Poles smelled the blood on their own hands, and therefore hated the Jews more than ever.

People in and around Karpy give yet another reason for the post-war violence against Jews and their protectors. Almost everyone Daniel and I asked informed us that Jews were communists. Polish resistance fighters—'their own' Armia Krajowa—fought not only the Germans, but also the Red Army and the Soviet-backed Polish People's Army. In other words, they fought communists, including the Jews. No one we asked knew of any violence against people who had protected Jews. The very suggestion was enough to anger some.

Of course, it was a radicalised group among the resistance who went on to commit violent attacks on Jews. Not all Polish resistance units continued fighting once the Germans had gone—far from it. Some recognised that further armed struggle was futile. On paper, Poland was among the victorious nations of the Second World War, but the geopolitical developments shaped at the conferences in Tehran, Yalta, and Potsdam soon made it clear that the country had been consigned to the Soviet sphere of influence. This spelled the end of Poland's main resistance force, the Armia Krajowa. The Red Army continued where the Germans had left off: disarming resistance fighters, arresting them in their thousands, and executing their leaders. But among those who battled on, there were plenty who saw Jewish survivors, even those who were unarmed, as guilty by association with the new Soviet-backed authorities.

One of the few people to survive Bełżec went on to meet his death in this wave of post-war violence. After escaping the extermination camp, Chaim Hirszman stumbled across not one but two groups of armed resistance fighters. The first was the Armia Krajowa. They refused to take him on, but let him live. Then he ran into a group from the much smaller Armia Ludowa. At its peak, this communist resistance army had 30,000 members at most, compared to the 300,000 Poles who fought for the Armia Krajowa. The Armia Ludowa did take Hirszman on. He proved himself as a useful fighter, and once the Germans had been driven out, he was given a post in the security apparatus of the new pro-Soviet government. In March 1946, he gave an eyewitness account of life in Bełżec to a representative of the Jewish Historical Committee in Lublin. After talking to her for several hours, he promised to return the following day to continue his testimony. He never got the chance. That same evening, he was shot dead outside his apartment. The killer, Jerzy Fryze, belonged to the youth wing of an anti-communist group.

The contrasting accounts that different historians give of Hirszman's death speak volumes about the controversy surrounding this phase of Polish history. British historian and Holocaust expert Martin Gilbert says Hirszman was shot 'because he was a Jew'. Polish writer Henryk Pająk argues that Hirszman was killed because he was 'an active and dangerous officer' of the new communist regime.

If Mala had travelled the twenty-five kilometres to Karpy in search of Mira, she would have passed Bełżec, the extermination camp where her little brother, Meir, and her sister Chaja almost certainly died. Mira and Chaja's husband, Majloch, may well have died there, too. The camp would gain far less notoriety than Auschwitz or Majdanek, but in and around the village of Bełżec, everyone knew what had gone on there. East of the Oder, the Holocaust took place under the noses of the local population. Unlike the people of Western Europe, they saw, heard, and smelled the killing. The bodies of those murdered in Bełżec were initially buried in deep pits. Later, the Germans made the Jewish prisoners dig up the bodies and burn them. The flames from these enormous pyres shot into the air, and the stench of burning flesh and bone spread for miles. On damp, windless days, it hung over the River Sołokija and reached Tomaszów Lubelski. Farmers as far away as

Susiec, fifteen kilometres west, spoke after the war of the black skies and the stink.

Local farmers occasionally found people at the side of the railway tracks: Polish Jews who had jumped from a train and landed badly. Unlike many deportees from Western Europe, they were keenly aware that the train was taking them to their death. The Germans forced the last few thousand inhabitants of the Warsaw ghetto to take off their clothes before herding them into the wagons; their nakedness would make it more difficult to escape or resist.

Around the time when Mala visited the Olszewskis, members of the Polish investigative committee for war crimes were writing down the stories of the people who lived nearby. The locals had no hesitation in talking about the camp. They all knew that trainloads of people had gone up in smoke there. The Olszewskis knew what had happened to Mala's family. And they probably knew what Mala would have seen if she had walked to Karpy in search of Mira and Amelka: people digging. The local police chief told the investigative committee he was always having to chase the diggers away, but they kept coming back. If so many Jews had been killed and cremated in one place, there had to be gold in the soil.

Instead of going to Karpy, Mala travelled back to Łódź, where no one seemed surprised to hear her sad news. They told her they already knew she would not find her family, but thought it was something she had to find out for herself.

It's difficult for Mala to talk about the sorrow she felt at that time. 'We need to stop for a bit. Otherwise I'll start to cry, and we can't have that.'

A little later, she says, 'Sometimes I think about Chaja, my sister. She had such a sweet little boy. Seven years old, he was. What did she tell him when she knew they were going to die? That little chap must have asked her: what's going to happen now?'

Then, as if forcing herself to tell a story that *can* be told, she adds, 'The eldest Olszewski girl joined the resistance in the forest and came riding back into Tomaszów Lubelski on a big brown horse.'

Instead of footnotes

The small resistance army led by Chil Grynszpan grew to become
one of the most successful Jewish partisan units. Success, however, is
a relative concept. Only about 200 of the 4,000 men and women who
fled into the forests around Parczew lived to see the end of the war.

In 2009, Frank Blaichman, one of Chil's fighters, wrote *Rather Die
Fighting: a memoir of World War II*. Directly after the arrival of the Red
Army, Poland's newly formed security police assigned him to track
down criminals, collaborators, and traitors in and around the small
town of Parczew, including people who had assaulted defenceless
civilians and Jewish fugitives. On 5 February 1946, as Blaichman was
out on an investigation in the countryside, between 100 and 120 armed
men surrounded Parczew. That day, they had tried in vain to free
the men being held at a police station run by the new Soviet-backed
authorities. Frustrated by their failure, they went on a five-hour spree,
ransacking houses recently reoccupied by Jews who had returned to
the town. In this pogrom, three 'unarmed Polish citizens of Jewish
nationality' lost their lives, as reported by the Committee for Polish
Jews in Lublin. 'Their goods were placed in wagons and carried off.' An
account of the events in Parczew can be found in David Engels' paper
'Patterns of Anti-Jewish Violence in Poland, 1944–1946' in *Yad Vashem
Studies*, vol. XXVI, Jerusalem 1998, pp. 43–85, which is accessible online.

As Blaichman wore a uniform and spoke fluent Polish, people often
assumed he was not Jewish. What he gleaned from his conversations
with the inhabitants of the region led him to conclude that, as a Jew,
there was no future for him in Poland. He emigrated several years after
the war, and eventually settled in the United States.

His memoirs and those of other Jewish partisans from the Grynszpan
group sparked repeated controversy in Poland due to their accounts
of anti-Semitism in the Armia Krajowa. Since the fall of communism,
Poland's main resistance army has become the object of national
celebration in Poland. Every city, and practically every village, has a
street named after the Armia Krajowa or a monument erected in its
memory. For many Poles, these resistance fighters are above all criticism
and, as they see it, the claims made by Chil's Jewish fighters must be
lies. The official history taught in Poland records the ban that senior

Armia Krajowa commanders imposed on the betrayal of Jews, under pain of death. A number of death sentences were indeed carried out for this crime. Even so, hundreds of eyewitness accounts—including some by veterans of the Armia Krajowa themselves—reveal that some of its fighting units killed Jews, especially in the east of the country, and especially if those Jews fought alongside the communist Armia Ludowa.

Hershel Zimmerman wrote his memoirs under the name Harold Werner, published as *Fighting Back. a memoir of Jewish resistance in World War II* (1994).

An account of what happened to Hirszman, the Bełżec survivor who was killed before he could complete his testimony, is given by Martin Gilbert in *The Holocaust: the Jewish tragedy* (1987), most specifically on pp. 816–18. Henryk Pająk wrote about Hirszman's fate in *Konspiracja mlodzieży szkolnej (Conspiracy of School Youth) 1945–1955* (1994), on pp. 130–31.

The peasants digging at the sites where the extermination camps of Aktion Reinhard once stood is described by Jan Tomasz Gross and Irena Grudzińska Gross in the book *Golden Harvest: events at the periphery of the Holocaust* (2012). They mainly focus on diggers at Treblinka, who are pictured posing proudly for the camera, spade in hand, but their book also contains information on digging at the Bełżec site. Their sources include the committee report quoted in this chapter.

In another of his books, *Fear: anti-Semitism in Poland After Auschwitz* (2006), Gross quotes Stanisław Ossowski, the Polish philosopher, who pointed out in 1947 that the downtrodden and the persecuted sometimes receive more loathing than pity. Ossowski wrote this in the magazine *Kuźnica*.

As recently as the 1980s, Dutch traveller Hans Fels discovered the persistence of the notion that Jews who had fled or been murdered had left behind caches of gold. Fels visited the old synagogue, or what was left of it, in Stary Dzików, a village where his grandparents once lived, not far from Bełżec, Karpy, and Tomaszów Lubelski. The local police took him in for questioning, and a comedy of errors ensued in which Fels thought he was being held for trespassing while the police were intent on finding out where he thought the gold was buried. 'We know the Jews buried their valuables around here, and you have come to find the treasure of the synagogue.'

The chapter's opening quote comes from Kalmen Wewryk's *To Sobibor and Back: an eyewitness account* (1999), translated by Howard Roiter from Yiddish into English.

15

The Nysa Kłodzka

'We must expel all the Germans, because countries are built on
national lines and not on multinational lines.'

–Władysław Gomułka, Polish political leader

To hear Polish at its purest, without a hint of a local accent or a
foreign twang, they say Lower Silesia is the place to go. It is spoken
in Wałbrzych, Kamienna Góra, Dzierżoniów, and Bielawa, towns near
the border with Germany and the Czech Republic, between the River
Bóbr and the Nysa Kłodzka (also known as the Bober and the Eastern
Neisse). Linguists suggest that this flawless Polish is related to the
background of the region's residents, people whose roots lie elsewhere.
They came here from all corners of pre-war Poland, but mostly from
the hilly farming country east of the River Bug, land that stretches far
into what is now Ukraine, Lithuania, and Belarus; a region that was
teeming with dialects. As in Karpy, the population spoke a mixture of
Polish and Ukrainian. From the spring of 1945, these people began
arriving in Lower Silesia and, in a quest for a communal spirit, they
began to cultivate a form of standard Polish, as if to quash any possible
doubts about their nationality. As if to say: we are more native than
the natives. We may not come from here, but we belong here. We are
Polish.

Lower Silesia did not become part of Poland until 1945. Two years
earlier, Stalin had already gained Roosevelt and Churchill's agreement

that he would retain control of eastern Poland, the part that Soviet forces had invaded in 1939. To compensate the Poles, Churchill came up with a plan that he illustrated by placing three matches end to end. Roosevelt and Stalin looked at them, intrigued. All German territory east of the rivers Oder and Neisse, Churchill proposed, would be given to Poland, including the former German provinces of Pommern and Upper and Lower Silesia. Poland would also be given the city of Danzig and the southern reaches of East Prussia. The three leaders were quick to agree.

In Polish, these lands became known as *Ziemie Odzyskane*, the 'recovered territories'. This recovery mainly involved expelling all the Germans and bringing in four million Polish-speaking people to replace them. Cities such as Nathan's hometown of Łódź, which had been subject to a demographic policy of Germanisation, saw their resident populations replaced by Poles after the German surrender.

By this time, the Jewish community of Łódź had been decimated, although the city was to remain the centre of post-war Jewish life in Poland for a number of years. Mala's next stop after Łódź was Wałbrzych, which lay deep in Lower Silesia, only twenty kilometres from the Czechoslovakian border. Formerly Waldenburg, the city had been completely German with no Polish or Jewish minority to speak of. But from May 1945, its German residents were displaced at a furious pace. In the terminology of the time, the city was Polonised.

Mala has few memories of Germans being driven out of the new Poland, though her own personal odyssey took her to the very heart of this ethnic cleansing. Her memory can be said to mirror the collective consciousness of Europe on this matter. Outside Germany, this ethnic cleansing is seldom given a place on the history curriculum, not even in Polish cities that prior to 1945 had been almost completely German, or in Czech cities where the same process occurred. The expulsion of Germans was certainly not exclusive to Poland: Hungarians, Soviets, Romanians, Czechs, and Slovaks were also involved. The estimates and calculations of the number of people who died or went missing as a result of the flight and forced displacement of the German-speaking peoples of Eastern Europe are sometimes sketchy, and vary enormously. They start at 200,000 and go all the way up to 2.5 million.

These figures are hard to verify for all kinds of reasons, but even the most conservative estimates are staggering.

Around seven million Germans in total were driven out of the new Poland. This calculation is not disputed and is the official figure used by the Polish authorities. In the new and considerably smaller Germany, some 12 million expelled persons or *Vertriebenen* arrived from all over Europe between 1945 and 1949. This influx meant that the population within Germany's new borders was higher after the Second World War than it had been before, despite the millions of German fatalities. In January 1947, 67 million people lived in the new, smaller Germany, an area that had been home to 60 million in 1939.

When Mala arrived in Wałbrzych, the remaining Germans were obliged to wear a white armband and to take off their hat to every Pole they met. Poles were allowed to evict them from their home at any time. In some instances, this happened in the middle of the night, in winter, in temperatures well below freezing. As British writer and historian Giles MacDonogh commented with reference to this post-war period, 'The boot was on the other foot.' By 1949, a mere 1 per cent of the city's population was German.

The transition to city life was often a culture shock for the new residents, many of whom came from villages such as Karpy. In terms of prosperity and development, there was a gulf to be bridged. One older woman remembers her amazement on arriving in Wałbrzych during the autumn of 1945 to find a toilet inside her house. My God, she thought, those filthy Germans used to shit in their own home! Running water, never mind a toilet, was unheard of in many eastern villages. For months, newly arrived families relieved themselves in Wałbrzych's gardens and parks. Heating radiators ended up on doorsteps outside the city's elegant nineteenth-century façades. The new residents had no time for these strange metal contraptions, which they saw as decoration that took up too much space.

The more unfortunate Germans in the east were held in camps before being put on transports to the new Germany. The Polish camp in Świętochłowice was especially notorious. During the war, it had been a subcamp in the extensive Auschwitz complex, and from February 1945, any German-speaking Pole could end up there: women, children, the elderly. It was a place where the Allies' Potsdam resolution that the transfer of the German population should be 'orderly and humane' collided with the harsh reality of sadistic violence and a desire for vengeance. Over 2,000 of the 5,048 prisoners held there died in a matter of weeks. Camp commandant Salomon Morel told prisoners that his family had been gassed in Auschwitz, and assured them, 'I will not rest until all Germans have had their rightful punishment.' He led a remarkably young group of guards who subjected prisoners to all manner of sadistic ordeals. They were made to eat dung, beat each other, and stand for hours chest-deep in ice-cold water. Survivors' statements recount how Morel forced prisoners to lie on top of each other to form a human pyramid. By the time it was finished, those at its base had passed out or suffocated.

At Łambinowice, which had gone by the name of Lamsdorf only weeks before, German women and children from a nearby village were ordered to exhume a mass grave close by. The bodies of the Soviet prisoners of war they uncovered were already badly decomposed. The stench was unbearable. Years later, a woman prisoner testified that German women and girls were forced to lie face down on the corpses while Polish militiamen shoved their faces deep into the slimy human remains with the butts of their rifles.

In Poland, the atrocities behind the figures have only recently become a focus of attention. In 2017, journalist Marek Łuszczyna wrote a book on the subject, the title of which translates as *A Little Crime: Polish concentration camps*. The title is controversial in itself, given that, shortly after the book's publication, a law was passed forbidding the use of the terms 'death camp' or 'concentration camp' in combination with the adjective Polish. The thinking behind the ban is that, by definition, concentration camps in Poland were German and not Polish. Anyone who says differently is guilty of maligning the country. A weekly publication interviewed Łuszczyna, and based its headline on the book's title. A court case ensued, and the publication lost. The judge demanded a rectification.

The verdict suggests a lack of clarity among modern-day Poles as to whether compatriots who committed crimes under communist rule were in fact Polish at all. They were communists, so doesn't that make them Soviets? In an interview after the ban on speaking of Polish camps, Poland's prime minister insisted, 'What happened after 1939 and later in 1944, 1945 is the responsibility of Germany, and what happened in communist Poland after 1945 is the responsibility of the communists or … the Soviet Union.' Journalist Marek Łuszczyna noted wryly that, by the same reasoning, his fellow countrymen had no right to be proud of Poland's 1974 World Cup team, which came third behind Germany and the Netherlands. This was the era of the Polish People's Republic, after all, so the footballers had been playing for communism, not for Poland.

The treatment of Germans on new Polish territory echoed the race politics of the Nazis. The numbers were of a completely different order, of course, and revenge was wreaked on collaborators across Europe. Yet it is striking that the violence against Germans in post-war Poland had nothing to do with how those German-speaking people had behaved during the war. As the British historian Keith Lowe observed 'Anti-fascists and German Jews were treated exactly the same as any other Germans—they were to be defined by their "Germanness", not their war record or political outlook.'

In short, they were to be given a dose of their own medicine. Polish general and old-time communist Karol Świerczewski told his troops, 'We are going to treat the Germans the way they did us.' And, 'You have to carry out your duties in such a harsh and decisive manner that the Germanic vermin do not hide in their houses but would rather flee from us of their own volition. And … will thank God that they are still alive.'

Harsh and decisive: that is probably how the Polish general's troops went about their duties. Yet the Poles by no means wrought on the Germans what the Germans had wrought on others. Their 'final solution' was not genocide, but expulsion. Millions of people were loaded onto trains, often crammed into the same closed cattle trucks in which Jews from all over Europe had been transported to the death camps in occupied Poland. These trains sometimes stood for days on a siding waiting for permission to enter the Soviet occupation zone in Germany. 'I have seen with my own eyes,' a priest testified in the early

1950s, 'that out of one wagon alone ten corpses were taken and thrown into coffins that had been kept on hand.' The priest was German and had witnessed the arrival in Görlitz, just over the new border along the Lausitzer Neisse. 'I noted further that several persons had become deranged … The people were covered in excrement, which led me to believe that they were squeezed together so tightly that there was no longer any possibility for them to relieve themselves at a designated place.' It was with good reason that *The New York Times* called the expulsion of the Germans from Central Europe 'the most inhumane decision ever made by governments dedicated to the defence of human rights.' The paper printed this in 1946. In the pages of the European press at the time, you will be hard pressed to find a note of disapproval as the Allies implemented their inhumane decision in favour of ethnic cleansing.

* * *

Mala would probably never have gone to Wałbrzych at all if Jakub Egit and Yitskhok Zuckerman had not gone before her. In May 1945, these two Polish Jews travelled to Lower Silesia to see whether the region lent itself to establishing a Jewish community.

Zuckerman, better known as Antek—a name he had picked up during the war—was one of the few leaders of the Warsaw Ghetto Uprising to survive. Others included Marek Edelman, Zuckerman's future wife, Zivia Lubetkin, and Simcha Rotem. Antek had been responsible for obtaining weapons from the Polish Armia Krajowa. One year later, he fought the Germans again, when the entire city of Warsaw rose up in a final act of resistance. Antek found himself in the thick of it for the second time.

The other man, Jakub Egit, was a committed communist, having joined the party in 1931. He survived the war in the Soviet Union, and returned as an officer in a Polish brigade under the command of the Red Army. He maintained good contacts with the new authorities, which had temporarily set themselves up in Łódź.

As soon as he arrived in Wałbrzych, Egit was convinced that this was the place. Not only was Lower Silesia rich in natural resources, but it was also full of textile factories, foundries, breweries, and sawmills, all of which would soon be standing idle. If Polish Jews were able to resettle quickly, there would be less chance of losing out to other Poles. Newcomers to the region could make use of the homes, food, and even clothes that expelled Germans had left behind. Another major advantage was that these cities had not been bombed. Names changed: Waldenburg became Wałbrzych, Landeshut became Kamienna Góra, and Reichenbach im Eulengebirge became Dzierżoniów. Perhaps the two men were also moved by the beauty of the local landscape, if such things still had the power to move them after everything they had seen during the war.

Egit saw a kind of righteous revenge in founding a Jewish settlement, a *yidisher yishev*, in what had been the proud industrial heart of the Third Reich. He envisaged a flourishing Jewish community, with places of worship, hospitals, schools, a couple of Yiddish newspapers, and even a publishing house. He wanted humanity to see that Hitler and his Nazis had not succeeded in their plan for a 'Europe free of Jews'.

Antek took a wholly different view. In his eyes, Lower Silesia's suitability lay in its proximity to the border. A Zionist before the war, the mass slaughter of the Jews had made him determined to join as many other Polish Jewish as possible in the promised land. Once they could cross the border with Czechoslovakia, he thought, the route would lead them via Prague and Vienna all the way to Haifa or Jerusalem.

The two men began their community in Lower Silesia with survivors of Gross-Rosen, a German concentration camp in the area. In fact, it had been a network made up of dozens of camps, and most of its prisoners had been forced to work in stone quarries or to dig an extensive system of underground tunnels. As word of the community spread, Jewish survivors from all over the country began to make their way to Lower Silesia, having discovered that their old shtetlekh and neighbourhoods had disappeared or been taken over by Poles who were not well disposed towards them. By the spring of 1946, over 70,000 had come to the region from eastern Poland and beyond. The largest concentration was in Dzierżoniów: at its peak, there were 18,000 Jewish residents in a town whose pre-war population of approximately

25,000 had included only the smallest of Jewish minorities. In 1946, over 10,000 Polish Jews were living in Wałbrzych, a town of around 60,000 people. This rapid growth was partly due to the connections Egit and Antek had established with the new authorities in Warsaw and Łódź. Based on the assurances of the two men, the Central Committee for Jews in Poland advised all survivors who, like Mala, had found a temporary refuge in Łódź to settle in Lower Silesia. The committee even organised trains to take them there.

Not that these Jewish pioneers were welcomed with open arms by Lower Silesia's lower-ranking officials, themselves newcomers to the region. Jews could seldom count on a job at one of the small factories, shops, and workshops the Germans had left behind—not even Jews with relevant knowledge and experience. The Jews had to work in the mines. 'The mineworkers are only given 160 grams of bread a day, which is not enough,' the local Jewish committee reported. The first Polish newspaper in this recovered territory ran the headline: 'In the new Poland, the Jew will serve the fatherland as labourer.' A newsworthy and unprecedented development, according to the author of the piece.

Nathan experienced these attitudes first-hand. In the autumn of 1945, he reported to the public officials responsible for housing allocation in Wałbrzych. From his appearance, it was still clear that he had narrowly escaped starvation in Auschwitz. 'A house?' the official said. 'First you have to get a job in the coal mines.'

The next day, Mala reported to the same department and presented her Polish papers, the documents issued to her by the policeman in Wolmirstedt. 'I was welcomed like a princess,' she recalls. She was given a wonderful house with five rooms and the right to turf out the German residents—a woman and her sixteen-year-old daughter.

By this time, Mala had already been living in Wałbrzych for a while, in a house she shared with a Red Army officer, his wife, and their baby. Her move from Łódź to Wałbrzych had been occasioned by a business deal she struck with two men in officers' uniforms. She had left Nathan behind at the Bursa.

She met her future business partners at the market in Łódź. This was after she had managed to sell all 200 of the medical thermometers Otto Möller had given her when she left Zerbst. The pharmacies in Łódź had given her a good price for them. This had opened up new possibilities to Mala, and she was hoping to find a new opportunity to trade. With this in mind, she walked up to the two soldiers—officers, by the look of them—who had just pulled up at the market square in a big car and were sizing up their surroundings. It turned out that they were looking to sell a pile of clothes in the boot of their car. Mala said she could help. The men introduced themselves as Moshe and Chaim, and promised Mala 10 per cent of the profits.

The clothes were sold in no time, and the three of them went for a drink together. Mid conversation, Mala switched to Yiddish. Moshe and Chaim stared at her, open-mouthed. You … Jewish? Even Polish Jews saw a Catholic girl in Mala.

Mala saw the men as deserters. During the war, they had fled to the Soviet Union, and had returned to Poland as soldiers. She thought they only wore their uniforms to give them an air of authority when they were out and about. Perhaps they were deserters, but it is just as likely that they had been discharged from military service and were unable or unwilling to return home. Whatever their motives, they had followed the avenue opened up by Jakub Egit, and had settled in Lower Silesia.

Mala told Moshe and Chaim that she came from an Orthodox family, that her father had been a religious teacher who despised lapsed and non-Orthodox Jews, and how her brother had once thrown all her Polish homework to the floor. Moshe and Chaim told her about their plan to make money by purchasing food in Łódź and selling it in their neck of the woods: in Wałbrzych, 240 kilometres south-west.

The plan made sense. The Germans expelled from Lower Silesia had left tons of clothing behind. At the same time, food was in short supply: the region's German farms had been abandoned in a hurry, and the new occupants were struggling to keep up production. Clothing was cheap, while food was expensive. Mala's fluent German made her a major asset, and the men were keen for her to come with them to Wałbrzych, so keen that they would only pay her the 10 per cent they had promised if she agreed. Mala had no qualms about going. Moshe and Chaim had been more than friendly to her. She also saw it as a way to distance herself from Nathan without hurting his feelings too much. She felt it would be for the best. Nathan was clearly besotted with her, but she still couldn't see a future with him.

Nathan took it badly. He had already lost his mother and his sister. Day after day, he went to the Central Committee offices hoping for news that they might still be alive, but always in vain. Now he was losing someone else, the one person he really wanted to be with. It left him feeling desperate. 'I can see no reason to go on living,' he told Mala's friend Różka, who had stayed behind in Łódź.

It is hard to know whether this confession came as a shock to Różka. In only six years, Poland had been transformed into a graveyard. Inside what had been the country's 1939 borders, one-sixth of the people who had lived, breathed, walked, played, made plans for the future, or looked back on a long and fulfilled life were dead. Would one more death, the suicide of a lonely man who had already lost his family, have caused a ripple in this sea of sorrow?

In Łódź that year, suicide was commonplace. American researcher Winson Chu studied the suicide rate among the population, and discovered that the numbers increased directly after the arrival of the Red Army, especially among Jewish survivors. Solomon Perel, the Jewish boy who found himself part of a German panzer division during the invasion of the Soviet Union, records a particularly tragic case in his memoirs. Before the war, when he lived in Łódź with his family, he used to play chess with two boys his own age. In his book, Perel records that one of them, Jerzyk Rappoport, went on to lead the underground Communist Party in the Łódź ghetto during the war, and how his brave deeds gave people courage. Rappoport managed to survive and, after liberation, fell deeply in love with a Jewish girl, a survivor of one of the camps. She did not return his affections, and married someone else. 'He could not cope with this loss,' Perel recalls. 'His instinct for survival and the enormous strength that had made it possible for him to endure the Shoah now deserted him, and he committed suicide.'

Even so, Nathan's words can't have left Różka entirely unmoved. We know this because she gave him Mala's address in Wałbrzych, despite having promised her that she wouldn't. For all his kindness, Mala had decided that Nathan was not the man for her. The realisation had dawned when they were eating at a restaurant in Łódź, shortly before her departure for Wałbrzych. They had spent the day searching for the grave of Nathan's father. He had died in the ghetto during the war, and Nathan thought he knew where he might be buried. They searched endlessly. Nathan's mood went from flat to dispirited to desperate: his mother and sister were already lost to him, and now he couldn't even find his father's grave.

Mala felt sorry for him, and invited him out for meal at her expense. Over dinner, she took pride in telling him that she had never once eaten pork during the war, despite having to hide her Jewishness at every turn, no matter what her circumstances or how far she had been from the watchful eyes of the Jewish community. Nathan saw no reason to be proud. To use a pre-war term popular in Amsterdam, he was a 'bacon Jew'. He had never adhered to Jewish dietary laws, nor had his parents. Only his grandmother ate kosher. In fact, he said, the war had only confirmed his conviction that there was no God.

Mala was shocked, and decided then and there that they could never be together. 'I wanted a kosher household and a husband who attended the synagogue.' It's a remarkable position for someone who was in love with a German. Mala still longed for Erich, a man for whom a kosher household would have been out of the question. 'But if I really had lost Erich and there was no chance of marrying him,' she reasons, 'I at least wanted a husband I could lead a Jewish family life with. The kind of life my father would have wanted for me. A real Jewish family and everything that went with it. It felt like Father's last hopes were pinned on me.'

Over seventy years on, she remembers thinking, 'If I can't be with Erich, I don't want to be with anyone. I'll work in an orphanage and be a spinster for life.' Later, she adds, 'The only thing that attracted me to Nathan was that he looked a little bit like Erich.'

In Wałbrzych, Moshe and Chaim took Mala to the house of an army officer, his wife, and their three-month-old baby. She had a lovely time — there was plenty to eat, vodka, and even a piano. In high spirits, the men showed off their military decorations and asked Mala to go into business with them long term, buying clothes from the Germans who were leaving, and selling them to Poles as they arrived. 'I saw instantly that it could be a goldmine, so I accepted,' Mala says. 'And they were right: because I could speak German, everyone preferred doing business with me.' Her lack of resentment towards Germans in general helped, too. She had no trouble being fair and reasonable in her dealings with them.

She wrote to Różka to let her know that she would be staying on in Wałbrzych. She told her about the business, how well things were going, and she asked Różka to consider moving to Lower Silesia, too, along with her new fiancé. It was a lovely part of the country, she said. The Jewish community was flourishing, and the town had not been bombed to rubble like so many other places. Różka decided to stay put, but she did give Mala's address to Nathan. And that would have consequences.

Mala moved in with the officer and his wife, and enjoyed their company. Moshe and Chaim often stopped by, and the vodka would flow freely. One evening, the two men—both bachelors—invited Mala to the pictures, each without the other knowing. Mala kept them guessing and was wondering who to choose when, out of nowhere, Nathan appeared. He threw his arms around her and held her tightly. Only then did he say hello to the others. He had a letter with him, a reply from Różka. In it, she gave her reasons for not wanting to move to Wałbrzych. She also told Mala how desperately sad Nathan had been.

The next day, Nathan and Mala went to the housing department with Moshe and Chaim. That was when Nathan was told he would have to work in the mines. In a fury, Moshe and Chaim drew their pistols and were ready to fight his corner, but Mala persuaded them to back down. War had taught her a different lesson from the two soldiers. She returned the next day, and her Polish papers plus a modicum of charm did the trick. Nathan no longer had to work in the mines, and instead came to live with her in the large house the department allocated to her, a house that, as we have seen, was already occupied by a German mother and daughter.

That afternoon, Mala had a long talk with Nathan, and admitted her love for Erich, the German aircraft engineer. She had to steel herself. 'In Łódź, and for a long time after, I couldn't bring myself to say that some Germans were good. I didn't dare, especially after hearing about the terrible things everyone had been through.'

Mala said she simply wasn't capable of falling in love with anyone but Erich. Nathan accepted this. He told her he was willing to wait. He moved in with her, but they slept in separate bedrooms. Mala says it gave them a chance to get to know each other better. In the meantime, she carried on trading in clothes, a business she now ran with Nathan's help. 'We earned good money every day,' she says.

Mala was nineteen years old, a successful businesswoman living with a young man so devoted to her that he was prepared to accept a platonic relationship. Two Germans completed the household. Mala hadn't had the heart to put the mother and daughter out on the street. 'I just couldn't. I knew from experience that Germans were people, too!' Grateful for the chance to stay, the two German women lived in one room, and took on the roles of cook and housekeeper.

After the episode at the housing department, Moshe and Chaim gave Nathan a pistol. It made him intensely happy. For the first time in his life, he was able to fend off danger, anything but a luxury in those days. Within weeks, Lower Silesia had become the Wild West of the new Poland. Resistance groups who had refused to disband and were now fighting the Red Army came to the region, as did other armed groups that embraced the outlaw life. The abandoned bunkers and tunnels in the wooded hills made a perfect base, and the Germans who had stayed behind made easy prey. As citizens, these Germans had next to no rights, and could expect little protection from new and inexperienced law enforcers, most of whom were less familiar with the local terrain than the outlaws themselves.

Scanning the newspaper reports and court archives from that time shows how blurred the lines were between outlaw and resistance fighter. These armed groups often went by abbreviations that referred to bona fide national resistance organisations, but in practice such names meant little. They fought Germans, Soviet soldiers, the new Polish authorities, or anyone they thought might have something worth taking. The manifesto of one Polish group even included 'completing the elimination of the Jews' as one of its official objectives.

Two such armed groups were native to the area and therefore German. One called itself *Freies Deutschland* (Free Germany); the other consisted of *Werwölfe* (Werewolves). The Werewolves had been established in late 1944 by Himmler as a special forces unit trained to carry out covert operations 'behind enemy lines'. By this stage, that phrase could be applied to all of Europe.

War had made violence part of everyday life, even among unarmed civilians. Teenagers had received no official schooling for six years, and the horrors they had witnessed had cut them adrift from their geographical, moral, and social moorings. In this, they were not alone. Historians use the term 'brutalisation': the slightest trigger led people to beat each other to a pulp, a state of heightened tension that lasted into the 1950s.

One example that has stayed with me comes from the world of football. The desire both to play and to spectate was so great that matches continued throughout the occupation, even when the terror was at its worst. These included legal matches involving Germans and ethnic Germans, and illegal matches between Poles. The professional club from Oświęcim — yes, Auschwitz — played a regular league fixture on 14 January 1945, just days before the first Soviet tanks rolled in and Red Army soldiers began liberating prisoners. The players must have been preoccupied with things to come, because they lost 10–1 to TuS Karwin, a team from a town that now lies in the Czech Republic, but then played in the Upper Silesian district league.

Only weeks after German forces had been driven from the region, the Silesian football clubs resumed their matches. A trip to the stadium was popular, but also dangerous. Matches often descended into brawls, especially if they ended in victory for AKS Chorzów, a club that had adopted the name Germania Königshütte during wartime and played on in a Germanised league. Now that the Germans had been defeated, it was payback time. In September 1947, at a match in Sosnowiec, a spectator heard one of the players speaking German. Dozens died in the rioting that ensued — over 100, according to some reports — while over 1,000 people had to be treated in hospital. The exact figures remain a mystery: in a desperate attempt to restore some semblance of order, the authorities suppressed all publications about the incident.

Suppression is a wider problem when it comes to forming a detailed impression of the violence in the region at this time. The new authorities gave clear instructions to the censor and the press: the country needs positive and uplifting fare, not the woeful reality of the day but the promise of a glorious future. As a historian, there is little point in relying on the contemporary news reports, awash with stories of reconstruction and repair, generic tales of camaraderie, and the desire for social justice, in stark contrast to the injustices committed by the defeated aggressor. Personal memoirs from the time are a far more accurate source, and speak of robbery, murder, rape, and violent clashes.

The rise of one particular form of violence meant that Mala and Nathan's days in Poland were soon numbered: the pogrom.

Instead of footnotes

In total, the Poles detained around 40,000 Silesians and other German-speaking Poles in the former subcamps of Auschwitz. Another 30,000 were deported by the Red Army to camps in the Soviet Union. Those who made it out of the Soviet camps alive, most of them only after the death of Stalin in 1953, stood a chance of being arrested on their return and locked up in a communist prison for having betrayed the Polish people.

The atrocities committed in the Polish camps have been extensively documented. In this chapter, I have based my account on Keith Lowe's book *Savage Continent: Europe in the aftermath of World War II* (2012); on Victor Sebesteyn's *1946: the making of the modern world* (2014); and on *After the Reich: from the liberation of Vienna to the Berlin Airlift* (2007) by Giles MacDonogh.

As regards the number of fatalities among expelled Germans, it is worth qualifying the figures and making a comparison with others driven from their homeland in the months and years following Germany's capitulation. In *Bloodlands* (2010), Timothy Snyder writes, 'In the postwar period, Germans were about as likely to lose their lives as Poles, the other group that was mainly sent west to a national homeland. Germans and Poles were much less likely to die than

Ukrainians, Romanians, Balts, and the Caucasian and Crimean peoples.
Fewer than one in ten Germans and Poles died during or as a direct
result of flight, exile, or deportation; among Balts and Soviet citizens,
the rate was more like one in five. As a general rule, the further east
the deportation, and the more directly Soviet power was involved, the
more deadly the outcome.'

Winson Chu, the American who carried out research into the
incidence of suicide among Jewish inhabitants of Łódź, published his
figures in *Zeitschrift für Genozidforschung* (*Journal for Genocide Studies*),
vol. 16 (2018) in an article called '»Wir sind keine Deutschen nur dem
Volke nach«. Multiethnische Vergangenheiten und Volksdeutsche in der
deutschen Kriminalpolizei in Lodz während des Zweiten Weltkriegs'
('"We are Germans not by ethnicity alone.": multiethnic pasts and
ethnic Germans in the German Criminal Police in Lodz during the
Second World War.') In the spring of 2018, he presented his analysis
of the statistics at the Warsaw German Historical Institute in a lecture
entitled 'Jewish Suicide Reports and the German Criminal Police in
Lodz/Litzmannstadt'.

16
The Bóbr

'I've got a lot of friends, and we've got a lot of makeup. So, the next time you're huggin' up with some really super, groovy white guy, or you met a really great, super keen white chick, don't be too sure. They might be black.'

–Eddie Murphy, comedian

Mala and Nathan got married on her twentieth birthday, 22 February 1946. A rabbi in Wałbrzych performed the ceremony, with ten members of the Jewish faith in attendance, the required number for a traditional Jewish wedding. The rabbi's wife gave Mala a white scarf to cover her head and face. He led her around Nathan seven times, after which the two of them went out into the snow-covered streets and took the tram back home. Mala was now Marilka Shlafer. She still hadn't fallen in love.

So why marry? 'Well, we were already living together,' Mala answers.

Besides, Nathan had promised her a kosher household, and that was something Mala appreciated. Her adaptability had brought her a long way, but now that she could be openly Jewish again, she cherished the idea of living by at least some of the rules she had been expected to obey as the child of Orthodox Jewish parents.

The pogrom that brought Mala and Nathan's life in Lower Silesia to an end took place 300 kilometres further east, in the central Polish city of Kielce. The events that unfolded there also snuffed out Jakub Egit's dream of a Jewish revival in a new corner of Poland, a communal life with Yiddish as its language, guided by specifically Jewish institutions. Those same events left Antek feeling utterly bereft, and strengthened his Zionist convictions.

The violence in Kielce was triggered by a 'blood libel' or 'ritual murder accusation', an anti-Semitic trope that goes back to the Middle Ages and played a part in the persecution of Jews in the Rhineland. The libel has taken various forms, but at its core is the claim that Jews abduct and murder Christian children to use their blood in Jewish rituals. As thousands of Jews left mainly German cities for a new life in the Kingdom of Poland, the blood libel followed them and appears in all kinds of memoirs. The most compelling account I have read is by Israel Joshua Singer, brother of Isaac Bashevis Singer, the only writer in Yiddish to win the Nobel Prize for Literature.

Eleven years older than his Nobel laureate brother, Israel Joshua Singer was born in Biłgoraj, a small town not far from Tomaszów Lubelski. Biłgoraj is a place where several strands in this book come together. Singer's father was a respected rabbi there. The grandfather of Daniel—my travelling companion on the search for the Gmitruks in much the same area—was mayor of the town. And the 'ordinary men' of Reserve Police Battalion 101 from Christopher Browning's book were billeted there during the war.

Around the turn of the century, the Singer family moved to Leoncin, a shtetl some forty kilometres north-west of Warsaw, and later to Warsaw itself. In the 1930s, the brothers emigrated to the United States: Joshua left first, followed by Isaac. Both men wrote about the world they had left behind in Eastern Europe. The accounts written by Joshua, who died of a heart attack in 1944, are anything but nostalgic: he describes the world he grew up in as a Hasidic boy in Leoncin as dull and narrow-minded. He was driven to despair by the intensity with which his obsessively strict parents practised their faith and the amount of religious study they demanded of him and of themselves. His rabbi father, Pinchas Mendel, spent countless hours poring over the Tanach and the Talmud.

'In our house everything was a sin. Calling my teacher, Reb Mayer, crazy was a sin. Catching flies on the Sabbath was a sin. Drawing was a sin. Running was also a sin, since it did not befit Jews to run, only gentiles. No matter what one did or didn't do, chances were it was sinful. Doing absolutely nothing was certainly a sin. "Why are you wasting time?" Father would complain each time he caught me looking out the window. "A Jew must never be idle. He must study instead."

'The Jew in question was a young child who spent ten hours a day in the heder [cheder], but apparently this wasn't enough.'

Fortunately for Joshua, every now and then something happened in Leoncin to make his young boy's heart beat a little faster. A blood libel, for example. Singer's description reads like a dark fairy tale, though he always insisted that things happened exactly as he describes. He was there and I was not, and Singer is a wonderful writer. In light of all this, the following account sticks close to the tale as he tells it.

It was shortly after the turn of the century on a day between Purim and Passover. As a state, Poland was non-existent; Warsaw and its environs were under Russian rule. On that day, the bath house caught fire. The attendant, a man called Eber, used water from the *mikvah*, the ritual bath, to douse the flames. He then refilled the almost empty bath with water from a nearby mud pond in which ducks swam and dived. When Joshua's father heard about this the next day, he ordered the bath house to be closed, as the *mikvah* now contained more swamp water than spring water, and was therefore no longer kosher enough. To correct the situation, the rules stated that the bath had to be drained completely and then filled with milk to purify it. Once it was kosher again, the attendant smeared the windows with red paint to stop any wayward schoolboys taking a peek at the women as they bathed.

Passover came, and to make their matzos the Hasidim wanted to use a special kind of dough with water that was drawn after the sun had gone down. The water was loaded onto a wagon with a big cask, and driven into town with great ceremony. 'The cask was wrapped in Passover tablecloths and the people marched behind it with veneration. A few gentiles witnessed the Jewish rite with complete astonishment.'

Among the gentiles who occasionally hung around Jews were two brothers from a nearby German colony. This was at the start of the twentieth century, and these events take place in a multicultural world. The two brothers were locked in a fierce competition to win the favour of the Jewish community, as both of them wanted the position of *Shabes goy*. This was a gentile who heated the ovens, took down the candlesticks, and chopped wood on the Sabbath, when Jews were forbidden to work or do so much as strike a match. All these jobs went to the elder brother, and with good reason: the man spoke Yiddish. Not only that, but he had familiarised himself with all the Jewish customs and holidays. He could recite the benediction over every glass of whisky he was offered. He knew that Jews were forbidden by law from drinking wine that had been touched by a gentile, and he would warn the housewives when he was at the door with the words 'A *goy* is coming ...' so that they could put away the wine in time.

Quite the man, you might think, except for the fact that he never left a job to his younger brother, who began nursing a deep resentment against him and all of Leoncin's Jewish community. After the cleansing of the ritual bath and the procession with the water, the brother spread a story among the gentiles that the Jews had lured a Christian child into the bath house to be killed by the ritual slaughterer. Not only that, he said, but Eber the keeper of the bath house had carried the Christian blood in a pail to the baker, who had mixed it with the holy water and kneaded it into the matzos.

The frustrated brother not only told the story to the German colony, but also to the surrounding Polish settlements. The rumour spread from village to village. 'Since it was close to Easter, when gentiles are generally incensed against the Jews for crucifying their Lord, the peasants' blood began to seethe.'

Witnesses began to appear, women who swore that they had seen with their own eyes how the child had been lured to its death. Jews who had gone to the surrounding villages to sell their wares came back wounded. The peasants were out to make the Jews pay for spilling innocent Christian blood. The ritual slaughterer was afraid to show his face.

A rumour spread that the gentiles were planning to come to the fair, which was only a few days away. The story went that they were going to murder all the Jews who had dared to consume the matzos made with Christian blood. The fear among the Jews was dreadful. Gates and doors were bolted at night, something that was unheard of in a shtetl such as Leoncin. Eventually, a few of the town's leading citizens decided to call on a prominent Polish landowner and district judge to ask for his protection.

Squire Christowski was not only a prominent citizen, but also a heretic who never set foot in a church. He scoffed at the accusation. Yet as a judge he had to be sure, and therefore demanded to know if any Christian children had recently been reported missing. It turned out that none had. Yet the gentiles continued to insist that the Jews had murdered a Christian child. At this, the town's lumber merchant, a wealthy man, had his coach and team harnessed, put on his best coat, and drove thirty kilometres to Sochaczew, where the real seat of power lay: a Russian *Nachalnik* or district head. The merchant asked the Russian to come back to Leoncin with him to solve the case. The red-bearded Nachalnik was far from amenable, but a juicy bribe soon changed his mind and he climbed aboard the merchant's carriage. He ordered ten of his men to accompany them with a view to restoring order in Leoncin by force if need be.

The Nachalnik, the policemen, and the lumber merchant arrived back on the eve of the fair. Groups of Polish peasants had already gathered in town. The Nachalnik went to the bath house, where a mob of gentiles had assembled. All the Jews were there, too, their heads bared to the Nachalnik. The younger of the German brothers was brought forward, and the investigation began. He gave a glib and detailed account of how he had seen the bath house keeper carrying a pail filled with red liquid.

'And where is this pail?' the Nachalnik asked sternly.

'Here it is, Illustrious Sire,' the bath house keeper said, and produced a pail stained with the red paint that had been smeared on the bath house windows.

Laughing, the Nachalnik held up the pail and asked the crowd, 'Is this blood or paint, peasants?'

'Paint, Illustrious Sire,' the peasants said.

'Are any of your children missing, peasants?' the Nachalnik asked.

'No, no one, Illustrious Sire,' the peasants answered in chorus.

'So if everyone is alive and well,' the Nachalnik demanded, 'how could a child have been killed?'

'We don't know, Illustrious Sire,' the frightened peasants replied, 'but the German told us he saw with his own eyes how the Jews killed a Christian child in the bath house …'

The Nachalnik grabbed the tall, thin German by the lapels of his oversized jacket and shook him. 'What did you see, you son-of-a-bitch?'

The man began to sputter, and the Nachalnik dealt him a hard blow, roaring, 'Tell the truth, you son-of-a-bitch, or I'll slice strips from your hide!'

The German sank to his knees and began to beat his breast. 'I made it all up, Illustrious Sire,' he blubbered, 'because these Jews would not give me any work. They give it all to my brother and leave me to starve.'

The Nachalnik thrust out his chest, blazing with medals, and cried, 'I will send you to Siberia for stirring up these people!'

The policemen were itching to tie up the kneeling German, but the Nachalnik told them to put their ropes away. 'Turn the son-of-a-bitch over and give him a dozen lashes on his bare ass,' he ordered. 'Then he can go.'

The policemen eagerly brought down their whips on the German's bony behind, counting the strokes slowly.

'Jesus!' he shrieked, in German.

And with every stroke, Singer claimed, the Nachalnik bellowed, 'That's what I'll give anyone who spreads lies and stirs up the people. In my district, peasants, order will prevail!'

Following the Treaty of Versailles, the Russian officials, or Nachalniks, disappeared from Poland, and the power of the country's large landowners increased. Although many of them were not exactly happy—or were no longer happy—about the presence of Jews in 'their' country, they chose order over chaos. All this changed again in the autumn of 1939. The German occupiers had no need of blood libels as a pretext for violence against Jews. And if the local population was willing to lend a hand, so much the better. They could be rewarded for their contribution. The Jews had nowhere left to turn, no hope of protection.

After the German withdrawal, power fell to the Soviets and the Polish communists. For a time, it was unclear how the new authorities would respond to the unrest that a blood libel could unleash. The first major test came in August 1945, when a rumour about the ritual slaughter of a Christian child at the synagogue in Kraków spread like wildfire. Jews throughout the neighbourhood were hounded and attacked. Jewish shops were destroyed and looted, as was the synagogue. A number of policemen and soldiers took part in the violence, but the majority of the security forces heeded their commanding officers, and order was restored. As a result, this urban pogrom led to only one confirmed death (although there were rumours of several more) and a few dozen casualties, some of them serious.

However, the outburst was a psychological blow to many, not least the surviving members of Poland's intelligentsia. A number of their articles expressed horror at the realisation that even the Holocaust had not consigned the blood libel to the past and that, if such violence could erupt in a cultured university city like Kraków, it could happen anywhere in Poland. Hanna Zajdman was one of those injured in the pogrom. She was shaken, not so much by the physical violence she suffered, but by the vicious comments made by the people whose job it was to help her. In the ambulance on her way to hospital, she heard a nurse talking to a soldier about how they shouldn't have to help 'this Jewish scum' because they were child killers who deserved to be shot.

Hanna Zajdman underwent an operation. As she was recovering on the ward, a soldier came to tell the patients that once they had been treated he would take them all to prison—child killers that they were—and proceeded to beat an injured man who was awaiting surgery. A short time later, two railway workers appeared. 'It's a scandal that a Pole does not have the civil courage to hit a defenceless person,' one of them said, and went on to demonstrate his own civil courage by striking one of the Jewish patients.

'One of the hospital patients hit me with a crutch,' Zajdman later testified. 'Women, including nurses, stood behind the doors threatening us, saying that they were only waiting for the surgery to be over in order to rip us apart.'

Before a year had passed, another pogrom would take place, an eruption of violence that would prove to be the tipping point for the community

of Jewish Holocaust survivors in Poland. The date was 4 July 1946; the
place, Kielce. The accusation that set the violence in motion was made
the night before by eight-year-old Henryk Błaszczyk; what ensued has
been the focus of a series of studies and books. Three days earlier,
Henryk's father had gone to the police to report him missing. The boy
returned of his own accord, and his father demanded to know where in
God's name he had been all this time. It later transpired that, without
telling his parents, young Henryk had hitched a ride to a village about
twenty-five kilometres away, where he and his family had lived six
months earlier.

The war had made giving your children a calm and consistent
upbringing a near impossibility for many parents. In the months and
even years that followed, thousands of young Henryks did whatever
they liked without paying undue heed to notions of parental authority.

His pockets stuffed with cherries, Henryk told his parents that he
had been kidnapped. Together with a bunch of other children, he had
been held captive in the basement of a building that was full of Jews.
The threat of murder hung over their heads, Henryk revealed: the
Jews wanted their blood to make matzos. Luckily, he had been able to
escape. At the age of eight, our Henryk was already well versed in local
myths and prejudices.

His father, Walenty, went straight to the police station to report
the crime, but, as he was blind drunk, the officer on duty told him to
come back the next day. Having sobered up, he returned the following
morning accompanied by a neighbour and his son. They went to the
supposed scene of the crime, a large building a few storeys high at 7
Planty Street by the River Silnica. There, Henryk pointed out a man in
a green hat as the person who had lured him inside.

At the time, the building was home to a kind of Jewish community
centre that also housed some 180 survivors of the German
concentration camps and repatriates from the Soviet Union. Six years
earlier, Kielce's Jewish community had been around 25,000 strong,
roughly 35 per cent of the population. In 1946, the people living on
Planty Street represented around half of the town's Jews.

Father, son, and neighbour returned to the building with nine plain-
clothes policemen to bring the man in the green hat in for questioning.

On their way, they told passers-by what was going on: that they were out to wreak justice on Jews who were kidnapping and killing Christian children.

From that point on, things quickly spiralled out of control. In police custody, the man in the green hat took a beating. The head of the Jewish Committee rushed to the police station to warn that a pogrom was imminent and to explain that there was no truth to the rumours of kidnappings and murders. The building on Planty Street didn't even *have* a basement. It was no use; he was sent packing. A police escort returned to the building, this time with a crowd in tow. Everyone was talking about the horrors taking place in the 'Jew house'.

The police gained entry to the building, and found no Christian children. Nor did they find a basement. Outside they gave young Błaszczyk a good telling-off in front of the crowd that had gathered. This might have been one of those familiar moments of release, similar to the one witnessed by young Israel Joshua Singer in Leoncin around the turn of the century: the instigator gets a spanking, and the angry mob sees sense and eventually slinks away. Not so in Kielce. Convinced the police were attempting a cover-up, people's anger grew.

The crowd won over a number of policemen who, to loud cheering, turned their weapons on the building as if to prevent people inside escaping. This encouraged onlookers to throw stones; no one stopped them. In the midst of the commotion, two trucks of military police arrived to restore order and replace or, if necessary, detain the policemen. But soon they, too, were caught up in the frenzy, spurred on by incensed civilians who hurled abuse like 'commie lovers' and 'Stalin's flunky', terms that clearly touched a nerve. Were the police really serving ordinary Poles, many wondered, or were they working for the Soviets? Years of nationalist and German propaganda had hammered home the message that all Jews were communists anyway. One soldier was slapped in the face. Another was berated by a member of the crowd, who shouted, 'If you're such a hero, go and beat the Jews!'

It wasn't long before a few members of the security service forced their way into the building, threatening and robbing the residents. Worse still, they began to drag them outside, where they fell into the hands of the raging crowd, which had been joined by a few hundred workmen from the nearby iron foundry. Wielding tools, they forced their way into the building and assaulted yet more residents.

Forty-two people lost their lives in the violence on 4 July 1946. They included a pregnant woman and a young mother and her child. The victims were stoned, shot dead, or their skulls bashed in with all manner of implements. Eighty of the building's residents were injured. A few of them survived by feigning death for hours on end.

The victims looked nothing like the Hasidim from Leoncin that Singer described, with their prayer shawls, sidelocks, hats, and wigs. In appearance, they were virtually indistinguishable from their murderers. Three had been highly decorated soldiers in the Polish army. Sources variously claim that two or three of the dead were not Jewish at all, and that they included two members of the security forces shot in self-defence by Jews. The reason for the pogrom had been identical to that in Leoncin. The major difference was that for one day in Kielce the authorities were on the side of the anti-Semites, and the impartiality of Leoncin's Nachalnik was nowhere to be found.

And what of the Catholic Church? The only institution still standing after six years of terror, it had considerably greater authority to address and admonish the population than did the country's new Soviet-backed leaders. But it had no real desire to do so. Of course, the church was willing to condemn the violence in general as it condemns every murder, regardless of who is the victim, to paraphrase a statement issued by Poland's most senior cleric at the time, Cardinal August Hlond. But the cardinal felt no need to dwell on the details of what happened in Kielce, or to reject the blood libel that had sparked the killings.

Seven days after the pogrom, Hlond told the international press that 'the miserable and deplorable events in Kielce' had not been triggered by racism. They formed an incident in 'an armed ... political struggle' against a regime that the majority of Poles did not want. In this conflict, 'some Jews' had unfortunately perished, 'but the number of Poles perishing is incomparably greater'.

The bishop of Kielce, Czesław Kaczmarek, went several steps

further. He argued that the security forces were controlled by Jews, and had started the pogrom 'as proof that anti-Semitism and fascism predominate in Polish society and as proof that the church ... is reactionary'. In an investigative report that he commissioned, witnesses were reported as saying that 'the Jews inside the house were defending themselves with grenades'. The first fatalities of the incident had been Poles, the report insisted, and not Jews.

Even more telling than the words of the ailing Hlond and the nationalist fanatic Kaczmarek were those of Stefan Wyszyński, a young man at the time. Not long before the pogrom, he had been appointed bishop of Lublin, and would go on to become the most influential spiritual leader in Poland and a hero in the country's fight against communism. Today his larger-than-life, slightly slumped stone effigy stares thoughtfully at passing shoppers from its seat on a plinth in the centre of Warsaw. Without Wyszyński's intercession, Karol Wojtyła would never have been elected Pope John Paul II.

A delegation of leaders from the community of Jewish survivors in Poland paid him a visit shortly after the pogrom in Kielce. They hoped to move the young and influential Catholic intellectual to make a strongly worded condemnation of anti-Semitism. A vain hope, as it turned out. The Jews had brought such hatred upon themselves, Wyszyński explained to the Jewish leaders, by collaborating with the new Polish government. A number of the ministers were Jewish, and were therefore accomplices to the atheism propagated by the Soviet Union. Wyszyński even went a step further. The Germans, he said, had attempted to destroy 'the Jewish nation' because it was 'an advocate of communism'. And the Germans had modelled the horrors of their camps on those of the Siberian camps. It was there that the origins of this recent evil lay.

He went on to give the Jewish leaders a piece of unsolicited advice. The best thing that Polish Jews could do, he told them, was to work hard to get a state in Palestine or some colonies in South America.

What Wyszyński presented to the Jewish delegation was an intellectual-sounding version of what for years had been known in Poland as *Żydokomuna*: the notion that communism had come to Poland as the result of a Jewish conspiracy. This notion had wide currency and the delegation were not surprised by it, although they had been hoping to hear something different. But it was another point made by Wyszyński that shocked them. It was far from certain, the young bishop explained, that the blood libel was unfounded. He referred to a notorious 1913 trial in Kiev, at which a Russian Jew called Mendel Beilis stood accused of ritual murder. Many Jewish books, both old and new, had been consulted during the trial, Wyszyński argued, without disproving the existence of the blood ritual. The Kiev court had acquitted Beilis, but the bishop saw no reason to suppose that the matter of the blood ritual had been laid to rest.

At the time of the pogrom, this was expressed in more forceful terms by an auxiliary bishop in a conversation with the British ambassador, Victor Cavendish-Bentinck. There was some proof, the cleric said, that the child in Kielce whose testimony had sparked the whole incident 'had in fact been maltreated and that the Jews had taken blood from his arm'. The ambassador concluded in a report to London that, if a bishop was prepared to believe such a thing, it was hardly surprising that 'uneducated Poles' were inclined to do the same.

Reading this report, it's hard not to hear the ambassador dismissing these Poles as medieval in their prejudices. But 'medieval' falls short as a term of reproach, given that, as far back as 1247, Pope Innocent IV had issued the first papal bull declaring the accusation of ritual murder levelled at the Jews to be a falsehood. Seven hundred years later, directly after the Second World War, the Catholic authorities in Poland had yet to toe the papal line. Things are different today. A 2014 survey revealed that most Poles agree with the thirteenth-century pontiff. The percentage of the population who believe in the blood libel has fallen to thirteen, which of course means that one in ten Poles do still consider the myth to be credible. They believe that Jews need Christian blood for their rituals or traditions, such as making matzo.

The Jewish leaders who went to see Wyszyński understood that an episcopal declaration against anti-Semitism was not on the cards. The people could interpret any such declaration as a show of support for the communist authorities who were calling on Poles to bury anti-Semitism once and for all in the aftermath of Kielce. Why would the church jeopardise its popular standing for the sake of a section of the population that many priests and other clerical foot soldiers had already been railing against for decades?

If communism was Jewish, then it stood to reason that anti-Semitism amounted to anti-communism. And anti-communist was exactly what the church was and wanted to be.

These tactical considerations were an extension of the behaviour that many Catholic clerics had exhibited during the occupation of Poland. In the eastern village of Radziłów, a ninety-minute drive from Czyżewo, Jews were being beaten, robbed, and worse in the summer of 1941. In the midst of the unrest, Chaja Finkelsztejn, one of the few Jews from Radziłów to survive the war, went to see the local priest. She suspected that he had given his blessing to the pogrom, and hoped he could stop the violence. On entering the presbytery, she saw a number of large copper pots that had belonged to Jewish acquaintances from the village. She made no mention of this, and showed the priest the bruises on her neck. The rest of her body was in the same state, she said, and men from the parish had tried to rape her and her daughter. She appealed to him to address his congregation. 'As their spiritual father, you should tell them from the pulpit that they shouldn't help the Germans because it besmirches the good name of Poles. The Germans alone do plenty of harm to the Jews.' The priest looked anxious. 'As big as I am …' he said, raising his hand above his head, 'I would become this small to my congregation.' He dropped his hand low, and said he was afraid they would lynch him. 'They might regret it later, but in the heat of the moment they could kill me, that's how great their hatred is of the Jews. Every Jew between twelve and sixty years old is a communist.'

Finkelsztejn then tried to explain that any Jews with communist leanings had already headed east with the Red Army when they'd had the chance. She reminded the priest that her children had even refused to wear communist red scarves to school, and that her family had been treated as class enemies by the Soviets. This he remembered, but it had little impact in a world that equated Judaism with communism.

In the wake of the Kielce pogrom, Polish newspaper columnists asked indignantly how such a thing could happen so soon after the German massacre of the Jews. The blood libel was a primitive superstition that had no place in the new Poland. Yet on another level, the pogrom appeared to spark a very different response, and thousands of Jews across the country found themselves confronted with open aggression. In one small town near Mala's home in Wałbrzych, a father who had lost sight of his daughter at the market told the police she had been kidnapped by Jews. Although the man was drunk, a few policemen took the accusation seriously and raided Jewish homes near the square. They even inspected the pots and pans on the stove, perhaps expecting to find the meat of a small child cooking away. On returning to the station, they found the missing seven-year-old waiting patiently. It had seemed to her the most likely place to be reunited with her drunken father.

Noach Lasman, who lived in the town, recalls sitting on a tram the next day and hearing a trio of apparently sensible citizens discussing a rumour that was doing the rounds. Some Jews, he heard one woman explain, had lost their sight as a result of the terrible things they had been through. The solution, a fellow passenger said, lay in using the blood of an innocent child. Yes, a third confirmed, rubbing the blood of an innocent child into their eyes could restore their vision.

One of the first murders in the Jewish community in Lower Silesia to be widely publicised was that of a dentist. Hundreds attended the funeral. For her part, Mala remembers the killing of a young Jewish mother who refused to hand over her money to a gang of thieves. 'The Poles stabbed her to death, in front of her young son.' A Polish historian who searched the police records of Wałbrzych and environs for this book could find no report of such a crime. But that needn't be the full story: these were chaotic times, and far from every incident was filed in records that are recoverable today.

One crime that was well-documented is the killing of twenty-six-year-old Becalel Mosze Zylberberg from Nowy Sącz. Mala remembers it well. Almost the entire Jewish community turned out to attend his funeral, which was reported by a newspaper with the words 'democratic' and 'Zionist' in its masthead. This was a few weeks after the pogrom in Kielce. Zylberberg was a Zionist activist who had helped guard a number of the Jewish agricultural collectives, or kibbutzim, being established across the region at the time. The funeral swelled into a public demonstration, attracting no fewer than 8,000 people. The reporter described the scene: 'The victim's young wife walked behind the coffin. They had been married just three weeks before.'

The newspaper included two speeches in its report: one by a representative of the provisional government; the other, by the vice-chairman of the Jewish Committee of Lower Silesia. In Polish, the government representative said the murder had been intended to intimidate the Jewish community, and in this it had failed. He assured those present that everything would be done to safeguard their security. 'The Jewish community will continue on its present path and build a new life in Lower Silesia.' Speaking in Yiddish, the representative of the Jewish Committee said Zylberberg had died 'for no other reason than that he was a Jew'. His death had come 'at the dawn of the fulfilment of a dream: life in a free Jewish state in Palestine'. Turning to the coffin, he added, 'Your blood, blood that was spilled in innocence, will strengthen us in our struggle for a national rebirth in Palestine.'

It soon became clear whose words struck a chord with the mourners. In the four months that followed, the Jewish population of Lower Silesia plummeted from 70,000 to about 8,000. During the month of September, Jews left the country at the rate of some 600 a day.

The government lent a hand. After Kielce, the authorities were keen to offer the Jewish community some form of reparation. Egit and Antek, the two founders of Lower Silesia's Jewish colony, were given what they had asked for: the seventy-two agricultural collectives across the region run by Jewish survivors were permitted to bear arms. A government assisting the Jewish community to obtain weapons: this was a unique state of affairs in Polish history — and it did not last long.

Antek, who helped train the security guards, secured another government concession. He convinced the defence minister to designate a formal border crossing, not far from Wałbrzych, through which only Jews were given passage. Christian Poles were condemned to a life in the People's Republic. The arrangement negotiated by Antek remained in force until February 1947, long enough for tens of thousands of Jews to cross from Poland into Czechoslovakia.

* * *

Several months before the Zylberberg murder, Mala and Nathan moved to one of the agricultural collectives in Lower Silesia, not far from the Wałbrzych home they had shared with the German mother and daughter. Before long, they resettled fifteen kilometres away at a second collective in Kamienna Góra on the banks of the Bóbr, a wide and relatively short river that flows down from the Krkonoše or Giant Mountains in what is now the Czech Republic.

The first kibbutz was set amid magnificent wooded hills, and had plenty of land for raising cattle, ducks, and chickens. There were even fruit trees to tend. Around eighty people lived and worked at the collective that, like many others, was affiliated with Gordonia, a Zionist youth movement launched decades earlier. Its founder, Aaron David Gordon, died in 1922, well before the outbreak of war. With his big grey beard, Gordon looked for all the world like a *zaddik* or religious mystic. A scholarly city-dweller, he rarely left the confines of his study, yet saw a future for the Jewish people in the great outdoors. He advocated agrarian schooling and a dynamic, physical life in preparation for working the land in Palestine, where the Jews faced the nigh-on impossible task of making the desert bloom if they were to become masters of their own destiny. His favourite expressions included the 'religion of work' and 'the idealism of the productive people'.

The ideal was one thing; the reality of working the land was another. Most Holocaust survivors came from a mercantile background, or were the children of tradesmen such as cobblers, tanners, and silversmiths. For them, the great outdoors was uncharted territory. Mala remembers getting lessons in farming, although her memories of Hebrew classes and the general sense of community are far more vivid. 'We ate together and sang a lot. We felt strong.'

That sense of solidarity grew stronger in Kamienna Góra, a kibbutz she and Nathan founded along with some fellow kibbutzniks when the collective near Wałbrzych became too crowded. In Kamienna Góra, Nathan and Mala were among the more experienced workers. The collective grew all its own food. Nathan's technical skills meant he had a key role in the running of the farm. 'Nathan worked very hard and could turn his hand to absolutely anything,' Mala remembers.

'Everyone was so fond of him. It was then that I fell in love with him, my own husband.'

The Kamienna Góra collective received regular visits from *shlichim*, Hebrew for 'emissaries', who gave the young farmers lessons on the geography of Palestine and taught them Zionist songs. These visitors often worked for a clandestine refugee operation called Bricha (Hebrew for 'flight'), which ran a network of safe houses, transport channels, smuggling routes, and unofficial border crossings in almost every Eastern European country. Through this network, they guided Holocaust survivors from Europe to Palestine: no easy task, given that the British authorities there were determined to prevent migration to the territory. Some Eastern European governments secretly lent their support to Bricha brigadiers, who they saw as ridding them of the problems associated with the Jewish survivors. In total, Bricha succeed in transporting some 200,000 European Jews to Palestine.

Mala discovered she was pregnant. In her typical no-nonsense way, she explains what this meant in the kibbutz. 'Women who were pregnant made sure they had an abortion. After all, we had no idea what the future held. One thing was certain: we would not be staying in anti-Semitic Poland. Besides, it was the country where our entire families had been murdered. Nathan and I decided to keep our baby. Nathan thought there would always be room for a child.'

Uncertainty about the future was certainly a factor in the high incidence of abortion among members of the new agricultural collectives, as was the transitional nature of these settlements. Most people in the Gordonia kibbutzim wanted to travel to the promised land the first chance they got, and they knew that Bricha preferred to help young people with no children. Such candidates were more likely to survive the long, clandestine journey and were better suited to the struggle against the British in Palestine.

But such was the impact of the Kielce pogrom that almost everyone left Poland, kids or no kids. Mala described how she, Nathan, and their whole group danced for joy when they crossed the border into Czechoslovakia.

Reading about the hardships and atrocities that the decimated Jewish community in Poland encountered in the aftermath of the Second World War, you can only empathise with that profound sense of release. And admire the Bricha agents, who were honoured in Israel decades later. Yet you can also say that the anti-Semites got their way. What Mala's father and many others before the war had thought impossible was about to become reality in its aftermath: Poland and other Eastern European countries became monocultural. The anti-Semitic Endek nationalists, whose resistance fighters had murdered both Germans and Jews, saw their dream come to pass: 'Poland for the Polish'.

Zionist activists had a very different take on things. 'Kielce was a good thing,' one Bricha veteran said years later at a convention in Tel Aviv. 'It was a catalyst.' This view was even expressed at the time, and from their perspective there is something to be said for it. Which does not alter the fact that the blood libel in Kielce led to a killing spree that left dozens dead and many more traumatised for life.

Jakub Egit had been nowhere near Kielce when the bloodshed occurred, but the pogrom also took a heavy toll on him, the man who had wanted to remain both Jewish and Polish, to be a Jew in Poland. As tens of thousands of Polish Jews made their way across the border, Egit stayed behind in Dzierżoniów, Lower Silesia with just enough people to maintain a small Yiddish-speaking community, a couple of schools, a theatre, and a hospital.

An enclave such as this was not considered appropriate in monocultural Poland. Egit fell out of favour with the regime, and was even jailed for a time. His crime? Attempting to found a Jewish province with the intention of making it part of Israel, an enemy state. After serving his sentence, he moved to Warsaw, where he worked as an editor for a Yiddish magazine. In 1956, Jews were once again permitted to leave Poland, and Egit took advantage of this opportunity. Still not a Zionist, he left for Canada and settled in Toronto. In the 1990s, he wrote his memoirs, published under the telling title *Grand Illusion*.

Antek's fate was very different. On hearing the news of the pogrom, he headed straight for Kielce with a carload of medical supplies. His 700-page memoirs give the impression of a man who could remain exceptionally cool in challenging, if not impossible, circumstances: in the ghetto, during the uprising, and in the resistance operations that followed. But at the hospital in Kielce, his composure temporarily deserted him. 'There was a moment when my nerves gave out.' These were fellow countrymen against fellow countrymen. He could see, hear, and feel how even the hospital staff had turned against the Jewish patients. He drew his pistol and ordered them to carry the patients out to the waiting ambulances within fifteen minutes. Under military escort, they were driven to the station where a train stood ready to take them and other Jews to Łódź.

After Kielce, Antek devoted much of his energy to getting as many Jews as possible out of Poland. He became a Bricha agent, and arranged his own departure a year later. In Israel, he settled in Lohamei HaGeta'ot, a kibbutz co-founded by surviving fighters of the Warsaw Ghetto Uprising.

His new homeland proclaimed him a hero of the nation, but even that level of recognition could not dull the pain of losing family, friends, an entire world. He started to drink heavily, and suffered from depression. One of his best-known quotes says nothing about his heroic battle against the Germans in the ghetto and everything about his permanently troubled mood after the war. In the nine-hour documentary *Shoah*, he tells director Claude Lanzmann, 'If you could lick my heart, it would poison you.' Like Egit, the man with whom he once sat on a terrace in Lower Silesia and decided to found a new Yiddish-speaking community, he came up with an emotionally charged title for his memoirs: *A Surplus of Memory*.

And what of Wałbrzych itself? In the company of Wojtek Szot, a Polish resident of the city, I go looking for traces of the Jewish world that existed in those months shortly after the war. He tells me how a small group of Jews held on until 1956, the year in which de-Stalinisation gathered momentum in Poland with the return of former strongman Władysław Gomułka. With the relative easing of Soviet control came a resurgence of nationalism, a development with immediate and troubling consequences for Poland's Jews. Windows were smashed, and there were skirmishes in the street. Polish soldiers had to be called in to restore order in Wałbrzych, and spent a night patrolling the streets to prevent further attacks on the Jewish minority.

Szot shows me all kinds of things. 'This building used to be ... And here's where the Yiddish theatre once stood.' I scribble pages of notes, but typing them up weeks later, I eventually put them to one side. It feels more honest to say that there is nothing left of Egit's community. A name or two at most.

One neighbourhood of Wałbrzych is referred to by the locals as 'Palestine'. Szot, who was born in 1987, explains, 'I always thought it owed its nickname to the state of the houses, many of which were damaged and reduced to rubble when an old mine exploded. The word "Palestine" conjures up images of war and bomb blasts. Only when I began to dig a little deeper into the history of my hometown did I discover that the neighbourhood owes its name to the tens of thousands of Jews who tried to build a new life for themselves here, with Yiddish as their language. It's such a pity they didn't succeed. A scandal, in fact. I'm sure hardly anyone here is still aware of it. I didn't even know myself.'

After a brief pause, he concludes, 'That makes me sad.'

Instead of footnotes

The opening quote comes from a short 1984 *Saturday Night Live* mockumentary. With the help of a team of make-up artists, US comic Eddie Murphy took on the role of a white man and 'discovered' that he was treated differently wherever he went. In a series of tongue-in-cheek scenes, other white men became his best pals. A bus full of white people turned into a cocktail party once the last black passenger had got off, and a banker offered him a loan without demanding security.

The story of the blood accusation in Leoncin comes from *Of a World That Is No More* by Israel Joshua Singer, posthumously translated from Yiddish into English by his son Joseph Singer in 1970.

The first known example of Jews accused of killing Christian children to use their blood in rituals comes from the English city of Norwich in 1144. The accusation centred on a twelve-year-old boy called William. Jews from the neighbourhood were supposed to have kidnapped him, placed a crown of thorns on his head, tied him to a cross, and stabbed him in his side.

The newspaper that reported on the funeral of Becalel Mosze Zylberberg was *Opinia. Pismo syjonistyczno-demokratyczne (Opinion: a Zionist-Democratic newspaper)*.

The quotes from the senior Catholic clerics in response to the pogrom in Kielce come from Jan T. Gross's book *Fear: anti-Semitism in Poland after Auschwitz* (2006), as does the reconstruction of this post-war pogrom. In a footnote, Gross mentions Chaja Finkelsztejn's account of going to see the priest to ask him to speak out against the violence in the village of Radziłów. He quotes from her memoirs, but also refers to journalist Anna Bikont's book *My z Jedwabnego* (2004), translated as *The Crime and the Silence* by Alissa Valles and published in 2015 by Farrar, Straus and Giroux. Primarily in Chapter 13, 'The Dreams of Chaja Finkelsztejn', Bikont reconstructs the murder of the Jews of Radziłów, Jedwabne, and Wąsosz, incorporating Finkelsztejn's 1946 testimony and a later interview she gave after moving to the United States.

In his book, Gross makes a point of debunking the position taken by Stefan Wyszyński: there was no basis for the claim that Poland's Jewish citizens in the 1930s were advocates of communism. Only a tiny minority of the 3.3 million Polish Jews at that time espoused the ideas of the banned communist party, although the percentage of communists among the Jewish community was higher than in the Polish population as a whole. Approximately 300,000 Polish Jews survived the Holocaust, and a comparably small fraction of them were communists. Most survivors came from the families of small-scale entrepreneurs, tradespeople, and craftsmen, a section of society that had never been sympathetic towards communism. Or, like Mala, they came from religious families who despised communism for its associations with atheism.

It is true that the new Soviet-backed government and security apparatus contained a disproportionate number of Jewish officials. They included Jakub Berman, the regime's second-in-command and the man in charge of the security services. There was a certain logic to the Jewish overrepresentation in government circles and the senior civil service, given that the provisional post-war government was the first in Poland's history to grant Jews the same rights as other citizens. This fell well short of running a public administration that was free from anti-Semitism, as Mala and Nathan experienced when they turned up at the housing department in Wałbrzych. Polish Jews who decided to remain in the country after the war, many ardent communists among them, would experience similar discrimination through the years. For where successive Polish governments began by expelling Germans, Ukrainians, and Belarussians from the ranks of officialdom, the government completed this process of ethnic cleansing in the late 1960s by purging the national administration of 'all foreign elements', a veiled reference to people of Jewish descent. In 1968, this culminated in a government-organised anti-Semitic witch-hunt that led over 10,000 Polish Jews to leave the country: some were compelled to leave; others were driven out by harassment. The government insisted that the campaign had nothing to do with anti-Semitism and spoke instead of anti-Zionism. Poles of Jewish descent were accused of having conflicting national loyalties: to Poland and to Israel. This was unacceptable, the party heads argued, especially when the Arab states that fought Israel in the Six-Day War were allies of the Soviet Union and its satellite states.

In an interview in 2016, Anna Zalewska, Poland's education minister at the time, appeared to deny that Poles were responsible for the pogrom in Kielce. She claimed not to know who the real murderers were. It was only when the journalist persisted that she answered 'anti-Semites.' And Poles were not anti-Semites, or anti-Semites were not Poles. And then there was the theory that communists had provoked the pogrom, in which case there is the argument that communists are not Poles.

The story of the drunken father at the market and his lost daughter comes from Noach Lasman, a Holocaust survivor who wrote his memoirs in 1997. They can be read at the Ringelblum Institute in Warsaw.

Egit's autobiography *Grand Illusion* dates from 1990, and did not trouble the bestseller lists — the opposite, if anything. Egit was a committed communist who believed in a Yiddish-speaking community in Poland, twin ideals that are enough to consign a person to historical obscurity.

17

The Tannenreutherbach

'One who would not be driven out must drive out.'

–Friedrich Schiller, poet and playwright

Historian Wojtek Szot says he loves to dig around in the past of his city. 'Because I love history, of course, but also because this is a region of diggers. And I don't just mean figuratively.'

Szot tells me how his grandparents, along with thousands of other Polish newcomers in the first months after the war, dug endlessly in parks, cellars, and gardens. They were searching for silver, gold, and other valuables, anything that the Germans might have consigned to the earth before they fled or were deported. A survey of the studies done on this phenomenon leaves me with the impression that digging was akin to playing the lottery. And every now and again, people did strike it lucky.

This wasn't as strange as it might seem. After all, what else was a fugitive or someone facing summary eviction supposed to do with their prized possessions? These Germans were afraid that they would be robbed as they fled (rightly so), and knew that everything they left behind would be seized upon by the new Polish residents (right again). Caught between a rock and a hard place, burying your belongings was not such an unlikely thing to do. Nor was digging: the new residents from eastern Poland, Ukraine, and Belarus arrived with little to nothing. How did they begin setting up a life for themselves? By taking

possession of whatever fittings, furnishings, and items they could lay
their hands on, above or below ground.

The newcomers took over just about everything. One fascinating
detail: they even hung onto their predecessors' photograph albums.
Until well into the 1950s, they were taken down off the shelf when
friends came to call. 'Look, here's the father of the house, these are the
children, and this is their aunty from Berlin. This is them on a sailing
trip, and in this one …'

The urge to dig did not extend to their dead. In those early days,
a great many newcomers were reluctant to bury their nearest and
dearest until they knew for sure that they would be allowed to stay
in the region and not be forced to move on. Anthropologists refer
to 'a culture of temporality'. This was grist to the mill of the new
authorities, as it meant new citizens who had come from the east to live
in the west were fervent supporters of the government's 'Polonisation
campaigns'. They wanted their new houses to remain theirs; Germans
should never be allowed to return. As historian Timothy Snyder writes,
'Communism had little to offer Poland as an ideology and was never
very popular. But Stalin's ethnic geopolitics took the place of the class
struggle, creating a durable basis of support, if not legitimacy, for the
new regime.'

Less temporary was the organised digging that took place. Coal
mining had always been a mainstay of the regional economy. The
mines only closed after the fall of communism in the 1990s, and even
then, mining did not stop completely: thousands of out-of-work
miners went on digging of their own volition, a tempting prospect in
the wooded hills of Central Europe, where seams of coal can be found
relatively near the surface. The holes dug by these enterprising diggers
are known in Polish as biedaszyby, which means something like 'poor
man's shafts'. Take a drive around Wałbrzych today, and you can still
see them everywhere.

* * *

During their time in Wałbrzych, Nathan took a shine to the piano that
belonged to the German mother and daughter in whose house he and

Mala were living. He taught himself the songs the Russian soldiers sang, and this did not go unnoticed. The couple came back from the theatre one evening to find two Soviet soldiers posted in front of the house. They had been ordered to wait for Nathan and Mala by the Russian general who had moved in across the street. He wanted the pianist he had heard playing to liven up the birthday party he was throwing for his girlfriend that night. The soldiers would not take no for an answer. Nathan had to agree, or the general would come down on them like a ton of bricks for failing to carry out an order.

At the party there were tables with glasses, booze, and butter. After every shot of vodka, the men took a spoonful of butter. Nathan joined in the drinking, but left the butter alone. He played his songs, and Mala danced with the Russians. Suddenly, the music stopped. Seconds later, Nathan was standing in front of Mala. All the colour had drained from his face. 'We have to leave,' Nathan said. 'Now.'

'He could barely get down the stairs,' Mala remembers. Outside, he fell in the snow. He told Mala to leave him there and go home. 'I'm going to kill some Germans,' he told her, and took out his pistol. Mala was beside herself. She told him she was not about to leave him out there in the snow, that the Germans were in bed asleep, and that it wasn't a good idea to go shooting them at this hour. She sat down beside him in the snow and begged him to come home with her.

'I was cold,' Mala says. 'At last he came with me, but he kept his pistol in his hand. When we got to the front door, he wouldn't give me the keys. Drunk as he was, he rang the doorbell. The daughter answered the door and of course I was terrified Nathan would shoot her, but she immediately saw how drunk he was and reached out to him kindly. At that, Nathan put the gun in his pocket.'

The German daughter undressed Nathan, who by this time had been sick. She washed him, and was able to get him into a clean pair of pyjamas. Mala managed to get hold of the gun.

That night, she was unable to sleep. 'I was so sad. It all felt so strange to me.'

On another occasion, she says, 'I was frightened. What if I was married to a drunk?!'

Lying awake that night, she recalled something Sewek, Różka's handsome boyfriend, had said when they were all living at the Bursa in Łódź. He had called Nathan a *schlemiel*, someone who would never be able to make a living for himself, never mind provide for a family. Of course, Sewek had had his reasons for being so dismissive. He saw how Nathan never left Mala's side, and this interfered with his plans: in Mala, he saw the perfect match for his associate, a man he had gone into business with in the diamond trade.

Watching over her husband that night in Wałbrzych, Mala wondered if there wasn't a kernel of truth in Sewek's words. 'And by then I had realised we were never going to have that kosher household he'd promised me.'

She needn't have worried. As her husband began to take on an ever more important role in the life of the kibbutz, first near Wałbrzych and then at Kamienna Góra, he gave the lie to Sewek's words. Nathan was no schlemiel. If anything, the former employee of Julian Weinberg, the engineer, was exceptionally skilled and therefore self-sufficient. At his graveside, decades later, his grandson summed this up with the simple words: 'My grand-dad could do anything.'

* * *

To leave Poland, Mala and Nathan did not have to travel far. The farm at Kamienna Góra was a mere ten kilometres from the border. They set off on a bright summer's day in 1946. Around seventy men and women between the ages of sixteen and forty walked a route that nowadays is popular with nature lovers. It took them past waterfalls and steep crags, through a rich and varied green landscape planted with beech, oak, and maple. Arriving at the border, the two shlichim guides told the group to wait until nightfall. That would give them more room for manoeuvre.

It wasn't to be. Shortly after nightfall, the group received a visit from Polish customs officials with weapons drawn. They separated the men from the women. Mala knew this was a very bad sign. This time, her luck had deserted her.

Hours dragged by, long uncertain hours in which the women had no idea what was happening to the men, and the men knew nothing about the women. The two shlichim had gone off with the border guards, returning now and then to give assurances couched in the vaguest of terms. Eventually, they returned with an ultimatum: leave all your possessions behind, or you can forget about a safe passage to Czechoslovakia.

Mala and many other members of the group had valuables with them and were well-off compared to the poverty that was the norm in those cold and lawless post-war days in Eastern Europe. Jewish partisans only accounted for a small proportion of Holocaust survivors, but in this group they were relatively well-represented. They had left the forests and returned to their hometowns to find their worst fears confirmed. With their families murdered and their possessions seized, the partisans were in a position to demand some restitution—they were armed, after all. Later, they heeded Jakub Egit's call, came to Lower Silesia, and wound up at the Kamienna Góra kibbutz, only to lose everything trying to cross the border. Mala also gave up everything, including the wedding ring she had only worn for a few months. 'I had been rich and now I had nothing. None of us had anything left.'

It is a source of pride to the Zionist-inspired people smugglers of Bricha that only one of the groups that tried to leave Poland under their guidance was killed at the border. Even so, the experience of Mala's group can hardly be termed 'safe passage'. But Mala's group is not mentioned in Bricha's annals, casting doubt as to whether the shlichim who guided them were even part of the organisation. When the men and the women were reunited after hours apart, the two people smugglers were nowhere to be found. Where had they gone? Many in the group believed they had been set up. They may well have been right, though the possibility that the smugglers met a worse fate than the fugitives cannot be ruled out.

Early the next morning, the group decided to keep moving, only now with no one to guide them. They walked on, unsure exactly where they were heading. Nathan knocked on the door of the first house they came to. The occupant asked them what they wanted … in Czech. That was when everyone began to sing and dance for joy. 'We had been stripped of our possessions and had lost our guides, but we were still alive and no longer in Poland.' Mala smiles at the memory.

With no money, it was hard to make progress, but the group managed to arrange horse-drawn carts that took them as far as the nearest station. There, a compassionate official let them board a train for Prague without paying. In the city, a delegation went in search of help from representatives of the Jewish community. Hours later, they returned, without any food but with train tickets for Vienna.

On their arrival, the group again sought contact with Jewish leaders. Again they were given no food but train tickets, this time to Pocking, a German border town on the banks of the fast-flowing River Inn where, for weeks, the US occupying forces had been providing food and shelter for thousands of refugees. 'We were given a wonderful meal and beds to sleep in.'

Mala was back in Germany, the land of the perpetrators. The Möllers' country, Erich's country. As she was coming to terms with this, her German sweetheart was being put on a train to the Soviet Union.

In Pocking, one of the women from the group was reunited with her fifteen-year-old brother. He had walked the same route to the Polish-Czech border days earlier, part of a group that met a terrible fate despite being guided by Bricha agents. The Polish border guards killed every last one of them. The boy was the only survivor. A shot was fired, and he fell forward into the mass grave, but he had not been hit. He lay still among the dead bodies of his brothers, sisters, and parents, waiting for the guards to leave the scene. When the coast was clear, he climbed out of the grave and crossed the border alone.

After a week or two, the group travelled on to Zettlitz near Gefrees in the north of Bavaria, where the Tannenreutherbach flows into the Lübnitzbach. There, Mala and Nathan found themselves in another agricultural collective. This one was called 'Lanegev', a reference to the Negev desert in what is now Israel. Like the Polish kibbutzim, life in Zettlitz was geared towards a future in Palestine. 'That's where everyone wanted to go,' Mala remembers. 'No two ways about it.'

Lanegev was not the first kibbutz to be founded with the help of the US authorities in the American occupation zone. Following an alarming report by American lawyer Earl G. Harrison, and the wave of indignation it triggered, over twenty kibbutzim were established there, mostly on farms that had belonged to former Nazis.

Before the war, Harrison had been a senior official in the US immigration department. His report, published on 24 August 1945, described the situation of Jewish survivors in the first months after the capitulation. He wrote of the 'crowded, frequently unsanitary and generally grim conditions' in which these displaced persons were living, in guarded camps fenced with barbed wire. Unable or unwilling to return to the places where they were born or raised, they were held there with nothing to do and 'no opportunity, except surreptitiously, to communicate with the outside world, waiting, hoping for some word of encouragement and action in their behalf'. He noted the high mortality rate among survivors who were incurably ill or debilitated, and observed that many of the Jews still had 'no other clothing than their concentration camp garb—a rather hideous striped pyjama effect'. Yet other former prisoners, he reported, had no choice but to wear SS uniforms. 'It is questionable which clothing they hate the more.'

In the spring of 1945, amid the chaos of a vanquished Germany, the Allies had found themselves faced with over seven million 'displaced persons' from at least twenty different countries, and had managed to repatriate around six million of them in the space of five months. But it took a while for the American authorities, both in Germany and back in the United States, to grasp that the real problem lay with the million or so displaced persons who were unable or unwilling to leave, either due to ill health or because they knew they had become outcasts in the places they used to call home. That million not only included Jewish survivors and refugees, but also people who had collaborated with the Nazis, many of whom came from the same parts of Eastern Europe. On the run from the Red Army, they had wound up in Germany. Among them were Ukrainians who had worked as concentration camp guards. Because the Allied allocation system operated on the basis of nationality, Jewish survivors often found themselves housed alongside Nazis and their accomplices in the former army barracks, convents, stables, and even labour camps and concentration camps that had been pressed into service to accommodate displaced persons. This system had a cruel twist in store for German and Austrian Jews who, in the months after the war, were classified as members of the 'enemy population'. The impact was not only psychological ('Sorry, you're German') but physical, too: they received fewer rations than displaced persons from countries that had been the victim of German aggression.

How had this situation arisen? Harrison believed the main cause lay in the military nature of the occupation. Soldiers are trained to fight and follow orders, not to attend to the needs of the traumatised. Soldiers value law, authority, and obedience, and so the displaced had to be contained within walls and barbed wire.

Harrison found his greatest adversary in US general George S. Patton, a military man through and through. Patton was resolutely unimpressed by Harrison, by the Jewish victims he encountered, and by the 'Judeo-Christian tradition' that had featured so prominently in US wartime propaganda. He wrote in his diary, 'Harrison and his ilk believe that the Displaced Person is a human being, which he is not, and this applies particularly to the Jews who are lower than animals.' He believed it was only right that they should be 'kept under guard'. Patton wanted the US army to go easier on the Germans, as the United States was going to need them badly in the coming conflict with the Soviet Union, an enemy he thought it was better to engage sooner rather than later.

The American press quoted Patton, and his conflict with commander-in-chief Dwight D. Eisenhower and other members of the military top brass threatened to escalate into a public row. Further embarrassment was averted by his death in December 1945, following a road accident in the Rhineland. He had been on his way to a pheasant hunt.

By that time, Harrison had won the battle with Patton and his military sympathisers. One sentence in particular had an impact on public opinion and was widely quoted: 'Beyond knowing that they are no longer in danger of the gas chambers, torture, and other forms of violent death, they see—and there is—little change … As matters now stand, we appear to be treating the Jews as the Nazis treated them except that we do not exterminate them.'

In response to the report, President Truman ordered special camps to be established for the victims of racial and religious persecution, camps where the food rations were far more generous. The minimum daily provision rose to 2,500 calories, which is in line with today's recommended dietary intake for a healthy adult. In addition, an Advisor on Jewish Affairs was appointed to US high command, and a Central Jewish Committee of the Liberated Jews was established, with elected members. President Truman wrote to General Eisenhower, 'We must make clear to the German people that we thoroughly abhor the Nazi policies of hatred and persecution. We have no better opportunity to demonstrate this than by the manner in which we ourselves actually treat the survivors remaining in Germany.'

And so it came to pass. By the time Nathan and Mala arrived in Zettlitz, the situation for Jewish survivors in the American zone had improved beyond recognition, a development that attracted the needy in increasing numbers. In the period when Mala and Nathan were trying to get on with their lives as members of the Lanegev kibbutz, a staggering 85 per cent of Jewish survivors on German soil were to be found in the American sector, approximately 157,000 people. A large proportion of them lived in agricultural collectives on farms and estates that had only recently been the property of senior Nazis, among them Hermann Göring.

At these farms, estates, and country houses, they sometimes came across some remarkable memorabilia. This was certainly true at the country residence of Julius Streicher, perhaps the most obsessively anti-Semitic Nazi apart from Hitler. In 1945 he was still living in Der Pleikershof near Cadolzburg, a property he had purchased with the profits from the Nazi weekly newspaper *Der Stürmer*. Stashed behind boxes of Nazi propaganda, the new residents found a large wooden sign bearing the motto *Ohne Lösung der Judenfrage gibt es keine Lösung der Weltfrage* ('Without a solution to the Jewish question, there is no solution to the world question'). Shortly before Streicher was tried and hanged at Nuremberg, only a few kilometres away, the new Jewish residents rehung Streicher's sign, a symbolic act. For them, the solution to the Jewish question had nothing to do with extermination: it stood for an independent Jewish state. One member of the group, Chaim Shapiro, later reflected, 'Pleikershof was our road to the motherland, the farming community was our corridor to Israel.'

The local Nazi leader who owned the farm where Mala and Nathan lived had been jailed. But in contrast to the cases of Streicher and Göring, his wife and two sons were allowed to go on living at the farmhouse. The Jewish refugees slept in four other buildings on the same grounds, among them a windmill and a sawmill.

The German family lived at loggerheads with the farm's new residents. They accused the kibbutzniks of fraud, claiming that they failed to hand over all the revenue from the mill and the sawmill to a district manager, as agreed. Endless complaints were filed with the American occupier. Mala doesn't remember all the allegations, but she does remember the German family, with whom no one associated. She also remembers the horses, cattle, chickens, and geese, and the twenty-two hectares of fields, the rough equivalent of thirty football pitches. The kibbutz was one of the finest and best equipped in the occupied zone, with agricultural machinery, an electrical workshop, and enough tools to produce clothes and shoes. This was a place for serious farming. There were tailors in the collective and even a dentist, though he lacked the medical supplies to treat his patients without inflicting a good deal of pain.

In the summer, they worked the land, and winter was spent operating the mill and the sawmill. 'We hardly owned anything,' Mala says, 'but that didn't bother us at all. We were always content and never fought with one another. We agreed to swap clothes so no one had to wear the same thing every Shabbat.'

The Yiddish newspaper for displaced persons in Germany, *Undzer Veg (Our Way)*, featured an item about the kibbutz in 1946. The reporter was impressed by the many partisans at the farming collective. Mala can still sing the partisan songs she learned there. Her own story chimes with the reporter's account of the kibbutzniks making a stone memorial, erected on the Nazi's farm in memory of the Jews who were murdered during the war. At the unveiling, members spoke about their wartime experiences.

While marriage was a common occurrence at the Zettlitz kibbutz, having a baby was not. 'I didn't know the first thing about it,' Mala says. 'No one had prepared me for what was coming. Contractions? I had no idea what they were.' In the middle of the night, she was taken by horse and cart to the small town of Münchberg, ten kilometres away, where the displaced Jewish community had set up a modest hospital, the only Jewish hospital in Germany at the time.

Mala watched from a distance as Nathan spoke to the doctor. He began to cry, but was unable to tell her what was wrong. Then a nurse came by and wished Mala good luck with her Caesarean. 'That came as a shock. One of the few things I did know was that a Caesarean was incredibly risky.' The baby was in an awkward position and, unsure how to proceed, the doctors at the small hospital arranged for Mala to be transferred to Hof. She made the twenty-kilometre journey by train and was welcomed at the town's hospital, the most advanced in Germany at the time. The vast Modernist building dated from 1931, and had survived the war relatively intact.

In her memoirs, Mala writes, 'They gave me a lovely room and asked me to lie down. A midwife came and sat at my bedside. She started knitting. I got it into my head that she didn't want to help me because I was Jewish. I became furious, snatched her knitting and pulled it apart. I started screaming at her. The midwife went to fetch the doctor, who tried to give me an injection to calm me down, but I pulled the syringe out of her hand and shouted, "I know all about your injections! You want to kill me!"

'For over an hour I lay there all alone, thinking about what was going to happen to me. Then another doctor came into the room. She managed to calm me and asked me to come with her to the operating theatre, where she examined me on the operating table. She sent for another doctor, and he examined me, too.'

Mala's baby was born safe and sound. She didn't need a Caesarean after all: by the time she went into labour, the baby had moved. Mala and Nathan called him Mosje, after Nathan's father. His second name was Icek, after Mala's father. It was 4 December 1946, a little over nine months since their wedding in Wałbrzych.

Mala asked the doctors and nurses who had cared for her to come to her bedside. She apologised for the way she had treated them, but everyone understood. 'The next day the doctors, the midwife, and the nurses returned with lovely presents for the baby.'

It was a happy time for Mala. 'Seven days later I returned to the kibbutz. It was 11 December. The snow was thick on the ground, but the whole kibbutz came out to meet us, every one of them with a gift for my little boy. There was hardly anything in the shops at the time, yet everyone had something for us.'

Mala's sudden fury at the midwife with her knitting and the bitter accusations levelled at the doctor with the needle seem completely out of character for the young woman who had acted so calmly and reasonably during the Polish occupation, at the workplace in Bremen, within the walls of the Magdeburg prison, and at the home of the pro-Nazi family in Zerbst, not to mention a far cry from her handling of the anti-Semitic housing officials in Wałbrzych. Had so much happened in the meantime? Perhaps it had. First and foremost, Mala had heard many of her fellow survivors talk about their wartime experiences, horrific accounts of immeasurable cruelty. Amplified by the hormones of imminent childbirth and her fear of a Caesarean, they could well have been enough to plunge her into a state of desperate paranoia.

On another occasion, she describes her behaviour as 'excessive'. But was it all that unreasonable for Mala to expect the worst? The reaction to Jews who came to settle in the Münchberg area in the years after the war suggests they felt similarly. The community began with a handful of survivors who had managed to escape a death march from Buchenwald by disappearing into the forests around Münchberg. Then Bricha agents brought thousands of other Eastern European Jews to the town. This did not go down well with the German population. *Undzer Veg* reported the tensions and how the local authorities would only allocate the very worst accommodation — often cellars and basements — to the Jewish newcomers '*vi es past far mentshn fun tsveyter klas*': as befits second-class citizens.

This rankled with the occupying forces. When the vocational college, originally founded to serve the local textile industry, lied to Jewish applicants about having no places left, the Americans intervened. When Jewish cemeteries were defaced with swastikas, the Americans demanded they be cleaned up. Three Jews were ordered off a train, despite having a valid ticket; the Americans published an indignant account of the incident. As late as March 1947, a barber was repeatedly refusing to cut the hair of Jewish customers; again, the Americans put a stop to this behaviour. A few kilometres south of Münchberg, a row about the milk quota led to locals throwing stones at a hotel that housed displaced Jews, yelling 'Down with the dirty Jews!' and 'Hang the Jews!' The Americans came down hard on the perpetrators, and a ringleader was sentenced to years in prison.

* * *

The resilience and energy of the young Zettlitz kibbutzniks did not go unnoticed by Bricha agents from Palestine, who were especially impressed by the combat experience of the partisans among them. From the winter of 1946, shlichim paid regular visits to the self-sufficient training farm to educate the residents and teach them Hebrew, but also to urge them to make haste: the *Yishuv*, the Jewish community in Palestine, was gearing up for an armed struggle with the region's Arab population, who were as vehemently opposed to the idea of a mixed government in an independent state as the Jews were themselves. The shlichim were eager for the kibbutzniks to join the struggle at the earliest possible opportunity.

Despite sharing the conviction that their future lay in Palestine, not every member of the kibbutz was wild about this prospect. The experience of crossing the Polish border had done little to inspire confidence, especially among Nathan and Mala's group. The kibbutzniks' discussions with each other and with the shlichim centred on whether it would be better to wait until an independent Jewish state had been established, a strategy that would enable them to emigrate legally and still join the fight to preserve their new homeland.

The shlichim talked to kibbutzim across the region, not only as a call to arms, but also to kindle solidarity with and love for a state that had yet to be created. They also wanted to boost morale, an important goal given that the collective life wasn't for everyone. Some struggled to cope with the emphasis on rules, the peer pressure, and the suffocating social ties that defined life in a kibbutz run by a socialist-Zionist youth movement like Gordonia. Others resented not being able to earn their own living or to decide what kind of work was best for them. And then there were those for whom working the land was too physically demanding. For all of these reasons, dozens left the kibbutzim in favour of much larger reception camps run by the military.

To dissuade members from leaving and to strengthen cohesion within the group, the cultural committee of a kibbutz in Lagersfeld organised a mock trial, enlisting the cooperation of its secretary, an outstanding musician by the name of Monish Einhorn. One day at lunch, Einhorn told the group he no longer wanted to prepare for a life in Palestine. Instead, he was leaving the collective in the hope of making a name for himself as a musician. A cousin in Frankfurt had offered to take him in. Einhorn's pretence must have been convincing, because his fellow kibbutzniks, including his closest friends, reacted furiously. They impressed upon him that the days of personal choices were over, that the Germans had seen to that. Choices were a community matter. Einhorn, who, like so many kibbutzniks had lost his entire Polish Jewish family in the war, then endured all kinds of abuse from the others, but he held firm. A close friend told him she could no longer respect him as a person, even if he ended up staying. Someone else wondered aloud, 'How could he take on the position of *mazkir* [secretary] when he always knew that he was going to leave?' Some simply cried and begged him to stay. Others remained in their room, sitting shiva as if he had died.

Einhorn consented to appear before an improvised court in the communal dining hall, complete with prosecutors, defence counsel, judges, witnesses, and Einhorn himself as defendant. The rest of the group spectated. Amid whistling and cat calls, Einhorn defended his decision. It had been motivated, he said, by the many shortcomings of the kibbutz and the Zionist movement. Einhorn's defence team, oblivious to the fact that this was all a sham, also blamed the Zionist movement and the rules in the kibbutz. One asked incredulously why the members still had to share each other's pyjamas. Another complained that the duties in the kibbutz were allocated unfairly, with all the good jobs going to those with connections. For his part, Einhorn condemned the entire concept of collective decision-making. 'If I want to smoke, the kibbutz will decide only five a day; if I want to go to the movies, do I have to wait until everyone is ready to go together?'

After the prosecutors' final arguments, questions from the audience, and a brief adjournment to allow the judges to reach their decision, the verdict was announced. 'Whether by or against his will, Monish must recognize the fact that Zionism is the only way to establish ... the nation, and the kibbutz the only way to actualization. He must stay!'

Einhorn accepted the verdict, which was binding. It was an outcome he had agreed to beforehand in any case. He stayed.

The historian Avinoam J. Patt, who recorded the events of the mock trial decades later based on the verbal accounts of several witnesses, observes that those involved were less shocked by Einhorn's criticism of the Zionist ideal than by his supposed betrayal of the kibbutz, his new family. Remember, Patt notes, that almost everyone was an orphan and that 80 per cent of all Jewish survivors on German soil were aged between fifteen and forty. Nathan and Mala fitted this profile exactly. The members of these new surrogate families hoped to find a way to overcome what the war had left them with — their fears, their depression, their anger, and their post-traumatic stress — or, if not overcome them, at least keep them at bay. For many kibbutzniks, someone deciding to leave such a family was tantamount to denying the importance of all this. It felt like a betrayal. You don't leave a grieving family to pursue your own career.

Surprisingly, there was no outburst of anger among the kibbutzniks when they found out that Einhorn had never intended to leave in the first place. They understood, witnesses said years later, that the mock trial had been a safety valve designed to release any unease brought about by group pressure. And, so the witnesses told Patt, it had fulfilled its purpose.

For Mala and Nathan, it was the other way around. They did not leave the collective; the collective left them. The shlichim wanted everyone who could be directly deployed in the armed struggle to set off for the promised land — everyone without children, in other words. The rest could follow later. At Lanegev, almost everyone was childless, and many had experience of combat. Those who were able heeded the call, and by the summer of 1947, with too few members to keep the farm running, Mala and Nathan moved with Icek to a displaced persons camp in Hessisch Lichtenau, where one of Nathan's aunts and her husband were staying.

Nathan made this discovery around the time of baby Icek's circumcision. The man who performed the ritual had brought along a copy of the Yiddish newspaper *Undzer Veg*. Displaced survivors living in camps had their names printed in the paper in the hope that relatives or friends would see them. Nathan was over the moon to see his aunt's name in print. He did have family after all.

In Hessisch Lichtenau, some 200 kilometres from Zettlitz, there were several camps that housed displaced persons. His aunt and uncle were staying in the barracks of a factory that had manufactured bombs during the war. Now it sheltered approximately 1,200 people who had access to a nursery, a primary school, and even a vocational college. Nathan went there, and learned carpentry. Mala studied English in a course funded by the Joint Distribution Committee — 'The Joint', for short — a Jewish-American charity. The Joint also gave her a job. In addition to her existing command of German, Polish, Yiddish, Hebrew, and a smattering of Russian, she learned to speak English in a matter of weeks.

Life at a displaced persons camp was very different from the communal experience of the kibbutz, and centred on the family or the individual rather than the collective. Trade was everywhere. Cocoa, coffee, and tea were especially valuable, arriving in aid parcels from 'every country where Jews still lived', to use Mala's words. These precious commodities were almost impossible to come by in post-war Germany, a country that had only just emerged from a harsh winter in which many starved. In those bitterly cold months, infant mortality among the German civilian population rose to double that in the displaced persons camps and the rest of Europe. People had to get by on less than 1,000 calories a day, and the freezing temperatures claimed hundreds of thousands of lives. The Germans called it 'the white death'.

At the camp, Mala was reunited with Chaim and Moshe, the two soldiers she had gone into business with in Łódź and Wałbrzych. On the night that Nathan came to Wałbrzych, she had been pondering which of them to go out with, until Nathan's sudden appearance changed everything. At the camp, it turned out that both had since met and married what Mala describes as 'lovely Orthodox wives' with whom they kept a strict kosher household. 'I was green with envy,' she says. Her own husband had made a real effort to do the same, Mala says, 'but he couldn't make it work'. For something as impractical and unreasonable as a life lived according to the precepts of faith, Nathan could not summon an ounce of enthusiasm.

Nathan's wartime ordeals reinforced his lack of faith, but also awakened a Zionism that was new to him. He came from Łódź, a city where, in the last pre-war elections, the majority of the Jewish population, Nathan's parents included, had voted for the Bund, a Jewish socialist party that consistently opposed Zionism. As the largest Jewish organisation in pre-war Poland, it had set its sights on a multicultural society, and saw Zionism as a pipe dream. Poland alone was home to over three million Jews; were they all just going to up sticks and settle in Palestine? Besides, in the eyes of the Bund's intellectuals, the whole idea was ideologically flawed: how could more nationalism be the answer to intolerant nationalists? The Bund's supporters were for staying.

While the Bund continued to play an active part in the lives of the Jewish survivors from Poland who had ended up in Germany, there is no doubt that the mass murder inflicted on the Jews by the Nazi regime had significantly strengthened support for the Zionist cause. And not only in Germany. Many articles and lectures published at the time can be summarised with a fatalistic 'I told you so.' In a survey held by UN refugee organisation UNRRA among 19,311 Jewish refugees in Germany, 18,072 gave Palestine as their preferred destination for migration. When asked to state a second preference, around 1,000 people wrote 'none'. Hundreds answered 'the crematorium'. Nathan might have been one of those respondents. While some did their best to obtain a visa for the United States, and for Canada, Australia, and a number of other countries, there were others for whom there was no alternative to a Jewish state, not anymore. For them it was a life among Jews, or no life at all.

This was not how Mala saw things. After the Zionist atmosphere of the Lanegev kibbutz, the camp in Hessisch Lichtenau brought her into contact with people who had their sights set on America, Nathan's aunt and uncle among them. In fact, they were already waiting on their visa. Mala would have loved to go with them. Through her work for The Joint, she was learning English and knew that times were tough for Jewish settlers in Palestine. In Münchberg, she had even met Jews who had reached the mandated territory, only to be turned back by the British. 'I told Nathan I would rather go to America first, and that we could travel on to Palestine from there.'

Nathan would not hear of it. They would leave for Palestine as soon as couples with children were given the opportunity. Mala remembers the endless discussions they had. She even enlisted the support of others to persuade her husband that America should be the first port of call for his young family. All in vain. Nathan was not about to be persuaded.

Looking back on those discussions, Mala suspects that Nathan's thinking was shaped by his betrayal at the hands of people he thought he could count on. 'That's something I never experienced, not in the same way,' she explains. 'I was betrayed by a Ukrainian I barely knew. And I was afraid of being given away by girls I didn't know that well, and before that by the neighbour in Karpy, again someone I barely knew. But Nathan had been betrayed by Polish people he took to be his friends. He had lived among Poles; my family hadn't. We were Orthodox, and that meant we didn't have Polish friends. We expected nothing from them, and they expected nothing from us. During the war, I was genuinely surprised to discover that people like Mrs Gmitruk were willing to be so kind to me. But Nathan's trust had been betrayed, and he no longer wanted to live in a country with non-Jews.'

The Americans were the first of the occupying Allied forces to understand that the displaced Jewish population would not be returning to Eastern Europe. Irving Heymont, a US major who was Jewish himself and in charge of a displaced persons camp in Landsberg, wrote in a letter home how his eyes had been opened by a speech made by Dr Jakob Oleiski, a Holocaust survivor and one of the camp's representatives:

'I Want to See My Home Again,' we sang with a feeling of homesickness in the first years of the 'Ghetos' [sic] looking through the fences over the Vilija to Kowno and other Lithuanian towns. Today, after all that, after the concentration camps in Germany, after we stated definitively that our former home was changed into a mass grave, we can only grope and clasp with our finger tips the shadows of our dearest, and painfully cry: I can never more see my home ... The victorious nations that in the twentieth century removed the black plague from Europe must understand once and for all the specific Jewish problem. No, no we are not Polish when we are born in Poland, we are not Lithuanians even though we once passed through Lithuania and we are neither Roumanians though we have seen the first time in our life the sunshine in Roumania. We are Jews!!!

The British did not agree. They went against the emphatic recommendation made in Harrison's report that Jewish displaced persons should be separated from others who were unwilling or unable to return home. In the autumn of 1945, Major-General Richard Henry Dewing wrote to the Ministry of Defence in a memorandum on behalf of the chief of staff of the British zone, 'It is undesirable to accept the Nazi theory that the Jews are a separate race ... Jews should be accommodated in camps appropriate to their nationality rather than their race or religion. Any form of racial or religious segregation will only give rise to anti-Jewish feelings and may well have far reaching repercussions.' The British Foreign Office employed a similar argument to combat the idea that stateless Jews should be allowed to leave for Palestine, stating that 'it would go far by implication to admit that [the] Nazis were right in holding that there was no place for the Jews in Europe'. By giving the victims of National Socialism preferential treatment, the Americans were simply echoing Nazi ideology. Ernest Bevin, the British foreign secretary, even argued that 'there had been no point in fighting the Second World War if the Jews could not stay on in Europe'.

Britain's words had little effect. They rubbed the Zionists up the wrong way, of course, but also failed to convince the rest of the world, even advocates of the multicultural ideal. No amount of high-flown rhetoric could mask Britain's pursuit of its own political interests: the desire to keep European Jews out of British-run Palestine. Since the 1930s, Britain had seen continuing Jewish immigration as a threat to its mandate, fearing it could spark a conflict with the Arab population that might engulf the whole of the Middle East, a region where the British were working to maintain a presence. The Labour Party's post-war rise to power did nothing to alter this position. Britain continued to dream of a global empire, much to the irritation of its ally America. In the summer of 1945, President Truman asked the British to allow at least 100,000 Jewish Holocaust survivors to settle in Palestine. Prime Minister Clement Attlee refused, informing Truman that most of the displaced persons did not come from German concentration camps at all, but from countries such as Poland and the Soviet Union. Countries that could take them back, if they so wished.

One year later, on 22 July 1946, the Zionist organisation Irgun, led by a Polish-born Jew by the name of Menachem Begin, bombed the King David Hotel in Jerusalem. Ninety-one people were killed. On 31 October that same year, the Irgun planted a bomb in the British embassy in Rome. On 1 March 1947, the organisation killed seventeen British officers.

Initially, this wave of violence, especially the hotel bombing, resulted in worldwide sympathy for the British. But the 3,000 arrests carried out in the wake of the attacks and leaked anti-Semitic statements by Evelyn Barker, Britain's commanding officer in Palestine at the time, soon turned the situation into an international PR disaster.

One year after the King David bombing, Britain started to pull its troops out of Palestine. The last British troops left on the termination of the mandate, on 14 May 1948. No sooner had the last High Commissioner for Palestine sailed from the port of Haifa than the Jewish Agency for Palestine proclaimed independence for the state of Israel.

Instead of footnotes

This chapter draws on the extensive research carried out by German Jim G. Tobias on the Jewish survivors in the post-war camps in

Germany, Austria, and Italy. His book *Vorübergehende Heimat im Land der Täter* (*Temporary Home in the Country of the Perpetrators*), 2002, is the source for my accounts of the Zettlitz kibbutz and Pleikershof, the former country residence of Julius Streicher. Tobias's work also led me to the US report by Earl G. Harrison, which can be found in its entirety online.

The mock trial at the Lagersfeld kibbutz is described in Avinoam J. Patt's book *Finding Home and Homeland: Jewish youth and Zionism in the aftermath of the Holocaust* (2009). Patt not only interviewed Monish Einhorn and other witnesses, but also had access to a diary kept by the kibbutz.

Giles MacDonogh writes about anti-Semitic incidents in the American occupation zone in his 2007 book *After the Reich*. The quote from General Patton comes from the second volume of *The Patton Papers*, compiled by Martin Blumenson and published in 1974.

The quote from Irving Heymont comes from the 2013 book *Year Zero: a history of 1945* by Ian Buruma. Heymont's letters were published as *Among the Survivors of the Holocaust, 1945: the Landsberg DP camp letters of Major Irving Heymont, United States Army* (1982).

The opening quote is from *Wallensteins Tod* (*Wallenstein's Death*), 1800, the third instalment of German writer Friedrich Schiller's trilogy of plays centring on General Albrecht von Wallenstein, a Bohemian and commanding general of the armies of the Holy Roman Empire. The action takes place in the Bohemian city of Pilsen during the winter of 1633, sixteen years into the Thirty Years' War.

18

The Ayalon

'If you want everyone to love you, don't discuss Israeli politics.'

–Saul Bellow, writer

September 1948. Two Amsterdam dock workers are painting 'Negbah' in bold white letters on the bow of a ship large enough to transport 660 passengers in relative comfort.

When the white letters on its bow still spelled 'Luxor', the ship spent years crossing the Atlantic. Its name change was occasioned by the Israeli government's decision to buy the vessel from the Netherlands for the sum of one million Dutch guilders. Its new purpose: to bring Jewish survivors to the newly founded state of Israel.

The ship was named after the Negba kibbutz in the Negev desert, where—days before the boat's purchase—a small group of Jewish fighters held off a major offensive by the Egyptian army. The fighters defending the kibbutz had relatively few weapons and no artillery, while the Egyptians threw everything they had at the settlement, including air power. The fact that the fighters held their ground was nothing short of miraculous and cause for jubilation in Israel, whose declaration of independence on 14 May 1948 had been greeted with attacks from all sides in an attempt to wipe it off the face of the Earth. The victory at Negba prompted intense and widespread celebration, of which the naming of the ship was one small expression.

On its maiden voyage, the Negbah set sail with 500 Jewish orphans on board, mostly Eastern European children who had been housed at an asylum in the Dutch town of Apeldoorn. When the ship left for Haifa a few weeks later, Mala's male counterpart Solomon Perel was among the passengers. He was one of 22,000 Holocaust survivors who signed up with the Israeli armed forces that year and who entered the conflict fresh from the boat.

These new arrivals could hardly be considered fresh after everything they had been through. Yet for many, the training, excitement, and camaraderie of military service helped chase away their demons, if only for a while. This can be read in the memoirs many of them wrote when they were older. Perel was happy to put the military training he received at an elite Hitler Youth boarding school to good use, fighting for a cause he believed in: the founding of the state of Israel. That said, he was the first to admit that he had once believed in the Soviet cause and, in a few isolated moments of utter confusion, even in the aims of the Nazis. As Perel puts it, 'From the moment I wore the uniforms with a swastika on, I became my own enemy ... I had to escape myself to survive.'

Two months later, in November 1948, Mala, Nathan, and Icek also boarded the Negbah. They joined the ship in Marseille, and celebrated their son's second birthday at sea. Families arriving in Israel did not have armed combat to distract them. They were housed in *ma'abarot*: guarded camps that accommodated the newcomers, often in tents, sometimes in small houses or barracks. Food was scarce, and the Israeli authorities were finding it hard to create work for these new arrivals. For although the existing population was willing to receive newcomers, opinion polls from the time show that they were also viewed with suspicion.

What kind of people were they, these survivors of mass slaughter in Europe? An educational director from The Joint, who worked in displaced persons camps in Germany, described the survivors as 'a marvelous example of a society without an élite. The élite of European Jewry were the first to be exterminated.' In public opinion, concern was growing that the mass slaughter inflicted by the Germans had been a process of unnatural selection that would ultimately harm the Zionist ideal.

With the benefit of hindsight, we know that the truth is more complex, that not only the elite were wiped out. After all, being wealthy and well connected was often the very thing that could get you a safe place to hide, especially in the west of occupied Europe. Yet in those first, uncertain post-war years, a particular perception, however inaccurate it might be, could work its way under the skin and become widely accepted as fact. This led some to draw even more extreme conclusions. There was a notion that Israel was being saddled with the outcasts of Eastern European Jewry. The insult 'soap' gained currency, based on the persistent rumour that the Germans had made soap from the remains of their Jewish victims.

After spending a few weeks in a camp, Mala, Nathan, and their young son were able to move to Lydda, also known for decades as al-Lydd. Until Israeli soldiers captured the city that summer, it had only been home to Muslims and Christians. The Israelis turned Lydda into Lod. In the Christian world, the city is known for the relics of St George, the martyr and supposed dragon-slayer who lived and died there. Mala and her family were given a place in street no. 11, Yod Alef, in a neighbourhood close to the old city centre.

It was a small house with three rooms: one for Mala, Nathan, and Icek, and one for another couple with their young son. Time passed, and the agency in charge of Jewish immigration to Israel decided to assign the third room, too, this time to a childless couple. The neighbourhood had no running water, electricity, or gas. The house had no toilet. The agency gave the residents food stamps, not money, and they had to stand in line for hours. Fortunately, Mala says, there was a strong sense of solidarity among the immigrants, and people took it in turns to wait in the long queues.

Nathan had no work to begin with, while Mala grew fruit and vegetables in their small patch of garden. 'That was what we lived on.' The city's temporary military government notified their superiors of the miserable conditions in which the newcomers were living. Hygiene was dire, and infectious diseases were rife. Shortages were leading to unacceptable situations on the black market, and, according to one delegate to the national agricultural conference held in Tel Aviv not long after Mala's arrival, there was even hunger and starvation in Lod.

In these conditions, Mala gave birth to a baby girl and named her Esther, after her mother from Czyżewo.

As the father of two children, Nathan was not required to serve in the army. Instead, he was permitted to find himself regular work, and took a job with the local police. The high hopes with which he joined up were dashed within a day, when he was ordered to patrol the old centre, a cluster of streets and houses around the Church of St George and the Great Mosque, the al-Omari. Barbed wire separated them from the rest of the city, and the 500 or so people fenced in were virtual prisoners. These were Christians and Muslims who had refused to leave when Lydda fell to the Jews, in addition to the inhabitants of local villages cleared by the Israeli army in the days that followed. In another section of what was now Lod, another fenced area was home to a further 500 people.

The two isolated neighbourhoods were a physical reminder of the driving-out of the city's residents a short time before. Both the Israeli soldiers and the new residents called the neighbourhoods 'ghettos', and in doing so they introduced this term to the region. In Arabic, it did not exist.

Nowadays, ask an older taxi driver in Lod to take you to the ghetto, and he will drive you straight to the old city centre. One Christian from Lod tells me he uses the word as often as he can 'to keep alive the memory of what happened to us Palestinians here'.

Mala uses the word, too. There is indignation in her voice. 'There it was, right in the middle of the city—a ghetto!' Nathan had not survived the Łódź ghetto only to patrol the barbed-wire fences of the Lod ghetto. 'He refused.'

* * *

For my part, I was astounded that Mala had yet again found herself in the thick of ethnic cleansing. To begin with, I was almost incredulous; it was as if brutal segregation followed her wherever she went. As a thirteen-year-old girl, she was living in Warsaw when the Germans isolated and later killed around 300,000 people. Mala fled the ghetto in time, only to find herself at the very heart of the 'bloodlands', where the biggest genocide of the twentieth century was gathering pace, much of it carried out with knives, clubs, and pitchforks. She escaped again, this time to the nation of the perpetrators, where she hunkered down with committed Nazis as ruthless air raids brought the war home to them. From there, it was back to Poland and the post-war violence inflicted on Jewish survivors and their protectors, while Germans were being driven from their homes, towns, and cities.

She had been through all this, only to arrive two years later in Lod, to live in a tiny house that only a short time before had belonged to Muslim or Christian residents. They had been driven out of Lod, a city that both friends and enemies of Israel regard as the place where one of the most significant or most troubling chapters of the Israeli war of independence unfolded, a war known to Palestinians as the *nakba*: the catastrophe. Israeli intellectual and public figure Ari Shavit goes so far as to call the city the epicentre of the conflict over the existence of Israel. 'Lydda is our black box,' he says. 'In it lies the dark secret of Zionism'.

The contents of that black box are summarised in a chapter of his book *My Promised Land*. Shavit leaves no doubt as to which side he is on: he is a Zionist. But as a Zionist who does not wish to deceive himself, he feels his only option is to acknowledge what was done to the city: 'Lydda is an integral and essential part of our story. And when I try to be honest about it, I see that the choice is stark: either reject Zionism because of Lydda, or accept Zionism along with Lydda.'

He makes this statement after presenting a reconstruction of the events in Lydda. Is it a biased reconstruction? Not really. In the minefield of Israel's historical narrative, historians of all nationalities give remarkably similar factual accounts of that scorching day in July 1948. (Needless to say, their political conclusions are another matter.) The events of that day stemmed from the conviction held by Israel's leader, David Ben-Gurion, and his military commanders that gaining control of Lydda and the surrounding villages was of crucial strategic importance. Without Lydda, Jerusalem could have been cut off from the rest of the country, including Tel Aviv.

The underlying concept was one of 'territorial continuum', a concept that becomes clear when you take a look at the UN's partition plan for the region. Lydda was also situated close to one of the largest airfields in the Middle East at the time. Where Israel was concerned, an airfield close to a hostile urban population that included soldiers from the Emirate of Transjordan was asking for trouble, present and future. A number of brigades therefore advanced at full speed and collectively captured the city in a gun battle that lasted around 45 minutes. Over 100 Arab-speaking civilians died in the fighting. Nine Israeli soldiers lost their lives.

That same evening, Israeli soldiers rounded up thousands of people and packed them together in the city's two mosques and the Church of St George, less than half a kilometre from the River Ayalon, Wadi Musrara in Arabic. In the days leading up to the fighting, the city had been flooded with refugees from nearby Ramla and the surrounding villages, bringing the total to around 50,000 people. The question of what was to be done with them quickly arose. One day after the capture of Lydda, an army commander called Yigal Allon put the question to Ben-Gurion. When he failed to get an answer the first time, Allon asked again, more forthrightly. Ben-Gurion made a gesture that was understood by everyone present. Among them was Yitskhok Rabin, later a Nobel Peace laureate and prime minister of Israel, who was brigade commander and staff officer for operations. He translated this wave of the hand into a written order: take them away, every last one of them, regardless of age.

It's an order Shmaryahu Gutman, the man appointed military governor of Lydda, is anxious not to give. He is hoping to present the expulsion of the population as an opportunity for a lucky escape when he meets the city's dignitaries in the Church of St George. As the minutes tick by, conditions in the Great Mosque are becoming unbearable. The heat is stifling. Thirst and lack of oxygen are driving people to despair. Gutman orders all kinds of people to be released: women and children, bakers to provide bread, and well operators to provide water, but this does nothing to relieve the distress. Those who leave are soon replaced by the dozens of young men Israeli soldiers continue to bring in from all corners of the city, their hands raised in the air.

Gutman tells the city dignitaries that a fierce battle for control of the nearby airfield could erupt around Lydda at any minute. No sooner has he said this than shots and explosions are heard. Gutman halts the conversation and dispatches one of his men to find out the cause. The soldier soon returns with the news that shots have been fired from the small mosque and a grenade thrown from the minaret. Israeli soldiers are under attack.

Later reconstructions reveal that two armoured vehicles belonging to the Arab Legion had driven into the city, probably by accident. The last armed Palestinians in Lydda took their arrival as a signal to attack.

The Great Mosque is packed with men; in the small mosque, there are women and children, too. Many have taken refuge there in the hope that the soldiers will spare a place of worship. Only now, fighters have opened fire from within.

Following the news of the hostilities, the soldiers in the rectory look to Gutman. How should they respond? The military governor decides that his troops should open fire on anyone acting suspiciously and on every house from which shots are fired. For the next thirty minutes, the din is deafening. Accounts of the death toll differ, although the consensus has grown in recent years. Historian Benny Morris quotes an internal report by the Israeli army that puts the number of Arab deaths at 250, with four Israelis killed. Morris is Israeli. Palestinian historian Aref al-Aref puts the death toll at 426.

Morris, whose authoritative book *1948* is anything but an indictment of the Israeli armed forces, expresses the view that the disproportion between Israeli and Palestinian fatalities at Lydda means that it should be characterised as a 'massacre' rather than a 'battle'. In his account, dozens die in the small mosque, among them women and children. A soldier armed with a PIAT anti-tank weapon blows a hole in the wall from a distance of six metres. The weapon resembles a bazooka and is fired from the shoulder. The shooter knows the grenade that hit his fellow soldiers was thrown from the minaret, but he hears voices behind the wall, and with a PIAT it makes sense to have a clear target to aim for, as firing is not without risk to the shooter himself. The blast is powerful, and the soldier does indeed sustain minor injuries. The pressure from the impact flattens dozens of people against the walls of the mosque.

Fear takes a hold of the delegation in the rectory. Shavit even describes 'the Arab dignitaries' as being 'in a state of hysteria'. They promise Gutman they will leave the city as long as he releases everyone being held in the Great Mosque. Gutman does not agree immediately, but retires for further deliberations. He returns accompanied by two young officers, whose role is to witness the crucial exchange that follows. Shavit presents this as a dialogue:

Dignitaries: What will become of the prisoners detained in the mosque?
Gutman: We shall do to the prisoners what you would do had you imprisoned us.
Dignitaries: No, no, please don't do that.
Gutman: Why, what did I say? All I said is that we will do to you what you would do to us.
Dignitaries: Please no, master. We beg you not to do such a thing.
Gutman: No, we shall not do that. Ten minutes from now the prisoners will be free to leave the mosque and leave their homes and leave Lydda, along with you and the entire population of Lydda.
Dignitaries: Thank you, master. God bless you.

Gutman then goes to the Great Mosque to tell the thousands being held there of the decision that he and their own leaders have reached. Everyone is allowed to leave the mosque, and will be given ninety minutes to leave the city. They are forbidden from leaving by car or truck, in case these vehicles fall into the hands of the Arab Legion, whose forces are stationed around twenty-five kilometres to the east. Gutman reckons the Legion will have no choice but to take care of the expelled civilians, a bonus for the Israeli forces: tending to a straggling column of needy refugees will only sap the Legion's operational strength.

Ari Shavit describes what happens next from Gutman's perspective:

The military governor can hardly believe his eyes. Thousands of men are leaving the Great Mosque, their heads bowed. No one complains, no one curses, no one spits in his face. With complete submission the masses march out and disperse. He climbs the tall minaret of the Great Mosque. From the top he watches chaos engulf the town. The people of Lydda grab anything they can: bread, vegetables, dates and figs; sacks of flour, sugar, wheat, and barley; silverware, copperware, jewellery; blankets, mattresses. They carry suitcases bursting at the seams, improvised packs made from sheets and pillowcases.

Tens of thousands of residents leave Lydda, their home. It is 13 July 1948. Israeli soldiers roam the streets, fire shots into the air and shout, 'Yallah, yallah', Arabic for 'Hurry up, hurry up'. Some hurl abuse; others amuse themselves by scaring the children. A few Arab residents produce letters of reference to show that they have worked well with the nearby Jewish settlement of Ben Shemen. This makes no difference to the soldiers. Once the column has started moving, they force the exiles to hand over their wristwatches, earrings, necklaces, and other valuables. 'Throw them in the bag.' The soldiers have jute sacks at the ready.

The aggression and lawlessness unleashed was powerful enough for brigade commander Yitskhok Rabin to be concerned about the effect the clean-up operation would have on the morale and social ethics of his soldiers. If they were to become constructive citizens in the new state, a corrective was needed. In his 1977 memoirs, Rabin recalls, 'Prolonged propaganda activities were required after the action, to remove the bitterness of these youth-movement groups, and explain why we were obliged to undertake such a harsh and cruel action.' This was written long before he came to international prominence as a peacemaker. Because he had been a government minister, a panel consisting of five members of the Israeli cabinet had the right to censor his book. They scrapped the passages about Lydda, including the above quote. The book's translator later leaked the offending text to *The New York Times*.

Binyamin Eshet, one year younger than Mala, is a Holocaust survivor from Poland. He went on to survive the pogrom in Kielce, where he had been one of the residents of the house on Planty Street. He joined the Israeli army, and took part in the expulsion at Lydda.

He is proud of the victory in the war of independence, but feels a profound sense of regret about that one day in Lydda, just as the American photographer and soldier Tony Vaccaro cannot condone the bombing of Zerbst.

Eshet was interviewed about Lydda in 2012. His head is bald, his face round, his expression permanently wide-eyed. As he talks, his thick, white eyebrows dance to the rhythm of his words. He recounts how the column left some refugees behind—old men, women, and children who were exhausted, abandoned by the side of the road. Everyone had to move on. *Yallah!* There is one thing he will not talk about, he says: the burial of the victims from the small mosque. He had spoken about this to a journalist once before, and had received a visit from a couple of furious secret service men. Sharing top secret military information? What did he think he was doing? They were particularly disappointed that, of all people, a veteran of the war that decided the future of the state of Israel should reveal such information. Even so, Eshet could not help returning to the subject in 2012. He spoke again about the burying of the dead, albeit in a faltering account, in veiled terms and counter-questions.

What happened to the bodies of those who were killed in the small mosque? It is the one aspect of the events in Lydda on which historians have reached no consensus whatsoever. Some, including Shavit, say they were buried by eight residents of Lydda on the orders of Israeli soldiers and that, once their work was done, the eight were killed and laid in the grave along with the victims, so that there would be no Arab witnesses. This version of events has led to heated debates in the Israeli press and among academics, not least because it summons up an image of all-too-recent massacres in Eastern Europe. Besides, not everyone believes it. Sceptical historians quote a man born and raised in Lydda who was twenty when his city fell. Abu Wadi was one of the Muslim residents who stayed behind. A few days after the PIAT strike, he says, the Israelis ordered him to remove the bodies from the mosque. The hands of the dead were already badly swollen. With a small group of others who had stayed behind, he dragged the bodies outside, where they were loaded onto a cart and taken to the cemetery. There they were not buried, but burned to ash.

Wadi died in 2011. A photograph shows him pointing at the place where the bodies were burned. Another controversial detail from his account is that the vast majority of the victims were grown men, not women or children. And after disposing of the bodies, he was not killed, but imprisoned in the ghetto that Nathan later refused to guard. In time, he and the others held in the ghetto were given Israeli citizenship.

War veteran Yerachmiel Kahanovich says he has no qualms about what happened in Lydda. Kahanovich, three years younger than Mala, is the man who fired the PIAT. In 2012, he spoke about the order to fire on the mosque to filmmaker Eyal Sivan.

> Sivan: How many got killed there?
> Kahanovich: I fired one and it was enough.
> Sivan: How many people were inside, do you know?
> Kahanovich: Plenty.
> Sivan: What do you mean?
> Kahanovich: Plenty. I opened the door, I looked inside, and I closed the door.
> Sivan: What did you see?
> Kahanovich: An empty hall—everyone on the walls.

Among the eyewitness accounts of those who were expelled, one in particular stands out. Not only because its author, a poet, writes so vividly and movingly, but also because it is the eyewitness account of a man who cannot see. Blind from birth, Reja-e Busailah was eighteen when the soldiers came to Lydda. He mainly remembers the siege as 'a time of inexpressible fear'. In his book *In the Land of my Birth: a Palestinian boyhood*, he recalls how the locals would refer to Lydda as 'the eighth Arab State'; no one ever imagined that the city could fall. Yet, like Ramla, Lydda fell with 'shockingly little resistance'. When the Israeli soldiers launched their attack, its defenders 'scattered like atoms, each in order to hide his meager weapon and look like an innocent civilian in the face of the conqueror with his anticipated, expected, limitless revenge'.

Busailah's book was published in English. Hardly surprising, considering that, by way of the West Bank and Cairo, he wound up in the United States, where he taught English literature for thirty years at the University of Indiana. 'It was only much later, after the fall of the town and the exodus, that I learned there had been scarcely more than three hundred fighting men [among us].' Their weapons included rifles that dated back to the Ottoman period. The British had left them three artillery guns; but, with insufficient shells and no one to operate them effectively, they were of little use. Each man carried his own weapon. For many, that was an axe, shovel, knife, stick, or club. Busailah notes dryly, 'That was enough to beat off the enemy. I believe we had three armoured cars fitted locally.'

The Arab Legion also sent several hundred Bedouins. They were famed for their courage, but turned out to be mercenaries and mainly interested in looting. One day before Lydda fell, they fled the city, as did the three military commanders supplied by Turkey. As the shooting began, Busailah took shelter inside a house with a number of other families, and waited for what was to come. The older university graduate they all looked to as their leader turned out to be more fearful than the rest. A very childish fear, Busailah recalls, which could have spelled disaster had it lasted long enough. 'Oh God, oh God, shield us, shield us. Oh God, I don't want to die. I am much too young to die yet, much too young,' the man moaned over and over, 'as though in consonance with the firing outside'. Much to everyone's relief, a younger cousin silenced him with what struck Busailah as 'a voice of startling dignity and authority.' He adds, 'If I believed, I would say that was God's answer to the helpless prayer.'

Gradually, the sound of explosions and gunfire began to recede. Busailah went to sit by the radio, tuned to a broadcast in Arabic on the Palestine Broadcasting Service. A newsreader announced that Lydda and Ramla were engaged in a heroic battle with the enemy. Busailah observes, 'We had long ago got used to this kind of lie. Indeed, I think we had long ceased to consider it a lie. It was a way of life.' Then came the news that everyone was to gather their belongings and leave the city as quickly as possible. Busailah remembers the relief he felt.

This memory corresponds to that of Gutman, the military governor who had sought to manipulate Lydda's Arab leaders into getting their people to leave of their own accord. Busailah writes, 'Salvation had come. They were going to let us go. And we should go, else they would kill us all ... We should return very shortly. It will not take the Arab armies long before they drive them [the Israelis] out of Lydda and Ramle [Ramla], out of Yafa [Jaffa] and beyond. In a matter of weeks, if not days, we should be back. Most believed this ...'

Jewish soldiers were stationed along the road, some with loudspeakers. Busailah remembers one soldier repeating that they had better leave to avoid a repeat of what had happened in the mosque. Another told them they would soon be allowed to return. Jewish officers and soldiers told them, 'You are going to King Farouk!', or 'You are going to King Abdulla, who sold you each for half a piastre.'

The sun beat down relentlessly, and the temperature reached 35 degrees in the shade. People threw off their loads, put down their suitcases and their food. Some collapsed. Everyone crowded around a well just outside the city. Watching the column from the top of the minaret, Gutman saw the crush and someone fall in. Busailah describes how people drove each other mad with talk of a pool or well in some ravine or just beyond a hill or a few metres from the road. One young man was pushed down into a well in which there was only a little muddy water at the bottom. When he clambered out, the rest of the group descended on him and began sucking water from his soaked clothes. This is Busailah's account, and of course his blindness meant that he did not witness these incidents himself. Afraid of losing his way, he stuck to the road, depending on those around him for guidance and for these descriptions of what took place.

After arriving at the first village in Arab hands, a friend told him a story about his sister. She had entrusted her two-year-old son to an older couple who had a cart pulled by a mule. In the evening, she found the couple safe in the village, but without the child. They told her the Jewish soldiers had shot into their tyres and killed the mule, and unable to carry the child, they had left him behind. 'The wailing and crying of the mother were uncontrollable, hysterical,' Busailah writes. 'Her brother Muhammad had to retrace much of the road and miraculously retrieved the child.'

Busailah ended up teaching at an American university. And, of course, that is what the Israeli leaders had hoped: that the people driven from their homes in Lydda would get on with their lives elsewhere. But not everyone was willing or able to leave the past behind. Some swore revenge. Among Lydda's thousands of exiles was George Habash, a young doctor from a Christian family. Twenty years after that thirsty, desperate walk in the burning sun, he would come to be viewed by many Israelis as the devil incarnate. His actions continue to shape our world: the lengthy security checks we go through before boarding a plane are a direct consequence of the series of hijackings carried out by Habash's group in the late sixties and early seventies. That group was the Marxist-Leninist-inspired Popular Front for the Liberation of Palestine, the PFLP for short: often regarded as a rebellious little brother to Yasser Arafat's PLO.

Habash was born six months after Mala, and grew up as the son of a relatively prosperous Greek Orthodox merchant in Lydda. As a boy, George sang in the choir at the Church of St George. After high school, he left for Beirut to study at the American University there, which at the time was a liberal bastion in the Middle East. As a paediatrician back in Lydda, he saw the British, not the Jewish immigrants, as the enemy. That changed on 12 July 1948, when Israeli soldiers burst into the clinic where Habash was working. 'I was gripped by an urge to shoot them with a pistol and kill them, and in the situation of having no weapons I used mute words. I watched them from the sidelines and said to myself: This is our land, you dogs, this is our land and not your land. We will stay here to kill you. You will not win this battle.'

But Habash did not stay. Hours before the people of Lydda were forced to leave their city, his ailing sister died. Habash blames her death on the Israeli soldiers who made it impossible for her to receive the care she needed. After arranging a hurried burial in the garden, he joined the column of residents flowing out of the city, holding his sister's children by the hand. That day, he lost his faith in God. Despite his disillusionment, he continued his work as a doctor for many years, in the Jordanian city of Amman and other places.

It was another twenty years before he founded the PFLP. The movement's founding document contains the sentence: 'The only language that the enemy understands is the language of revolutionary violence.' One year later, the group hijacked its first plane, an El Al Boeing, and succeeded in securing the release of sixteen Palestinians in exchange for ten Israeli passengers and the air crew. The following year, the group hijacked four planes and diverted them to an old military airfield in the Jordanian desert. The world was stunned as, once again, Habash succeeded in exchanging his hostages for Popular Front members being held in Israeli and European prisons. He ordered the planes to be blown up. Only one person died in these hijackings, a hostage-taker and member of Habash's organisation.

Which is not to say that innocent civilians never died at the hands of the PFLP. In interviews, the former paediatrician made it clear that he did not mourn the loss of what he called enemy lives. Even into old age, when asked what had made him go from treating sick children to committing terrorist attacks, Habash always gave the same reply: 'Lydda.' That day in July had taught him an important lesson, he explained: 'The Israelis took our country because they are powerful, and that is why we have to attain power.'

'Justice without power,' he often repeated, 'means nothing.'

* * *

As the blind poet Busailah was being reunited with his family in a refugee camp in the West Bank city of Ramallah, Mala and Nathan were moving into a small house in Lod. Mala had escaped from the blackest hell in European history and would never return to the world of her youth, neither geographically, nor in terms of culture or religion. Paradoxically, her arrival in the promised land of the Jewish people saw her abandon her desire to live the Orthodox life to which she had been raised. 'Most of my time was spent with Holocaust survivors from Poland, and there were very few Orthodox Jews among them. Where we were in Lod there wasn't a single one!'

She had lost the battle for her faith to Nathan, although it's not entirely clear how much of a fight she put up. 'Whenever Nathan and I had a row and he thought I was getting above myself, he would always say, "If it hadn't been for the war, you'd have twelve children and a wig on your head." And yes, there was some truth to that.'

The Israeli authorities also had a hand in ensuring that, in cultural terms, Mala never returned to the streets of her youth, to Miła, Dzika, and Nowolipki. Although many of the country's leaders had Polish roots—over half of Israel's prime ministers were born in Poland—they were equally determined that the hundreds of thousands of newcomers should adopt the culture that had originated in the years of the British mandate, and that meant no more Yiddish. Hebrew was the language of the Zionist. With this came a rejection of urban frivolity. It was physical labour that would enable the new state of Israel to rise from the soil of Palestine. This meant retraining almost everyone, as before the war most immigrants had been merchants, businesspeople, or craftsmen, or had been born to parents from such a background. Israel's first president, Chaim Weizmann, could hardly have been more specific when he said, 'It is essential to remember that we are not building our National Home on the model of Djika [Dzika] and Nalevki [Nalewki].' Dzika was the Warsaw street where Mala's father had been born and where Mala had slipped in and out of the ghetto. Nalewki was the street where her sister Chaja and her family had lived.

During the 1948 war, approximately 700,000 Muslim and Christian inhabitants were driven from the region that went on to become Israel. Most ended up in the surrounding countries, often in refugee camps that took on a semi-permanent character. In the space of four years, almost the same number of people came to Israel, the majority from mainly Muslim countries in the Middle East and North Africa, such as Morocco, Yemen, and Iraq. About 300,000 came from Europe, the vast majority from Poland and Romania. Between 1941 and 1951, about 75 per cent of the population was replaced.

Some streets, neighbourhoods, and kibbutzim—sometimes, entire villages—started to be populated solely by European Holocaust survivors. Especially after the Eichmann trial in 1962, these places became the scenes of endless discussions about what people had done, seen, and endured. How did this woman's brother die? And what had the Germans done in that one town, while in that other village they

…? And remember that man the Germans appointed *Judenälteste* in the ghetto of such-and-such?

Take the Israeli village Meishar, for example, which used to be called Bashit before the expulsion of the Muslim population. The authorities decided to allocate a group of survivors from Poland to this small settlement. Avishag Rudich, my guide to the world of European Holocaust survivors in Israel, often went there in her youth. It was where her mother grew up and where her grandmother lived until her death in 2019. Like many of the other residents, her grandmother wore short-sleeved tops, so her Auschwitz tattoo was always visible. She could tell the most chilling stories, though the horror did not lie in how they were told. The lively and unsentimental way that Rudich's grandmother and her fellow residents talked about their experiences showed that the horrific had been absorbed into the everyday. 'Horror stories were the soundtrack of my youth,' Rudich says. 'But the rhythms and melodies were not always sombre or in a minor key.'

The most popular stories in Meishar centred on the miraculous ways in which people had survived and the coincidences that had led to the narrowest of escapes. There was the tale of a former partisan, the only Jew in his unit, with the Polish resistance movement Armia Krajowa. A few weeks before the German withdrawal, he got word that he was to be transferred to another unit holed up in the forest a few hours' walk away. He was handed directions and a top-secret message. On no account was he to open the envelope. The going was tougher than expected, and it soon became clear that he would have to spend the night in the forest alone. Perhaps it was mistrust or just idle curiosity that made him open the envelope and read the two words written on the note inside: *'Zabij Żyda'*. 'Kill the Jew.'

Avishag Rudich's grandfather, Eliezer Fuchs, had a scar that ran the length of his jaw, a lifelong reminder of the bullet that had grazed him. A German soldier had taken aim from no more than a metre away, at the edge of a freshly dug mass grave. Though it all but missed its target, the bullet was enough to send Grand-dad Fuchs tumbling head-first into the grave, which was more of a broad ditch. When the Germans left, he was able to climb out. This was not long after he had been told to leave the extremely confined quarters where he had been hiding with his family. His father sent him on his way with the words, 'You are a survivor.' It was neither a slight nor a compliment. Fuchs made it out of the mass grave with his injured jaw, but ended up in German hands after all. This time he was sent to Bergen-Belsen. But his father had been right. Apart from two distant cousins, he was the only member of his family who lived to see liberation.

In Meishar, Fuchs lived next door to a man who was unable to use his hands. His wrists had been shattered. He told anyone who would listen how the Germans had done this to him. His wife never contradicted him, but if her husband left the room she made a point of saying, 'It wasn't the Germans, it was us.' 'Us', meaning the Jewish ghetto police. 'He used to steal from his own. Plenty and often.'

The horror stories told by Meishar's residents in those first decades after the war may have been lively, but nobody pulled their punches. As Rudich puts it, 'They took their suffering out on one another.'

She continues, 'There was one woman who had all her teeth knocked out by her husband. Situations like that were not uncommon. Most of these people were the only members of their family to survive the war. They were deeply traumatised and all packed in together. Looking back, as a mother of three, I reckon by today's standards that child protection would have taken every child from Meishar into care. But this is now. And that was Israel in the fifties and sixties.'

At Warsaw's Ringelblum Institute, genealogist Noam Silberberg—who grew up in Israel—tells me, 'In Western Europe, there is a strong focus on survivor's guilt: why did I survive when the rest of my family did not? In Israel, this is accompanied by another phenomenon. Not "Why did I survive?" But "Why did that irritating, unreliable neighbour of mine survive?" For years, this was a source of huge mistrust. People were highly disapproving of each other's war stories.'

It's a tendency Rudich recognises. One that is exacerbated, she says, by the experience many had of being betrayed by their Polish compatriots. Not to mention the added blow of the indifference they encountered from non-Jewish neighbours, acquaintances, and sometimes even friends after the Germans had gone. For many, that more than anything motivated them to leave the country. After the turn of the century, Rudich moved from Israel to live in Warsaw for a while when her husband was posted there for work. This did not go down well with her grandmother. 'She had never been back to Poland, and had no desire to go.' To many Israelis, Poland is first and foremost 'the biggest Jewish graveyard in the world'.

Rudich's grandmother let the news of her granddaughter's move to Poland sink in, and got in touch a few days later to tell her what to do while she was there. She was to go to Ożarów, the small town about 160 kilometres south of Warsaw where her grandmother had lived as a young girl. Before the war, half the population of Ożarów had been Jewish. Now, not a single Jew lives there. Rudich was to go there and tell them how well her grandmother was doing. 'Make sure they know that I have a big family, here in Israel, and that we are all doing well. Tell them you were an officer in the army and that we are strong. Very strong. That is what you should say.'

Rudich tells me all this with a smile, but her voice is muted. 'I took a trip to that small town. It's nothing to write home about. I didn't do what my grandmother asked of me. Where could I start? Whose doorbell should I ring? And it hit me how moving her request was, the wish of a remarkable but deeply traumatised woman. Her life in Israel had restored the balance that had been disrupted by war. That's how she felt about it, and I was to go and tell that to her past.'

After Nathan had refused to guard one of the small ghettos in Lod, he teamed up with Władek, a friend from Poland, and they set about renovating one of the ruins in the city for Władek and his family to live in. With a third man, whose Hebrew was already fluent, the two friends tried to set up a cooperative to repair and renovate houses. They were given the job of installing electricity in a school. Before long, the man who spoke good Hebrew found himself a good job with the airline El Al. He put in a good word for Nathan.

* * *

Today, Lod is home to over 75,000 people. It is the most diverse city in Israel, home to Bedouins, Christians, Muslims, and Jews, ultra-

Orthodox, religious, and secular. Almost half of this last group have arrived from Russia and Georgia in the last twenty years, along with a wave of newcomers from Ethiopia. The airport is the city's main employer.

Lod's Muslim community numbers around 20,000. They are descended from the small group who stayed behind — the inhabitants of the two ghettos — and descendants of Palestinians who in the months after their expulsion from Lydda were then driven out of other villages in the region, such as Az-Zakariyya (which became the Israeli settlement of Zekharia) and Barqusya (which was wiped off the map). The fact that these descendants exist at all shows that comparisons with the ghettos in Nazi-occupied Europe do not hold up. The people of the Lod ghettos survived and were released, some time after internal memos at the government department for Minority Affairs concluded that the ghettos in Lod were entirely unnecessary. Nathan's refusal became government policy. The city's military authority was replaced by a civilian government. The barbed wire came down. Even so, Lod remained a place that people in Israel preferred to avoid.

The city's streets have the air of a place that has fallen on hard times. Its bad reputation in the rest of the country was cemented as tensions rose between Israelis and Palestinians in the territories occupied during the Six-Day War of 1967. Those tensions spread to Lod, with its sizeable Arab minority, and segregation once again took on a physical form. In a move to combat crime, a three-metre wall was built in 2010, separating the Arab section of the city from the Jewish section. Public amenities are considerably better on one side than they are on the other. On the Muslim side, there are no house numbers or street names. The GPS responds as if there are no streets at all. The city's garbage trucks have been known not to show up for weeks on end.

The Church of St George, at the heart of one of Lod's former ghettos, turns out to have a wonderful iconostasis that features St George, the inevitable dragon, and Christian texts in Arabic script. Outside, litter rattles and drifts along the unpaved street, and three goats graze on the minuscule patch of land between the motorway and an exit road. We are only fifteen kilometres from cosmopolitan Tel Aviv, the wealthiest city in Israel.

In the same year that the wall went up, a bill came before parliament to ban schools from teaching that Israel expelled most of the region's Arab residents in the war of 1948. The ban was presented as move to bolster patriotism. The bill was defeated, and even Lod's anti-crime wall is now in disrepair. Yet recent election results indicate that the people living on either side of the wall are becoming ever more radicalised. Residents working to combat segregation in Lod find themselves being pushed further into the margins. In 2018, the man who reached the office of deputy mayor and fought for years to bring understanding between the two sections of the population threw in the towel. He and his family moved away, and now live somewhere that his wife feels is 'a better place to raise a family'.

Mala and her young family experienced none of these tensions. Thanks to his technical skills, Nathan quickly rose through the ranks at El Al. He earned a decent salary, and after living in Lod for almost ten years, the family bought a house in Holon, closer to Tel Aviv. A few years later, the airline's management gave him a posting at Amsterdam's Schiphol Airport, and the family lived as expats in the Netherlands for a while. In 1979, they moved to the Netherlands again after their daughter finished her military service and married a Dutchman. This time, they stayed for good. Mala's children had children of their own, and those children in turn had children. Mala now has four grandchildren and nine great grandchildren.

Having settled into Dutch suburban life, Nathan aged more rapidly than Mala. He died at the Beth Shalom old folks' home in March 2015. Earlier that day, Mala had visited him at his 'house of peace' and they had sung Yiddish songs together:

> Oyfn veg shteyt a boym,
> Shteyt er ayngeboygn,
> Ale feygl funem boym
> Zaynen zikh tsefloygn.

> On the road stands a tree
> It stands bent and deserted

All the birds from that tree
Have flown away.

Instead of footnotes

This chapter opens with an observation from Canadian-born American author Saul Bellow. It comes from *To Jerusalem and Back: a personal account*, a book he wrote after a series of trips to Israel in 1975. Bearing these words in mind, this chapter proved far from simple to write. What I take to be a neutral statement can come across as anything but to any number of readers. While this applies to everything a journalist or historian writes about any part of the world, when it comes to Israel and the Palestinians (or Arabs — to give but one example) a whole new level of sensitivities arises: every statement on the Middle East conflict printed in the newspaper I write for invariably prompts a flurry of angry or indignant reader responses.

The battle for the Negba kibbutz is a case in point. Initially, I wanted this chapter to include a comparison made by Abba Kovner, a Holocaust survivor from Vilnius (formerly Wilno in Polish). In an article, he referred to the battle as 'Negbagrad', his way of saying that it had been as decisive a turning point in the 1948 War as the Battle of Stalingrad had been in the Second World War, which explains why the ship that brought Mala, Nathan, and Icek to Israel had 'Negbah' painted on its bow. At the same time, I could already hear readers saying, 'How could you even think of comparing the two? The death toll alone makes the comparison absurd: a few hundred versus a million!'

This is true, of course, but I still believe that such a comparison is worth noting, if only because it says something about what the 1948 War means to the Israelis — and specifically to a man like Kovner, a Holocaust survivor who was badly in need of a sense of purpose and euphoria in the here and now. Two years earlier, without the support of the Jewish leaders in Palestine, he had set out to murder millions of Germans. His plan had been to travel to Germany with a small team and poison the drinking-water supply in a number of major German cities. The plan failed. However, a few of Kovner's group did succeed in poisoning the bread given to SS officers in custody.

Several thousand became ill. Oddly, none of them died.

Kovner called the group he formed with a number of close associates Nakam, Hebrew for 'revenge'. Without vengeance, he thought, it was only a matter of time before someone made another attempt to exterminate the Jewish people. And so he travelled to Germany in 1946 with cans of deadly chemicals in his luggage. In the end, he got no further than the port of Toulon, where he panicked when his name was called over the ship's Tannoy, and dumped his cans overboard. His plan had not been rumbled, but he was arrested for travelling on false papers. Jewish military leaders wanted nothing to do with vengeance on an epic scale; their focus was on a future in Palestine.

The outbreak of the 1948 war gave Kovner a renewed sense of purpose. The poet became a captain in the Israeli armed forces, and made a name for himself as a propagandist. He directed his fury at the Egyptians, whom he referred to as dogs, and at fellow countrymen who in his eyes showed too little courage in the face of hostility, such as the fighters of the Nitzanim kibbutz. Channel 4 in the UK produced a TV documentary *Holocaust: the revenge plot* (2018) based on recordings Kovner made on his deathbed. A 2009 biography of Kovner by Dina Porat was published under the title *The Fall of a Sparrow: the life and times of Abba Kovner*. Ian Buruma also gives an extensive account of Abba Kovner's revenge plot in his book *Year Zero: the history of 1945* (2013).

In the end, I didn't leave Kovner out of the main body of the book for fear that a comparison between Negba and Stalingrad might invite the wrath of readers. It was simply a matter of keeping things readable by being selective about which side streets to wander down. And yes, the appeal of this kind of footnote is that it gives me room to tell a story like Kovner's despite such considerations.

The quotes from Reja-e Busailah are largely taken from his article, 'The Fall of Lydda, 1948: Impressions and Reminiscences', *Arab Studies Quarterly*, vol. 3, no. 2 (Spring 1981), pp. 123–151, and from his book *In the Land of My Birth: a Palestinian boyhood* (2018). And, as previously mentioned, my account of the events in Lydda also owes a great debt to Ari Shavit's 2013 book, *My Promised Land*.

Martin Kramer is one of the historians who do not believe that Israeli soldiers had the bodies from the small mosque buried by

Palestinian 'volunteers' who were executed when the work was done. Kramer wrote about this subject in an extensive article entitled 'What Happened in Lydda?', which is a response to the work of Ari Shavit and Benny Morris. It was published in an edition of *Mosaic* in July 2014, and is freely available online.

The two Lydda veterans quoted—Kahanovich, who fired the PIAT at the small mosque, and Eshet, who was troubled by his conscience—gave their testimonies in 2012. They were interviewed by filmmaker Eyal Sivan at the request of Zochrot, an Israeli NGO.

Elias Khoury, a Lebanese writer, wrote a book about one of the two small ghettos in Lod, called *My Name is Adam: children of the ghetto*. It takes the form of a novel, but his descriptions of life in the Lod ghetto are based on historical research.

The memoirs of Yitskhok Rabin, which date from 1979, were published in English under the title *The Rabin Memoirs*.

In Israel, Mala also encountered the sisters she had met on the train to Tomaszów Lubelski, the young women armed with pistols who were searching for the daughter one of them had left behind with a Catholic farmer. It was Nathan's friend Władek who put them in touch. During the war he had fought in Chil Grynszpan's militia. Władek's real name was Velvl Litvak, but in Chil's group he was known as 'Velvele der patsan', from the Polish slang word 'pacan', meaning 'slowpoke' or 'dummy'. The two sisters told Mala they never found the daughter they had been looking for. Władek eventually left Israel for Brazil, where he lived not far from his beloved leader Chil.

I read about the hardships faced by the first post-war immigrants to Israel and the nascent country's misgivings about Holocaust survivors in *Survivors of the Holocaust. Israel after the war* (1999), by Hanna Yablonka, translated from the Hebrew by Ora Cummings.

A great many articles have been published about Lod and its recent history. One particularly informative piece is 'Israel and its Arabs: pulled apart', which appeared in *The Economist* on 14 October 2010.

The song 'Oifn veg sjtejt a boim' is considered a Yiddish classic. The lyrics are by Itzik Manger, a poet from Czernowitz (now Chernivtsi) who rose to fame in 1930s Warsaw, the capital of the Yiddish world. He left Poland in 1938. Just in time.

EPILOGUE
The Bosbaan

'Few are able to remember the bloodshed and hardship of those years without recapitulating the very categories of exclusionary identity that caused so much agony.'

–Brian Porter-Szücs, historian

People tend to construct a view of the world based on their own experiences. They are less inclined—even less able—to accept that distinct realities can exist side by side. Mala understood this, and decided not to tell the story of her survival to the often emaciated and traumatised young men and women she met at the Bursa, the school building in Łódź where she lived for a time. For her part, she found it hard at first to believe their accounts of the horrors of Auschwitz. 'I just wasn't able to. Not after Germans had taken me in with such kindness.' And when the truth of those horrors did hit home, Mala felt it would be wrong to share her own story, to explain how well she had been treated by a German family. 'And not just any old Germans!' Mala emphasises. 'Committed Nazis!'

The Yad Vashem archives give an impression of how conflicted Mala felt about her story and of the shame she felt in relation to her new countrymen and women. Survivors go to the organisation in Jerusalem to bear witness to the murder of their family members during the occupation. Mala made that trip for the first time in 1955, two years after Yad Vashem was founded, to register the deaths of her

parents, her sisters, and her younger brother, Meir. To do so, she had to
fill in a form that asked a number of questions about her, as a witness.
It asked if she herself was a survivor of the Shoah and, if so, how she
had survived. There were five options:

One: in a camp.

Two: in a forest.

Three: in a ghetto.

Four: in hiding.

Five: had false papers.

Circle the option that applies to you. More than one possible
answer. Mala opted for 'forest' and 'ghetto', not for 'false papers'.

Fifty-seven years later, she went back to Yad Vashem, this time to
report her brothers Pinie and Azriel as murdered. This was in 2012,
and Mala had already committed her memoirs to paper. Again, she
stated that she was a Shoah survivor, and again she circled 'forest' and
'ghetto'.

This was true, of course: she had been in the forest near Karpy,
and she had survived the Warsaw ghetto. Yet throughout the war, 'false
papers' had been crucial to her survival. Twice she chose not to circle
that option.

I ask her about it, and she tells me she can't remember why. What
does it matter, she says. I've told my story, haven't I?

What we tell people about our past says as much about the present.
This applies just as much to historians and others who piece together
stories from the past, whether at a slight remove or from a greater
distance. It's not so much the past they study as what has been handed
down from the past, and their findings speak volumes about the times
in which they live, and about themselves as producers of history. For
Mala, the past changed—everything changed—when she discovered
that her family was lost to her, though at first she could not believe they
were all dead. Speaking about the new world she entered on returning
to Poland, she once said, 'It had never occurred to me that the war
would end and what the world would be like when it did.' So many
of the concerns that filled her days and occupied her mind during the
war suddenly fell away. Only when there was no longer a need to fear

exposure — 'I was always afraid, always' — did she realise how her every action had been ruled by that fear and the agonising question of how far she could take her pretence.

At the little church in Karpy, a priest handed her a certificate of baptism, a document that ultimately played very little part in escaping the genocide. Mala does not think it was a factor in the investigation into her background in Magdeburg, where she waited, worked, and improved her German in a prison that was one step away from a concentration camp. But for Mala it felt like a defining moment. That day at the church, a memory of Alter came rushing back to her, the brother who, years before in Warsaw, had dashed her Polish schoolbooks to the floor with a furious sweep of his arm. Roaring the words 'Get rid of the church!', he bitterly predicted that she, his own sister, would one day abandon her faith.

Later, in Germany, Mala agonised about proving her devout brother right, and wondered how her father would have judged her. In his eyes, how high a price could a young woman pay for survival? Was conversion permissible? Despite the priest's insistence that he was giving her the document to save her life and not her soul, Mala could not escape the feeling that she had committed an act of betrayal.

Her father would no doubt have taken his question to a rabbi. And he would not have been alone in this. An answer to the question exists, given by one of the few rabbis to survive the German occupation. In the ghetto of Kaunas, Ephraim Oshry was presented with all kinds of questions that shone a stark light on the extreme degradation suffered by the city's Orthodox Jews. The rabbi, relatively young for one so learned, recorded the questions and his answers on scraps of paper torn from cement sacks, and buried them for safe keeping. He retrieved them immediately after liberation, and they were later published in a series of volumes under the title *She'eilot u-Teshuvot mi-Ma'amakim*, which roughly translates as 'questions and answers from the depths'. One of these questions was: is it permissible for a Jew to purchase a baptismal certificate if it would enable him to escape into the forest and join the partisans? No, was Oshry's steadfast answer. Purchasing a baptismal certificate could not be condoned under any circumstances. Even if it meant the difference between life and death, this was too great a betrayal of God, the faith, and the Jewish people.

This sounds like an extreme position, as does the answer he gave to a man whose testicles were stomped on by a German policeman. According to Jewish law, an infertile man cannot sleep with his wife. Oshry ruled that Deuteronomy 23:1 gave him no leeway to make an exception in this particular case.

Yet it would be selling Oshry short to dismiss him as a rigorous hardliner or a rabidly legalistic rabbi; that would only trivialise the significance of his answers. In other situations, he could give far more leeway and even show a measure of pragmatism. After the war, for example, he allowed the faithful to enter churches and monasteries in search of Jewish children who had gone into hiding there, something that was far from self-evident for Orthodox Jews. After 7 May 1942, he also allowed contraception, following a German decree that all pregnant women in the ghetto would be killed. And shortly after liberation he gave permission for a circumcision to take place under anaesthetic, something that was unheard of in his world. The boy in question had spent so long among non-Jews, Oshry reasoned, that to inflict pain on him was to run the risk that he would rebel against other commandments of the Torah—a risk that justified deviating from the law. And despite Deuteronomy, he ruled that the man whose testicles had been crushed could still be called to read the Torah: the exceptional circumstances gave Oshry scope to apply the Halacha leniently on this point.

But conversion or the pretence of conversion to save your own skin? Out of the question.

Mala's longing to live by the tenets of her faith may have been prompted by nostalgia or the love she felt for her parents. She understands why it was a longing that Nathan could not share. Their differences echo a debate that took place in Jewish theological circles and thousands of Jewish households as the years passed. On one side, the conviction that to abandon the Jewish faith is to sound the death knell for Judaism and Jewish culture, and to hand Hitler a posthumous victory. On the other side, the position that if God can permit something like the Holocaust, He does not deserve our faith.

At a conference in 1975, two men who embodied these positions squared up to one another in a discussion that resonated throughout Israel. The first side was taken by Emil Fackenheim, a theologian who regarded Auschwitz as a divine order to preserve and practise the Jewish faith and, in doing so, to save the Jewish people. Then there was Alexander Donat, a chemist, journalist, and survivor of the Warsaw ghetto who had settled in New York and was working to keep the memory of Holocaust victims alive. At the conference, he spoke out in admiration for those in the ghetto who put God in in the dock and found Him wanting. Contemplating whether God was in the ghetto, Donat said, 'I saw the face of God. It was not the face of a child on the gallows. It wore the helmet of an SS man.'

Mala tended towards the position of the theologian, Nathan towards that of the journalist with a scientific background. But as time went on, Mala's views gradually shifted towards Nathan's. She bridles at this suggestion, then concedes 'Well, maybe a little bit.' Something of that shift is revealed as she tells me about her release from the Magdeburg prison camp where she had ended up, thanks to Iwan the pockmarked Ukrainian. 'Because I was so religious, I was convinced my release was the work of God,' she says sheepishly. And throwing her hands in the air, she exclaims, 'What did I know, back then?!'

As for Nathan, Mala believes that towards the very end of his life, he was moved by something spiritual. It was a Friday, and a young rabbi had come to the Jewish care home to say Kiddush, a blessing at the start of Shabbat. Nathan let the rabbi come and sit by his bed, something that was completely out of character—Mala had practically had to drag him to the synagogue for his own son's bar mitzvah. Yet there was the rabbi, reading verses from the Torah at Nathan's bedside. Mala had never thought it possible, and, whether it was true or not, the thought that Nathan had given up his battle with God five minutes before he died gave her comfort. She saw it as a sign that God does exist.

Nathan was the first loved one Mala had seen after death. The others had disappeared into thin air, and for a long time it was hard for her to accept that they had all been murdered. It was 2012 before she went to Yad Vashem to report the deaths of her brothers Pinie and Azriel, who had fled to the Soviet Union before the Nazis launched their eastern offensive. At the Bursa in Łódź, Mala met people who had survived the war by escaping to Russia, and she cherished a hope that her brothers might turn up one day. Psychologists advise people, if possible, to see the body of a loved one — a parent, a brother, or sister — who has died. It makes acceptance less complicated. This was an experience that Holocaust survivors seldom had.

From Israel, Mala wrote to the Jewish cemetery in Warsaw in the hope of finding a family member. 'If a brother or sister had survived, I thought one day they might leave a sign at our mother's grave.' The grave was the family's only existing physical point of reference. But the family no longer existed. 'The people at the cemetery were kind enough to answer. Nothing had ever been found.'

Mala's story is shot through with an irresolvable tension between fearful secrecy and the desire to be open with others. 'I was afraid,' Mala tells me, 'but I didn't want to be alone.' She had the ability to charm, she says so herself, and she is sure that this helped her. But she also knows that this same outgoing, sociable nature could lead her into trouble or take her to the brink of the abyss. The need to seek contact makes it harder to conceal your identity. It was one small step from sleeping over after a friend's party to being locked up in a prison camp. There, her charm worked to her advantage once again, or perhaps it was more her credibility: they believed her story, not the story told by the Ukrainian.

And then there was Ela, the most anti-Semitic of the Polish girls at the Magdeburger Bierhaus. But to Mala she was also the smartest and the nicest, and so much of her time was spent with Ela, even though she presented the greatest danger. If one of the others had discovered Mala's secret, they might have been inclined to take pity on her. Not Ela. Mala was repelled by Ela's anti-Semitism. She feared it, too. Yet she felt no need to answer her friend's racial hatred with hatred of her own, for Ela as an individual.

When the Americans arrived, she felt only the faintest of urges to tell her friend she was Jewish. She kept her secret till the end, even as they said their last goodbyes on a railway platform in Poland. Nor did she tell the Möllers that they had welcomed a Jewish girl into their family home. Solomon Perel, Mala's male counterpart, did speak out and went on to keep in touch with the Nazi girlfriend who would almost certainly have reported him had she known he was Jewish.

This highlights a striking similarity between Mala and Solomon: neither of them felt an overwhelming sense of outrage, or the desire for revenge. Both are open-hearted about the love shown them by surrogate families who wanted to see 'their 'kind' exterminated and, in Solomon's case, who were even taught and trained to exterminate. 'Jupp the Nazi has never left me,' Perel said at the start of this century, using the nickname given to the boy from the Hitler Youth he once was, or pretended to be. Like Mala, he lived among Nazis and—the cruellest of ironies—had to sing along with them every evening on their way to the dining hall: '*Erst wenn vom Messer spritzt das Judenblut, dann geht's uns nochmal so gut.*' ('We'll be even better off once Jewish blood spurts from our knives.')

Not to arouse suspicion, he wanted to be the best pupil in the class. He succeeded, but this also meant spouting the Third Reich's racial doctrine for the edification of his classmates. Almost everything Solomon learned shocked and terrified him. But as Jupp he learned all this deeply disturbing material off by heart and presented it with verve. Perel has given the world more, in my view, by talking about how he was able to do this than by shouting his outrage from the rooftops.

The same is true of Mala. At the Bursa in Łódź, there were times when she wept for joy to be among Jews again. Yet part of her longed for what she'd had in Germany. 'Sometimes I wanted to go back to that family, to that world where no one knew I was Jewish.' With disarming honesty, she tells me how she missed the Möller family. If the war had lasted for another few months, she says, she might have stayed with them. 'They were so kind to me. And they genuinely felt for me, a Polish girl of German descent, who had come from so far away. They honestly wanted to take care of her.' What surprised Mala most, she says, was that she didn't have to work for her keep, something that had become second nature to her at the factory, on the farm in Lublin, with the Gmitruks, and at the Junkerhof. 'They cooked and cleaned for me, I didn't do it for them.' The Möllers expected no gratitude in return.

During our last conversation, I need to know for sure. 'And Erich?' I ask. 'Was he really the love of your life?'

'Yes, Erich was the love of my life,' she answers. 'And I was very fortunate that Nathan was able to live with that.'

On another occasion, she tells me, 'Nathan was wonderful. I remember once in Israel when we were out walking together. We had two children by this point, and there was no question of me returning to Germany to look for Erich. "My goodness, it's cold," I said to Nathan. "Nonsense," he replied, "it's not cold at all." And then I said, "If I were here with Erich, he'd have offered me his pullover by now!" Nathan didn't say a word. I'd been married ten years by then. Strange, isn't it? That's love.'

'And what if you had actually gone back to Germany and found Erich?' I ask.

'Then everything would have been different,' she replies. 'But isn't that true of all life's big decisions?'

* * *

It's human nature to see the decisions we have taken as the ones that were right all along. Just as we are drawn to information that reinforces the views we already hold and gloss over anything that might lead us to doubt them. Psychologists believe this tendency to be particularly strong in people of a cheerful disposition, people who take life as it comes and see no need to look over their shoulder and wonder where the path not taken might have led. Perhaps it's this knowledge that explains why, time after time, I am not only impressed, but also surprised by the open-heartedness and honesty with which Mala reflects on her life. That said, maybe at heart she is less cheerful than she lets on—to me, at least. One thing is certain: as a teenager she showed all the resourcefulness and flexibility demanded by a phase of life in which certainties are hard to come by.

Mala's memoirs were published on too small a scale to expose her to reactions from people she did not know. However, Solomon Perel's book was adapted for the big screen, reached a wide audience, and prompted countless reactions, some of them critical. It was only on reading them that I came to understand that admiration is not the only possible reaction to the resourcefulness, intelligence, and self-insight that enabled him to survive the war. One review described the Perel portrayed in the film as 'opportunistic and cynical', and a young woman on a radio talk show had no qualms about calling his morality into question. 'What is there in this situation about morality?' Perel responded later. 'You think only about how to survive. If I had shot others, that would be different. When the Russian Army came near Berlin and the SS officers took off their uniforms and changed into the clothes of death camp inmates, now that was immoral.'

Perel insisted the criticism did not affect him, though he was shocked by the opinion of one young German woman who argued that committing suicide would have been the moral thing to do. Perel disagrees: 'I wanted to live. For me, the moral thing was to live. There's nothing more holy in life. I didn't want to die as a martyr, I wanted to live as a human being.'

Mala also had critical questions to deal with, in her case from the German government. In 1953, after much wrangling, an arrangement was reached that gave Jewish Holocaust survivors the right to a modest sum in compensation for their suffering and the loss of their loved ones. Mala applied, for the murder of her family, but objections were raised: because she had used different names during the war, her entitlement to payment could not be confirmed. 'But it was the Germans who had forced me to use all those names. "What did you expect me to do?" I said. "Stick to my own name, no matter what? And if I'd done that, would I be here today? Well, would I?!"'

It is one of the rare moments when I hear indignation in her voice.

Long stories leave more room for interpretation than short stories. If only because, in the time it takes for the story to unfold, any interpretation that surfaces can take on a form that is fixed enough to convince. Besides, a single interpretation is easier to write: it allows you to dispense with any observations that may seem interesting but fail to support or illustrate your central premise. It keeps the page-count down. But a human life, by definition, is so much more than an illustration or a courtroom exhibit. By sticking with that one interpretation, you rule out other interpretations that are every bit as interesting and just as valuable.

This was brought home to me the first time I heard Mala's story from her grandson Amir at the Jewish cemetery in Warsaw. There and then, he drew a different conclusion from his grandmother's story than I did. 'To me, your grandmother's life is one big indictment of our obsession with clear-cut identities,' I told him, gearing up for a conversation in which Amir and I would explore the fluidity of national, religious, and personal identity. After all, his grandmother's appreciation of the layers of her identity did not come from her upbringing, and certainly wasn't ideologically inspired. These were things worth discussing, it seemed to me.

But Amir had a different take on things. 'As I see it,' he said, 'her survival story is all about the value of little white lies.' The lies his grandmother told saved her life, Amir said, and meant she was the only one of her large family to survive. But by lying she had also turned her back on one of her father's most sacred commandments. 'If there's one thing he taught her,' Amir said, 'it was never to tell a lie, no matter what.'

Amir then told me an anecdote that, as it turned out, his grandmother was also fond of telling. One day, she and her younger brother Pinie — so close they were practically twins — found a coin. They sneaked off together to buy chocolate, and ate it hiding under their parents' bed. Father saw Mala's feet sticking out, and pulled the children out from under the bed. Their faces and their clothes were covered in chocolate, but they both swore blind that they hadn't eaten any. Mala had seldom seen her father so angry. 'Father thought lying was just about the worst sin there was.'

'What if it had been the other way around?' Mala said one day. 'I've often wondered. Suppose the Germans had wanted to kill all the Catholics instead, what would the Jews have done? Would they have told the Germans where the Catholics were hiding? Would Jews have betrayed Catholics the way Catholics betrayed so many Jews? What would my father have done if our Catholic housekeeper had asked him for help?'

Mala's story is an indictment of thinking in boxes, but it's hard to leave those boxes behind. Perhaps this applies more to me than it does to Mala herself. A few chapters in, one of my readers asked, 'Do you always need to point out everyone's nationality? Polish this and Polish that?' It's a valid point.

Later, without any prompting from me, Mala answers the question she has so often asked herself: 'My father would have helped our Polish housekeeper. I'm sure of it.'

'But it's something you often wonder about?'

'Yes, I wonder. I mean, the Poles were raised with anti-Semitism, but we never had a good word to say about Catholics either. As Orthodox Jews, we wanted nothing to do with the Polish. We didn't want to speak their language, took no interest in their culture, their national heritage. In hindsight, I don't think that was right: living in a predominantly Catholic country, yet wanting nothing to do with Catholics.'

It's exceptional *not* to judge people based on the group they belong to. Mala talks about how remarkable her friend Janek the Priest was for never asking whether the accusation Iwan made against her was true; he never once asked her if she was Jewish. At first, I thought her praise was excessive, inspired more than anything by her fondness towards him. But having arrived at the epilogue to this book, I find myself thinking that perhaps Janek the Priest *was* a very special man. History has swallowed him whole.

This book begins in Godlewo Wielkie, a hamlet not far from the shtetl where Mala's mother was born. I stood there on a farmer's land, only to find that the pigsty and the five people who hid beneath it had also been swallowed by life and time. Days later, at a farm in Poland's 'reconquered territories', I listened to an old man tell the sad tale of his father, Cholewicki the farmer. He dug the pit beneath the sty together with the Jews who hid there, he gave them food, and he died of the injuries inflicted by Poles who, when the Germans had gone, came looking for him and for 'the Jews' gold'.

We talked, and the old man told me what was on his mind. He talked about Polish politics and the storm clouds he saw gathering on Poland's horizon. He grew animated as he spoke of the Russians and the danger they posed, sharing countless illustrations of his thinking on this topic. He recommended a book to me: *The Russian Soul.*

'Read it and you'll understand us Poles better. Then you'll know what we're dealing with.'

Back in Warsaw, I bought the book. It made dispiriting reading. In brief: the Russian has a soul formed by nature and history, which is irreconcilable with the national character of Europeans who live further west. And, whatever he might claim, the Russian is driven by conquest and subjugation.

After a chapter or two, I laid it aside. It wasn't so much the faulty reasoning that got to me. It was more that, even for a book in which I have taken so many detours, this felt like one detour too far. But later, as is so often the case, I changed my mind. The old farmer near Wrocław, his book, his fear and dread of an entire people, a people he did not know, had never met, and whose language he did not speak: these things are at the heart of this journey through time, the story of Mala's survival. Before an outsider can count on a measure of humanity and compassion, they first have to convince us they are one of our own.

Instead of footnotes

Rafael F. Scharf, our guide to the lost world of Mala's father in this book's opening chapters, gave a lecture about Rabbi Oshry. In it, he reflects on the answers or 'responsa' Oshry wrote to the questions his followers asked him and what they tell us about the issues the Jews of the Kaunas ghetto were facing. Entitled 'Saints or madmen? A meditation on Ephraim Oshry's Responsa from the Holocaust', the lecture is included in the 1996 collection *Poland What Have I to Do with Thee.* A number of Oshry's responsa can be found online, for example at https://jewishaction.com/ jewish-world/history/responsa_from_the_holocaust/.

A word of thanks

It is simply not possible to mention everyone who has helped me on my journey of several years to trace the people, events, and places from Mala's story. Even so, it's worth a try. Beginning with Amir Swaab, of course, since the journey began with him and a piano. Then I met Noam Silberberg, again in the company of a piano. I regularly sat down with him at a table in Warsaw's Ringelblum Institute, where he never failed to provide answers to my challenging and convoluted questions about Mala's family history in Czyżewo, Warsaw, and Tyszowce.

Thanks are also due to Charlotte Pothuizen, whose knowledge of Polish saved me from many a slip-up. Thanks to the many people who read the manuscript, often friends and loved ones; they include Theo van den Bogaard, Guusje Korthals Altes, Sjeng Scheijen, Ewa Stanczyk, Roeland Termote, and Pim Vos. And not forgetting proofreader Jan van de Laar, illustrator Hester Schaap, and chief editor at Prometheus (and good friend) Job Lisman. And, of course, my gratitude goes to everyone who helped me with particular passages or formulations, among them Kamil Bałuk, David Barnouw, Ilan Cohn, Rachel Corner, Bas Jacobs, Bartosz Józefiak, Kunera Korthals Altes, Hugo Logtenberg, Hans Steketee, and Jeroen de Willigen.

Throughout the book, I give the names of many experts who helped me on my way, and my alternative footnotes highlight the help I received from the likes of David Cohen, Magdalena Kicińska, Isa van Eeghen, and Hubert Smeets. I have yet to mention Renata Glinkowska, Justus van de Kamp, Ola Krysiak, Adrianna Trypus,

Robbert Baruch, Matan Shefi, Janne de Vries, Agata Szepe, Hilde Pach, and Esther Shlafer. Esther not only shared her expert advice, but was also responsible for the final edit of her mother's written memoirs, which were an indispensable source for this book.

While I could not have done without these invaluable contributions, the responsibility for the choices and any errors I have made is entirely my own.

Lastly, of course, I would like to thank Mala — Mrs Shlafer to me — for her courage and open-heartedness.

Index of persons